P9-AGU-146

Doing Web Development: Client-Side Techniques

DEBORAH KURATA

WITHDRAWN
UTSA LIBRARIES

Apress™

Doing Web Development: Client-Side Techniques
Copyright ©2002 by Deborah Kurata

All rights reserved. No part of this work may be reproduced or transmitted in any form
or by any means, electronic or mechanical, including photocopying, recording, or by
any information storage or retrieval system, without the prior written permission of
the copyright owner and the publisher.

ISBN (pbk): 1-893115-87-9
Printed and bound in the United States of America 12345678910
Trademarked names may appear in this book. Rather than use a trademark symbol
with every occurrence of a trademarked name, we use the names only in an editorial
fashion and to the benefit of the trademark owner, with no intention of infringement
of the trademark.

Editorial Directors: Dan Appleman, Gary Cornell, Jason Gilmore, Karen Watterson
Technical Reviewer: Don Kiely
Managing Editor and Production Editor: Grace Wong
Copy Editor: Kim Wimpsett
Composition and Art Services: Impressions Book and Journal Services, Inc.
Indexer: Nancy Guenther
Cover Designer: Tom Debolski
Marketing Manager: Stephanie Rodriguez

Distributed to the book trade in the United States by Springer-Verlag New York,
Inc.,175 Fifth Avenue, New York, NY, 10010
and outside the United States by Springer-Verlag GmbH & Co. KG, Tiergartenstr. 17,
69112 Heidelberg, Germany
In the United States, phone 1-800-SPRINGER, email orders@springer-ny.com, or visit
http://www.springer-ny.com.
Outside the United States, fax +49 6221 345229, email orders@springer.de, or visit
http://www.springer.de.

For information on translations, please contact Apress directly at 901 Grayson Street,
Suite 204, Berkeley, CA 94710.
Phone 510-549-5930, fax: 510-549-5939, email info@apress.com, or visit
http://www.apress.com.

The information in this book is distributed on an "as is" basis, without warranty.
Although every precaution has been taken in the preparation of this work, neither the
author nor Apress shall have any liability to any person or entity with respect to any
loss or damage caused or alleged to be caused directly or indirectly by the information contained in this work.

The source code for this book is available to readers at http://www.apress.com in the
downloads section. You will need to answer questions pertaining to this book in order
to successfully download the code.

Library
University of Texas
at San Antonio

To my daughters, Jessica and Krysta, for your understanding and support. Thank heaven for little girls who are not afraid to build hand-coded Web sites for their friends, scale a climbing wall, get a black belt, fly a plane, learn to snowboard, beat every level in Nintendo, and still be little girls.

Brief Contents

Contents

Chapter 7: Understanding Object Models *171*

Chapter 8: Using JavaScript *199*

Chapter 12: Using XSL *335*

Chapter 13: Defining Schemas and DTDs *383*

Chapter 14: Reading XML with JavaScript *397*

Chapter 15: Web Application Architectures

Acknowledgments

THIS BOOK HAD SEVERAL starts and stops over an 18-month period. During this time, I have had help from many different people at Apress. I want to thank Dan Appleman and Gary Cornel for their interest in this book. I'd like to especially thank Grace Wong for her work as the production editor, Alexa Stuart for providing the project management, and Kim Wimpsett for copy editing the book. They have been very patient with my challenging schedule and special requirements, such as Try Its and complex tables.

I also had a great set of technical reviewers. I'd like to thank Jim Beattie, Kevin Bell, Erik Buljan, Jason Gilmore, Larry Hansen, Kathleen Dillard-Joeris, Deborah Smith, Michael Souder, and Garth Unwin who all gave of their free time to review and comment on chapters. A special thanks to Don Kiely for his role as the official technical editor. I appreciate all of your time, Don!

Finally, I would like to thank my family for their understanding and support. To my husband and partner, Jerry, thanks for your help with research and for reminding me just how case sensitive Unix can be. To my 11-year-old daughter, Jessica, thanks for working through the first drafts of my chapters; you are an HTML wizard! To my 8-year-old daughter, Krysta, thanks for keeping the sound of your video games off while I wrote. And to my parents, Jerre and Virginia Cummings, I apologize for all of those times during my childhood that I ignored you when you said "get to sleep." I was actually just practicing for the sleepless nights required to fit writing a book into an already busy life.

—*Deborah Kurata, August 2001*

About the Author

Deborah Kurata is a professional software designer and developer. She is the author of several best-selling books including *Doing Objects in Microsoft Visual Basic 6.0* (SAMS). That book details the GUIDS Methodology for software design, a Unified Modeling Language (UML)–based design process used by professional software designers throughout the world.

Deborah is a contributor to several software development magazines and is among the highest-rated speakers at software development conferences worldwide. For her work in support of software development and software developers, she has been recognized with the Microsoft Most Valuable Professional (MVP) award.

Deborah is the cofounder and president of InStep Technologies (www.insteptech.com), a leading software consulting and training firm. InStep assists clients with the design and development of object-oriented, component-based software for Windows and the Web. InStep provides premier software consulting services to the most successful companies in Silicon Valley, the San Francisco Bay Area, and other locations nationwide. Reach InStep at (925) 224-7280 or info@insteptech.com.

Deborah has degrees in physics and mathematics from the University of Wisconsin-Eau Claire and an MBA from the College of William and Mary.

Introduction

THIS BOOK IS AN introduction to client-side Web application development for professional programmers. Appropriate use of client-side scripts, style sheets, and XML is essential for building high-performance Web applications that provide a rich user experience. This book addresses the client-side technologies that every Web application developer needs to know.

This book provides comprehensive coverage of all aspects of client-side Web development. It includes the basics of HTML and Cascading Style Sheets (CSS), scripting with JavaScript, dynamically displaying data with XML and XSL, and patterns for Web application architecture.

Who Should Read This Book?

Many professional C, C++, Java, and Visual Basic developers are moving to the world of Web application development. Some of these developers are adding browser-based user interfaces onto their existing applications, others are "converting" existing Windows-based applications to run enterprise-wide business processes through a browser, and others are building entirely new Web applications. This book is for all of those developers.

There are also many Web developers who specialize in technologies such as ASP, JSP, or PHP. For these developers, this book provides detailed information on leveraging client-side features such as XHTML, CSS, and JavaScript.

I have many opportunities to talk with software developers at conferences, via newsgroups and e-mail, and through my consulting company. The key concern for many developers is how to come up to speed quickly on the many technologies involved with Web development. There are shelves of books on each technology, but it is hard to know where to begin, how the technologies interrelate, or even how to find time to do that much reading. The goal of this book is to provide an overview of all of the key client-side technologies in one place.

This book assumes you have not done much client-side Web development, so it starts with the basics. The first several chapters introduce the Web and key Web technologies such as HTML, XHTML, and CSS. These chapters are useful for anyone wanting to get started with Web application development

Later chapters of the book cover JavaScript, the Document Object Model (DOM), and then XML, schemas, and XSL. Much of this information is more advanced and aimed at professional developers who want to leverage client-side techniques in their browser-based applications.

Will I Get Hands-on Practice?

Most of the techniques in this book include a Try It section that presents steps for you to try the technique. This provides a facility for you to practice what you are reading.

You can try these exercises using a Microsoft Windows or Unix system. Because all of the demonstrated technologies are client-side, you don't need Web server software. All you need is a Web browser.

The Try It exercises were tested using Microsoft Internet Explorer version 5.5 and Microsoft Internet Explorer version 6 on Microsoft Windows. They were also tested using Netscape version 6 on Microsoft Windows and on Unix.

Following each Try It exercise is a code listing that demonstrates a possible solution to the exercise. Most of these solutions follow XHTML standards.

 **NOTE** *If you don't want to type in all of the code, you can download it from*
`www.apress.com/catalog/book/1893115879/`
To download the code, you need to know the last word on page 280.

Many of the Try It exercises build upon prior Try It exercises to demonstrate how the technologies build upon one another and work together to form a complete Web application. When this is the case, the solution code shows in bold the new or revised code lines.

What Will This Book Tell You?

This book is organized as follows:

- **Chapter 1: Introduction to the Web**. To build great Web applications, you need to understand how the Web works and know the many terms used in Web development. This chapter provides this introductory information. If you are already familiar with these basic concepts, you can skip this chapter.

- **Chapter 2: Designing Web Applications**. When designing a Web application, you have many design aspects to consider. Managing all of these aspects is easier if you follow a design methodology. This chapter presents the GUIDS Methodology, a pragmatic approach to design for Web applications.

- **Chapter 3: Using HTML**. This chapter provides the foundation you need to work with HTML elements and attributes. It also covers XHTML, the new HTML standard.

- **Chapter 4: Using Style Sheets**. CSS allows you to separate the content of your Web pages from the style of those pages. This chapter presents techniques for defining and using styles. It includes techniques for creating visual effects without using images to improve the performance of your Web application.

- **Chapter 5: Building Tables**. HTML tables can display tabular data. They can also help you to line up page elements on an invisible grid. This chapter describes how to build a basic table, give the table some style, and add a scroll bar to the table. It also demonstrates how to use a table for a multi-column layout as is used on news sites.

- **Chapter 6: Building Forms**. Forms are a key part of a Web application. They allow you to collect information from the user. This chapter demonstrates how to create a simple form, a stylish form using CSS, and a precise form using absolute positioning.

- **Chapter 7: Understanding Object Models**. To add client-side interactivity to a Web application, you need to access the Web browser's capabilities and reference the HTML document's elements. You do that using an object model. This chapter describes what an object model is and details how to work with the browser object model and DOM.

- **Chapter 8: Using JavaScript.** JavaScript adds client-side logic to your Web application. This chapter provides an introduction to JavaScript and demonstrates how to use JavaScript to react to a user's action, dynamically add text to a Web page, hide and show Web page elements, and perform image rollovers.

- **Chapter 9: Validating Form Data.** Forms are a key part of a Web application and validating the form data is critical. Using JavaScript to validate the data allows you to perform the validation on the client, before submitting the form to the server. This chapter demonstrates how to use JavaScript and regular expressions to perform client-side data validation.

- **Chapter 10: Saving Data with Cookies.** Though most Web applications store data in a database on the Web server, you may have the need to store information, such as user preferences or application state, on the client. This chapter presents the JavaScript code for reading and writing cookies on the user's computer. It also discusses the security issues surrounding the use of cookies.

- **Chapter 11: Introduction to XML.** With XML you can define the data needed by your Web application separate from the Web pages. This allows you to more easily update that data without having to update how that data is displayed. This chapter describes how to build an XML document and when you would want to use one. It also provides an introduction to namespaces.

- **Chapter 12: Using XSL.** An XML document defines the data, but not a way to display the data. You can use XSL to transform an XML document into HTML for display in the browser. This chapter defines XSL and describes how to build XSLT stylesheets using XSLT elements and XPath.

- **Chapter 13: Defining Schemas and DTDs.** DTDs and schemas specify the valid structure and content of an XML document. You can use a DTD or schema to validate your XML document contents. This chapter describes DTDs and schemas and then presents how to build a schema for your XML documents.

- **Chapter 14: Reading XML with JavaScript.** Instead of using XSL to format your XML data, you can read an XML document into an HTML file using JavaScript. This chapter details the steps required to read the XML document and then navigate through the document to dynamically build a table of XML data for display in the browser.

- **Chapter 15: Web Application Architectures.** This chapter describes the technologies needed for client-side and server-side architectures and presents several architectural design patterns. It also presents the benefits of using a three-tiered architecture for a Web application.

How Do I Use This Book?

You can use this book to come up to speed quickly on client-side Web application technologies. Or, you can use this book as a single reference to common client-side features such as displaying data in a table using XSL or validating a form. You can also use this book as a tutorial, working through all of the exercises. You can use this book as it best suits your needs.

I have made every effort to describe the concepts presented in this book in a clear and concise fashion. I have tried to ensure it is up to date as of this writing. If you have suggestions for improving the content of the book or find something that is incorrect or unclear, I would like to hear from you. I can then incorporate your comments in future editions of this book. You can reach me via email at deborahk@insteptech.com.

CHAPTER 1

Introduction to the Web

THE WEB. GRANDMOTHERS USING EBAY, five-year-olds accessing barney.com, and just about everyone in between are now using the Web. It has become as much a part of our lifestyle as Automated Teller Machines (ATMs) and cell phones. (Does anyone even remember what life was like before ATMs and cell phones?)

The Web started out as a way to share simple textual information, primarily for government and research purposes. As the Web became more graphical, it became more interesting for other uses. Now most companies include Web pages as part of their marketing materials, cities present their services on Web pages, and people display their photos on personal Web pages. You can find everything from movie listings to local weather to information for your child's history report on the Web.

At first, the Web primarily consisted of documents displayed in a browser. Users could view the documents and link to other documents, but they could not interact with these static documents. Much of the Web is still static Web pages.

Then along came e-commerce (electronic commerce)—the idea that companies could sell anything on the Web. For e-commerce, companies need to display product listings and availability, take orders, accept credit cards, schedule deliveries, track user contact information, and so on. This requires much more than static Web pages; it requires Web *applications* that can display information contained in a database or other file, react to user selections, and store user-entered information.

Soon, many other industries were providing Web applications. Most banks now allow you to view your account and perform financial transactions on the Web. You can order pizza, book airline tickets, buy flowers, download your favorite music, check on your stocks . . . the list goes on and on.

As more and more people worked with these Web applications, it became apparent that the same type of functionality could be used for internal business applications. Instead of building Microsoft Windows or X-Windows applications that require deployment on user desktops or building mainframe applications that provide limited flexibility, companies can build Web-like applications that run on their private networks. Anyone with access to the company network can then access the applications and perform business functions such as tracking customers, entering expense reports, reviewing company policies, changing company benefit information, managing the quarterly budget, or producing invoices.

This book takes you through the process of building Web applications. It starts by describing how to create static pages and then covers technologies for adding interactivity to your pages. It also covers how to build Web pages dynamically using data from an external file. There are many technologies available for Web application development, so the last chapter focuses on how to put these technologies together to achieve your desired result.

In order to build great Web applications, you first need to understand what the Web is and how it works. It also helps to have a good handle on the many terms used in Web development. That is the purpose of this first chapter. If you are already familiar with these basic concepts, you can skip this chapter.

What Will This Cover?

This chapter covers the following key concepts:

- Describing what the Web is

- Defining basic terminology

- Understanding how the Web works

By the end of this chapter, you will know how the Web works and be familiar with the basic Web terminology used throughout this book.

What the Web Is

When you think of the Web, you may think of a spider web–like network of computers that contain Web pages you can view from a browser. Technically speaking, the network of computers upon which the Web exists is the *Internet*.

The *Internet* consists of millions of computers around the world that communicate with each other electronically. The Internet is public and accessible to anyone through an *Internet Service Provider* (ISP). You probably have access to the Internet through a modem, cable modem, or *Digital Subscriber Line* (DSL).

An *intranet* is similar in concept to the Internet, but the computers within the network are private. Access is only permitted by direct access to the private network. Most internal corporate browser-based applications are developed for a company's intranet.

An *extranet* is an extension of a company's intranet. It allows external users, such as customers or suppliers, to have access to parts of the intranet.

The *Web*, a.k.a. *World Wide Web* (www), is a large collection of documents on the Internet that are linked together. You can navigate from one document to another by clicking on a *hyperlink*. A hyperlink is normally defined with specially marked text, a symbol, or an image.

A document available on the Web is called a *Web page*. Anyone can view a Web page using a *Web browser* such as Internet Explorer, Opera, or Netscape. A Web browser fetches a requested Web page and displays it.

The browser is referred to as a *Web client* because it uses the services of the Web. The phrase *client-side* refers to anything happening within the browser.

A *Web server* is a computer that stores or generates the Web pages. It provides the pages to the client when the page is requested. The phrase *server-side* refers to anything happening on that Web server computer.

For example, a user can launch a browser such as Internet Explorer or Netscape and access a page such as `www.hollywood.com`. That page is found on a Web server somewhere on the Internet, downloaded to the client, and displayed in the user's browser. When the user clicks on a hyperlink on that page, the page referenced by that hyperlink is located on a Web server, downloaded to the client, and displayed in the browser.

A Web *site* is a collection of Web pages, usually on the same server or provided by the same company. A Web *application* is distinguished from a simple Web site in that it performs a business function, such as taking an order.

The Web was invented in the early 1990s by Tim Berners-Lee and Robert Cailliau, but it did not grow significantly until about 1994. Berners-Lee is still actively interested in his invention. He is now Director of the World Wide Web Consortium (W3C), which is an organization that coordinates standards for Web development.

Berners-Lee also created the Hypertext Markup Language (HTML) that is used as the language for the Web. Every Web page is comprised of content and HTML elements that define how the content is to be displayed in the browser. (HTML is described in detail in Chapter 3, "Using HTML.")

Even though the term *Web* is technically the public World Wide Web, convention allows the term to refer to the Internet or any intranet/extranet. In this book, the term *Web* is used to encompass the public Web and any private intranet or extranet. If you want to be technically accurate, you could instead refer to *Web applications* as *browser-based applications*.

How the Web Works

It is useful to know a little about what actually goes on behind the scenes. There is a lot that happens between the short time that the user types in a Web page address or clicks on a hyperlink and the time that the Web page is displayed in the browser.

The user first selects the Web page to be viewed either by typing the address of the page into the address area of the browser or by clicking on a hyperlink that identifies the address of the desired page.

URI = Address

The address of a Web page is defined with a *Uniform Resource Identifier* (URI). The URI provides a uniform naming scheme for all of the resources on the Internet or an intranet, including Web pages, images, video clips, applications, and so on. Two types of URIs are a *Uniform Resource Locator* (URL) and a *Uniform Resource Name* (URN).

A URL is an address for a resource on the Internet or on an intranet. It normally consists of three parts:

- The protocol used in the request

- The name of the Web server machine storing the resource

- The path to the resource on that machine

For example, the URL `http://www.hollywood.com/movies/coming_soon.html` consists of the protocol (`http:`), the name of the machine (`www.hollywood.com`), and the path to the resource (`/movies/coming_soon.html`). Many Web applications use the `http:` protocol, but you may have seen other protocols such as `ftp:` or `mailto:`.

For intranet resources, a common URL is of the form `file:\\fileserv\Training\TrainingWelcome.htm`. This URL consists of the protocol (`file:`) and the path to the resource (`\\fileserv\Training\TrainingWelcome.htm`).

A URN is a unique name for a resource on the Internet. This name does not identify where the resource is located and does not normally include the protocol, Web server name, or path. Rather, it is a logical name defined for the resource.

Every Web server has a unique address called an *Internet Protocol* (IP) address. That IP address looks something like this: `216.219.242.10`. You can access a Web server using the IP address instead of the URI by using this format: `http://216.219.242.10`. However, the IP address is not very user friendly or easy to remember, so URIs are used more often.

Normally, a user enters the Web page address as a URI such as `www.hollywood.com` or clicks on a hyperlink that has an associated URI. The URI must be converted into an IP address in order to locate the Web server. This is done using the *Domain Name System* (DNS). The DNS knows how to convert the logical URI name into the physical IP address of the Web server.

Once the Web server is located, the browser (client) communicates with the Web server through the Hypertext Transport Protocol (HTTP), the network protocol for the Web. With HTTP, Web servers can deliver any Web page, image, stylesheet, or any other file to any client.

The client begins communication with the Web server by opening a *Transport Control Protocol* (TCP) connection and sending a request message to the server. That Web server generates an HTTP response containing the requested resource, which in this example is a Web page. The Web server then sends that response to the client and closes the connection. Figure 1-1 shows this process.

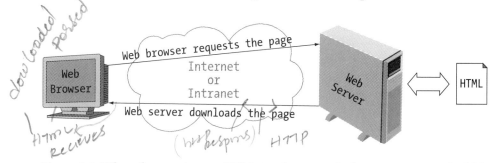

downloaded parsed (handwritten)

Web browser requests the page

Web Browser

Internet or Intranet

Web Server

HTML

Web server downloads the page

HTTP *recieves* (handwritten) *(http response) HTTP* (handwritten)

Figure 1-1. *When the user types a URI into a browser, the browser requests the Web page from a Web server, the Web server downloads the page to the browser, and the browser interprets and displays it.*

Once the Web server has closed the connection, it no longer has any information about the client. HTTP does not keep track of the client that it sent the page to or which other pages it has delivered to that client. Because HTTP does not maintain connection information between request transactions, it is a *stateless* protocol.

As the client receives the response from the Web server, the browser parses and interprets the HTML it receives. (The HTML processing is described in detail in Chapter 3, "Using HTML.")

The resulting page is displayed in the browser's window. This process is repeated again and again as the user links to other pages.

Instead of requesting a Web page, the user can select a Web application by entering the address of the application into the address area of the browser or by clicking on a hyperlink that identifies the address of the desired application.

The process for locating the application is the same as with a Web page. However, instead of downloading the application to the client, the application is executed on the Web server. The application can access a database to collect or store data, execute business logic, or perform any other operation. In many cases, the application generates HTML that is returned as a result.

The application then returns the result to the client, most frequently in the form of HTML that is downloaded, parsed, and displayed in the browser. Figure 1-2 shows this process.

5

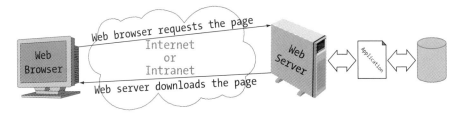

Figure 1-2. When the user accesses a Web application, the application is executed on the Web server, the Web server downloads the output of the application to the browser, and the browser interprets and displays it.

Many Web applications use several technologies and application programming languages such as HTML, JavaScript, Extensible Markup Language (XML), Java, Visual Basic, Active Server Pages, Java servlets, PHP, and so on. This book provides a detailed look at the technologies most commonly used for client-side development. Chapter 15, "Web Application Architectures," presents how to put all of the technologies together to successfully build a full-featured Web application.

What Did This Cover?

In order to build Web applications, it is important to understand some basic Web concepts. This chapter provided a basic overview of the Web and covered many of the basic terms.

The next chapter takes you through the steps for designing a Web application. The remaining chapters present the details you need to start building one.

Additional Resources

One chapter could not begin to cover everything there is to know about the Web. This section provides some additional resource suggestions by way of books, articles, and links to Web resources.

The books, articles, and links all existed at the time of this writing. There is a good chance that the books and articles still exist as you read this. However, the same cannot be said of Web links. Ignore the suggested links if they no longer exist.

Books and Articles

Gralla, Preston. *How the Internet Works.* **Indianapolis, IN: Que, 1999.**
This is a beautiful book with many full-page color pictures. This is a great book to get for your boss or users if they don't quite "get" the Web.

Links

`http://hotwired.lycos.com/webmonkey/backend/protocols/index.html`: This page provides links to articles on HTTP and DNS.

`http://webservices.web.cern.ch/WebServices/`: This site provides a wealth of information about the Web.

`http://www.w3.org/Addressing/`: This is the W3C site on URLs and URIs.

CHAPTER 2

Designing Web Applications

WHEN DESIGNING A GREAT Web site, the look and feel is frequently the most important aspect of the design. The focus is on color schemes, graphics, and attitude. When designing a great Web application, there are many more design aspects to consider.

A Web application normally performs a set of business processes or other tasks so you need to design the logic required to complete those tasks. You also need to define the layout of the Web pages to most efficiently help the user accomplish the tasks. Most Web applications also use data, so you need to design the structure of that data.

Managing all of the aspects of the Web application's design is easier if you follow a specific design methodology. This chapter presents the GUIDS Methodology, a pragmatic approach to software design. This methodology steps you through the process of designing your Web application.

The purpose of this chapter is to describe the GUIDS Methodology and walk you through the design of a simple Web application.

What Will This Cover?

This chapter covers the following key design concepts:

- Understanding the purpose of design

- Goal-centered design to define the business processes or tasks

- User-interface design to define the look and feel

- Implementation-centered design to define the architecture

- Data design to define the data structure

- Strategies for constructing the application, including project planning and scheduling

By the end of this chapter, you will know how to design all aspects of a Web application.

The Purpose of Design

Today's Web tools make it easy to develop Web pages and even simple Web applications without any forethought. You can just start building pages and keep modifying them until they work, then modify them further until they actually perform the task for which they were intended. A more proactive approach is to think through the Web application before you build it.

Before a house is built, for example, the house is designed and the blueprints document this design. Before a car is built, the car is designed and the CAD drawings document this design. So too should it be with Web applications.

Thinking through the design of your Web application before you build it ensures you are building the right application. It ensures you understand what it is that the application is supposed to do. It ensures you are communicating with the users and subject matter experts about what the application is to do. It helps you select the appropriate set of technologies for the Web application from the dozens of available Web technologies. It identifies the data that the application needs and how to work with it.

Without design, you have no plan or strategy for the application's development. Without a design you could build the application based on a guess as to what the users really need. Then you could continue to modify the application until it really does what the users need.

It is far better to know ahead of time the application's real goal. In other words, you need to understand the tasks that the users need to accomplish with the application.

The amount of time spent on the Web application's design depends on the application's complexity. You would spend some time and money designing a new home, for example, but not much time or money designing a tree house for the kids. The same applies to your Web application. You may not spend much time designing the application to track the team scores for your bowling league, but you will want to take the time to do a careful design of your company's order entry/inventory/invoicing application.

You may be thinking you really don't have time for design. Management wants completion of the Web application in "Web time" where expectations are weeks, not months. My company, InStep Technologies, has successfully completed several Web applications in "Web time" by following these guidelines:

- Use a good design methodology.

- Overlap the application's design and development.

- Follow some extreme programming (XP) techniques.

A design methodology helps you to develop a plan for defining the design. Using a methodology, you can logically and efficiently think through all aspects of the design. A methodology also defines the expected outputs from the design process, giving you guidelines and templates for building a set of design documents or specifications. We use the GUIDS Methodology for our design process; this methodology is covered in the next sections of this chapter.

Many design methodologies assume you need to design all aspects of every possible feature of an application before you can begin to build it. This is not necessarily true. If you can define an architecture for your Web application that supports change and allows future changes to be easily implemented, then you can design and build the application in small pieces. Because each piece is relatively small, you can deliver them quickly.

You can design the first piece of the application and then develop it, design the second piece of the application and then develop it, and so on. If you have a team working on the application, the design and development can overlap. So, the developers on the team can begin development of the first piece while the designers are working on the design of the second piece. The developers can then build the second piece while the designers are designing the third piece, and so on.

Much of these "just-in-time design," "build for change," and "iterative development" concepts stem from what has become known as *extreme programming (XP)*. The following quote summarizes the basics of XP:

> *"So you code because if you don't code, you haven't done anything. You test because if you don't test, you don't know when you are done coding. You listen because if you don't listen you don't know what to code or what to test. And you design so you can keep coding and testing and listening indefinitely."* —Kent Beck

For more information on XP, see the "Additional Resources" section of this chapter.

The GUIDS Methodology

The GUIDS Methodology for software design provides an object-oriented approach to software design and can be used with any languages, technologies, or modeling tools.

Each letter in the word GUIDS represents one of the phases of the design process:

G – Goal-centered design. This phase involves defining the basic goals of the Web application. What is the application trying to achieve? This phase then looks at how the user will use the application to perform tasks to meet those goals. Each task is called a *use case,* and the steps required to perform that task is called a *scenario.*

U – User-interface design. This phase involves defining the basic look and feel of the Web application, including the navigation techniques. It also includes converting each use case from the prior phase into a Web page or set of pages needed to perform the task. The focus is on defining a user-interface centered on the user's goals. This phase frequently results in a prototype of the user interface.

I – Implementation-centered design. This phase involves defining the technologies that will be used and how the technologies will work together within a cohesive Web application architecture. With the large number of technologies available for Web application development, this is a key step in the design process.

D – Data design. This phase involves defining any data that the application needs or uses and selecting the appropriate data stores to persist that data. If the application requires a new database, this phase also defines the structure of that database.

S – Strategies for construction. This phase involves defining the approach for the construction. This includes identification of the tools to be used, standards followed, and basic development approach. It also includes the definition of the development project plan and schedule.

The remainder of this chapter describes each of these phases in further detail.

Goal-Centered Design

The primary purpose of the Goal-centered design ("G") phase is to ensure you understand the underlying business issues or logic that must be handled by your Web application.

The "G" phase normally includes the following steps:

- Define the goal of the Web application.

- Define the use cases.

- Define the scenarios for each use case.

- Optionally, define a domain model.

When these steps are complete, you will have a better understanding of the purpose of the Web application and the tasks that the user must perform when using the Web application.

The result of the "G" phase is a document that defines the goal statement, set of use cases with scenarios, and an optional domain model. The scenarios in this document are used during the User-interface design phase to define the appropriate user interface required to perform each task. It can also be used during functional testing of the application to understand the functions that the application must perform.

Defining the Goal

The first step in the "G" phase is to define the basic goal of the Web application. The goal statement should be short (one to two sentences) and should reflect the main purpose of the Web application.

Let's walk through an example.

You are asked to develop a Web application to support a company that provides training courses. The application must allow the user to access the course catalog, sign up for a mailing list, and register for courses. After discussions with the subject matter experts, you define the goal of the Web application as:

> *The goal of this project is to provide an easy to use Web application that allows potential attendees to review the course catalog, register for courses, and sign up for a mailing list.*

Review the goal with the project sponsors and subject matter experts. This ensures that there is no miscommunication as to the Web application's main purpose. The goal statement sets the scope of the project by defining the high-level set of features that the Web application will support.

Defining the Use Cases

The next step in the "G" phase is to define the use cases for the Web application. The use cases define how the application will be used to meet the goal.

Normally, there is one use case for each primary task that a user must perform. The use case should define how a user would perform the task within the context of the new Web application, not how the task is currently performed.

Several types of users may use the Web application. For example, you may have business personnel entering or processing application data, external customers reviewing the data, and managers wanting summary information. Thinking about all of these users, called *actors*, helps ensure you define all of the appropriate use cases.

Going back to the example, from the goal statement and further interviews with the subject matter experts, you define several use cases as follows:

- Display the list of courses with their dates and locations.

- Add the user to the training mailing list.

- Enroll an attendee in a course.

- Enroll a set of attendees in a course.

- Enroll an attendee in multiple courses.

- Modify the enrollment of an attendee.

The number of use cases that you define depends on what your Web application must do. You can have anywhere from a few dozen to hundreds of use cases.

> **TIP**   *If you have more than about 25 use cases, break the project into separate, smaller projects with each project having no more than about 25 use cases. If you want to make deliveries in "Web time," where expectations are weeks not months, you can select an even smaller number of use cases. A smaller project is easier to manage, has less risk, and has a higher chance of success. It is then easier to get that second project approved when the first project was such a success!*

Defining the Scenarios

After defining the use cases, you need to detail the scenarios that define the steps performed for each use case. This provides the level of detail required to turn the use case into a user interface and associated business logic.

Each scenario is normally of the form: subject + verb + object. The subject defines who does the step, the verb defines what is done, and the object defines what is affected. Notice that this defines *what* is done and not necessarily *how* the Web application will do it.

Let's detail the scenario for one use case: "Add the user to the training mailing list."

1.   The user selects to be on the mailing list.

2.   The user defines a name and e-mail address for the mailing list.

3. The user defines information on how the user found the site, and the number of people at the user's location that may want training for use by the Marketing department.

4. The user selects to save the entered information.

5. The application validates the user-entered information.

6. The application saves the validated data.

If you are familiar with the Unified Modeling Language (UML), you can model these use cases visually. (For more information on the UML, see the "Additional Resources" section at the end of this chapter.)

To make the scenarios easier to work with, the primary scenario should not contain much "if" logic. For example, between steps 5 and 6 in the previous list, another set of steps could define how to handle the errors: "If the name is not defined, then . . . ." "If the e-mail address is wrong then . . . ." "If something other than a number was entered into the number of people box then . . . ." In many applications, the amount of error handling exceeds the amount of basic logic thereby making the basic logic more difficult to see.

The recommended approach is to define the "if" logic as one or more separate scenarios for the use case. In this example, a separate scenario could be defined for: "User entered invalid data" and all of the "if" logic could be defined within that scenario.

Defining the Domain Model

Another step that you can perform in the "G" phase is to develop a domain model. A *domain model* is a visual representation of the business area (domain) described by the Web application.

The most common syntax for defining a domain model is the UML. With the UML, you can define the basic things, or *objects*, with which the Web application must work. The easiest way to select these objects is to pick the nouns from the goal statement and use cases.

From the example, objects are the course, attendee, registration, and mailing list. These are the nouns from the use cases.

For each object, you can define the data elements for which the object is responsible. These are called the *properties* of the object. You can also define the sets of business logic for which the object is responsible. These are called the *methods* of the object.

In UML, each object is drawn as a box divided into three sections. The name of the object is defined at the top of the box, the list of properties are defined in the middle of the box, and the list of methods are defined at the bottom of the box.

Lines are drawn between the boxes to represent the relationships between the objects. For example, an attendee has a registration for a course. An attendee can also be on the mailing list. Figure 2-1 shows these relationships.

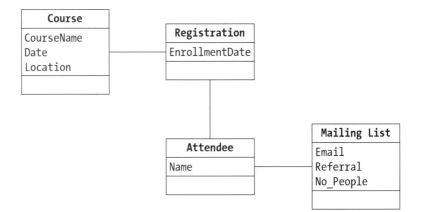

Figure 2-1. This simplified domain model uses UML to depict the relationships between the objects in the Web application.

User-Interface Design

The primary purpose of the User-interface design ("U") phase is to define the look and feel, navigation, and layout of the visual elements of your Web application.

The "U" phase normally includes the following steps:

- Define the conceptual design of the Web application.

- Define the navigation techniques.

- Define the page layouts.

- Optionally, build a prototype.

When these steps are complete, you have the design of the application's visual components. This design could be done with a Web design tool, such as Microsoft FrontPage or Macromedia Dreamweaver. Some Web designers prefer to use graphic design tools such as Adobe Photoshop or Paint Shop Pro for this design process. Other designers prefer products such as Microsoft Powerpoint or just paper and crayons. The tool does not matter as long as the design step is completed.

The result of the "U" phase is the visual design of the Web application and optionally a prototype of that design.

Defining the Conceptual Design

The first step in this "U" phase is to develop conceptual designs that provide different colors, styles, and visual elements. The users or subject matter experts can then select the conceptual design for the Web application based on these choices.

For instance, when you go to buy a car you don't want the salesperson to ask you what you want the car to look like. It would be hard and very time consuming to define all aspects of what you want the car to look and feel like. Instead, you would probably rather leave it to the designers to simply give you a few choices. It is frequently hard enough just selecting the model and color!

The same is true with your Web applications. You, as the designer, should not just ask the users what they want the application to look like. Rather, you should provide the users with about three conceptual design choices. The users can then select the best parts from the three choices to define the basic design.

As you develop the conceptual designs, consider these factors:

- **What browsers will be supported?** Does your Web application need to support every browser ever developed? Can it be limited to more recent versions of the most common browsers? For intranet applications, frequently you can define one or two specific browsers and browser versions, such as Internet Explorer 5.5 or Netscape 6. The more older browser versions you need to support, the more limited you may be in your conceptual designs. Alternatively, you may need to provide separate conceptual designs for older browsers and versions.

 NOTE *Defining the supported browsers and versions is important to complete before the "I" design phase because the choice may limit which Web technologies can be used. Some older browsers do not support some of the newer technologies.*

- **Are you converting an existing application?** Too frequently management wants an existing application "converted" to work on the Web without really understanding what that means. They think that the users want the Web application to work the same as the original Windows application. From a functional point of view, this may be true. But just because the users liked the Windows application does not mean that they will like a Windows-like user interface on their Web application. Don't get stuck trying to make the Web application work like Windows. Leverage the benefits of a true Web-based application.

- **What kinds of Web pages are needed?** Include an example of each type of Web page included in your application. Most Web applications have search and select pages, data entry pages, report pages, and so on. Include concepts of each type as part of the conceptual design.

- **How many data-entry elements are needed on the screen?** Some Web applications require twenty or more data entry elements on the page. To provide enough space for these, limit the amount of excess spacing or graphics along the left and right margins of the page.

- **How can you make the Web pages visually appealing?** Just because a page is used for data entry or a report does not mean that it should be boring. How many data-entry pages have you seen that are black and white, use the system font, and have a tedious vertical layout? You can add color, lines, and some style to make all of the pages of your Web application look interesting.

 NOTE *If users work with your Web application during the majority of their work time, they will be spending more time with your application than with their families. So anything you can do to make that time more enjoyable . . .*

Defining the Navigation Techniques

Web applications normally consist of many Web pages, sometimes hundreds. So, it is important to provide an easy way for the users to know where they are and how to navigate to where they want to go.

Many different navigation choices exist, but a few seem to be more common in Web applications.

One of the most common navigation mechanisms is a drop-down menu system. This may be a common choice because most Web applications are replacing Microsoft Windows or X-Windows applications that use a menu-based navigation system. Figure 2-2 shows an example of drop-down menu navigation.

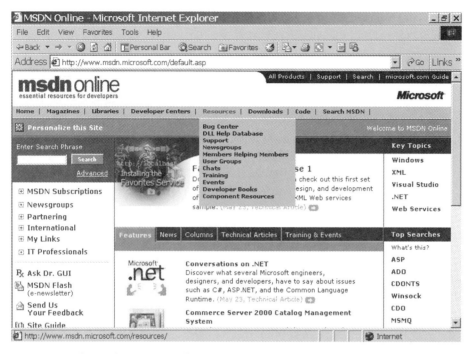

Figure 2-2. This Web page provides an example of a drop-down menu navigation technique.

A technique similar to drop-down menus provides for horizontal menus, as shown in Figure 2-3. When deciding on vertical drop-down versus horizontal menus, keep in mind that horizontal menus are limited by the horizontal width of the page.

Another common navigation mechanism for Web applications is the left navigation tree, as shown in Figure 2-4. As you can see, this style of navigation takes up some of the horizontal space on the page. This may not be desired if you have data-entry pages that require large amounts of horizontal space.

Web pages lend themselves to many more design choices. For example, instead of a text-based navigation tree, you can use graphics, as shown in Figure 2-5.

You can also combine these techniques. Figure 2-2 includes both a drop-down menu and a left navigation tree.

Another nice navigation feature for use in Web applications is called *breadcrumbs*, as shown in Figure 2-6. The idea behind breadcrumbs is to show the user how they got to where they are so they can logically navigate backward. This can be useful when several pages are required to complete a task or if the user can drill down to more detailed information.

Whatever navigation technique you select, be sure to use it consistently within your Web application.

Figure 2-3. This Web page provides an example of a horizontal menu navigation technique. Each menu option on the first horizontal menu bar, such as Resource Center, displays a different second horizontal menu bar.

Figure 2-4. This Web page provides an example of a left navigation tree. A search feature is also provided to quickly find desired information.

Figure 2-5. This Web page provides an example of a graphical left navigation tree.

Figure 2-6. This Web page demonstrates breadcrumbs. The hand cursor is over the navigation bar displaying the breadcrumbs.

Defining the Page Layouts

The page layout defines the placement of the visual elements for each of the primary pages in the application. It should also define where the information for the page would come from.

The visual layout of each page is defined as part of the design process to ensure that the users understand what they will get when the application is complete. This helps the users to picture the "G" phase use cases. The visual layouts also help the users to define whatever other tasks, steps, or data-entry elements that may have been missed during the "G" design phase.

There are several guidelines to keep in mind as you define the visual page layouts.

- **Layout for maximum productivity.** The layout should optimize the user's productivity on completing the tasks defined in the "G" phase use cases.

- **Be consistent.** The Web pages should provide a consistent look and feel, navigation, and basic functionality. For example, if one data-entry page uses a button called "Save" and another uses a button called "Submit" for the same purpose, the user may be confused.

- **Visually group content.** If a Web page contains thirty data-entry fields, it is easier for the user to find the desired field if they are logically grouped together on the page.

- **Define required fields.** Clearly show fields that the user must enter. This is frequently done using an asterisk next to any field that is required and then displaying a key stating that all asterisked fields must be entered.

The page layouts should also be used to identify where the data for the page is stored. If the page displays data, where did that data come from? If that page collects data from the user, where should it go?

Some of the information on the Web page is *static*; that is, it will not change. So the information may be hard-coded directly into the Web page as text. Other information on the page comes from an existing database, such as a corporate accounting system, or from a new database that will need to be designed in the "D" phase.

Defining the location of the data for the Web pages is critical for the next phase in the design process. In that phase, you need to select the technologies you will use to build the Web application. The technologies needed for static pages are different from those that need to access a database and build the pages from that data.

Building a Prototype

A *prototype* is a working example of the pages of your Web application. There are many pros and cons of developing a prototype, which is why this is an optional step.

The benefit of creating a prototype is to allow the users to visually see and possibly navigate between the pages of the Web application. This gives them a better feel for how the application will work.

In some cases, however, the user can mistake the prototype for the completed application. This can cause difficulty if the application is complex and will take a significant amount of time to be finished.

If you are going to build a prototype, there are several tools you can use to build it quickly. These are discussed in Chapter 3, "Using HTML."

Implementation-Centered Design

The primary purpose of the Implementation-centered design ("I") phase is to define the technologies that will be used in the development of the Web application and how they will work together within a Web application architecture.

The "I" phase normally includes the following steps:

- Define the architecture.

- Define the technologies needed to support the architecture.

- Optionally, build a proof of concept.

To define the architecture and technologies and to build the proof of concept, you need to be familiar with the technologies available for Web development. You need to understand what each technology is, when it should be used, and how to combine them to build a full-featured and efficient Web application.

This book covers many of these technologies to provide you with this understanding. The architecture design is revisited in Chapter 15, "Web Application Architectures," after these technologies have been introduced.

When these "I" phase steps are complete, you have the technical design of the application. The result of the "I" phase is the architecture of the Web application, the identification of the technologies to be used and optionally a proof of concept of the architecture.

Data Design

The primary purpose of the Data design ("D") phase is to define the data structures needed for your Web application.

In most cases, the data for your Web application is defined in a database such as Oracle or Microsoft SQL Server. In other cases, the data may be defined using XML as described in Chapter 11, "Using XML." In either case, design the structure of the data in the "D" phase.

Defining the data structures during the design improves developer productivity. This is most important when a team of developers will be working on the Web application.

The result of the "D" phase is the design of the data structures. This could include a database design or design of XML documents. Detailing good database design is beyond the scope of this book. Please refer to the "Additional Resources" section at the end of this chapter for more information on this topic. XML document design is presented in Chapter 11, "Using XML."

Strategies for Construction

The primary purpose of the Strategies for construction design ("S") phase is to develop the strategies and plan for the construction of the Web application.

The "S" phase normally includes defining the following:

- The tools to be used during the development

- Coding standards and conventions

- Source code control requirements

- Planned testing procedures

- Launch strategies

- Project plan

- Project schedule

By defining a standard set of tools, development conventions, and strategies a team of developers can successfully work on the application. Even if it is just you, defining these strategies gives you a good starting point for the development.

When these steps are complete, you are ready to begin the construction phase and build the application!

What Did This Cover?

In most other industries, there is a design phase before building anything complex, be it a car, a house, or a better mousetrap. The same should be true for your Web applications.

This chapter presented the GUIDS Methodology for software design. You can work through this methodology, adjusting it as needed, to define the goal, tasks the users perform to accomplish that goal, the user interface, the architecture, and the data structures for your Web application. After completing this design, you have what you need to efficiently construct the application.

The next chapter starts a series of chapters on Web technologies, beginning with the most basic, HTML.

Additional Resources

One chapter could not begin to cover everything there is to know about Web application design. This section provides some additional resource suggestions by way of books, articles, and links to Web resources.

The books, articles, and links all existed at the time of this writing. There is a good chance that the books and articles still exist as you read this. However, the same cannot be said of Web links. Ignore the suggested links if they no longer exist.

Books and Articles

Beck, Kent. *Extreme Programming Explained: Embrace Change.* **Upper Saddle River, NJ: Addison-Wesley, 2000.**
This is the classic book on extreme programming. It defines techniques for development that allow you to define your Web application as smaller sets of functionality, which you can rapidly develop and test.

Cooper, Alan. *About Face: The Essentials of User Interface Design.* **Foster City, CA: IDG Books, 1995.**
This is an insightful and entertaining book on user interface design concepts. Though many of the examples are shown using Microsoft Windows applications, the concepts can be applied to your Web applications.

Cooper, Alan. *The Inmates Are Running the Asylum.* **Indianapolis, IN: SAMS, 1999.**
The focus of this book is on designing for people, not for engineers. The subtitle of this book: "Why High-Tech Products Drive Us Crazy and How to Restore the Sanity" sums it up.

Fowler, Martin. *UML Distilled: Applying the Standard Object Modeling Language.* **Reading, MA: Addison-Wesley, 1997.**
This approachable book defines the basics of UML.

Hernandez, Michael. *Database Design for Mere Mortals: A Hands-On Guide to Relational Database Design.* **Addison-Wesley, 1997.**
This book provides an overview of relational database design that is unintimidating for those new to this concept.

Kurata, Deborah. *Doing Objects in Microsoft Visual Basic 6.* **Indianapolis, IN: SAMS, 1999.**
Though this book has "Visual Basic" in the title, the first several chapters cover the GUIDS Methodology in detail.

McConnell, Steve. *Code Complete: A Practical Handbook of Software Construction.* **Redmond, Washington: Microsoft Press, 1993.**
This book is highly recommended for every person writing any type of application. It provides details on topics such as variable naming, commenting, and good code construction techniques.

Links

`http://www.conallen.com/whitepapers/webapps/ModelingWebApplications.htm`: This page presents a white paper on modeling Web applications with UML.

`http://www.insteptech.com`: This Web site provides additional information on the GUIDS Methodology for application design.

CHAPTER 3

Using HTML

HYPERTEXT MARKUP LANGUAGE (HTML) is the basic language of the Web. It is with HTML that you define the user interface of your Web application. Since the Web is very visual, a good user interface is important. Whether you are building that next great dotcom site or an intranet application, the importance of a great user experience can be critical to the success of your Web application.

Each page that you view on the Web is comprised of one or more HTML documents. Each HTML document contains text and HTML syntax. Web browsers, such as Internet Explorer and Netscape, interpret the HTML syntax and display the Web page accordingly.

The purpose of this chapter is to provide you with the foundation you need to begin developing Web applications using basic HTML elements and attributes. Later chapters expand on these basics to add style sheets, tables, and forms to your user interface.

What Will This Cover?

This chapter covers the following key HTML concepts:

- Understanding HTML basics

- Using HTML tags to define elements

- Using attributes to define the properties of the elements

- Examining the anatomy of an HTML document

- Looking at XHTML

- Understanding how HTML interacts with your browser

- Creating a Web page using HTML

- Working with absolute and relative URIs

- Working with colors

27

- Working with fonts

- Linking to other Web pages

- Learning the basic set of HTML elements and attributes

- Handling different browsers and browser versions

By the end of this chapter, you will know how to leverage HTML to build the basic visual layout for your Web applications. These pages form the basis of the user interface of your Web application.

HTML Basics

HTML is a markup language that defines standard syntax for marking up a document. The markup syntax allows you to specify formatting, layout, and style for the document. Web browsers then interpret the markup syntax and display your document as a Web page.

In order for a Web browser to distinguish the document content from the markup syntax, all markup commands in HTML are surrounded by angle brackets (< >). These are called HTML *tags*. A Web browser parses these tags to determine how to display the document content as a Web page.

Most browsers provide an option to view the HTML source showing the HTML tags. With Internet Explorer, you can select Source from the View menu or right-click on the page and select View Source. With Netscape, you can select Page Source from the View menu or right-click on the page and select View Page Source. If you currently have access to the Web, try it. Access your favorite Web page and view the source. Notice the HTML markup commands surrounded by angle brackets (< >) throughout the page.

HTML tags contain *elements* that represent structure, layout, formatting and behavior, such as paragraphs, images, lists, and hypertext links. These are the building blocks of your HTML document.

Many HTML elements have properties, called *attributes*, which give you more control over the look or behavior of the element. For example, attributes can define the size of an image or the color of a font.

HTML is not case sensitive. Element and attribute names can be uppercase, lowercase, or proper case. For compatibility with the current standards, lowercase is recommended.

TIP *A common recommendation was to define the element and attribute names in the HTML document as uppercase so they stood out from the textual content of the page. The current recommendation is to use lowercase for compatibility with the new XHTML standards, discussed later in this chapter.*

Defining Elements

An HTML element is defined with a beginning tag and an ending tag. The beginning tag consists of a left angle bracket (<), the element name, and a right angle bracket (>) with no spaces between the angle bracket and the element name. The ending tag consists of a left angle bracket (<), a forward slash (/), the element name, and a right angle bracket (>). The text contained between the beginning and ending tags is the *content* of the element. For example:

```
<h1>Welcome to our Training Page</h1>
```

The <h1> tag denotes the beginning of the h1 (or heading level 1) element, and the </h1> tag denotes the end of that element. The text contained between the beginning and ending tags is the content of the element and is formatted as a level 1 heading.

TIP *Some browsers can interpret some elements using the beginning tag with no ending tag, such as the p (paragraph) element. Provide both beginning and ending tags for compatibility with the new XHTML standards, discussed later in this chapter.*

If an element has no content, it is *empty*. For example, the br (line break) element has no content; it simply breaks to a new line. For example:

```
View a list of our courses.<br></br>Or, sign up for our mailing list.
```

With empty elements, you can combine the ending tag with the beginning tag as follows:

```
View a list of our courses.<br />Or, sign up for our mailing list.
```

Elements can contain other elements. Between the beginning and ending tag of one element you can insert the beginning and ending tag of another element. For example:

```
<head>
<title>Training Welcome Page</title>
</head>
```

Notice how the `title` element tags are nested entirely within the `head` element tags. This capability to nest elements allows you to nest fonts within paragraphs, rows within tables, and controls within forms.

HTML tags should not overlap. That is, if a tag begins within another tag, it should also end within that tag.

If all of the elements in your HTML document are defined with beginning and ending tags and the tags do not overlap, the HTML document is *well-formed*. For example, the following is not well-formed:

```
<h1>Welcome to our <font color="red">Training Page</h1>
Our training courses are the best in the industry.</font>
```

In the previous example, the `<font>` tag resides within the `<h1>` tag, but the `</font>` tag appears after the `</h1>` tag. These tags are overlapping and are therefore not well-formed. The correct HTML is:

```
<h1>Welcome to our <font color="red">Training Page</font></h1>
<font color="red">Our training courses are the best in the industry.</font>
```

Notice how both the beginning and ending `font` element tags for the heading are nested within the `h1` element tags. Since the first `font` element is then only applied to the heading, the `font` element is repeated for the additional text.

TIP   *Some browsers, like Internet Explorer, are very forgiving. They accept overlapping tags such as the previous example that is not well-formed. However, it is good coding practice to always build well-formed HTML documents and ensure your tags do not overlap. Well-formed documents are a requirement for compatibility with the new XHTML standards, discussed later in this chapter.*

There are two basic types of elements, inline and block-level. *Inline* elements define HTML commands. Inline elements can only contain text or other inline elements. Generally, inline elements are not displayed on a new line. Both font and b (bold) elements are examples of inline elements. They change the content's attributes but don't display the content on a new line.

Block-level elements define the HTML document structure. Block-level elements can contain other block-level elements, inline elements, or text. Generally, block-level elements are displayed on a new line. Both h1 and p are examples of block-level elements.

Specifying Attributes

Attributes provide a greater level of control over how the element looks or behaves. You can modify the behavior of an element by assigning values to the element's attributes.

An attribute is defined by an attribute name followed by an equal sign (=) and a value. The attribute value should be quoted using either double quotes (" ") or single quotes (' '). Quotation marks are not required unless the attribute value contains special characters.

 TIP *Use quotation marks around all attribute values for compatibility with the new XHTML standards, which are discussed later in this chapter.*

Attribute name and value pairs are defined within the beginning tag for the element, after the tag name and before the right angle bracket (>). You can specify multiple attributes for an element by separating the attributes with a space. For example, the font element has face and size attributes that identify the font name and size:

```
<font face="arial" size="4">Our training courses are the best in the
industry.</font>
```

This example defines a specific font type and size for the text between the beginning and ending tags.

TIP *You can create your own attributes for many of the elements. See Chapter 9, "Validating Form Data," for information on enhancing form validation by adding attributes to* form *elements.*

The Anatomy of an HTML Document

Most HTML documents follow the same basic structure. They contain a standard set of element tags, text specific to the page, and comments. This structure is shown next and discussed in the text that follows.

```
<html>
<!-- Welcome Page -->
<head>
<title>Training Welcome Page</title>
</head>
<body bgcolor="#D2B48C">
<h1>Welcome to our Training Page</h1>
<font size="4">Our training courses are the best in the industry.</font>
</body>
</html>
```

Every well-formed Web page includes the tags for the html element (lines ❶ and ❿). This is the *root* element of the page and defines that the content of the file is HTML. The rest of the page is divided into two main sections, the header and the body.

TIP *Be sure to include the* html *element as the root element of your HTML document for compatibility with the new XHTML standards, discussed later in this chapter.*

A *comment* (line ❷) can exist anywhere in the page. Any text between the beginning comment marker (<!--) and the ending comment marker (-->) is considered to be a comment and won't appear within the browser window. However, the comments appear if the user views the source of the HTML or saves that page as HTML. So don't put anything in your comments that you would not want a user to read.

The *header* section of an HTML document (lines ❸through❺) is nested within the html element. This section contains the preparatory information for the page. The header section of the page can also include styles and scripting. It should not contain content to be displayed on the page. This section minimally includes the page title (line ❹), which should provide a good description of the page.

The page title is important because it is used in many ways. The browser displays this title in the browser's title bar, search engines list this title when the page is found by a search, the browser defaults to this title when the user saves favorites, and this title is used in the history list.

The *body* section of an HTML document (lines ❻ through ❾) is also nested within the html element. This section contains the information to be displayed in the browser, including the content for the page and the elements that define the format of the page. All of the static text, all of the graphic elements, and any other visual elements required for the page are defined within the body.

NOTE *Every HTML document has* head *and* body *elements, even if the document does not contain a* <head> *or* <body> *tag. You may have seen, or even written, HTML documents without these tags and the documents are displayed correctly since these elements exist without the tags. Be sure to use the* head *and* body *element tags for compatibility with the new XHTML standards, discussed later in this chapter.*

The first element within the body section (line ❼) defines a line of text to appear on the page using the level 1 heading style. The heading style is different from the title (line ❹) in that the title element defines the logical name of the page and the h1 element simply defines a style of text on the page.

The second element within the body (line ❽) defines text to appear with the defined font. When a browser interprets this HTML, the result appears as in Figure 3-1.

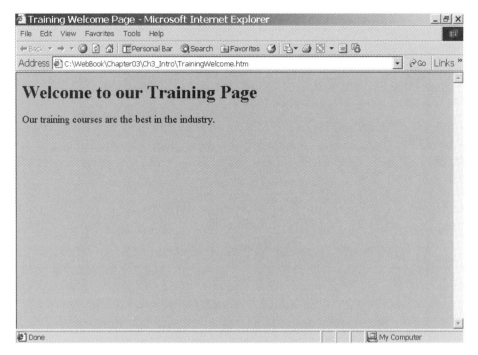

Figure 3-1. A simple and visually uninteresting example of a Welcome page provides a starting point.

Any text in the HTML document that is not associated with an element is displayed in the browser as is. For example, the following will display the text on the page:

```
<body bgcolor="#D2B48C">
<h1>Welcome to our Training Page</h1>
Our training courses are the best in the industry.
</body>
```

However, all text for a Web page should be defined as content within an element in the HTML document. Normally text is defined within a block-level element such a p (paragraph) or div (division). For example:

```
<body bgcolor="#D2B48C">
<h1>Welcome to our Training Page</h1>
<div>Our training courses are the best in the industry.</div>
</body>
```

TIP *It is good programming practice to define all textual content for the Web page within a block-level element. This ensures compatibility with the new XHTML standards, discussed later in this chapter.*

You can indent or add white space to the HTML document as needed for readability without impacting the display of the page. Tabs, carriage returns, and all extra white space in the text of your HTML document are ignored. For example, the HTML from the prior example could contain extra spaces and lines without impacting how that HTML is displayed:

```
<font size="4">
    Our training courses are the best in the industry.
</font>
```

To display a carriage return in the body of the Web page, use the br element or start a new paragraph with the p element. To insert white space, use the   (non-breaking space) character entity. There is no HTML equivalent for a tab, but you can set margins using styles as defined in Chapter 4, "Using Style Sheets."

XHTML

Everyone in the high-tech field knows that as soon as you finally feel comfortable with a technology, it changes. So, now that you are familiar with the basics of HTML, let's look at XHTML.

The "X" in XHTML represents the application of the eXtensible Markup Language (XML) to HTML. The World Wide Web Consortium (W3C) has recommended the XHTML specification as the newest version of HTML and calls it "a reformulation of HTML 4 in XML 1.0."

XML allows definition of a precise syntax. By applying XML to HTML, you can develop HTML that conforms to a rigorous standard. The goal of that standard is to provide a more consistent interpretation and display of your HTML documents in all browsers. XML is discussed in further detail in Chapter 11, "Using XML."

The greatest impact XHTML has on your HTML development is as follows:

- The root element of the document must be defined with the <html> tag.

- Tags must be in lowercase (<p> instead of <P>).

- You must add a trailing slash to any empty tags, with a preceding space (`<br />`). Adding the space ensures that the element is parsed appropriately in browsers that don't support the trailing slash syntax.

- Tags not specified as empty must have an ending tag (`</p>`).

- Attribute values must always be in quotation marks (`<input type="text" />` instead of `<input type=text />`). You can use either double quotes (" ") or single quotes (' ').

- Attribute values cannot be inferred; they must be defined (`<input type="checkbox" checked="checked" />` instead of `<input type="checkbox" checked />`). The W3C refers to the original shortcut as *attribute minimization*, which is no longer supported in XHTML.

- The `id` attribute must be used when defining identifiers. The value of the `id` attribute must be unique on a page. The `id` attribute replaces the `name` attribute but because older browsers support the `name` attribute and not the new `id` attribute, you may want to provide both attributes and give them identical values. See Chapter 6, "Building Forms," for more information on using both the `name` and `id` attributes.

- The `body` element content must be contained within block-level elements, such as `p` (paragraph), `div` (division) or `table`.

- Thought has been given to support of nontraditional browsers, such as cell phones and other devices. These devices can support a subset of the standard through device profiling, called a Composite Capability Preference Profile (CCPP). The W3C is working on CCPP with the Wireless Access Protocol (WAP) Forum.

Follow these requirements as you define your standards for HTML development if you want to be XHTML compliant.

See the W3C Web site and other XHTML references in the "Additional Resources" section of this chapter for more information and details on XHTML.

Specifying the HTML Version

To follow XHTML standards, declare the version of HTML that is in your HTML document. You can define HTML 4 or the newest XHTML version.

You define the version with a document type (DOCTYPE) declaration as the first line of your HTML document as follows:

```
<!DOCTYPE html PUBLIC "-//W3C//DTD XHTML 1.0 Transitional//EN"
    "DTD/xhtml1-transitional.dtd">
```

This specifies the version of HTML in your HTML document, in this case, XHTML 1.0. The DOCTYPE declaration also identifies the *Document Type Definition* (DTD) for the HTML document. A DTD defines the set of elements and attributes that are valid for the HTML version you specified.

The DTD can be used by a browser or HTML validator to validate your HTML. See Chapter 13, "Defining Schemas and DTDs," for more information on DTDs. See the "Additional Resources" section of this chapter for links to Web sites that will validate your HTML using the defined DTD.

You have three DTD choices with XHTML 1.0:

- Validate your HTML based on the strict XHTML standard. Use this when you want clean structural HTML without any tags that have been replaced by style sheets. (See Chapter 4, "Using Style Sheets," for more information.)

```
<!DOCTYPE html PUBLIC "-//W3C//DTD XHTML 1.0 Strict//EN" "DTD/xhtml1-strict.dtd">
```

- Validate your HTML based on the transitional standard between HTML 4 and XHTML. Use this when you want to use the new XHTML features but also support older browsers.

```
<!DOCTYPE html PUBLIC "-//W3C//DTD XHTML 1.0 Transitional//EN"
    "DTD/xhtml1-transitional.dtd">
```

- Validate your HTML based on using frames. Use this only when you want to use HTML frames.

```
<!DOCTYPE html PUBLIC "-//W3C//DTD XHTML 1.0 Frameset//EN"
    "DTD/xhtml1-frameset.dtd">
```

 CAUTION *These declarations are case sensitive. If you don't have the appropriate case, the declaration may not work as you expect.*

The strict standard does not allow many of the tags used to define element style information, such as background color and font information. So, the HTML shown in this chapter does not validate against the strict standard. For the purposes of this chapter, you need to use the transitional standard. The next chapter replaces the style related tags with style sheets, which is the recommended approach. After that point, the HTML shown in this book validates against the strict XHTML standard.

How HTML Works

To best understand the effect of your HTML coding, it is useful to know what actually goes on behind the scenes as the browser interprets your HTML document.

When the user selects or opens a Web page, the user's browser parses and interprets the HTML on the page. All of the tags in the header section of the HTML document are fully parsed and interpreted first. The tags in this section are not displayed, but provide instructions to the browser.

Then the tags in the body section are processed serially. The browser interprets and displays content in the browser's window based on its own interpretation of the HTML tags surrounding that content.

A standards body called the World Wide Web Consortium (W3C) (www.w3.org) defines the specification for HTML. With such a standard in place, one would think that your Web page would appear the same in every browser on any machine. However, this is not the case. Different versions of different browsers on different operating systems process the HTML slightly differently. Several techniques for dealing with these differences are presented later in this chapter. More advanced techniques for handling browser differences are presented in later chapters.

Since it is the browser and not a Web server that interprets the HTML, you can view local HTML files in your browser. You can create an HTML document as a file on your computer and open it in your browser. The browser then interprets the HTML the same way as if you had accessed the HTML from a Web server. You will be using this technique if you work through the Try Its later in this chapter.

Creating a Static Web Page Using HTML

You can create static Web pages using only HTML. Static pages don't provide interactivity, but they can look good and provide an interesting user experience. Each Web page can contain text content, graphics, and links to other pages. If you view the source of several Web pages, you will find many pages that are developed exclusively with HTML.

You can use a basic text editor—such as Notepad or WordPad for Windows and Emacs or vi for Unix—to create a file containing your HTML document. Using a simple tool has the benefit of simplicity, but it requires that you know the necessary HTML and spend the time typing in all of the correct HTML syntax.

Several tools are available to help you create your HTML. Tools such as Microsoft FrontPage or Macromedia Dreamweaver allow you to lay out your page using a WYSIWYG (what you see is what you get) style of editor. With these tools, you can visually place elements on the page and the tool builds the appropriate HTML behind the scenes. Most of these tools allow you to view and edit the HTML directly within the tool as well.

There are also more advanced tools that validate your HTML for conformance to standards and warn you about broken links and potential conflicts between browsers. Some tools evaluate your pages for performance bottlenecks and make recommendations for improvement. See the "Links" section at the end of this chapter for links to several such tools.

The basic steps for building an HTML document using an HTML file are:

1. Create a text file and save it with an .htm extension.
    Alternatively, use an .html extension for your HTML file, which is common for Web pages hosted on Unix machines.

2. Add the DOCTYPE declaration to define the HTML version you plan to use.

3. Add the `html`, `head`, and `body` elements.

4. Add elements and attributes to the header section of the HTML document to define basic preparatory information such as the page title.

5. Add elements and attributes to the body section of the HTML document to provide the desired page content and formatting.

6. Try out your HTML document in a browser to ensure it appears as you expect.

Follow these steps to get started creating your Web application.

Try It 3-1.

Creating a Simple Web Page

Try It 3-1 begins development of a Welcome page that welcomes the user to the application and provides general introductory information. You can, of course, tailor this example to any static page.

1. Using Notepad or your tool of choice, create a new text file.

2. Add the DOCTYPE declaration and the basic HTML tags to the file: `<html>`, `<head>`, `</head>`, `<body>`, `</body>`, and `</html>`.

3. Add a `title` element to the header section of the page. You could give the page a title like "Acme Training Welcome Page".

4. Add a `bgcolor` attribute to the body element to give the page background an interesting color. Alternatively, add a `background` attribute to display a background graphic. (See Table 3-1 for reference information on these elements and attributes.)

5. Add an `h1` element to the body section of the page with text such as "Welcome to the Acme Training Page".

6. Define text such as "Our training courses are the best in the industry." in a specific font size and/or font face.

7. For an added challenge, add `ul` and `li` elements to define a list of course offerings on the page. (See Table 3-1 for reference information on these elements.)

8. Optionally, define graphics to add to the page using the `img` element. Be sure to use consistent color schemes and graphics appropriate for the application. (See Table 3-1 for reference information on this element.)

9. Save the file as TrainingWelcome.htm.

 CAUTION   *Be sure to save the file as text-only. The default file type may not be text-only in the tool you are using.*

10. Open the TrainingWelcome.htm file in your browser.

If you have an association set up for the .htm extension and you are using Windows, you can double-click on the page in Windows Explorer and it will appear in your default browser. If you don't have an association set up for the .htm extension, launch your browser and use the File ➢ Open menu option to open the TrainingWelcome.htm file.

The resulting page will appear similar to Figure 3-1, depending on how many optional features you added to the page. If your page does not appear as you would like, modify it using the elements and attributes presented in this chapter.

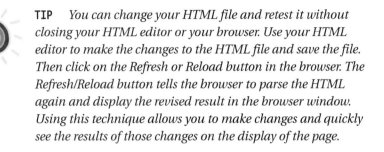

TIP *You can change your HTML file and retest it without closing your HTML editor or your browser. Use your HTML editor to make the changes to the HTML file and save the file. Then click on the Refresh or Reload button in the browser. The Refresh/Reload button tells the browser to parse the HTML again and display the revised result in the browser window. Using this technique allows you to make changes and quickly see the results of those changes on the display of the page.*

The HTML document with the optional list of courses is presented in Listing 3-1.

Listing 3-1. The TrainingWelcome.htm file contains the HTML needed to display a simple Welcome page.

```
<!DOCTYPE html PUBLIC "-//W3C//DTD XHTML 1.0 Transitional//EN"
    "DTD/xhtml1-transitional.dtd">
<html>
<!--
    Try It  3-1
    Title:  Welcome Page
    Author: InStep Technologies
            www.insteptech.com
    Purpose:To demonstrate the basic techniques for
            creating an HTML document
 -->
<head>
<title>InStep Training Welcome Page</title>
</head>
<body bgcolor="#D2B48C">
<h1>Welcome to the InStep Training Page</h1>
<font face="arial" size="4" color="red">
    Our training courses are the best in the industry.
</font>
<br />
<br />
```

```
<font size="4" color="navy">Here are a few of our course offerings:</font>
<ul>
    <li>OO Design</li>
    <li>OO Programming with VB</li>
</ul>
</body>
</html>
```

HTML Techniques

There are some basic techniques that can help you work more successfully with HTML. These techniques are especially important as you go through the "HTML Reference" section of this chapter because many attributes require use of these techniques.

Working with URIs

Some HTML elements, such as anchors and images, require specification of an URI, or Uniform Resource Identifier. An URI defines the protocol (such as FTP or HTTP) to be accessed along with the specific location of an HTML document, graphic, or other file somewhere on the Web.

 **NOTE** *You may be more familiar with the commonly used name, Uniform Resource Locator (URL). A URL is actually a special case of a URI as discussed in Chapter 1, "Introduction to the Web." URI is the W3C standard name that will be used throughout this book.*

If you use graphics on your page, you need to define the source location of the graphic by setting the src attribute to the URI so the browser knows where to locate it. If you want to link to another page, you need to set the href attribute of the link to the URI of that page.

URIs can be *relative* or *absolute*.

An absolute URI defines the entire path to the page including the protocol, the Web server name, the complete path, and the filename. The example below is an a (anchor) element that defines a hyperlink to a Course Catalog HTML file:

```
<a href="http://www.insteptech.com/CourseCatalog.htm">View the course catalog.</a>
```

CAUTION *Some systems, such as Unix, have case sensitive filenames. So, if you are specifying a location on a Unix Web server, watch the casing on the path and filenames.*

Use absolute URIs when you are referencing pages that do not exist on the same Web server as the page you are creating.

A relative URI describes the location of the desired file with reference to the location of the current page. If the file is in the same directory on the Web server as the current page, you can use relative referencing and specify the filename with no path. For example:

```
<a href= "CourseCatalog.htm">View the course catalog.</a>
```

If the page is in a subdirectory, you can relatively reference the file as follows:

```
<a href= "Catalog/CourseCatalog.htm">View the course catalog.</a>
```

If the page is in a subdirectory of the parent directory, you can relatively reference the file using the double dots (..) to back up one directory:

```
<a href= "../Home/Catalog/CourseCatalog.htm">View the course catalog.</a>
```

TIP *If the referenced page is part of your Web application, use a relative path. This gives you more flexibility in working with the pages in development, testing, and production environments. It is also more efficient.*

Working with Colors

Many HTML elements have attributes, such as bgcolor, which require specification of a color. A color can be defined by a logical name or by its red, green, and blue (RGB) color values.

The logical names include simple colors such as "black" and "navy" and fancier color names like "cornflowerblue" and "sandybrown."

An RGB color value is comprised of three hexadecimal numbers that specify the intensity of each of the three colors: red, green, and blue. The values range from 00, defining none of that color, to FF, defining the maximum amount of that color. For example, #FF0000 is max red, no green and no blue, resulting in red.

#00FF00 is no red, max green, and no blue, resulting in green. #00FFFF is aqua, which is an equal mix of green and blue with no red.

 TIP *Not all color names are recognized by all browsers. All browsers should recognize RGB color values. To provide cross-browser compatibility, use RGB values.*

With the RGB values, you have thousands of colors to choose from. However, some users' computer systems may only display 256 colors. Of these 256, 40 vary on different computer systems. By starting with the most common set of 256 and eliminating the 40 variable colors, you are left with a palette of 216 colors optimized for cross-browser and cross-platform use. This palette is called the *browser-safe palette.*

If you use colors that are not in this set of 216 colors, those colors may dither, appear blocky, and make the text on the page more difficult to read on systems that support only 256 colors. To see what your pages look like in other color resolutions, set your system color scheme to 256 colors. This tip is described in detail at www.smartisans.com; see the "Links" section for more information on this site.

The browser-safe palette is supported by both Internet Explorer and Netscape. Limiting your color use to these colors ensures that your colors appear correctly. See the "HTML Reference" section of this chapter for a table of standard color names and their associated RGB values. See also the "Links" section at the end of this chapter for links to sites that can help you work with the browser-safe palette and select the colors that you want.

Working with Fonts

When you have a lot of information to display on a Web page, varying fonts can help set information apart. Font definition includes the style or face, size, and color.

The font face includes the font name, such as "arial" or "helvetica." When you specify a font face, you can provide several options separated by commas:

```
<font face="arial, helvetica, courier">
```

The browser attempts to use the first font on the list. If that font is not found on the user's system, the browser tries the second font name. If none of the fonts are found, the browser's default font is used. The most commonly available font faces are Times and Courier. Most Windows users also have Arial.

Font sizes can be defined using specified values 1 through 7. These values don't map to pixels or points, but to the browser's default font, which has a font size of 3. As you may expect, font size values larger than 3 give you larger than average fonts, and values smaller than 3 give you smaller fonts.

You can also define relative fonts by using plus (+) or minus (–). For example, a font size value of –2 is two sizes smaller than the browser's default font. A font size value of +1 is one size larger than the default font.

Font colors are defined using color attributes as defined in the prior section, "Working with Colors."

Linking to Other Web Pages

One page does not a Web application make. To develop a real application, you need a set of pages and one or more ways for the user to navigate between those pages.

There are several different ways you can provide page navigation. The most common way to navigate between pages is with a hyperlink. A hyperlink is defined using an a (anchor) element as follows:

```
<a href="TrainingCourseList.htm">View the course catalog.</a>
```

The text between the beginning and ending tags is displayed on the page. The browser displays the text underlined and in a link color to identify that the text is a link to another location. When the user clicks on the link, the browser navigates to the page identified in the href attribute.

For a more visual look, you can use an image as the link. To do this, insert an img element between the anchor tags as follows:

```
<a href="TrainingMailingList.htm">
   <img src="../images/MailingList.gif" alt="Mailing List" align="middle" />
   Sign up for our mailing list
</a>
```

This displays a graphic along with text as a link. The user can click on either the graphic or the text to navigate. The alt attribute of the img element defines the alternate text that is displayed in place of the image while the image is downloading. This is especially useful if the user has the image-loading feature of their browser turned off. It also makes your page more accessible because an agent or other text-to-speech tool could read the image text.

 **TIP** *Use the* width *and* height *attributes of the* img *element to specify the size of the image. By specifying these attributes, the image is rendered with the correct dimensions and the user will not see a visual shifting of the page when the image is finished downloading.*

Try It 3-2.

Adding Links to a Web Page

Try It 3-2 adds links to the Welcome page created in Try It 3-1.

1. Open the Welcome page file (TrainingWelcome.htm) from Try It 3-1 in your HTML editing tool.

2. Define a text link with the a (anchor) element that allows the user to navigate to another page. Use TrainingCourseList.htm as the link reference. This linked page is created in Chapter 5, "Building Tables."

3. Define a graphic link to another page. Use TrainingMailingList.htm as the link reference and use any graphic. This linked page is created in Chapter 6, "Building Forms."

4. Save the file.

5. Open the TrainingWelcome.htm file in your browser. You should see both links on the page.

6. Click on the link. You will get nothing (or an error) because the new page is not yet created.

The resulting page will appear similar to Figure 3-2.

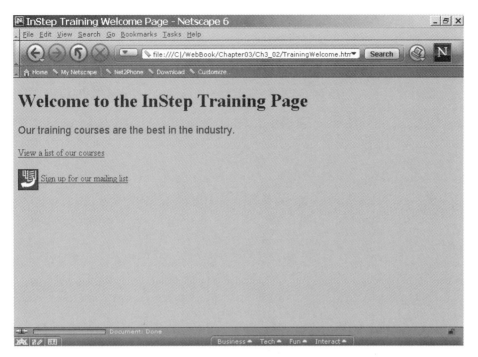

Figure 3-2. This Welcome page has links to related pages.

The code used to generate the page shown in Figure 3-2 is presented in Listing 3-2.

Listing 3-2. The TrainingWelcome.htm file was modified to include two links.

```
<!DOCTYPE html PUBLIC "-//W3C//DTD XHTML 1.0 Transitional//EN"
    "DTD/xhtml1-transitional.dtd">
<html>
<!--
    Try It  3-2
    Title:   Welcome Page
    Author:  InStep Technologies
             www.insteptech.com
    Purpose: To demonstrate linking to another Web page
-->
<head>
<title>InStep Training Welcome Page</title>
</head>
<body bgcolor="#D2B48C">
<h1>Welcome to the InStep Training Page</h1>
```

```
<font face="arial" size="4" color="red">
   Our training courses are the best in the industry.
</font>
<br />
<br />
<div>
<a href="TrainingCourseList.htm">View a list of our courses</a>
<br />
<br />
<a href="TrainingMailingList.htm">
   <img src="MailingList.gif" alt="Mailing List" align="middle" />
   Sign up for our mailing list
</a>
</div>
</body>
</html>
```

NOTE *The listing includes* div *element tags around the* a *(anchor) tags. This is for XHTML compliance, which requires that body element content must be contained within block-level elements. See the "XHTML" section earlier in this chapter for more information.*

HTML Reference

There are many HTML elements and attributes, but you will find that most Web pages use a core set. These elements and attributes are defined in Table 3-1. This list should get you started with most of what you want to do with basic HTML.

> **CAUTION**   *The HTML elements and attributes marked with an asterisk (*) in Table 3-1 are deprecated in HTML 4. A deprecated element or attribute is one that has been outdated by newer constructs and is no longer recommended. The W3C may drop these elements in the future. Many of these deprecated elements and attributes provide for formatting, such as the* font *element and* bgcolor *attribute. Instead of using these deprecated elements and attributes, use cascading style sheets for formatting your page as defined in Chapter 4, "Using Style Sheets." See* www.w3.org *for more information.*

Table 3-1. Frequently Used HTML Elements and Attributes

ELEMENT	MEANING, USE, AND COMMON ATTRIBUTES	EXAMPLE
a	Anchor. An inline element that defines a hypertext link to another page or page location. Common attributes:	<a href= "CourseCatalog.htm" target="_blank">View the course catalog.</a>
	href - Defines the URI of the page that is displayed as the result of the link.	
	target - Opens the link in a defined window. Use _blank to open the link in a new window. This is useful if you want to keep the user in your application in one window but show summary or help information in another window.	
b	Bold. An inline presentational element that styles the text between the beginning and ending tags as bold.	You can register for <b>any</b> of our courses here.
body	Body of the HTML document. Defines the body section of the HTML document where the page content is defined. If you want to ensure compliance with XHTML, the body can only contain block-level elements. The block-level elements can then contain the inline elements or text. Common attributes:	See the prior section for an example.

Table 3-1. Frequently Used HTML Elements and Attributes (continued)

ELEMENT	MEANING, USE, AND COMMON ATTRIBUTES	EXAMPLE
body *(cont.)*	**background*** - The background graphic for the page.	
	bgcolor* - Background color for the entire page.	
	link* - Hyperlink color.	
	text* - Text color for the entire page.	
br	Break. An empty inline structural element that generates a new line.	`For more information, contact:` `  Acme, Inc.`

div	Division. See also: span. A block-level structural element that defines a section or fragment of the page that shares a common format. It is used to contain and position other elements or text. Common attributes:
	
	align* - Aligns the text within the division. Valid values are: left, center, right, and justify.
		`<div align="center">Here is`
		`what developers are saying`
		`about our courses:</div>`

font*	Font. An inline element that styles the text between the beginning and ending tags using the defined font attributes. Common attributes:
	
	color* - Font color.
	
	face* - Font face. Defines a list of font names. The browser attempts to use the first font on the list. If that font is not found on the user's system, the browser tries the second font name and so on. If none of the fonts are found, the browser's default font is used.
	
	size* - Size of the font. The value is 1 through 7, with 3 being the default value.
		`<font face="arial, helvetica,`
		`courier" size="4"> Our training`
		`courses are the best in the`
		`industry.</font>`

Table 3-1. Frequently Used HTML Elements and Attributes (continued)

ELEMENT	MEANING, USE, AND COMMON ATTRIBUTES	EXAMPLE
h1	Heading. A block-level phrasal element that defines a heading style where 1 represents the heading level. Use 1 for main headings, 2 for sub headings, and so on down to 6 heading levels. You can control the look of the headings using styles. Common attributes: **align*** - Aligns the text. Valid values are: `left`, `center`, `right`, and `justify`.	`<h1 align="center">Welcome to our Training Page</h1>`
head	Header of the HTML document. Defines the header section of the HTML document where the page preparation occurs. There should not be any content for the Web page in this section of the HTML document.	See the prior section for an example.
hr	Horizontal rule. An empty block-level presentational element that adds a horizontal line to the page. Though this has several attributes, they are deprecated in HTML 4. Use styles instead to define the look of the rule.	`Here is the main section.<hr />` `Here is the subsection.`
html	Root element. Defines to the browser that the page should be interpreted as HTML. This is the root element of the page.	See the prior section for an example.
i	Italics. An inline presentational element that styles the text between the beginning and ending tags as italics.	`You can register for <i>any</i> of our courses here.`
img	Image. An inline element that defines an image on the page. Common attributes: **align*** - Aligns the image with respect to the surrounding text. Valid values are: `top`, `middle`, `bottom`, `left`, and `right`. **alt** - Alternative text that should be displayed if the image cannot be displayed. Under Windows, this text also appears as a tool tip. This attribute is also important for accessibility because the alternate text can be read to the user.	`<img src="images/courses.gif" alt="Course Offerings" />`

Table 3-1. Frequently Used HTML Elements and Attributes (continued)

ELEMENT	MEANING, USE, AND COMMON ATTRIBUTES	EXAMPLE
img *(cont.)*	**border*** - Thickness of the image border in pixels.	
	height - Height of the image in pixels or a percentage. If the height is different than the image height, the browser shrinks or expands the image to fit the defined height.	
	hspace* - Horizontal space on both sides of the image in pixels.	
	src - URI of the image.	
	vspace* - Vertical space on the top and bottom of the image in pixels.	
	width - Width of the image in pixels or a percentage. If the width is different than the image width, the browser shrinks or expands the image to fit the defined width.	
li	List item. Defines an item within a list.	See ol or ul for an example.

link	Link to an external file. Establishes a link to an external file, such as a style sheet or font definition file. This element is placed in the header section of the HTML document. Common attributes:	`<link rel="stylesheet"`
		`type="text/css"`
		`href="TrainingStyle.css" />`

	href - URI of the external file.	
	rel - Defines the relationship between the element and the linked file. The only value recognized by both Netscape and Internet Explorer is stylesheet.	
	type - Provides an advisory on the content type of the linked file.	
meta	Meta data. Allows definition of information about a document, such as the author name, content description, or keywords. This must be defined in the header section of the HTML document. Common attributes:	`<meta name="author"` `content="Deborah" />`

Table 3-1. Frequently Used HTML Elements and Attributes (contiued)

ELEMENT	MEANING, USE, AND COMMON ATTRIBUTES	EXAMPLE
meta *(cont.)*	**content** - Specifies the value of the meta data property. **http-equiv** - Used in place of the name attribute to create HTTP response message headers. **name** - Specifies the name of the meta data property. Some valid values are: author, copyright, description, and keywords. **scheme** - Specifies the scheme to be used to interpret the property's value.The valid meta data properties and their valid values are not predefined. The scheme defines the location of the property definition.	

ol	Ordered list. Defines a numbered list. Each list item (li element) is indented within the list. You can control the look of the list using styles. Common attributes:
	
	start* - Defines the starting number for the list.
	
	type* - Defines the type of number. Valid values are: A for capital letters, a for lowercase letters, I for Roman numerals, i for lowercase Roman numerals, 1 for Arabic numbers.
		`<ol>`
		`    <li>OO Design</li>`
		`    <li>OO Programming</li>`
		`</ol>`

p	Paragraph. A block-level structural element that styles the text between the beginning and ending tags as a paragraph. Adds a blank line before and after that paragraph. You can control the look of the paragraph using styles. Common attributes: **align*** - Aligns the text. Valid values are: left, right, center, and justify.	`<p>This is one paragraph</p>` `<p>This is another paragraph</p>`

Table 3-1. Frequently Used HTML Elements and Attributes (continued)

ELEMENT	MEANING, USE, AND COMMON ATTRIBUTES	EXAMPLE

pre	Preformatted. A block-level phrasal element that styles the text between the beginning and ending tags as preformatted text. All spaces, tabs, and carriage returns are retained as defined in the text. This is useful for displaying preformatted information like code listings.	```<pre>```
		```for i = 0 to 5```
		``` ' Do Something```
		```next i```
		```</pre>```

span	Span. See also: div. An inline structural element that defines a subsection of text that is formatted differently than the other text. It is primarily used to apply a style to an element or text within a sentence or other block-level structure.	```Our course is <span```
		```style="color:purple">```
		```GREAT!</span>```

title	Page title. An element that does not appear in the Web page; rather it defines the text that appears in the browser's title bar when the page is displayed. This element is placed in the header section of the HTML document.	```<title>Training Welcome``` ```Page</title>```

ul	Unordered list. Defines a bulleted list. Each list item (li element) is indented within the list. You can control the look of the list using styles. Common attributes:
	
	type* - Defines the type of bullet. Valid values are: disc (default), circle, and square.
		```<ul>```
		``` <li>OO Design</li>```
		``` <li>OO Programming</li>```
		```</ul>```

NOTE   *Additional HTML elements and attributes are presented in Chapter 5, "Building Tables," and Chapter 6, "Building Forms." Styles are detailed in Chapter 4, "Using Style Sheets."*

See the "Additional Resources" section of this chapter for a reference to a complete listing of valid HTML elements and their associated attributes.

Some of the elements in Table 3-1 have color attributes. These colors can be defined using a named value or an RGB value as described in the "Working with Colors" section earlier in this chapter. The W3C defined standard color names and their associated RGB values are presented in Table 3-2.

Table 3-2. Standard Color Names and Their RGB Values

COLOR NAME	RGB VALUE
Black	#000000
Silver	#C0C0C0
Gray	#808080
White	#FFFFFF
Maroon	#800000
Red	#FF0000
Purple	#800080
Fuchsia	#FF00FF
Green	#008000
Lime	#00FF00
Olive	#808000
Yellow	#FFFF00
Navy	#000080
Blue	#0000FF
Teal	#008080
Aqua	#00FFFF

HTML Character Entities

As you build your Web page, you will find that there are certain characters that cannot easily be added to your HTML or don't display correctly in the browser. In some cases, this is because the character has special meaning to HTML (such as the < character). To display these types of characters, you need to use HTML *character entities.*

HTML character entities simply replace a specific character. They are not elements or attributes and are not defined using tags. They are character combinations that begin with an ampersand symbol (&) and end with a semicolon (;). There are a large number of these entities and Table 3-3 presents only a few. See the "Additional Resources" section of this chapter for a reference to a complete listing of valid HTML character entities.

Table 3-3. Common HTML Character Entities

ENTITY	MEANING	EXAMPLE
&	Ampersand. Since the ampersand has special meaning in HTML, this entity allows you to define an ampersand in the text.	The course is at a great bed & breakfast.
'	Apostrophe.	The instructor's lectures were great.
©	Copyright symbol.	© InStep Technologies, 2001
>	Greater than. Since the greater than sign indicates the ending of a tag, this entity allows you to define an actual greater than in the text.	7 > 5
<	Less than. Since the less than sign indicates the beginning of a tag, this entity allows you to define an actual less than in the text.	5 < 7
	Nonbreaking space. Inserts one space at the defined location without a carriage return.	
"	Quotation mark. Since quotation marks have special meaning in HTML, this entity allows you to define a quote in the text.	Here is what an attendee said: "The course was great!"

Browser Compatibility

Even though the W3C has defined standards for HTML and XHTML, not all browsers follow these standards. Some browsers add their own extensions. Some browsers were built before the standards were defined or are not up to date with current standards. And in many cases, the user may just have an older version of a browser that does not support the latest standard.

If a browser does not support a particular element or attribute, or supports it differently, the browser may not display your Web page as you intended. This is even more of a concern when you are supporting Web applications that may not appear the same to all of the users.

In some situations, such as an internal application in a corporate environment, you may be able to develop your Web application to run on one standard type and version of browser. In that case, you can write your HTML specifically for that browser. In many other situations, like any public Web site, you want to ensure compatibility with many browsers and browser versions.

There are several ways in which you can provide support for different browsers and browser versions. One alternative is to limit yourself to a very basic set of HTML that is the most standard across the browsers. This, of course, has the adverse effect of limiting your control over the look and format of the page.

Another choice is to determine the user's browser type and version and make adjustments as needed as the page is processed. This requires some scripting as discussed in Chapter 8, "Using JavaScript."

A common alternative is to develop separate pages for separate browsers. The first Web page of your Web application could determine the user's browser type and version (again with scripting) and then display a page specifically tailored for that browser and version. This will, of course, require more time to develop and fully test the set of pages.

There is also a middle-of-the-road choice. You can decide that you will only support a specific set of browsers such as only browsers that run HTML Version 4 or greater. This limits the amount of work you must do to support all browsers yet provides for some amount of browser choice for the user.

Whichever approach you choose, you need to ensure that you have access to each browser and version that you plan to support so you can view your page in that browser. As you develop more complex pages, it is important that you view the page with every browser on which the page could appear. Otherwise, you could be surprised to find out how your page appears.

If you have more than one browser available on your system, you may want to view the TrainingWelcome.htm file from the prior Try It in each browser. You can then see the differences in the browser support of the HTML that you have created.

Basic HTML Tips and Tricks

This section includes basic tips and techniques when working with HTML.

Visual Design

The Web is a very visual medium so visual design is an important aspect of your Web development.

Define the Resolution

The optimal solution for handling screen resolution is to have your Web page correctly resize based on the size of the browser window. However, this may not always be feasible. In that case, you need to design the layout of your Web pages based on a selected screen resolution.

The resolution you select depends on the audience for your Web application. If you are working on an intranet application and you know that most users will, or could, run 800×600 resolution you can design for that size. If you are building a public Internet application, you may need to limit yourself to 640×480.

Unlike Windows applications, you cannot easily determine the user's screen resolution within the Web page. Even if you could, most users may want to display the Web page in only a portion of their screen. If you need to lay out your page to a specific resolution, you may want to consider developing the pages in several resolutions and then allowing the user to select the desired size.

Whichever technique you chose, be sure to remain consistent for all of the pages in your Web application.

Commenting

Commenting is just as important in HTML as it is in any other programming language. Here are a few commenting tips.

Use Comments

Use comments to describe the purpose of the Web page and to detail any complex layout or effects on the page.

Watch Your Comment Content and Length

Be aware that comments are downloaded to the user, so you don't want to add too many comments. Also, the user can view the source of your page to view the comments, so you don't want to say anything personal or confidential.

Defining Your Directories and Files

Every HTML file that you create needs to reside somewhere on your Web server. Here are several tips on defining the path and filenames and on the structure of your Web application source directories.

Create Logical Filenames

Give each HTML file and each support file a logical name. You may define hundreds of Web pages, graphics, and other files in your application, so the more logical the filenames, the easier it is to remember which file is which.

You can prefix the filename of your Web pages with the name of the primary object represented by the page. For example, all of the pages supporting training are named TrainingXXX.htm. All of the pages for an address book are named AddressXXX.htm.

Ensure You Have a Default Page

If a user types your URI without a page name, the Web server tries to locate a default page such as index.html (Unix) or default.htm (Windows). If you don't have a page by that name, the user may not get what you would like.

Select your Welcome page and rename it to the appropriate default page name. Alternatively, some Web server products allow you to change the name (or set of names) that is used as the default page.

Define the Correct Extension

The extension is the primary way for the browser to know what type of file it is receiving. Be sure to include an .htm or .html extension on each of your Web pages. Either extension can be used, but for consistency it is good to select one and use it throughout a single Web application.

Use Lowercase Names for Entering URIs

Any path name, directory name, or filename that the user needs to enter as a URI should be in lowercase. This makes it easier for the user to remember the URI and ensures that the desired page is found. For example:

```
www.insteptech.com/courses/register.htm
```

Use Proper Case Names for Code Readability

In many Web applications, you don't want the user to jump into a page by typing in the URI. Rather, you want the user to come through a login page. So there is no need to ensure the filename is lowercase.

If the page does not need to be entered as a URI by the user, you can continue to use lowercase or you can use proper case (capitalization) to define filenames that are easier to read. For example, TrainingMailingList.htm is easier to read than trainingmailinglist.htm.

Set Up a Logical Directory Structure

Define your working directory structure such that all of the files for your application are in one directory and its subdirectories. Put all of your HTML files into the application's directory, any graphics in an image subdirectory and any include files in an include subdirectory.

For larger applications, you should break your HTML files into logically related groups and store them within subdirectories of the application's main directory.

Use Relative Paths Where Possible

If you follow the suggested directory structure, you can define the location of images, includes, and other pages in the application using relative paths. This makes it easier to move the Web application, such as from a test system to a production system.

Working with Images

Images are important to a Web-based application. They're eye candy. Here are some tips for working with images. More image tips are provided under the "Performance Tips" section later in this chapter.

Use Existing Images

It will save you a lot of time if you can locate existing images for your Web page instead of creating them from scratch. (And if you are like me, creating from scratch may not even be an option.) You can download images from several Web sites like www.altavista.com or you can purchase a library of images. You can also scan in photographs for use on your page.

CAUTION *Be careful when you use existing images. Some images are copyrighted; others have complex permission schemes. Some prevent use on commercial sites; others can be used but cannot be modified. Be sure to check the site or CD for license requirements or disclaimers and read the small print.*

Use the Right Tool

Creating images requires a full-featured tool to ensure you can achieve the look you want. One of the most commonly used tools is Adobe Photoshop. Another choice is Paint Shop Pro for Windows. If you must create images from scratch, select the tool that works best for you.

Use the Right Graphics File Format

The most widely used graphics file formats are: GIF, JPEG, and PNG.

GIF is normally used for graphics and is limited to 256 colors. It has a reasonably small size and it supports transparency. GIF images can be animated for a more interesting look.

JPEG is used more often for photographs and high color images. It does not support transparent images.

PNG (Portable Network Graphics) is similar to GIF and is optimized for graphics use on the Web. PNG supports image depths up to 24-bit and provides a better lossless compression than that found in GIF files. PNG has been accepted as an image standard by the W3C.

Use one of these formats to ensure that your images appear as you expect in both major browsers.

Watch Your Image Colors

If your images contain colors that are not in the browser-safe palette, those colors may dither, appear blocky, and make the text on the page more difficult to read.

To see what your pages look like in other color resolutions, set your system color scheme to 256 colors. This tip is described in detail at www.smartisans.com, see the "Links" section for more information on this site.

Getting Your Application Noticed

A public Web application is of no use if no one ever finds it. So, it is important that your application be noticed and easily found.

Here are some tips for getting your site noticed. See the "Links" section of this chapter for a reference to additional tips on getting your pages to the top of search engine results.

Index Your Page for Search Engines

Internet search engines, called *Web crawlers*, search through Web pages in order to build search indexes. To ensure that your page is found during a search, include appropriate keywords describing your page. Normally you do this with meta element tags.

For instance, say your Web page lists all of the Visual Basic (VB) courses that you train. You want search engines to find your page if the user searches for "VB" or "Visual Basic" courses. In this example, you would add the following to the header section of your Web page:

```
<meta name="keywords"
    content="VB courses,Visual Basic courses,VB training,Visual Basic training"/>
<meta name="description"
    content="Visual Basic Training from InStep - The best in the industry"/>
```

The keywords entry should include the relevant keywords. The more specific the match to what the user is entering, the higher your page gets ranked with the search engines.

The description entry should include a good description of the page. Frequently, the description appears below the page title in the search results page. This is the place to define why the user should click through to your page.

The meta element tags are also a good place to put misspelled variations of your company name or products. An urban legend has it that one travel Web site does more business than any other in the Mediterranean because their pages show up in searches for many alternative spellings of the word.

Don't Forget the Title

If a search engine finds a match to one of your Web pages, the search engine displays the title of your page if one is provided. Be sure to provide a good title that compels people to check out your application. Standard practice is to limit the title to no more than sixty-four characters.

Performance Tips

Even as users get better computers and higher speed connectivity, performance is still an issue. The biggest performance delays on most pages is attributed to downloading graphics, so many of the following tips are focused on graphics issues.

Minimize the Size of Background Images

Many Web page designs include a background image. If the image is simply a repeating pattern, you can create the image file as one line of the pattern, just large enough to contain the entire description of the pattern. When a page defines this image as the background, the browser quickly downloads the small file and repeats (tiles) the image vertically to cover the full size of the screen. If you had built the graphic to the size of the screen, the graphic would download more slowly and cause a delay in the display of your page.

 CAUTION *Using a background image can make it more difficult to read the text on the page. This is especially true if the image contains colors that are dithered on some systems because they are not within the browser-safe palette.*

Minimize the Size of Color Block Images

To add a nice design element, you may want blocks of a single color on your page to visually offset other text or graphics. Instead of creating the entire block with an image, you can create a very small (few pixels) image. Then use the `width` and `height` attributes of the `img` element to expand the image to the desired size. This smaller image downloads much faster than a larger image.

Optimize Image Display

Text around an image won't begin to appear in the browser until the image file is opened and the size is determined. To shortcut this process, use `width` and `height` attributes of the `img` element to predefine the correct image size. Text on the page then displays before the image download is complete.

Another image optimizing tip is to create a low resolution (and smaller) image that quickly appears on the page. Also, create a second, higher quality image that redraws over the lower quality image. Using the `lowsrc` and `src` attributes for the img element, you can define both images and the browser handles the download to display both images.

Reuse Images on Other Pages

Once a graphic is downloaded, it is cached. If you reuse the same graphic on multiple pages, you won't take the hit of downloading it again.

Debugging Tips

Sometimes it is difficult to see why a page does not display as you expect. Here are some tips for debugging your HTML.

Recognize Browser Differences

Text and layouts that appear correctly under Internet Explorer may not appear the same in Netscape or vice versa. It is important to understand the differences between the two browsers and ensure that you code your HTML to account for these differences.

Don't Forget Missing Ending Tags

Internet Explorer is very forgiving of missing ending tags. Netscape is not as forgiving. If your page appears correctly in Internet Explorer and not in Netscape, check your beginning and ending tags.

Use a Validator

There are several HTML validators available on the Web. These validators evaluate your HTML syntax and describe any syntax errors. Some validators even provide extensive help on correcting the errors. See the "Links" section at the end of this chapter for links to several of these validation tools.

What Did This Cover?

The first tier of a multi-tiered architecture is the user-interface, or presentation layer. For Web applications, the user interface is normally created using the HyperText Markup Language (HTML). This chapter was a whirlwind tour though HTML.

This chapter provided a basic introduction to building an HTML document. It examined the basic anatomy of an HTML document so you can better understand its fundamental structure. You learned how to use HTML elements with their associated attributes to liven up the text on the pages of your Web application.

The Try Its in this chapter worked through a simple HTML example that displayed a static page to the user. Anchor tags were added to link to pages that will be built in upcoming chapters.

But what if you just finished creating the fifty-third page of your Web application and the user decides that all of the headings should be navy and all of the background colors should be yellow? Wouldn't it be nice to make the change in one place and have all of your pages recognize the changes?

The next chapter defines how to use style sheets to define the basic styles of your Web application and reuse those styles on all of your pages. So, when the user wants to change the look, you can change all of the pages by changing just the style sheet.

Additional Resources

One chapter could not begin to cover everything there is to know about basic HTML. This section provides some additional resource suggestions by way of books, articles, and links to Web resources.

The books, articles, and links all existed at the time of this writing. There is a good chance that the books and articles still exist as you read this. However, the same cannot be said of Web links. Ignore the suggested links if they no longer exist.

Books and Articles

Castro, Elizabeth. *HTML 4 for the World Wide Web*. Berkeley, CA: Peachpit Press, 2000.
I read through a lot of HTML books before I found one that really told me what I wanted to know. Yes, those HTML reference books were very useful. But just knowing what the elements and attributes are did not tell me how to put them together to visually display something that looked nice. This book provides a very task-based approach to using HTML that expands on the information provided in this book.

Musciano, Chuck, and Bill Kennedy. *HTML: The Definitive Guide*. Cambridge, MA: O'Reilly & Associates,1998.
This is an excellent reference book. It takes a complete tour of HTML in reference fashion. Though this book is very approachable for a beginner, this is a true reference book and not the best learning tool if you are just starting out.

Musciano, Chuck, and Bill Kennedy. *HTML & XHTML: The Definitive Guide.* Cambridge, MA: O'Reilly & Associates, 2000.

This is the updated version of the prior book covering XHTML.

Williamson, Heather. *Writing Dynamic Cross Browser HTML.* Berkeley, CA: Apress, 2001.

This is the first book to address how HTML can be used effectively with the latest versions of Netscape and Internet Explorer, in addition to supporting legacy versions. It provides an in-depth discussion of the features that can be used safely, which features must be avoided, and how to use scripting languages to overcome differences between HTML implementations.

It also teaches you how to incorporate cross-platform disciplines into the development process.

Links

`http://hotwired.lycos.com/webmonkey/99/31/index1a.html/`: This article defines three techniques for successful search placement for your Web pages: get crawled, get ranked, and get clicked.

`http://watson.addy.com/`: Dr. Watson is a free service that analyzes your Web pages to ensure they conform to the latest HTML standards. Watson can also check out many other aspects of your site including link validity, download speed, search engine compatibility, and link popularity.

`http://www.15seconds.com`: This Web site provides a wealth of information on Web site design and on Web application development. It also contains links to many other Web development resources.

`http://www.cast.org/bobby/`: This site provides a Web-based tool that evaluates the accessibility of Web pages. The tool, called Bobby, identifies changes to Web pages that are needed so people with disabilities can more easily use them.

`http://www.htmlhelp.com/tools/validator/`: This Web site validates your HTML syntax. You can validate from a URI or from a file on your computer.

`http://www.htmlvalidator.com/`: This tool validates your HTML syntax. You can download a demo version to try it out.

`http://www.libpng.org/pub/png/`: This site provides information on the PNG graphics file format.

`http://www.lynda.com/hexh.html`: This Web site provides a color chart of the nondithered colors that work well on the Web along with their associated RGB values. This chart can be helpful for selecting colors for your Web pages.

`http://www.macromedia.com/software/dreamweaver/`: This site is the home to Dreamweaver, a full-featured HTML editing tool.

`http://www.netmechanic.com/`: This site provides tools for improving, promoting, and monitoring your Web pages.

`http://www.smartisans.com`: This site covers many Web page design tips and techniques.

`http://www.w3.org`: The standard site for the World Wide Web Consortium (W3C) that is responsible for setting standards for the Web.

`http://www.w3.org/People/Raggett/tidy/`: This site provides a link to HTML Tidy. This free utility fixes basic HTML errors and tidies up sloppy editing into nicely laid out markup. It also identifies where you need to pay further attention on making your pages more accessible to people with disabilities.

`http://www.w3.org/TR/xhtml1/`: This site contains the specifications for XHTML.

`http://www.wdvl.com/Authoring/HTML/`: This site provides a complete reference to the valid HTML 4 elements and attributes.

`http://www.wdvl.com/Authoring/Languages/XML/XHTML/`: This site provides an introduction to XHTML with some examples.

CHAPTER 4

Using Style Sheets

As you use HTML to implement your Web page design, you will quickly discover HTML's limitations and how little control you have over the formatting of a page. HTML does not provide for indentation, justification, line spacing, character spacing, absolute position, or other layout attributes. This is where Cascading Style Sheets (CSS) fit in.

CSS allows you to separate the content of your Web page from the style. You can use HTML to specify the content and structure of your page and use CSS to define the color, indentation, justification, spacing, positioning, and other important style properties. And since you can define these styles in a separate CSS file, you can apply the styles to all of the pages in your Web application. This gives you much more control and helps you provide a consistent look throughout all of the pages in your Web application.

The purpose of this chapter is to provide you with the basics for defining and using styles. Later chapters expand on these basics to define styles for tables and to use absolute positioning to lay out forms.

What Will This Cover?

This chapter covers the following key CSS concepts:

- Understanding style sheets

- Working with styles

- Applying inline styles for greater control

- Using embedded styles for standardization

- Defining style classes for flexibility

- Declaring styles using IDs

- Using styles to add visual effects

- Creating an external style sheet for reusability

- Understanding how styles cascade

- Learning the basic set of style properties

By the end of this chapter, you will be able to define style rules, apply styles to elements on a Web page, and create interesting visual effects. You will also understand how style sheets cascade.

Cascading Style Sheet Basics

CSS is a specification that defines formatting styles and the rules by which they are applied. The World Wide Web Consortium (W3C) maintains this specification, defining the standard style properties and rules.

Ever use the style feature of Microsoft Word? It allows you to apply a specific formatting style to text in your Word document. There are styles such as Heading 1, Bullet, and Normal. If you want to have a certain look for some of the text in your Word document, you can define the font, paragraph style, and other attributes and then save this set of attributes as a named style. You can then apply this style to text in the document and that text is displayed with the defined font, paragraph style, and other attributes.

CSS provides for the same type of functionality in your Web pages. If you want to have a certain look for some HTML elements on your Web page, you can define a specific set of properties such as font name, font size, and font color as a CSS style. You can then apply this style to an HTML element and the element is displayed with the defined font name, font size, and font color.

Style Sheets

You define the CSS formatting styles and rules that you want to use with a style sheet. A *style sheet* is a set of style rules that describe how HTML document elements are to be displayed on the page. Each style rule in the style sheet looks similar to this:

```
p {font-family:arial; font-size:20pt; color:red}
```

The style rule is comprised of two parts, a selector and a declaration. The *selector* part of the style rule specifies which HTML elements are to be affected by the rule. The style rule above is defined for p (paragraph) elements. This rule is applied automatically to every p element in every HTML document that uses this style sheet.

A selector can specify more than one element by separating the elements with commas. The following style rule applies to all h1 and h2 heading elements:

```
h1, h2 {font-family:arial; color:navy}
```

The *declaration* part of a style rule, contained within braces ({ }), defines the style properties to be applied to the specified elements. The properties are comprised of name and value pairs. Each name is followed by a colon (:) and one or more values. The property name defines the attribute, such as color or font family. The property value defines the specification of that attribute. Each name and value pair is separated by a semicolon (;). The declaration in this example defines a specific font family, size, and color:

```
p {font-family:arial; font-size:20pt; color:red}
```

As a result of this style rule, all of the p elements on the Web page are displayed in red, 20-point Arial font.

At this point, you may be thinking that you can achieve the same result using HTML elements and their associated attributes. For this particular example, you are correct:

```
<p><font face="arial" size="20pt" color="red">Some text</font></p>
```

NOTE *Notice the difference in syntax between the attributes of the HTML* font *element versus the properties of the style rule. The names of the HTML attributes are not necessarily the same as the style properties (*face *versus* font-family *in this example)—the attributes use an equal sign (=) where the style properties use a colon (:) and the style properties are separated by semicolons (;) instead of spaces as with the attributes.*

But what if you have twenty paragraphs? Do you want to repeat that font definition within every paragraph? What if you decide later that you really want the text to be blue? Do you want to find and update every place you added this font definition? Now you may be seeing some of the benefits of using style sheets.

The Benefits of Style Sheets

Using style sheets has many benefits:

- **You can save time.** Instead of setting the font attributes for every header or paragraph in your page with all of the correct beginning and ending tags, you simply set the heading or paragraph style.

- **You can simplify maintenance.** If the look of your page needs to be changed (for example, all paragraph text needs to be blue instead of black), a simple change to the style is all you need.

- **You can ensure style consistency on your page.** If you define a paragraph style, every paragraph reflects that style.

- **You can ensure style consistency throughout your Web application.** You can save the style rules to an external CSS file, then link this file to every page in your application. This ensures that all pages in the application have a consistent style.

- **You can improve the appearance of your Web page.** Style properties extend the capabilities provided by HTML attributes. For example, styles provide for setting a margin. There is no standard attribute for this in HTML.

- **You can make your Web page more interesting.** You can use styles to define interesting visual effects, such as background text, shadowing, absolute positioning, and other advanced effects not available with HTML.

There is one primary down side to CSS—not all browsers support it.

NOTE *As of this writing, CSS Level 2 is the current W3C standard and is supported by Internet Explorer 4 and above and in Netscape 6 (Mozilla). CSS Level 1 was (more or less) supported by Internet Explorer 3 and above and Netscape Navigator 4 and above. CSS Level 3 is currently under development.*

Defining Styles

There are three basic techniques for defining styles for your Web pages:

- **Inline.** You can specify a style rule directly within an HTML element using the `style` attribute of the element. This is useful when you want a style applied only for a particular element on your Web page.

- **Embedded.** You can specify the style rules within a Web page. This is useful if you want to apply special styles specifically for that one Web page.

- **External.** You can specify the style rules in an external file. This is the recommended technique to apply styles consistently to all pages of a Web application.

These techniques are discussed in detail in the sections that follow. In many cases, you will want to use a combination of inline, embedded, and external styles.

Follow these steps to give your Web application some style:

1. Determine if you want to define inline, embedded, or external styles. You may decide to use each of these techniques for different styles on your page.

2. If you plan to use any external styles, create a text file using any text editor and save it with a .css extension. Normally, the CSS file is stored in the same directory as the Web page files.

3. Add style rules to the CSS file for any externally declared styles.

4. Add style rules to the Web page for any styles to be embedded in a particular page.

5. Add the `style` attribute to any element on the Web page for any style to be declared inline, thus affecting only that particular element.

Using Inline Styles for Greater Control

Inline styles allow you to specify a style rule directly within an HTML element. This is useful when you want a style applied only to a particular element on your Web page. The style properties specify a set of attributes for the HTML element. Style properties provide more functionality than standard HTML attributes, giving you more control over the layout and appearance of the element.

Use the `style` attribute of an HTML element to give that element a specific style. The specified style is applied to that particular HTML element. Since the style rule is defined within the element's tag, there is no need for a selector, only the declaration. For example:

```
<p style="margin-left:0.5in; font-family:arial; font-size:20pt; color:red">
    Our training courses are the best in the industry.
</p>
```

This style declares a specific left margin, font family, size, and color for this particular paragraph. Notice how the style is declared using the `style` attribute of the p element.

Using an inline style in this case is better than using individual element attributes because many of the formatting attributes have been deprecated. In addition, there are more style properties than element attributes, giving you more control over the look of the element. In the previous example, the `margin-left` style property allows you to set a left margin for the paragraph. There is no comparable paragraph attribute.

Applying a style inline for an individual element gives you better control over the layout of that element, but it does not give you other benefits of styles, namely the ability to reuse the style and apply it to multiple elements. For these benefits, you need to use embedded styles.

Try It 4-1.

Using an Inline Style

Try It 4-1 declares and applies an inline style on the Welcome page from Try It 3-2.

1. Open the Welcome page file (TrainingWelcome.htm) from Try It 3-2 in your HTML editing tool.

2. Add a paragraph or two to the page.

3. If desired, remove the `font` element and replace it with a p element.

4. Add the `style` attribute to define an inline style for one of the p (paragraph) elements.

5. Save the file.

6. Open the TrainingWelcome.htm file in your browser. You should see the paragraph with your defined style.

7. Experiment with other style properties.

The resulting page will appear similar to Figure 4-1.

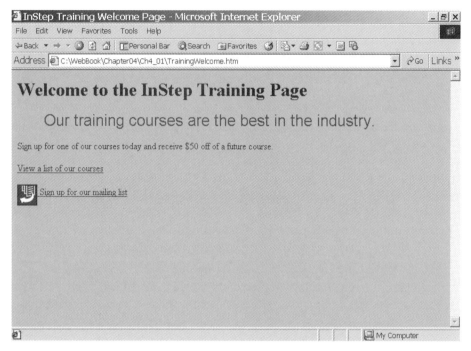

Figure 4-1. This Welcome page demonstrates an inline style. The indented text on this page is the result of that style.

Listing 4-1 presents the code used to generate the Web page shown in Figure 4-1. The transitional DTD is specified in the document type declaration for this code because there are still deprecated attributes in this example. You will be replacing the last deprecated attributes with styles in the next Try It.

Listing 4-1. The TrainingWelcome.htm file uses an inline style to define the look of one of the elements.

```
<!DOCTYPE html PUBLIC "-//W3C//DTD XHTML 1.0 Transitional//EN"
    "DTD/xhtml1-transitional.dtd">
<html>
<!--
    Try It  4-1
    Title:  Welcome Page
    Author: InStep Technologies
```

```
                www.insteptech.com
      Purpose:Define an Inline style
   -->
<head>
<title>InStep Training Welcome Page</title>
</head>
<body bgcolor="#D2B48C">
<h1>Welcome to the InStep Training Page</h1>
<p style="margin-left:0.5in; font-family:arial; font-size:20pt; color:red">
   Our training courses are the best in the industry.
</p>
<p>
   Sign up for one of our courses today and receive $50 off of a future course.
</p>
<div>
<a href="TrainingCourseList.htm">View a list of our courses</a>
<br />
<br />
<a href="TrainingMailingList.htm">
   <img src="MailingList.gif" alt="Mailing List" align="middle" />
   Sign up for our mailing list
</a>
</div>
</body>
</html>
```

Using Embedded Styles for Standardization

You can define a consistent style for all elements of a specific type, such as every
h1 (heading 1) element, using embedded styles. The style is automatically applied
to that element type throughout the page, giving you a standard look on the page.

You declare an embedded style with a style element in the header section
of the HTML document. The style element contains one or more style rules.
For example:

```
❶  <head>
❷  <title>Training Welcome Page</title>
❸  <style type="text/css">
❹  <!--
❺  p {font-family:arial; font-size:15pt; color:navy}
❻  h1 {color:navy}
❼  -->
❽  </style>
❾  </head>
```

The style element (lines ❸ through ❽) has a type attribute that indicates the types of style rules to use; in this case, it is CSS. This type attribute is required for strict conformance to XHTML. The HTML comment markers within the style element (lines ❹ and ❼) are not required but are highly recommended so that older browsers that don't understand the style element ignore the style definition.

A style element can contain any number of style rules. The style rule selector identifies the elements to which the declaration is applied. The style rule declaration defines the set of style properties defined with name and value pairs separated by semicolons and enclosed within braces ({ }).

The style rules in this example define the style properties for two elements. The p element style (line ❺) is automatically applied to every paragraph element on the Web page. The h1 element style (line ❻) is automatically applied to every h1 element, overriding the default h1 style.

Notice the similarities between the inline and embedded styles. In both cases, the style properties are the same. With inline styles, however, you use the style *attribute* of an element within the body section of the HTML document. For embedded styles, you define a style *element* in the header section of the HTML document.

Using an embedded style allows you to define a particular set of style rules for a Web page. These styles provide a consistent look throughout your page and allow you to change the look of the entire page by simply adjusting the style definition.

The examples in this section define a style for all elements of a particular type, such as all p or h1 elements. What if you have two different styles of paragraphs that you want to use? The next section introduces embedded style classes, which can give you the flexibility you need to handle multiple styles for one type of element.

Try It 4-2.
Using an Embedded Style

Try It 4-2 adds embedded styles to the Welcome page from Try It 4-1. During this Try It, you can remove any remaining deprecated attributes from the Web page so it conforms to the strict specifications of XHTML.

1. Open the Welcome page file (TrainingWelcome.htm) from Try It 4-1 in your HTML editing tool.

2. Add a style element in the header section of the page.

3. Declare a style rule for a p (paragraph) element within the style element.

4. Optionally, define a style rule for the h1 element.

5. Optionally, define a style rule for the body element. If you define a body element style, you can remove the deprecated bgcolor attribute within the body tag.

6. Optionally, remove the deprecated align attribute from the img element.

7. Save the file.

8. Open the TrainingWelcome.htm file in your browser. All of the elements, except the one with the inline style from Try It 4-1, should appear with your defined style.

9. Experiment with other style properties in the style rules.

The resulting page will appear similar to Figure 4-2.

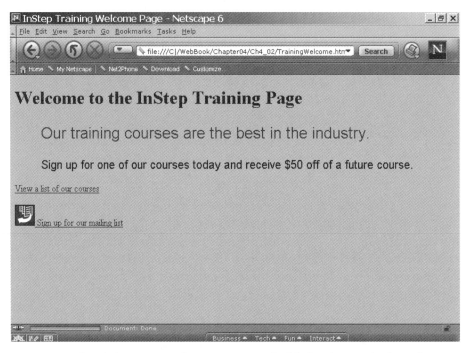

Figure 4-2. This Welcome page demonstrates embedded styles. Notice how the inline style takes precedence over the embedded style for the paragraph.

The new style rules are applied automatically to the defined elements. You did not need to update any of the existing HTML on the page to apply these styles.

Notice that the new style rules did not apply to the paragraph with the inline style. This is because the inline style takes precedence over the embedded style. This cascading effect is discussed later in this chapter.

The code used to generate the page shown in Figure 4-2 is presented in Listing 4-2.

NOTE *If you removed the deprecated* bgcolor *attribute from the* body *element and the deprecated* align *attribute of the* img *element as described in the steps above, you can set the DOCTYPE to the strict DTD instead of the transitional DTD used in the prior Try Its. The declaration of the strict DTD is shown in the first line of the code in Listing 4-2.*

Listing 4-2. The TrainingWelcome.htm file contains the HTML with an embedded style.

```
<!DOCTYPE html PUBLIC "-//W3C//DTD XHTML 1.0 Strict//EN" "DTD/xhtml1-strict.dtd">
<html>
<!--
    Try It   4-2
    Title:   Welcome Page
    Author:  InStep Technologies
             www.insteptech.com
    Purpose:Define an embedded style
 -->
<head>
<title>InStep Training Welcome Page</title>
<style type="text/css">
<!--
p {margin-left:0.5in; font-family:arial; font-size:15pt; color:navy}
h1 {color:navy}
body {background-color:#D2B48C}
-->
</style>
</head>
<body>
<h1>Welcome to the InStep Training Page</h1>
<p style="margin-left:0.5in; font-family:arial; font-size:20pt; color:red">
   Our training courses are the best in the industry.
</p>
<p>
   Sign up for one of our courses today and receive $50 off of a future course.
</p>
```

```
<div>
<a href="TrainingCourseList.htm">View a list of our courses</a>
<br />
<br />
<a href="TrainingMailingList.htm">
    <img src="MailingList.gif" alt="Mailing List" />
    Sign up for our mailing list
</a>
</div>
</body>
</html>
```

Declaring Style Classes for Flexibility

The styles defined so far have been for specific elements or specific types of elements such as p or h1. *Style classes* allow you to declare named styles that can be applied to specific elements on a Web page. This allows you to define styles for sets of elements, instead of all elements of a defined type. This gives you more flexibility in defining the styles for your page.

When you specify a particular HTML element as the selector of a style rule, the style properties are automatically applied to all occurrences of that particular type of element. For example, a style rule with a selector for the p element affects all text within any p element tags on the page.

Using style classes, you can define different styles for different types of the same element. For example, you can define two types of paragraphs: key points and normal information. If you want the key points to stand out when your page is displayed, you could make the key point paragraph font bigger and red. You can define two different styles for the two different types of paragraphs by defining two style classes.

You declare a style class using a dot (.) and a style class name in the selector part of the style rule. The style class names can be any name that provides a good description of the usage of the style. If the style class is only to be used for a particular type of element, the element name precedes the style class definition. For example:

```
❶  <style  type="text/css">
❷  <!--
❸  p {margin-left:0.5in; font-family:arial}
❹  p.key {font-size:20pt; color:red}
❺  p.normal {font-size:15pt; color:navy}
❻  .margin {margin-left:0.5in}
❼  -->
❽  </style>
```

The style element (lines ❶ through ❽) includes the definition of a style for a p element (line ❸) and three style classes that were given names of key, normal, and margin (lines ❹ through ❻).

> **NOTE** *The style class names can be any name that you want. Because of the large number of styles that you may have for your Web application, you may want to define some standard naming conventions for your style classes.*

Both the key (line ❹) and normal (line ❺) style classes can only be used with p elements. The margin style class (line ❻) is not associated with any particular element type. It can be used with any relevant element.

Styles are additive, meaning that the p element style properties are added to any p element style class properties. If there is a conflict, the style class takes precedence.

For example, the key style class defines a style to be used for key points. It has all of the style properties of the p element style (line ❸) plus all of the style properties of its style class definition (line ❹). The normal style class defines the style for informational paragraphs. It has all of the style properties of the p element style (line ❸) plus all of the style properties of its style class definition (line ❺).

The p element style is applied automatically to every p element on the Web page. But to assign a style class to a particular HTML element, you must set the class attribute of that element to the style class name. For example:

```
❶    <body>
❷    <h1 class="margin">Welcome to our Training Page</h1>
❸    <p class="key">Our training courses are the best in the industry.</p>
❹    <p class="normal">Sign up for one of our courses today.</p>
❺    </body>
```

The h1 element (line ❷) uses the margin style class. The important paragraph on the page (line ❸) uses the key paragraph style class. The normal paragraph (line ❹) uses the normal paragraph style class. Any paragraph element without a class attribute uses the standard p element style.

You can also assign multiple style classes to one particular element. For example:

```
<p class="key best">Our training courses are the best in the industry.</p>
```

The style rules from both the key class and from the best class (not shown) are applied to that paragraph. See the "Cascading Style Sheets" section later in this chapter for more information and an example on cascading multiple styles for one element.

Style and style class declarations assume that you want to apply a style to *several* elements. There may be situations where you want to define a *unique* style for an individual element. You can do this with inline styles by setting the `style` attribute of the element as discussed previously. However, you may want to keep all of your style information together as embedded styles. In that case, you can define a style rule using the value of the element's `id` attribute.

To define a style for a particular element, use a pound sign (#) and the value of the element's `id` attribute as the style selector. This ID must match the `id` attribute of the element for which it was defined. For example, an element on the Web page has an `id` attribute of `LastName`. The style rule for that element could be:

```
#LastName {font-size:15pt; color:brown}
```

This technique of declaring styles based on the unique ID of an element is used when absolutely positioning the element. See Chapter 6, "Building Forms," for more information and an example of using style IDs.

Style classes are a great way to define the styles for your Web applications. You can even use them to create cool visual effects. The next section presents a simple effect you can create by adding a few more style classes to your embedded style sheet.

Try It 4-3.

Using Style Classes

Try It 4-3 adds style classes to the Welcome page from Try It 4-2.

1. Open the Welcome page file (TrainingWelcome.htm) from Try It 4-2 in your HTML editing tool.

2. Declare a style class for a p (paragraph) element within the `style` element tags. You could name it "key."

3. Declare a second style definition class for a p element within the `style` element tags. You could name it "normal."

4. Declare a third style definition class that is not associated with a particular element. You could name it "margin" if you want to use it to set a page margin.

5. Replace the inline style inserted in Try It 4-1 with the `class` attribute for the paragraph to apply one of the p element style classes that you created.

6. Add the `class` attribute to another paragraph on the page and set it to the second p element style class that you created.

7. Add the `class` attribute to the h1 and div tags on the page and set them to the third style class that you created.

8. Save the file.

9. Open the TrainingWelcome.htm file in your browser. Each paragraph should be displayed with its appropriate style.

10. Experiment with other style properties in the style definition.

The resulting page will appear similar to Figure 4-3.

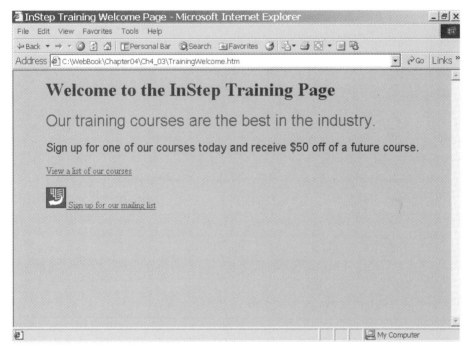

Figure 4-3. This Welcome page demonstrates the results of several style classes. Notice how all of the elements now have a left margin.

The code used to generate the page shown in Figure 4-3 is presented in Listing 4-3.

Listing 4-3. The TrainingWelcome.htm file contains the HTML and styles needed to display the Welcome page.

```
<!DOCTYPE html PUBLIC "-//W3C//DTD XHTML 1.0 Strict//EN" "DTD/xhtml1-strict.dtd">
<html>
<!--
    Try It   4-3
    Title:   Welcome Page
    Author: InStep Technologies
           www.insteptech.com
```

```
    Purpose:To demonstrate style classes
            using an embedded style
 -->
<head>
<title>InStep Training Welcome Page</title>
<style type="text/css">
<!--
p {margin-left:0.5in; font-family:arial}
p.key {font-size:20pt; color:red}
p.normal {font-size:15pt; color:navy}
.margin {margin-left:0.5in}
h1 {color:navy}
body {background-color:#D2B48C}
-->
</style>
</head>
<body>
<h1 class="margin">Welcome to the InStep Training Page</h1>
<p class="key">
   Our training courses are the best in the industry.
</p>
<p class="normal">
   Sign up for one of our courses today and receive $50 off of a future course.
</p>
<div class="margin">
<a href="TrainingCourseList.htm">View a list of our courses</a>
<br />
<br />
<a href="TrainingMailingList.htm">
   <img src="MailingList.gif" alt="Mailing List" />
   Sign up for our mailing list
</a>
</div>
</body>
</html>
```

Using Styles to Add Visual Effects

So far, the style examples have focused on defining the desired properties of the basic page text. But styles can do so much more. You can add background text, drop shadows, embossing, and many other visual effects by using styles.

Figure 4-4 displays a simple example of the type of effect that you can do with styles. Listing 4-4 presents the style rules used to generate the effect shown in Figure 4-4. These style rules are listed in the more conventional vertical layout used by many Web developers. Since browsers ignore extra spacing, this vertical layout is only for easier reading and has no affect on the display of the page.

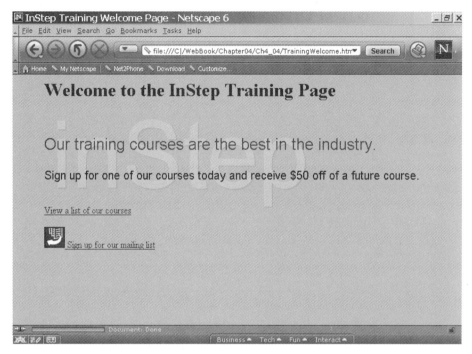

Figure 4-4. Get better performance by using text and styles instead of graphics for visual effects such as this embossed logo.

Listing 4-4. These styles provide an interesting embossed effect.

```
div.foreground {
    margin-left:0.5in;
    color:#E2C48C;
    font-family:arial;
    font-size:120pt;
    position:absolute;
    top:50px;
    left:20px;
    z-index:0
}
```

```
div.shadow {
    margin-left:0.5in;
    color:#C2A48C;
    font-family:arial;
    font-size:120pt;
    position:absolute;
    top:52px;
    left:22px;
    z-index:0
}
p {
    margin-left:0.5in;
    font-family:arial;
    position:relative
}
```

The `foreground` style class defines a margin and the font color, style, and size. The `position`, `top`, and `left` style properties define an absolute position of the text on the page. The `z-index` style property is 0 to ensure that the text appears behind any other text or graphics on the page.

NOTE   *A* `z-index` *value of –1 works well for placing elements in the background, but this value only works in Internet Explorer, not in Netscape.*

The `shadow` style class is almost identical to the `foreground` style class. It has a slightly darker color and is offset down and to the right by two pixels.

Use these two style classes in combination to give the text an embossed look. First, define the text to be embossed. Add the text to the body section of the HTML document within a `div` element defined with the `shadow` style class. Add the text again, this time within a `div` element defined with the `foreground` style class. The resulting HTML is as follows:

```
<div class="shadow">inStep</div>
<div class="foreground">inStep</div>
```

Notice that the text for the shadow is drawn first and then the foreground is drawn on top. Otherwise, the shadow appears on top of the text, which is not the desired effect.

The p element style was modified to ensure the paragraph elements were positioned relatively on the page, over the special effect.

NOTE   *This change to the p element style is not necessary if the* z-index *is set to –1. However, the resulting effect would not work in Netscape.*

Doing visual effects with text and styles instead of graphics is much more efficient because there are no graphics files to download. Experiment with the available style properties and consult the "Additional Resources" section at the end of this chapter for references to other style ideas.

Style classes are a great way to define the styles for your Web applications. However, you are still faced with the need to cut and paste the style classes into every one of your HTML documents. Wouldn't it be nice if the style rules could be stored in an external file and referenced by all your HTML documents? That is the purpose of the external styles discussed in the next section.

Try It 4-4.

Using Styles to Create a Visual Effect

Try It 4-4 adds a visual effect to the Welcome page from Try It 4-3.

1. Open the Welcome page file (TrainingWelcome.htm) from Try It 4-3 in your HTML editing tool.

2. Add style rules to the style element in the header section of the page to define a visual effect of your choice. If desired, you can use the example presented in this section.

3. If the style rules define absolute positioning, as in the example presented in this chapter, add the position style property to the p element style rule to define relative positioning for the text.

4. Apply the styles to specific text on your page.

5. Save the file.

6. Open the TrainingWelcome.htm file in your browser. The visual effect should appear as you had specified.

7. Experiment with other style properties or other visual effects.

If you used the example presented in this section, your result will appear similar to Figure 4-4. The code used to generate the page shown in Figure 4-4 is presented in Listing 4-5.

Listing 4-5. The TrainingWelcome.htm file contains the HTML and styles needed to display the Welcome page with a visual effect.

```
<!DOCTYPE html PUBLIC "-//W3C//DTD XHTML 1.0 Strict//EN" "DTD/xhtml1-strict.dtd">
<html>
<!--
    Try It  4-4
    Title:  Welcome Page
    Author: InStep Technologies
            www.insteptech.com
    Purpose:To demonstrate visual effects
            using embedded styles
  -->
<head>
<title>InStep Training Welcome Page</title>
<style type="text/css">
<!--
p {margin-left:0.5in; font-family:arial; position:relative}
p.key {font-size:20pt; color:red}
p.normal {font-size:15pt; color:navy}
.margin {margin-left:0.5in}
h1 {color:navy}
body {background-color:#D2B48C}
div.foreground {margin-left:0.5in; color:#E2C48C; font-family:arial;
    font-size:120pt; position:absolute; top:50px; left:20px; z-index:0}
div.shadow {margin-left:0.5in; color:#C2A48C; font-family:arial;
    font-size:120pt; position:absolute; top:52px; left:22px; z-index:0}
-->
</style>
</head>
<body>
<div class="shadow">inStep</div>
<div class="foreground">inStep</div>
<h1 class="margin">Welcome to the InStep Training Page</h1>
<p class="key">
    <br />
    Our training courses are the best in the industry.
</p>
<p class="normal">
    Sign up for one of our courses today and receive $50 off of a future course.
</p>
<div class="margin">
```

```
<br />
<a href="TrainingCourseList.htm">View a list of our courses</a>
<br />
<br />
<a href="TrainingMailingList.htm">
    <img src="MailingList.gif" alt="Mailing List" />
    Sign up for our mailing list
</a>
</div>
</body>
</html>
```

Creating an External Style Sheet for Reusability

In the last several sections, you have seen different ways to define and use style rules in an embedded style sheet. These rules are defined in the HTML document that uses the styles. To reuse the styles throughout multiple pages of your Web application, you can instead create your styles in an external file and link that file to all of your HTML documents. Later, if you want to change the way all of your pages look, simply change the external style sheet file and all of the pages in your application linked to the style sheet file reflect the change.

To create an external style sheet, simply create a text file for the style rules. This file is called a style sheet file and is normally given a .css extension. Add your style rules to that file. The style rules are the same as for the embedded styles. If you have existing embedded styles that you want to move to an external style sheet file, you can cut the style rules and paste them into the style sheet file.

Any HTML document that wants to use the styles from the style sheet file can link to that style sheet file. Use the link element in the header section of the HTML document to link to the desired external style sheet file:

```
<link rel="stylesheet" type="text/css" href="TrainingStyle.css" />
```

The rel attribute of the link element defines the nature of the relationship between the linked resources; in this case, the link is to a style sheet. The type attribute defines the type of the linked file (always text/css for cascading style sheets). The name of the style sheet file is defined with the href attribute using relative or absolute paths. In this example, the style sheet file (TrainingStyle.css) is located in the same directory as the Web page.

The style rules in the external file can then be applied to elements in the HTML document as described with embedded styles.

External styles provide the best of all worlds. They allow you to identify styles that can be used to define the look for your HTML elements. They are defined external to the HTML page, making maintenance easier. The style sheet file can be linked to any HTML document, making the styles reusable throughout your Web application.

TIP   *Use style classes in an external style sheet for defining standard styles for your Web application and embedded styles for defining page-specific styles.*

As your Web application goes through those inevitable user-interface changes, you will be glad you have those styles!

Try It 4-5.

Using an External Style Sheet File

Try It 4-5 adds an external style sheet to the Welcome page from Try It 4-4.

1. Open the Welcome page file (TrainingWelcome.htm) from Try It 4-4 in your HTML editing tool.

2. Cut the embedded style rules out of the Welcome page.

3. Delete the `<style>` and `</style>` tags and the comment marks.

4. Create a new text file and save it as TrainingStyle.css.

5. Paste the style rules into the style sheet file.

6. Save the file.

7. In the header section of the Welcome page, add the `link` element to link the Welcome page to the external style sheet.

8. Open the TrainingWelcome.htm file in your browser. Each element should be displayed with its appropriate style.

9. Experiment with other style properties in the style sheet file.

The resulting page will appear similar to Figure 4-4. This Try It did not change the look itself, only *where* the look is defined.

The code in the style sheet file is shown in Listing 4-6. The code in the HTML file is shown in Listing 4-7.

Listing 4-6. The TrainingStyle.css file contains the styles that can be used by any page in the Web application.

```
/*
   Try It   4-5
   Title:   Style Sheet
   Author: InStep Technologies
           www.insteptech.com
   Purpose:To demonstrate external style sheets
```

```
*/
p {
    margin-left:0.5in;
    font-family:arial;
    position:relative
}
p.key {
    font-size:20pt;
    color:red
}
p.normal {
    font-size:15pt;
    color:navy
}
.margin {
    margin-left:0.5in
}
h1 {
    color:navy
}
body {
    background-color:#D2B48C
}
div.foreground {
    margin-left:0.5in;
    color:#E2C48C;
    font-family:arial;
    font-size:120pt;
    position:absolute;
    top:50px;
    left:20px;
    z-index:0
}
div.shadow {
    margin-left:0.5in;
    color:#C2A48C;
    font-family:arial;
    font-size:120pt;
    position:absolute;
    top:52px;
    left:22px;
    z-index:0
}
```

Listing 4-7. The code in the TrainingWelcome.htm file simply needs the link to the style sheet.

```
<!DOCTYPE html PUBLIC "-//W3C//DTD XHTML 1.0 Strict//EN" "DTD/xhtml1-strict.dtd">
<html>
<!--
    Try It   4-5
    Title:   Welcome Page
    Author:  InStep Technologies
             www.insteptech.com
    Purpose: To demonstrate style classes
             using an external style sheet
  -->
<head>
<title>InStep Training Welcome Page</title>
<link rel="stylesheet" type="text/css" href="TrainingStyle.css" />
</head>
<body>
<div class="shadow">inStep</div>
<div class="foreground">inStep</div>
<h1 class="margin">Welcome to the InStep Training Page</h1>
<p class="key">
   <br />
   Our training courses are the best in the industry.
</p>
<p class="normal">
   Sign up for one of our courses today and receive $50 off of a future course.
</p>
<div class="margin">
<br />
<a href="TrainingCourseList.htm">View a list of our courses</a>
<br />
<br />
<a href="TrainingMailingList.htm">
   <img src="MailingList.gif" alt="Mailing List" align="center" />
   Sign up for our mailing list
</a>
</div>
</body>
</html>
```

Cascading Style Sheets

A key feature of CSS is that style rules can *cascade.* This means that you can define a number of style rules for the same set of elements and all of the rules can influence the presentation of those elements.

As discussed throughout this chapter, you can define style rules using inline, embedded, or external styles, or any combination of these. If any one particular element has multiple style rules defined, the styles rules are all applied for that element in a cascading fashion.

The following example aids in demonstrating how styles cascade. Say you create a style rule for a p element in an external style file such as the one you created in Try It 4-5:

```
p {
    margin-left:0.5in;
    font-family:arial;
    position:relative
}
```

Then you want to add some styles just for a particular page so you define an embedded style for the p element in the header section of the page as follows:

```
<style type="text/css">
<!--
p {font-size:12pt; color:green}
-->
</style>
```

You also want to give one particular p element on the page some additional style rules. You can use an inline style as follows:

```
<p style="width:350px; background-color:#FFFF9C">
    Call us for more information: (925)225-1016
</p>
```

This paragraph appears with a yellow (#FFFF9C) background that is 350 pixels wide. The font for the paragraph is 12-point green as per the embedded style sheet rule for p elements. The paragraph has a 0.5 inch left margin, uses the Arial font, and is relatively positioned on the page as defined in the external style sheet rule for the p element.

All of these styles cascade, each adding the defined style properties. The result is a combination of all of the style rules.

As you may expect, there is the possibility that two style rules conflict. For example, say the inline style was instead:

```
<p style="font-size:10pt; color:lightblue; width:350px; background-color:#FFFF9C">
   Call us for more information: (925)225-1016
</p>
```

In this case, there is a conflict because the inline and embedded style rules for the p element specify different font-size and color properties.

If there is a conflict, the style property that is used depends on the following:

- Specific selectors always take priority over general selectors. A style rule with a class defined in the selector beats a style rule without a class. For example, a style rule with a selector of p.key always beats a p selector. And a style rule with an element ID beats a style rule with a class. For example, a style rule with a selector of p#FirstParagraph beats a selector of p.key.

- Inline styles take precedence over embedded styles.

- Embedded styles take precedence over external styles.

- When multiple style rules apply to the same element, the style rule defined last takes precedence. An example of this is shown below.

You can cascade styles by combining styles classes. Say you create an embedded style as follows:

```
<style type="text/css">
<!--
p {font-size:12pt; color:green}
p.offer {text-align:center; color:purple}
p.best {font-weight:bold; color:yellow}
-->
</style>
```

You can then assign both of the style classes to one element as follows:

```
<p class="best offer">$50 off if you sign up now!</p>
```

In this example, both the offer style class and best style class are applied to the element. The element appears bold and centered. But notice that the color is defined in both rules. The precedence in this situation depends on the order of the style rule definitions in the style element (not the order in the class attribute) with the last style rule taking precedence. Since the best style class is defined last, the text is yellow. If you shifted the order of the rules in the style element, the color would change appropriately.

These cascading rules can get much more complex. See the "Additional Resources" section at the end of this chapter for references to more information on cascading rules.

There are cases where this cascading effect can be useful for the development of your Web application. However, overuse of this technique can make your Web pages more difficult to maintain because the style properties affecting any one element may be defined in several places.

Cascading Style Sheet Reference

There are many CSS properties. Table 4-1 shows the most commonly used properties.

Table 4-1. Common Cascading Style Sheet Properties

PROPERTY	MEANING	EXAMPLE
/* */	Comment marker.	/* This style sheet defines the basic background styles */
background-attachment	Defines whether or not the background image should scroll or remain fixed when the text is scrolled. Valid values are: scroll (default) or fixed.	background-attachment:fixed
background-color	Color of the background. Valid values are: transparent (default) or a color defined with a logical name or RGB value.	background-color:yellow
background-image	Image to be used as the background. Valid values are: none (default) or the URI to the image.	background-image:url (background.gif)
color	Color of the text attribute for any element defined with a logical name or RGB value.	color:red
display	Specifies how an element should be displayed. Valid values are: none (to hide an element), block (to start a new paragraph - default), inline (no new paragraph), or list-item (to display as if it were an li element).	display:none

Table 4-1. Common Cascading Style Sheet Properties (continued)

PROPERTY	MEANING	EXAMPLE
float	Specifies how an element should float on the page. If the value is left, the element will be displayed on the left and text will wrap to the right and vice versa. Valid values are: left, right, or none (default).	float:none
font-family	Defines the list of desired fonts. The browser attempts to use the first font on the list. If that font is not found on the user's system, the browser tries the second font name. If none of the fonts are found, the browser's default font is used. Most commonly available fonts are Times and Courier. Most Windows users also have Arial.	font-family:arial, helvetica, courier
font-size	Defines the size of the font. Values can be an *absolute size* using one of these constants: xx-small, x-small, small, medium, large, x-large, or xx-large. Values can be a *relative size* using one of these constants: larger or smaller. Values can be a specific *length* defined in points (pt), inches (in), centimeters (cm), or pixels (px). Values can be defined as a *percentage* of the parent element's font size.	font-size:20pt
font-style	Defines the slant of the font. Valid values are: normal, italic, or oblique.	font-style:italic
font-weight	Defines the weight (boldness) of the font. Valid values are: normal, bold, bolder, lighter. You can also specify a multiple of 100 between 100 and 900 where 400 is normal and 700 is bold.	font-weight:bold

Table 4-1. Common Cascading Style Sheet Properties (continued)

PROPERTY	MEANING	EXAMPLE
height	The height of the element. Valid values are auto (default) or a length. Length can be in pixels (px), points (pt), inches (in), or centimeters (cm). If the element, such as text, does not fit into the defined height and width, the excess content flows below the element. See overflow to control this.	height:20px
left	Defines how the left side of an element is positioned. If the position property is set to absolute, this is the position from the left side of the document window. If the position property is set to relative, this is the position with respect to the prior element on the page. Values can be in pixels (px), points (pt), inches (in), or centimeters (cm).	left:20px
line-height	Defines the leading, which is the distance between the bottom of one line and the bottom of the next line. Values can be in pixels (px), points (pt), inches (in), or centimeters (cm) or a percentage of the font size.	line-height:10pt
margin-bottom	Defines a bottom margin specifying the distance from the bottom edge of the page. Values can be in pixels (px), points (pt), inches (in), or centimeters (cm).	margin-bottom:0.5in
margin-left	Defines a left margin specifying the distance from the left edge of the page. Values can be in pixels (px), points (pt), inches (in), or centimeters (cm).	margin-left:0.5in

Table 4-1. Common Cascading Style Sheet Properties (continued)

PROPERTY	MEANING	EXAMPLE
margin-right	Defines a right margin specifying the distance from the right edge of the page. Values can be in pixels (px), points (pt), inches (in), or centimeters (cm).	margin-right:0.5in
margin-top	Defines a top margin specifying the distance from the top edge of the page. Values can be in pixels (px), points (pt), inches (in), or centimeters (cm).	margin-top:0.5in
overflow	Defines how excess text is handled if the text does not fit within the defined height and width. Valid values are: visible (default), hidden, auto (adds scroll bars as needed), and scroll (adds scroll bars).	overflow:hidden
position	Defines how an element is positioned on the page. Valid values are: relative and absolute. *Relative positioning* positions an element relative to the prior element on the page. *Absolute positioning* positions an element relative to its position on the page. See Chapter 6, "Building Forms," for an example of absolute positioning.	position:absolute
text-align	Justifies an HTML element. Valid values are: left, center, right, and justify.	text-align:center
text-decoration	Applies a specific decoration to a font. Valid values are: none, underline, overline, line-through, blink. However, blink did not blink in Internet Explorer 5.	text-decoration:underline

Table 4-1. Common Cascading Style Sheet Properties (continued)

PROPERTY	MEANING	EXAMPLE
top	Defines how the top of an element is positioned. If the position property is set to absolute, this is the position from the top of the document window. If the position property is set to relative, this is the position with respect to the prior element on the page. Values can be in pixels (px), points (pt), inches (in), or centimeters (cm).	top:20px
visibility	Defines whether the element is visible on the page. Used to dynamically hide or show elements on a page. Valid values are: hidden or visible.	visibility:hidden
width	The width of the element. Values can be in pixels (px), points (pt), inches (in), or centimeters (cm). If the element, such as text, does not fit into the defined height and width, the excess content flows below the element. See overflow to control this.	height:20px
z-index	Defines the stacking order of elements that overlay each other. Use –1 with Internet Explorer to specify that the element is behind the text. Use increasing numbers to stack the elements from bottom to top.	z-index:3

 **CAUTION** *Notice that many of the properties in the table are similar to element attributes. However, the names of the properties and the valid values are not consistent with the attribute names and values. For example, font names are defined with attributes using the* face *keyword and with style properties as* font-family.

See the "Additional Resources" section of this chapter for a reference to a complete listing of valid style properties.

Basic CSS Tips and Tricks

This section includes basic tips and techniques when working with CSS.

Visual Design

The Web is a very visual medium so visual design is an important aspect of your Web development.

Watch the Font Size

Many browser users set their text size to meet their individual preferences. This may be because the user wants to see more on their screen and thereby wants to make the font smaller. Or it may be for accessibility reasons that the user wants to make the font larger. Or perhaps a particular computer resolution looks better with specific font sizes.

If you set a font size in your style sheet to a hard-coded size using an absolute size or a specific length measurement, you prevent the user's default font selections from having an effect.

It is recommended that you instead use either the relative size specifications or the percentage values. That way you can adjust fonts up for emphasis or down for detail with respect to the user's font selections. See Table 4-1 for more information on these property values.

Use Scrolling Areas

An interesting visual technique you can do with styles is to define scrolling areas on your page, as shown in Figure 4-5.

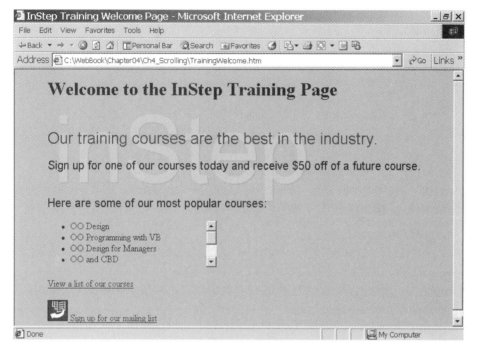

Figure 4-5. Use styles to define scrollable areas on your pages.

The trick here is to use the overflow style property as follows:

```
<style type="text/css">
<!--
div.scrollarea {margin-left:0.5in; height:80px; width:300px; overflow:auto}
</style>
-->
```

This style snippet defines a specific size of a scrollable viewport using the height and width properties and uses the auto value of the overflow property to automatically add scroll bars as needed.

The code that demonstrates the use of this style class is as follows:

```
<p class="normal">
   <br />
   Here are some of our most popular courses:
</p>
```

```
<div class="scrollarea">
<ul>
   <li>OO Design</li>
   <li>OO Programming with VB</li>
   <li>OO Design for Managers</li>
   <li>OO and CBD</li>
   <li>OO for the Web</li>
   <li>OO in .NET</li>
   <li>OO for Java</li>
</ul>
</div>
```

You can add other style attributes to make this scrolling area look more interesting. For example, you can add a border using:

```
div.scrollarea {margin-left:0.5in; height:80px; width:300px;
   border:solid #E2C48C; overflow:auto}
```

Debugging Tips

Sometimes it is difficult to see why a page does not display as you expect. Here are some tips for debugging your style sheets.

Recognize Browser Differences

Text and layouts that appear correctly under Internet Explorer may not appear the same in Netscape or vice versa. It is important to understand the differences between the two browsers and ensure that you code your CSS to account for these differences.

Don't Use Invalid Syntax

Internet Explorer is forgiving of invalid syntax but other browsers are not. A common mistake is in the declaration syntax. Ensure that you use a colon (:) instead of an equal sign (=) between the property name and the property value:

```
p {font-size:12pt; color:green}
```

Use a validator (see the next tip) to check your syntax.

Use a Validator

There are several CSS validators available on the Web. These validators evaluate your CSS syntax and describe any syntax errors. Some validators even provide extensive help on correcting the errors. See the "Links" section at the end of this chapter for links to several of these validation tools.

What Did This Cover?

This chapter covered techniques for defining style rules. By using style rules, you can define a standard look for your Web pages and apply those styles to every page of your Web application.

Without style sheets, you are limited to the attributes available for a specific HTML element. By applying an inline style, you can have more control over the look of each element.

Embedded styles allow you to define a style rule for all elements of a specific type on a Web page. The defined style properties are automatically applied to every occurrence of the HTML element on that page. This promotes consistency through the page.

If you want different styles for different occurrences of an HTML element, you can define style classes. A style class can be applied to a specific occurrence of an HTML element by setting that element's `class` attribute.

If you define the style rules in an external file, you can apply the style to all of the pages of your application. This ensures consistency, makes it easier to change the look of the application, and simplifies maintenance.

The Try Its in this chapter demonstrated how to use inline, embedded, and external style sheets. Styles were used to create visual effects and to format the paragraphs on the Welcome page.

The next chapter defines how to use tables to organize the display of information on your page. It also presents how to use styles with tables to add visual appeal to table-based information.

Additional Resources

One chapter could not begin to cover everything there is to know about CSS. This section provides some additional resource suggestions by way of books, articles, and links to Web resources.

The books, articles, and links all existed at the time of this writing. There is a good chance that the books and articles still exist as you read this. However, the same cannot be said of Web links. So, ignore the suggested links if they no longer exist.

Books and Articles

Goodman, Danny. *Dynamic HTML: The Definitive Reference.* **Cambridge, MA: O'Reilly & Associates, 1998.**
This is an excellent reference book. It contains an HTML reference and a CSS reference.

Graham, Ian. *HTML Stylesheet Sourcebook.* **New York: John Wiley & Sons, Inc., 1997.**
This book focuses on style sheets and provides a thorough reference to the style properties and their use.

Lie, Hakon Wium, and Bert Bos. *Cascading Style Sheets: Designing for the Web.* **England: Addison Wesley Longman, 1999.**
The authors of this book are part of the World Wide Web Consortium (W3C), making this book the definitive reference for CSS. This book includes a chapter on cascading and inheritance, providing additional examples of the cascading mechanism used by CSS.

Links

`http://jigsaw.w3.org/css-validator/`: This site, which is part of the W3C site, validates your CSS. You can provide a URL to your page, upload a local file, or insert a snippet of CSS code to be validated.

`http://www.w3.org/Style/CSS/`: This is the site for the World Wide Web Consortium's (W3C) discussions on CSS.

`http://www.wdvl.com/Authoring/Style/Sheets/`: This site provides many articles and reference materials on using CSS.

`http://www.webreview.com/style/`: This site provides browser compatibility charts specifically for CSS. This can be very helpful when developing cross-platform applications.

`http://www.zvon.org/xxl/css1Reference/Output/`: This site provides a summary of the CSS style properties.

Building Tables

HTML TABLES PROVIDE A NICE way to display tabular data. More importantly, HTML tables allow you to define multicolumn text, line up graphics with text, define sidebars, and much more. You can design your pages with a multicolumn newspaper or magazine layout, such as www.msn.com and www.yahoo.com, by using borderless HTML tables.

The purpose of this chapter is to provide you with the basics you need to build tables using HTML and CSS. The next chapter covers how to use these techniques to build nicely formatted data entry forms. Additional table creation techniques using XML and XSL are covered in Chapter 12, "Using XSL."

What Will This Cover?

This chapter covers the following key HTML table concepts:

- Understanding the basics of creating tables with HTML

- Creating a simple HTML table

- Giving a table some style

- Building scrollable tables

- Using tables for a multicolumn layout

- Learning the basic set of HTML table elements and attributes

By the end of this chapter, you will know how to leverage HTML and CSS to build a table-oriented or multicolumn user interface for your Web application.

HTML Table Basics

An HTML table is comprised of horizontal *rows* and vertical *columns*. The intersection of each row and column defines a *cell*.

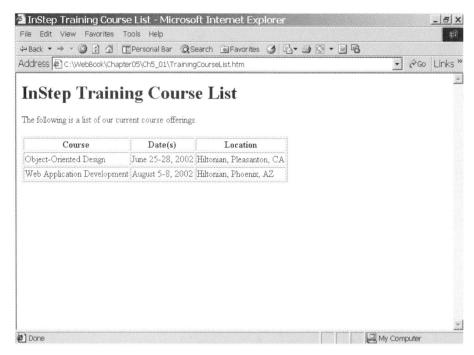

Figure 5-1. You can use a table to display tabular information in rows and columns.

You can build tables with HTML to display rows and columns of data as shown in Figure 5-1. You can define column headings, designate table border widths, and define the content of each cell.

You can also define cells that span columns, align data within a cell, and define spacing between cells. You can apply CSS styles to rows, columns, and cells to enhance the look of the table.

Borderless HTML tables provide an invisible grid in which to arrange the elements on the page. You can lay out information in a columnar fashion similar to a newspaper or magazine as shown in Figure 5-2. View the source of several of your favorite Web pages to see if they use tables to control the layout of the page.

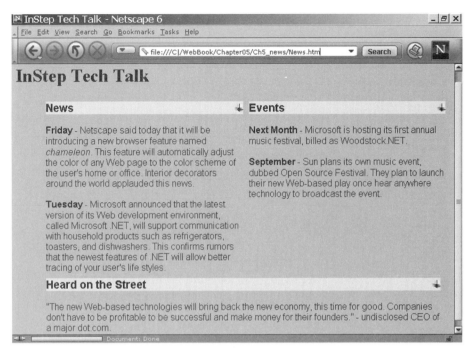

Figure 5-2. You can use a table to lay out information in magazine-style columns.

Whether you are using tables to display tabular data or to lay out your page, the basic HTML techniques are the same. To create a table with HTML, you start by declaring a table. Then define each table row. Within each row, define the cells either as a column heading or as column data. This is demonstrated in Listing 5-1.

Listing 5-1. A simple table example

```
❶   <table border="1">
❷      <tr>
❸         <th>Course</th>
❹         <th>Date(s)</th>
❺         <th>Location</th>
❻      </tr>
❼      <tr>
❽         <td>Object-Oriented Design</td>
❾         <td>June 25-28, 2002</td>
❿         <td>Hiltonian, Pleasanton, CA</td>
⓫      </tr>
```

⑫ `<tr>`
⑬ `    <td>Web Application Development</td>`
⑭ `    <td>August 5-8, 2002</td>`
⑮ `    <td>Hiltonian, Phoenix, AZ</td>`
⑯ `  </tr>`
⑰ `</table>`

The table element tags (lines **❶** and **⑰**) define the beginning and ending of the table. The border attribute of the table defines the size of the border around the cells. Use a value of 0 to hide the table borders, which basically defines an invisible grid.

Each tr element (lines **❷** through **❻**, for example) identifies a table row. Any attributes on the tr element affect all of the cells in the row.

The th elements (lines **❸**, **❹**, and **❺**) specify the heading for each column in the table. These are normally inserted into the first row of the table.

The td elements (lines **❽**, **❾**, and **❿**, for example) specify the data in each column of that row. These elements must always reside within a tr element specifying the table row.

TIP   *Indent your HTML, as in Listing 5-1, to help you visualize the table rows and columns. Any extra spaces or tabs you enter makes the code easier to read and has no affect on the resulting display in the browser.*

In this example, the td element contains textual information, basically, the course names, dates, and locations. The td element could contain other types of information such as links or images. For example, the location could be a link to more information about the hotel. The course name could be a link to the syllabus for the course. Or you could add another column to the table for the instructor and add the instructor's picture using an image.

Creating a Simple HTML Table

Building even the simplest tables requires some work to ensure that each row and column is correctly identified with beginning and ending tags. Building a hidden table to lay out a complex page is even more challenging.

The basic steps for creating an HTML table are:

1. Ensure that you lay out the look of the table during the design phase of the project. For more complex layouts, sketch the page on paper and

draw in the desired rows and columns. This helps you visualize the rows and columns needed to achieve your design.

2. Determine the desired location of the table on the page and add the table element tags with the desired attributes.

3. Add tr (table row), th (table header), and td (table data) element tags as appropriate to build your table.

4. Add the contents of each cell in the table within the td element tags.

TIP   *Put something in each cell, otherwise the table cell may not appear correctly. For example, the browser may not display a cell's border if the cell is empty. To insert a space in the cell of a table, use*   *for a non-breaking space.*

5. Try out your page to ensure that it appears as you expect.

TIP   *When maintaining or debugging hidden tables, temporarily set the* table *element's* border *attribute to a nonzero value. This allows you to see where the cells appear on the page.*

To get the right look, you may need to combine standard table layouts with cells that span rows or columns or use nested tables (tables within tables), as demonstrated later in this chapter.

TIP   *Use a tool like FrontPage to build your table without having to enter all of the table tags. You can then use an HTML editor to modify the table if necessary.*

Try It 5-1.

Building a Table with HTML

Try It 5-1 begins development of a new Course List Web page. This page presents a table of the courses that are offered along with their dates and locations.

1. Using your tool of choice, create a new text file.

2. Add the DOCTYPE declaration and the basic HTML tags to the file: `<html>`, `<head>`, `</head>`, `<body>`, `</body>`, and `</html>`.

3. Add a `title` element to the header section of the page. You could give the page a title such as "Acme Training Course List."

4. Define any other text or images to give the page a nice look and introduce the table.

5. Add a `table` element to define a table on the page. Optionally, give the table some attributes, such as `border`.

6. Define a `tr` element for every row in the table.

7. Define `th` elements within the first `tr` element to create a heading for each column.

8. Define `td` elements within the remaining `tr` elements to define the data within each row.

9. Save the file as TrainingCourseList.htm.

10. Open the TrainingCourseList.htm file in your browser. If you defined a link to a page of this name in your Welcome page from the prior Try Its, you will be able to access this page through the link on your Welcome page.

11. Experiment with other table elements and attributes.

The resulting Web page will appear similar to Figure 5-1. If your table does not appear as you expect, ensure that you have the beginning and ending tags for each element that you defined. Missing ending tags are the most common error in building tables.

Listing 5-2 shows the code used to generate the Web page displayed in Figure 5-1.

Listing 5-2. The TrainingCourseList.htm file uses a table to display a list of courses.

```
<!DOCTYPE html PUBLIC "-//W3C//DTD XHTML 1.0 Strict//EN" "DTD/xhtml1-strict.dtd">
<html>
<!--
    Try It   5-1
    Title:   Course List
    Author:  InStep Technologies
             www.insteptech.com
    Purpose:To demonstrate basic tables
 -->
<head>
<title>InStep Training Course List</title>
</head>
<body>
<h1>InStep Training Course List</h1>
<p>The following is a list of our current course offerings.</p>
<table border="1">
    <tr>
        <th>Course</th>
        <th>Date(s)</th>
        <th>Location</th>
    </tr>
    <tr>
        <td>Object-Oriented Design</td>
        <td>June 25-28, 2002</td>
        <td>Hiltonian, Pleasanton, CA</td>
    </tr>
    <tr>
        <td>Web Application Development</td>
        <td>August 5-8, 2002</td>
        <td>Hiltonian, Phoenix, AZ</td>
    </tr>
</table>
</body>
</html>
```

Giving a Table Some Style

The table in Figure 5-1 was informative but not very exciting. To give your tables a nicer look, you can add styles using Cascading Style Sheets (CSS).

A common style for tables of data on the Web uses one style for odd lines and one for even lines. Figure 5-3 presents an example of this style.

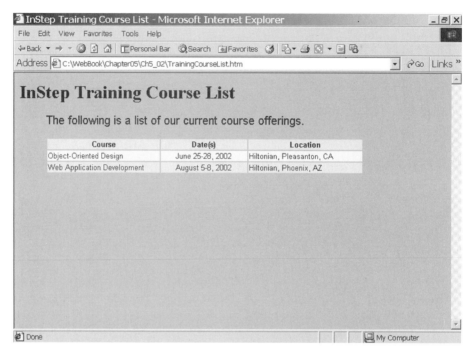

Figure 5-3. Using styles improves the look of your tables.

To accomplish this look, use CSS to define style classes for the even and odd rows. You can also define a style for the basic table. The style rules could look something like this:

```
❶   table {margin-left:0.5in; font-family:arial}
❷   .odd {font-size:10pt; color:navy; background-color:#FFFF9C}
❸   .even {font-size:10pt; color:navy; background-color:#C6EFF7}
❹   .wide {width:200px}
❺   .narrow {width:150px}
```

The `table` style rule (line ❶) defines a font for all of the text in the table. It also defines a margin for the table, offsetting it from the left margin. The odd style class (line ❷) defines one particular background color, and the even style class (line ❸) defines a second background color. In both cases, the text in the row is navy.

The wide style class (line ❹) defines a wide column width, and the narrow style class (line ❺) defines a slightly smaller column width. These are used to define the widths of the columns in the table.

TIP *If a width is not specified, the table size expands to fit the elements or to the edge of the browser window, whichever comes first. Use the* width *style property to specify a fixed column width.*

The next step is to apply these styles to the rows and columns. For example, you can apply the odd style to odd rows of the table. Apply the style to the tr element using the class attribute as follows.

```
<tr class="odd">
    <td>Object-Oriented Design</td>
    <td align="center">June 25-28, 2002</td>
    <td>Hiltonian, Pleasanton, CA</td>
</tr>
```

Use additional element attributes, such as align in the previous example, to further control the layout of your cells.

Try It 5-2.

Building a Table with Style

Try It 5-2 adds table layout styles to the TrainingStyle.css file from Try It 4-5. It then uses those styles in the Course List page from Try It 5-1.

1. Open the TrainingStyle.css file containing the Cascading Style Sheet from Try It 4-5.

2. Add a style rule for the table element.

3. Add four style classes, one for the even rows, one for the odd rows, one for a wide column width, and one for a narrow column width.

4. Save the TrainingStyle.css file.

5. Open the TrainingCourseList.htm file from Try It 5-1.

6. Add the link element to link the TrainingStyle.css file to this HTML file. See Chapter 4, "Using Style Sheets," for the syntax of the link element.

7. Add the class attribute to each tr element to assign the style to the row in the table. Be sure to use the even style class for the even rows and the odd style class for the odd rows.

8. Add the `class` attribute to each `th` element to define the width style to the column in the table.

9. Optionally, remove the `border` attributes from the `table` element.

10. Save the file.

11. Open the TrainingCourseList.htm file in your browser. The table should appear with alternating row colors.

12. Experiment with other table styles.

The resulting page will appear similar to Figure 5-3. If the page does not appear as desired, ensure that you updated the CSS with the defined styles.

The HTML used to generate the page shown in Figure 5-3 is presented in Listing 5-3. The revised style sheet is presented in Listing 5-4.

Listing 5-3. The TrainingCourseList.htm file uses the style sheet to give the table some style.

```
<!DOCTYPE html PUBLIC "-//W3C//DTD XHTML 1.0 Strict//EN" "DTD/xhtml1-strict.dtd">
<html>
<!--
    Try It   5-2
    Title:   Course List
    Author:  InStep Technologies
             www.insteptech.com
    Purpose:To demonstrate basic tables with styles
 -->
<head>
<title>InStep Training Course List</title>
<link rel="stylesheet" type="text/css" href="TrainingStyle.css" />
</head>
<body>
<h1>InStep Training Course List</h1>
<p class="normal">The following is a list of our current course offerings.</p>
<table>
    <tr class="even">
        <th class="wide">Course</th>
        <th class="narrow">Date(s)</th>
        <th class="wide">Location</th>
    </tr>
    <tr class="odd">
        <td>Object-Oriented Design</td>
        <td align="center">June 25-28, 2002</td>
        <td>Hiltonian, Pleasanton, CA</td>
    </tr>
```

```
    <tr class="even">
        <td>Web Application Development</td>
        <td align="center">August 5-8, 2002</td>
        <td>Hiltonian, Phoenix, AZ</td>
    </tr>
</table>
</body>
</html>
```

Listing 5-4. The TrainingStyle.css file was modified to include the table styles.

```
/*
    Try It   5-2
    Title:   Style Sheet
    Author:  InStep Technologies
             www.insteptech.com
    Purpose:To demonstrate external style sheets
             for tables
*/
p {
    margin-left:0.5in;
    font-family:arial;
    position:relative
}
p.key {
    font-size:20pt;
    color:red
}
p.normal {
    font-size:15pt;
    color:navy
}
.margin {
    margin-left:0.5in
}
h1 {
    color:navy
}
body {
    background-color:#D2B48C
}
```

```
div.foreground {
   margin-left:0.5in;
   color:#E2C48C;
   font-family:arial;
   font-size:120pt;
   position:absolute;
   top:50px;
   left:20px;
   z-index:0
}
div.shadow {
   margin-left:0.5in;
   color:#C2A48C;
   font-family:arial;
   font-size:120pt;
   position:absolute;
   top:52px;
   left:22px;
   z-index:0
}

table {
   margin-left:0.5in;
   font-family:arial
}
.odd {
   font-size:10pt;
   color:navy;
   background-color:#FFFF9C
}
.even {
   font-size:10pt;
   color:navy;
   background-color:#C6EFF7
}
.wide {
    width:200px
}
.narrow {
    width:150px
}
```

Adding Scroll Bars to Tables

The table in Figure 5-3 looks much nicer than the table in Figure 5-1. But what if you have a lot of data and you don't want the table to take over your page? You can add scroll bars to allow the user to scroll to additional table data as shown in Figure 5-4.

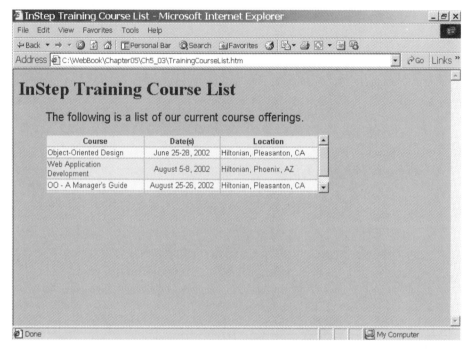

Figure 5-4. Use scroll bars to allow access to more table data without expanding the size of your table.

To accomplish this look, use CSS to define a `div` style class and apply it around the table. The style would look something like this:

```
div.scroll {height:100px; width:550px; overflow:auto}
```

The height and width defined in this style is the desired size of the table. By specifying auto for the `overflow` property, scroll bars only appear if they are needed, that is, when there is more data than can fit into the defined size.

The user can then scroll the table without scrolling the entire page. This is useful if you want to keep stationary headers or other graphics on the page, yet allow the user to scroll through a long table.

Try It 5-3.

Building a Table with a Scroll Bar

Try It 5-3 adds a div style to the TrainingStyle.css file from Try It 5-2. It then uses that style in the Course List page from Try It 5-2 to add a scroll bar to the page.

1. Open the TrainingStyle.css file containing the Cascading Style Sheet from Try It 5-2.

2. Add a style class for a div element that defines the scrollable region size and an overflow property value of auto.

3. Save the TrainingStyle.css file.

4. Open the TrainingCourseList.htm file from Try It 5-2.

5. Add div element tags around the table element tags and set the class attribute to the new style class you defined in step 2.

6. Save the file.

7. Open the TrainingCourseList.htm file in your browser. The table should appear with alternating row colors and a scroll bar.

The resulting page will appear similar to Figure 5-4. If the page does not appear with the scroll bar, ensure that the size of the scrollable area is set small enough such that scroll bars would be necessary or add more rows to the table to increase the table size.

The HTML used to generate the page shown in Figure 5-4 is presented in Listing 5-5. The revised style sheet is presented in Listing 5-6.

Listing 5-5. The TrainingCourseList.htm file uses a scroll bar to efficiently present a large list of information.

```
<!DOCTYPE html PUBLIC "-//W3C//DTD XHTML 1.0 Strict//EN" "DTD/xhtml1-strict.dtd">
<html>
<!--
   Try It  5-3
   Title:  Course List
   Author: InStep Technologies
           www.insteptech.com
   Purpose:To demonstrate a scrollable table
  -->
```

```
<head>
<title>InStep Training Course List</title>
<link rel="stylesheet" type="text/css" href="TrainingStyle.css" />
</head>
<body>
<h1>InStep Training Course List</h1>
<p class="normal">The following is a list of our current course offerings.</p>
<div class="scroll">
<table>
    <tr class="even">
        <th class="wide">Course</th>
        <th class="narrow">Date(s)</th>
        <th class="wide">Location</th>
    </tr>
    <tr class="odd">
        <td>Object-Oriented Design</td>
        <td align="center">June 25-28, 2002</td>
        <td>Hiltonian, Pleasanton, CA</td>
    </tr>
    <tr class="even">
        <td>Web Application Development</td>
        <td align="center">August 5-8, 2002</td>
        <td>Hiltonian, Phoenix, AZ</td>
    </tr>
    <tr class="odd">
        <td>OO - A Manager's Guide</td>
        <td align="center">August 25-26, 2002</td>
        <td>Hiltonian, Pleasanton, CA</td>
    </tr>
    <tr class="even">
        <td>.Net Application Development</td>
        <td align="center">September 5-8, 2002</td>
        <td>Hiltonian, Phoenix, AZ</td>
    </tr>
</table>
</div>
</body>
</html>
```

Listing 5-6. The TrainingStyle.css file was modified to include the scroll style.

```
/*
   Try It   5-3
   Title:   Style Sheet
   Author:  InStep Technologies
            www.insteptech.com
   Purpose: To demonstrate external style sheets
            for tables that scroll
*/
p {
   margin-left:0.5in;
   font-family:arial;
   position:relative
}
p.key {
   font-size:20pt;
   color:red
}
p.normal {
   font-size:15pt;
   color:navy
}
.margin {
   margin-left:0.5in
}
h1 {
   color:navy
}
body {
   background-color:#D2B48C
}
div.foreground {
   margin-left:0.5in;
   color:#E2C48C;
   font-family:arial;
   font-size:120pt;
   position:absolute;
   top:50px;
   left:20px;
   z-index:0
}
```

```
div.shadow {
    margin-left:0.5in;
    color:#C2A48C;
    font-family:arial;
    font-size:120pt;
    position:absolute;
    top:52px;
    left:22px;
    z-index:0
}
div.scroll {
    height:100px;
    width:550px;
    overflow:auto
}
table {
    margin-left:0.5in;
    font-family:arial
}
.odd {
    font-size:10pt;
    color:navy;
    background-color:#FFFF9C
}
.even {
    font-size:10pt;
    color:navy;
    background-color:#C6EFF7
}
.wide {
    width:200px
}
.narrow {
    width:150px
}
```

Using Tables for a Magazine-Style Layout

There are a few additional techniques that you need to know to get the magazine-style layout used by the news page shown in Figure 5-2. These are better explained in context, so this section steps through the code used to generate the news page.

The HTML for the news page is valid XHTML syntax so you can define the strict DTD for this page. As with all pages, the code continues with an explanatory comment:

```
<!DOCTYPE html PUBLIC "-//W3C//DTD XHTML 1.0 Strict//EN" "DTD/xhtml1-strict.dtd">
<html>
<!--
    Try It   None
    Title:   News Page
    Author:  InStep Technologies
             www.insteptech.com
    Purpose: To demonstrate a newspaper-like layout
 -->
```

The header section of this page includes a title and a link to the external style sheet used in the prior examples. The header also contains an embedded style sheet. These styles are embedded in this page instead of added to the external style sheet because they are only valid for this page and won't be reused for any other page.

The styles define the font style to be used for the table text and the height and width of the cells. In some cases, there is a "wide" version of a style. This is used for the text at the bottom of the news page that spans both columns. The wider columns could have different style properties so they were specified as a separate style, though in this example, many of the properties were the same. The resulting header section of the HTML document is as follows:

```
<head>
<title>InStep Tech Talk</title>
<link rel="stylesheet" type="text/css" href="TrainingStyle.css" />
<style type="text/css">
.tableSubHeader {
    margin-left:0in;
    font-size:14pt;
    font-weight:bold;
    color:navy;
    background-color:#C6EFF7;
    height:18px;
    width:350px
}
.tableSubHeaderWide {
    margin-left:0in;
    font-size:14pt;
    font-weight:bold;
    color:navy;
```

```
    background-color:#C6EFF7;
    height:18px;
    width:700px
}
.tableCell {
    width:350px;
    font-size:12pt;
    color:navy
}
.tableCellWide {
    width:700px;
    font-size:12pt;
    color:navy
}
.italics {
    font-size:12pt;
    font-style:italic
}
.bold {
    font-size:12pt;
    font-weight:bold
}
</style>
</head>
```

The body of the news page starts with a heading:

```
<body>
<h1>InStep Tech Talk</h1>
```

If any additional text were required prior to the content that appears in the columns, you would insert it after the heading and before the table.

All of the content of the news page is within one primary table:

```
<!-- Main table -->
<table border="0" cellspacing="0" cellpadding="5px">
```

The border attribute value of 0 prevents any border from appearing in the table. You may want to set the border attribute to a nonzero value during debugging in order to see the table cells. The cellspacing attribute of the table defines the spacing between the cells. The cellpadding attribute defines the space between the table border and the contents of the cell.

The first row of the table contains two cells. The first cell contains the "News" subheading and its associated content. The second cell in the first row contains the "Events" subheading and its associated content. (Refer back to Figure 5-2.)

The top of the first cell contains a subtitle and a graphic. To line these up correctly within the cell, you can define a nested table with a single row. The first cell in the nested table contains the subtitle. The second cell contains the graphic. The graphic is right justified using an inline style that sets the `float` property. The `align` attribute could have been used, but the `align` attribute of the img element is deprecated. The HTML for the nested table is as follows:

```
<tr>
  <td class="tableCell" valign="top" align="left">
  <!-- Example of a nested table -->
  <table class="tableSubHeader" border="0" cellspacing="0" cellpadding="0">
    <tr>
      <td>News</td>
      <td><img src="NewsGraphic.gif" alt="" style="float:right" /></td>
    </tr>
  </table>
```

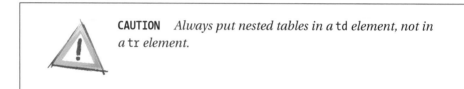

CAUTION *Always put nested tables in a* td *element, not in a* tr *element.*

The remaining text within the "News" cell is inserted in the same cell, after the nested table. You can define span elements within this text to offset important words or phrases:

```
<br />
<span class="bold">Friday</span> - Netscape said today that it will be
introducing a new browser feature named
<span class="italics">chameleon</span>.
This feature will automatically adjust the color of any Web page to the
color scheme of the user's home or office. Interior decorators
around the world applauded this news.
<br />
<br />
<span class="bold">Tuesday</span> - Microsoft announced that the latest
version of its Web development environment, called Microsoft .NET,
```

```
will support communication with household products such
as refrigerators, toasters, and dishwashers. This confirms
rumors that the newest features of .NET will allow better
tracing of your user's life styles.
</td>
```

The top of the second cell also contains a subtitle ("Events") and a graphic, so a nested table was inserted. The first cell in the nested table contains the subtitle. The second cell contains the graphic. In this case, the same graphic was used but any graphic could be used. Notice that this code is similar to the prior nested table:

```
<td class="tableCell" valign="top" align="left">
<!-- Example of a nested table -->
<table class="tableSubHeader" cellspacing="0" cellpadding="0">
   <tr>
      <td>Events</td>
      <td><img src="NewsGraphic.gif" alt="" style="float:right" /></td>
    </tr>
</table>
```

The remaining text within the "Events" cell is inserted in the same cell, after the nested table:

```
<br />
<span class="bold">Next Month</span> - Microsoft is hosting its first
annual music festival, billed as Woodstock.NET.
<br />
<br />
<span class="bold">September</span> - Sun plans its own music event, dubbed
Open Source Festival. They plan to launch their new Web-based
play once hear anywhere technology to broadcast the event.
</td>
</tr>
```

The second row of the primary table contains quotes heard on the street. This row spans both columns, so the colspan attribute is set to 2. Within this doublewide cell, the subtitle and graphic are again inserted using a nested table:

```
<tr>
   <td class="tableCellWide" colspan="2" valign="top" align="left">
   <!-- Example of a nested table -->
   <table class="tableSubHeaderWide" cellspacing="0" cellpadding="0">
      <tr>
         <td>Heard on the Street</td>
         <td><img src="NewsGraphic.gif" alt="" style="float:right" /></td>
      </tr>
   </table>
```

The remaining text within the doublewide cell is inserted in the same cell, after the nested table:

```
   <br />
   "The new Web-based technologies will bring back the new economy,
   this time for good. Companies don't have to be profitable to
   be successful and make money for their founders." - undisclosed
   CEO of a major dot.com.
   </td>
 </tr>
</table>
</body>
</html>
```

The result of Listing 5-4 is a two-column, two-row table that appears as shown in Figure 5-2.

HTML Table Element and Attribute Reference

Common HTML table elements and attributes are presented in Table 5-1. These elements add to the list of basic HTML elements presented in Table 3-1.

Table 5-1. Commonly Used HTML Table Elements and Attributes

ELEMENT	MEANING, USE, AND COMMON ATTRIBUTES
caption	Table caption. Defines a caption for the table. If you use scroll bars, the caption is within the scrollable region, which is not very useful. Common attributes: **align*** - Aligns the caption with respect to the table. Valid values are: top (default), bottom, left, right.

Table 5-1. Commonly Used HTML Table Elements and Attributes (continued)

ELEMENT	MEANING, USE, AND COMMON ATTRIBUTES
table	Table. Defines the beginning and ending of a table. Common attributes:
	align* - Aligns the table on the page. Valid values are: `left` (default), `right`, `center`.
	bgcolor* - Sets one color as the background of a table. (Internet Explorer only)
	border - Sets the border thickness around each cell, in pixels. Set border to 0 (the default) if you don't want a border to appear.
	bordercolor* - Defines the color of the border. (Internet Explorer only)
	cellpadding - Defines the internal distance between the border of the cell and the cell contents in pixels or a percentage of the available space. Use `cellpadding` to add white space around the table data. Default is 1 pixel.
	cellspacing - Defines the distance between the border of one cell and the next cell or the table border in pixels or a percentage of the available space. Use `cellspacing` to add white space between columns. Default is 2 pixels.
	width - Defines the width of the table in pixels or as a percentage of the screen. Use the percentage width if you want the table to resize to the width of the user's browser window. A fixed width speeds display of your table because the browser does not need to calculate the column widths.
td	Table data. Defines a cell within a row in the table. Common attributes:
	align - Defines the right/left alignment of a cell. Valid values are: `left` (default), `right`, `center`, and `justify`.
	bgcolor* - The background color of the cell.
	colspan - The number of columns this cell spans. The default is 1.
	nowrap* - Text within the cell does not wrap.
	rowspan - The number of rows this cell spans. The default is 1.
	valign - The top/bottom alignment of a cell. Valid values are: `top`, `middle` (default), or `bottom`.

Table 5-1. Commonly Used HTML Table Elements and Attributes (continued)

ELEMENT	MEANING, USE, AND COMMON ATTRIBUTES
td *(cont.)*	**width*** - The width of this column in pixels or as a percentage of the screen. Use the percentage width if you want the table to resize to the width of the user's browser window. A fixed width speeds display of your table because the browser does not need to calculate the column widths. **wrap*** - Text wraps within the cell.
th	Table header. Defines a heading for a column of the table. Headings are displayed in bold in the center of the column. Common attributes: **align** - Defines the right/left alignment of a heading. Valid values are: left (default), right, center, and justify. **bgcolor*** - Defines the background color for the header. **colspan** - The number of columns this header spans. The default is 1. **rowspan** - The number of rows this header spans. The default is 1. **valign** - The top/bottom alignment of a cell. Valid values are: top, middle (default), or bottom. **width*** - The width of this column in pixels or as a percentage of the screen. Only use the percentage width if you want the table to resize to the width of the user's browser window. A fixed width speeds display of your table because the browser does not need to calculate the column widths.
tr	Table row. Defines a row in the table. Common attributes: **align** - Defines the right/left alignment of all cells in the row. Valid values are: left (default), right, center, and justify. **bgcolor*** - Defines the background color for the row. **valign** - Defines the top/bottom alignment of all cells in the row. Valid values are: top, middle (default), or bottom.

CAUTION *HTML 4 has deprecated several of the style-based attributes for tables. These are marked with an asterisk (*) in Table 5-1. W3C recommends use of styles instead of these deprecated attributes.*

HTML Version 4 and later includes several other elements that are useful in working with tables. These are listed in Table 5-2. See the "Additional Resources" section of this chapter for more information and examples on the use of these elements.

Table 5-2. Additional Table Elements Available in HTML 4.0 and Later

ELEMENT	MEANING, USE, AND COMMON ATTRIBUTES
col	Column. Allows formatting of an entire column. Common attributes:
	align - Defines the right/left alignment of the column. Valid values are: left (default), right, center, and justify.
	valign - Defines the top/bottom alignment of all cells in the column. Valid values are: top, middle (default), or bottom.
colgroup	Column group. Allows formatting of a group of columns. Note that this element must be before any of the tbody, tfoot, or thead elements. Common attributes:
	align - Defines the right/left alignment of the columns. Valid values are: left (default), right, center, and justify.
	valign - Defines the top/bottom alignment of all cells in the columns. Valid values are: top, middle (default), or bottom.
tbody	Table body group. Allows formatting of the table body. You can have one or more tbody elements in a table to define horizontal sections of a table and apply formatting to those sections. Common attributes:
	align - Defines the right/left alignment of the table. Valid values are: left (default), right, center, and justify.
	valign - Defines the top/bottom alignment of all cells in the table. Valid values are: top, middle (default), or bottom.

Table 5-2. Additional Table Elements Available in HTML 4.0 and Later (continued)

ELEMENT	MEANING, USE, AND COMMON ATTRIBUTES
tfoot	Table footer group. Allows formatting of a table's footer. You can only have one tfoot element in a table. Common attributes:
	align - Defines the right/left alignment of the table footer. Valid values are: left (default), right, center, and justify.
	valign - Defines the top/bottom alignment of all cells in the table footer. Valid values are: top, middle (default), or bottom.
thead	Table header group. Allows formatting of a table's header. You can only have one thead element in a table. Common attributes:
	align - Defines the right/left alignment of the table header. Valid values are: left (default), right, center, and justify.
	valign - Defines the top/bottom alignment of all cells in the table footer. Valid values are: top, middle (default), or bottom.

HTML Table Tips and Tricks

This section includes basic tips and techniques when working with HTML and CSS to create tables. There are many uses for tables and these techniques can help you lay out and debug your tables.

Performance Tips

Tables can impact the performance of the display of your page because the browser has to interpret and format the table. Use these tips to optimize performance.

Set Browser Width

Tables frequently take longer to display than expected. This is because the browser needs to calculate the widths of all of the columns before the table can be displayed. Improve your table display performance by defining fixed widths for the table and for each column in the table when feasible.

Minimize Tables within Tables

Nested tables can severely impact performance. Limit the use of nested tables wherever possible.

Debugging Tips

Sometimes it is difficult to see why a table is not displayed as you are expecting. Here are some tips for debugging your tables.

Use a Tool

If you build and update your table using an HTML tool like FrontPage, the tags are taken care of for you.

Turn on Table Borders

By setting the border attribute of the table to a nonzero value during debugging, you can more easily see how the table is laid out. This is frequently useful for debugging your table.

Check Your Tags

Missing ending tags are the most common error in working with tables. Frequently, there are so many `tr` and `td` element tags that it is easy to miss an ending tag.

If some of the text that is supposed to be in the table appears before the table on the page, you are probably missing a `td` element tag.

Put Something in Every Cell

A cell with no contents may not appear correctly. For example, a cell may not appear with any borders even though all other cells have their borders. To prevent this problem, put something in every cell. Use ` ` for an empty cell.

What Did This Cover?

This chapter covered the basic techniques for building a table and giving it a nice look using styles. You can create tables to display tabular data or to control the layout of your page elements. In either case, creative use of tables and table styles can energize an otherwise dull page.

The Try Its in this chapter demonstrated how to build a simple table to display tabular data. They also presented some ideas on how to use styles to format the table and to add scroll bars.

The next chapter looks at creating data entry forms on the page. There, you will leverage what you learned in this chapter to lay out forms using borderless tables.

Additional Resources

This section provides some additional resource suggestions by way of books, articles and links to Web resources with tips on creating tables.

The books, articles, and links all existed at the time of this writing. There is a good chance that the books and articles still exist as you read this. However, the same cannot be said of Web links. So, ignore the suggested links if they no longer exist.

Books and Articles

Castro, Elizabeth. *HTML 4 for the World Wide Web.* **Berkeley, CA: Peachpit Press, 2000.**
This book has some very detailed suggestions for laying out tables on the page and then creating the appropriate HTML to achieve the desired layout.

Links

http://home.netscape.com/assist/net_sites/table_sample.html: This Web site provides many different examples of creating tables and demonstrates rowspan, colspan, and several other table elements.

http://www.w3.org/TR/REC-html40/struct/tables.html: This is the standard site for the World Wide Web Consortium (W3C) that specifically addresses tables.

CHAPTER 6

Building Forms

THE HTML DESCRIBED SO FAR in this book presents static content to the user. This is great for welcome pages and other content but does not provide the main functionality you need to develop a Web *application*. To build a Web application, you must allow the user to enter and update information.

You can use HTML forms to build Web pages comparable in purpose to Windows-based forms. You can present a login page for security into your application. You can track the users of your application with a guest book. You can provide online registration for courses or social events. You can present pages to maintain basic application data such as customers in a sales application, parts in an inventory application, or addresses in a personal assistant application. You can allow the user to identify purchases and take credit card numbers in an e-commerce application. The possibilities are limitless.

The purpose of this chapter is to provide you with the basics you need to develop data-entry forms using HTML. This chapter leverages the table and style sheet techniques you learned in the prior chapters to give your forms a nice layout and style.

What Will This Cover?

This chapter covers the following key HTML form concepts:

- Understanding the basics of creating forms with HTML

- Creating a simple HTML form

- Improving the look of HTML forms with tables and styles

- Adding a selection box to a form

- Submitting HTML form data

- Passing data with hidden fields

- Specifying the layout of HTML forms with absolute positioning

- Learning the basic set of HTML form elements and attributes

By the end of this chapter, you will know how to build data-entry forms with HTML. You will learn how to use tables to align labels and data-entry boxes. You will also learn how to use absolute positioning for complete control over the look of your form.

HTML Form Basics

An HTML form is comprised of form elements, such as data-entry boxes and radio buttons. These form elements are sometimes called *controls* or *fields* on the form. A form can be added to any HTML page to allow a user to review, enter, or update information. Figure 6-1 presents a simple form without a nice layout or style.

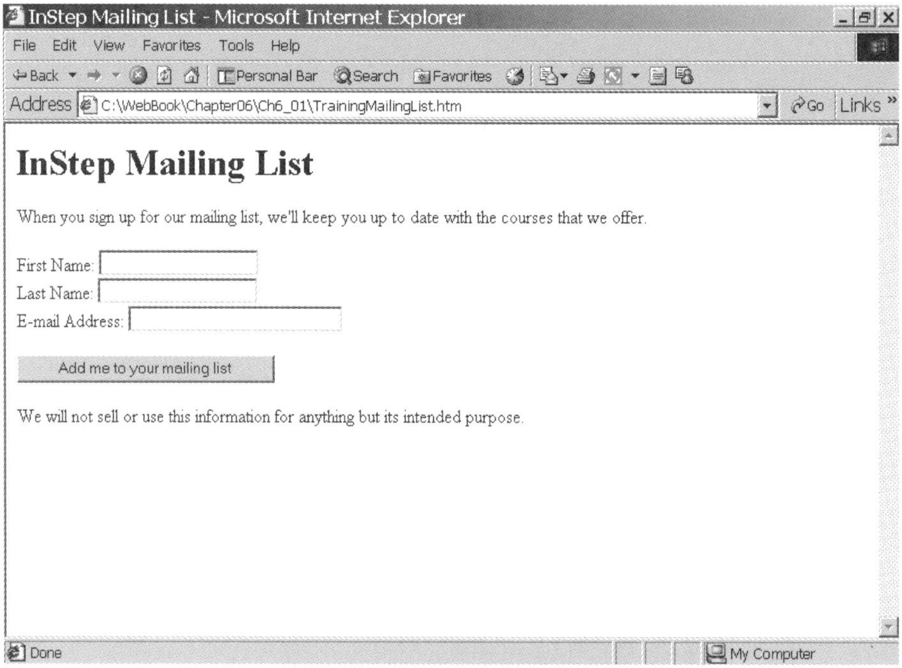

Figure 6-1. You can use a form to collect information from the user.

Users normally complete a form by modifying its controls, such as entering text into a text box, and then submitting the form by clicking on a button on the form. The data obtained from the form is then sent through HTTP to the Web server for processing.

You create the visual display of the form using data-entry boxes, command buttons, other controls, and other visual elements. You then write the code on the Web server to receive and process the form data. This section covers the basic HTML required to define the visual display of the form. Later sections in this chapter describe the code required to accept and process the form data.

You define the visual display of a form on a Web page using `form` element tags. All of the elements between the beginning and ending `form` element tags define the content of the form. This is demonstrated in the following example:

```
❶    <form id="MailingList" method="get" action="">
❷    <div>
❸      <label for="FirstName">First Name:</label>
❹          <input type="text" id="FirstName" name="FirstName" size="20" /><br />
❺      <label for="LastName">Last Name:</label>
❻          <input type="text" id="LastName" name="LastName" size="20" /><br />
❼      <label for="Email">E-mail Address:</label>
❽          <input type="text" id="Email" name="Email" size="28" /><br />
❾      <button type="submit" name="Save" value="Save">Add me to your list</button>
❿    </div>
⓫    </form>
```

The `form` element tags (lines ❶ and ⓫) define the beginning and ending of the form. User input in response to any of the elements within these `form` element tags is submitted to the Web server when the form is submitted.

The `id` attribute uniquely identifies the form. To make it easier to assign an ID, define a consistent naming convention that you can use for all of your form IDs. Some developers prefix the form ID with "frm" to indicate that it is a form. More commonly, proper case logical names are used. The latter is the convention used in this book.

NOTE   *The* name *attribute of a form has been deprecated. Use the* id *attribute instead.*

The `method` and `action` attributes of the `form` element define how the form data is submitted to the Web server. These are discussed in detail in the "Submitting HTML Form Data" section later in this chapter.

A `form` element that is XHTML compliant can contain block-level elements but not inline elements. This means that you cannot simply add text or controls within the `form` element. Rather, the text and controls must be within a block-level element like the `div` element in this example (lines ❷ and ❿).

There are many HTML elements specifically defined as controls for use within a `form` element. These controls provide for different types of user response. For example, the user can type information into a text box, select from a list of entries in a select box, pick a choice from a set of radio buttons, or perform an action such as saving using a command button.

Each label element (lines ❸, ❺, and ❼) appears as the label for the control defined in the for attribute of the label element. Label elements are not required for labels or any other text displayed on the form, but using a label element allows an agent or other text to speech tool to associate the label with the control making your Web page more accessible.

The input elements with the type attribute set to text (lines ❹, ❻, and ❽) identify text box controls on the form. The id attribute provides a unique identifier for the control. You can use this ID to define control styles as shown later in this chapter or to access the control with script as shown in Chapter 9, "Validating Form Data."

The name attribute defines the control's name. This name is submitted to the Web server with the control's data when the form is submitted. See the "Submitting HTML Form Data" section of this chapter for details on submitting the form to the server.

CAUTION *If you don't define the* name *attribute for a control, the value of that control is not submitted to the server when the form is processed.*

As with form IDs, define a consistent naming convention for the id and name attributes of your controls. Some developers use prefixes such as "txt" for text boxes. The most common convention is to use the proper case description of the control's contents. The latter is the convention used in this book.

NOTE *In most cases, the value of the* id *and* name *attributes should be identical. See the "Add Keyboard Shortcuts" tip toward the end of this chapter for an example of an exception to this.*

The size and maxlength (not shown) attributes of the input element allow you to define the size of the data-entry box and the maximum number of characters that can be entered. You can use the value attribute (not shown) to define a default value. The user-enter text is automatically assigned to the value attribute.

You may want several buttons on the form to provide for different actions that the user can perform. At a minimum, you need to provide a mechanism for the user to submit the information they have entered or selected to a Web server.

In this example, the button element (line ❾) has its type attribute set to submit so it provides the submit mechanism. When the user clicks on this button, the form is submitted and the `name` and `value` attributes of all controls within the `form` element tags are submitted to the Web server for processing.

You can add any number of HTML forms to any page to provide for data entry in your Web application. Each form must have a submit type button or image within the `form` element tags to send the user-entered values to the Web server for processing. (You can also submit using scripting code.) The submission process is discussed in detail in the "Submitting HTML Form Data" section later in this chapter.

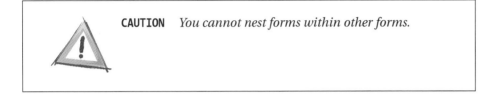

CAUTION *You cannot nest forms within other forms.*

Creating a Simple HTML Form

Building forms with HTML is easy. Simply define the `form` element tags and add the desired control element tags. As you will see, however, there is little beauty in this simplicity.

The basic steps for building an HTML form are:

1. Ensure that you lay out the look of the data-entry form during the design phase of the project.

2. Create the HTML document that will contain the form.

3. Optionally add the graphics, text or other elements for the introduction to the form, instructions, data-entry tips, and so on.

4. Add the `form` element tags.

5. Within the `form` element tags add `label` elements and other descriptive text.

6. Add the desired control element tags to define the data entry or data selection mechanisms desired for your form.

7. Within the `form` element tags, add a button or image that the user can click to submit the data entered on the form.

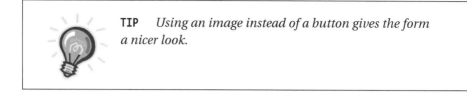

TIP *Using an image instead of a button gives the form a nicer look.*

8. Try out your page to ensure that it appears as you expect.

When you display your form, you may find that it does not look very good. It does not line up nicely or have any style. You need to do some additional work to make the form look good as discussed in the next section.

Try It 6-1.

Building a Data Entry Form

Try It 6-1 begins development of a new Mailing List Web page. This page presents a form that allows a user to sign up on a mailing list.

1. Using your tool of choice, create a new text file.

2. Add the DOCTYPE declaration and the basic HTML tags to the file: `<html>`, `<head>`, `</head>`, `<body>`, `</body>`, and `</html>`.

3. Add a `title` element to the header section of the page. You could give the page a title such as "Acme Mailing List."

4. Define any other text or images to give the page a nice look and to introduce the form.

5. Add a `form` element to define a form on the page. Set the standard form attributes such as `id`, `method`, and `action`.

6. Define `label` elements for the controls on the form. You could add labels for name, address, e-mail, and so on.

7. Define `input` elements for text boxes on the form. You could add text boxes for name, address, e-mail, and so on.

8. Define a `button` element for a submit button. Be sure to set the `type` attribute to `submit`.

9. Save the file as TrainingMailingList.htm.

10. Open the TrainingMailingList.htm file in your browser. If you defined a link to a page of this name in your Welcome page from the prior Try Its, you will be able to access this page through the link on your Welcome page.

11. Experiment with other control elements and attributes.

The resulting Web page will appear similar to Figure 6-1. If your form does not appear as you expect, ensure that you have both the beginning and ending tags for each element that you defined. Missing ending tags is the most common error in building forms.

Listing 6-1 displays the code used to generate the Web page shown in Figure 6-1.

Listing 6-1. The TrainingMailingList.htm file displays a simple form for data entry by the user.

```
<!DOCTYPE html PUBLIC "-//W3C//DTD XHTML 1.0 Strict//EN" "DTD/xhtml1-strict.dtd">
<html>
<!--
    Try It  6-1
    Title:  Mailing List
    Author: InStep Technologies
            www.insteptech.com
    Purpose: To demonstrate a basic data entry form
  -->
<head>
<title>InStep Mailing List</title>
</head>
<body>
<h1>InStep Mailing List</h1>
<p>When you sign up for our mailing list, we'll keep you up to date with the
    courses that we offer.</p>
<form id="MailingList" method="get" action="">
<div>
    <label for="FirstName">First Name:</label>
        <input type="text" id="FirstName"  name="FirstName" size="20"
            maxlength="40" />
        <br />
    <label for="LastName">Last Name:</label>
        <input type="text" id="LastName" name="LastName" size="20"
            maxlength="40" />
        <br />
    <label for="Email">E-mail Address:</label>
        <input type="text" id="Email" name="Email" size="28" />
        <br />
        <br />
    <button type="submit" name="Save" value="Save">
        Add me to your mailing list
    </button>
</div>
</form>
```

```
<p>We will not sell or use this information for anything
   but its intended purpose.</p>
</body>
</html>
```

Improving Forms with Tables and Styles

When you look at a form created with the steps in the prior section, such as Figure 6-1, you can see that the controls on the form are not laid out very nicely. The labels aren't justified. The text boxes are not aligned properly. The form does not make good use of horizontal space. There is no color or style. The form just does not look good.

There are two techniques for improving the layout of the form: tables and absolute positioning. The most common technique is to lay out forms with borderless tables as described in this section. The more complex technique of absolute positioning is described later in this chapter.

To define the layout of a form using a table, begin by designing the look of your form on paper. (You may have done this during the design phase as described in Chapter 2, "Designing Web Applications.") Then sketch a table over the form contents by drawing cells around the visual elements of the form. With a table, you can justify and align controls within columns on the page.

Once you have the desired layout on paper, create the HTML document and add the `form` element tags. Add `table` element tags within the `form` element tags to define the table within the form. Then place the labels and controls into the cells of the table according to your design. For example:

```
❶  <form id="MailingList" method="get" action="">
❷     <table>
❸        <tr>
❹           <td><label for="FirstName">First Name:</label></td>
❺           <td><input type="text" id="FirstName" name="FirstName"></td>
❻           <td><label for="LastName">Last Name:</label></td>
❼           <td><input type="text" id="LastName" name="LastName"></td>
❽        </tr>
❾        <tr>
❿           <td><label for="Email">E-mail Address:</label></td>
⓫           <td><input type="text" id="Email" name="Email" size="28"></td>
⓬        </tr>
⓭        <tr>
⓮           <td> </td>
```

```
⑮        <td  colspan="3" align="center">
⑯            <button type="submit" name="Save" value="Save">Add me </button></td>
⑰      </tr>
⑱    </table>
⑲ </form>
```

The `table` element tags (lines ❷ and ⑱) reside within the `form` element tags (lines ❶ and ⑲). Make the table invisible by setting the `border` attribute of the `table` element to 0, which is the default.

The `tr` elements (lines ❸ through ❽, for example) define a row and the `td` elements (lines ❹, ❺, ❻, and ❼ for example) define each cell in the row. A label or control can reside within each table cell.

Notice that the first row has four columns of labels and controls (lines ❹, ❺, ❻ and ❼) while the second row only has two columns (lines ❿ and ⑪). In this example, you could add two additional empty columns to the second row (before line ⑫) to make each row consistent. Use the nonbreaking space (` `) within any empty cell to ensure that cell is displayed properly (similar to line ⑭).

NOTE *Empty cells without a nonbreaking space are not always formatted correctly, especially if your table has a border.*

The empty `td` element (line ⑭) defines an empty cell. The `colspan` attribute of the `td` element (line ⑮) is used to display the submit button across the remaining three columns of the table.

Using a table within your form improves the layout, taking a big step toward improving the look of your form. But for a really nice looking form, you can add styles as presented in Chapter 4, "Using Style Sheets." You can use styles to define font sizes, background colors, and other attributes that can give all of your forms a consistent look.

To add styles, you can embed style rules within the Web page or link to an external style sheet:

```
<link rel="stylesheet" type="text/css" href="TrainingStyle.css">
```

You can then use any styles you have defined within the style sheet or add additional styles to the style sheet for the form. Use an external style sheet if you plan to use the styles in several forms. Use an embedded style within the HTML document if the style rules only apply to the form within the HTML document.

Figure 6-2 shows the result of adding a table and styles to the simple form shown in Figure 6-1. Notice how much better this form looks than the original form.

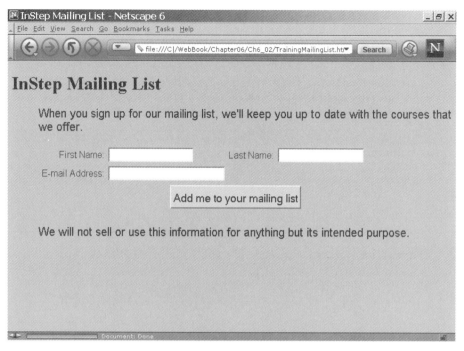

Figure 6-2. Using a table and some styles can greatly improve the look of your forms.

Try It 6-2.

Building a Form Using a Table and Styles

Try It 6-2 adds a table, a style sheet, and some embedded styles to the Mailing List page from Try It 6-1 to align the labels and controls on the form.

1. Open the TrainingMailingList.htm file from Try It 6-1 in your HTML editing tool.

2. Add the link element to link the TrainingStyle.css file to this HTML file. See Chapter 4, "Using Style Sheets," for the syntax of the link element.

3. Apply the normal style class to any standard paragraphs on the page.

4. Add an embedded style definition for an input element and tr element.

   The input element style defines the style of the text that the user types into the input element and the tr element style defines the style for the row such as row height and font.

5. Optionally, add a `tr` element class and a `button` element class to define a specific style for the row containing the button and for the button itself.

6. Add `table` element tags within the `form` element tags.

7. Remove the `div` element tags that were added in Try It 6-1 to define a block-level element within the `form` element. The `table` element is a block-level element and contains all of the other elements for the form.

8. Add `tr` elements for each row needed to contain the elements for the form.

9. Add `td` elements to contain each label and control on the page.

10. Save the file.

11. Open the TrainingMailingList.htm file in your browser.

The resulting page will appear similar to Figure 6-2. If the form does not appear as you expected, set the `border` attribute of the table to a nonzero value to see the table borders during your debugging.

Listing 6-2 displays the code used to generate the page shown in Figure 6-2.

Listing 6-2. The TrainingMailingList.htm file uses tables and styles to improve the layout and look of the form.

```
<!DOCTYPE html PUBLIC "-//W3C//DTD XHTML 1.0 Strict//EN" "DTD/xhtml1-strict.dtd">
<html>
<!--
    Try It  6-2
    Title:  Mailing List
    Author: InStep Technologies
            www.insteptech.com
    Purpose:To demonstrate laying out a form using a table and styles
  -->
<head>
<title>InStep Mailing List</title>
<link rel="stylesheet" type="text/css" href="TrainingStyle.css" />
<style type="text/css">
<!--
input {
    font-size:12pt;
    color:navy
    }
tr {
    font-size:12pt;
    color:navy;
    height:30px
    }
```

```
            tr.rowButton {
                height:50px
                }
            button.rowButton {
                font-size:14pt;
                color:navy;
                height:40px
                }
            -->
            </style>
            </head>
            <body>
            <h1>InStep Mailing List</h1>
            <p class="normal">
                When you sign up for our mailing list, we'll keep you up to date with the
                    courses that we offer.
            </p>
            <form id="MailingList" method="get" action="">
                <table>
                    <tr>
                        <td align="right">
                            <label for="FirstName">First Name:</label>
                        </td>
                        <td align="left">
                            <input type="text" id="FirstName"  name="FirstName" size="20"
                                maxlength="40" />
                        </td>
                        <td align="right">
                            <label for="LastName">Last Name:</label>
                        </td>
                        <td align="left">
                            <input type="text" id="LastName" name="LastName" size="20"
                                maxlength="40" />
                        </td>
                    </tr>
                    <tr>
                        <td align="right">
                            <label for="Email">E-mail Address:</label>
                        </td>
                        <td align="left">
                            <input type="text" id="Email"  name="Email" size="28" />
                        </td>
                        <td> </td>
                        <td> </td>
```

```
        </tr>
        <tr class="rowButton">
            <td> </td>
            <td colspan="3" align="center">
                <button class="rowButton" type="submit" name="Save" value="Save">
                    Add me to your mailing list
                </button>
            </td>
        </tr>
    </table>
</form>
<p class="normal">
    We will not sell or use this information for anything
     but its intended purpose.
</p>
</body>
</html>
```

Adding a Selection Box to a Form

Another common data-entry technique is a dropdown selection box. A dropdown selection box provides the user with a predefined set of choices as shown in Figure 6-3. This is similar to a combo box in a Windows application.

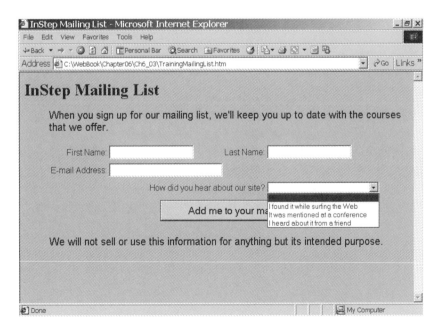

Figure 6-3. A dropdown selection box gives the user a specific set of choices.

The values for this selection box can be predefined in the HTML page. More commonly, the selection box is built dynamically on the Web server using information from a database. See Chapter 15, "Web Application Architectures," for more information on server-side techniques. In this section, the selection box is created with HTML.

A selection box requires two different types of elements. The select element defines the selection box itself. The option elements contained within the select element define the entries listed in the dropdown box. For example:

```
❶ <select id="Referral" name="Referral">
❷   <option value="Empty" />
❸   <option value="Surfing">I found it while surfing the Web</option>
❺   <option value="Conference">It was mentioned at a conference</option>
❻   <option value="Person">I heard about it from a friend</option>
❼ </select>
```

The select element tags (lines ❶ and ❼) define the selection box. The id attribute defines the logical name used to access the selection box with code. The name attribute defines the name submitted to the Web server with the control's data when the form is submitted. See the "Submitting HTML Form Data" section of this chapter for details on submitting the form to the server.

The option element tags (lines ❷ through ❻) define the entries that are available for selection within the dropdown selection box. The value attribute defines the value that is submitted to the server. The content of each option element tag is the text that appears within the selection box. Providing an empty option (line ❷) allows the user to select none of the defined choices.

Try It 6-3.

Adding a Selection Box to a Form

Try It 6-3 adds a selection box to the Mailing List page from Try It 6-2 to provide a dropdown selection box on the form.

1. Open the TrainingMailingList.htm file from Try It 6-2 in your HTML editing tool.

2. Add a row to the table within the form above the submit button. This row contains the control label and selection box.

3. Add select element tags within the td element tags.

4. Add option elements within the select element tags for each item to be listed in the dropdown selection box.

5. Save the file.

6. Open the TrainingMailingList.htm file in your browser.

The resulting page should appear similar to Figure 6-3. The code used to generate the selection box on the page shown in Figure 6-3 is presented in Listing 6-3.

Listing 6-3. This code snippet shows the HTML needed to display the selection box. See the prior section for the code displaying the other elements on the form.

```
<tr>
    <td colspan="3" align="right">
        <label for="Referral">How did you hear about our site?</label>
    </td>
    <td align="left">
        <select id="Referral" name="Referral">
            <option value="Empty" />
            <option value="Surfing">I found it while surfing the Web</option>
            <option value="Conference">It was mentioned at a conference</option>
            <option value="Person">I heard about it from a friend</option>
        </select>
    </td>
</tr>
```

Submitting HTML Form Data

So far, you have created the visual part of the form for display to the user. In order for the form to be useful, the data the user enters on that form needs to be submitted to the Web server for processing.

When the user clicks on a button or graphic that submits the form, the form data is sent to the Web server. This data is submitted in name and value pairs. The name comes from the name attribute that you defined for the data-entry element. The value comes from the value attribute, which is automatically set to the user-entered or user-selected data for that element.

For example, if the user entered information on the form as shown in Figure 6-4, the name and value pairs passed to the server would be:

FirstName=Deborah
LastName=Kurata
Email=deborahk@insteptech.com
Referral=Person
Save=Save

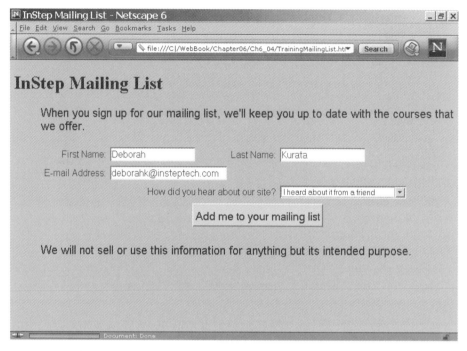

Figure 6-4. This completed form is ready for submission to the Web server.

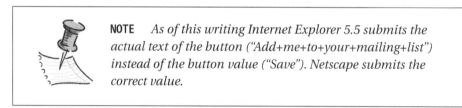

NOTE   *As of this writing Internet Explorer 5.5 submits the actual text of the button ("Add+me+to+your+mailing+list") instead of the button value ("Save"). Netscape submits the correct value.*

For a data-entry element's name and value pair to be included in the submission, the data-entry element must:

- Reside within the same form element tags as the element (button or graphic) used to submit the form.

- Have the name attribute defined.

When the Web server receives these name and value pairs, code on the Web server processes the data. For example, this Web-server code could validate a user-entered ID and password from a login page. It could store user identification information from a guest book entry page. It could process purchase requests and validate a credit card number for an online purchase page. It can perform calculations, validation, and database storage and retrieval.

The form element's action attribute defines the name of the Web-server application that processes the form's data. You have many choices for the technique and language used to develop this Web-server application. For example, you could write a CGI (Common Gateway Interface) script using a language such as Perl. You could write a Java servlet to process your form. You could use Microsoft Active Server Pages (ASP) and a server-side scripting language like VBScript. See Chapter 15, "Web Application Architectures," for more information on these server-side techniques. See the "Additional Resources" section of this chapter for links to prebuilt and reusable server-side applications.

Some examples of action attributes are:

```
<form name="MailingList" method="post"
   action= "http://www.insteptech.com/cgi-bin/ProcessMailing.cgi">
```

```
<form name="MailingList" method="post" action="ProcessMailing.asp">
```

The first example references a CGI script defined with a fully qualified path. The second example uses an Active Server Page (ASP) that resides in the same directory as the Web page containing the form.

The method attribute of the form element defines how the name and value pairs are sent to the server. Valid values are get or post.

The get method appends the name and value pairs to the URI in the Address field of the browser when the form is submitted. This means that the user can see (and potentially modify) those names and values.

For example, if the user submits the form shown in Figure 6-4, the Address field of the user's browser contains:

```
file:///C:/WebBook/Chapter06/Ch6_04/TrainingMailingList.htm? FirstName=Deborah
   &LastName=Kurata&Email=deborahk@insteptech.com&Referral=Person&Save=Save
```

This submission contains the URI from the `action` attribute, which defaults to your current Web page if it is not specified. After the question mark (?) are the name and value pairs separated by ampersands (&). Spaces within any value are replaced with a plus sign (+) so there are no empty spaces in the submission.

The `post` method sends the data as part of the HTTP request instead of appending it to the URI making it more difficult for the user to view or modify the data. Post is normally the recommended value for the `method` attribute as shown in Table 6-1.

You may want to test your form submission process without having to complete your server-side application. You can do this by submitting the form data to an e-mail address as follows:

```
<form name="MailingList" method="post" enctype="text/plain"
action="mailto:youraddress@yoursite.com">
```

For this test to work:

- The `method` attribute must be set to `post`. This does not work with `get`.

- The `enctype` attribute is set to `text/plain` to ensure that the data is formatted as text.

- The `action` attribute must be set to a valid e-mail address.

- The browser you are using must support the `mailto:` protocol. Some older browsers don't.

- You must have a working mail system (installed and configured) on the computer from which this Web page is displayed. For example, if you are trying this from your computer, you need to ensure you have a mail system such as Microsoft Outlook. (Before you attempt to use this technique, be sure you can send and receive mail from that computer.)

If you cannot test using the mailto technique, you can achieve a minimal level of testing of your submission by using the get method and reviewing the resulting URI in the Address field of the browser.

Table 6-1. Comparing the Form *Element's* Method *Attribute Values:* post *and* get

POST	GET
Recommended value.	Default value.
Form is submitted as an HTTP Post request with the form data submitted in the body of the request.	Form is submitted as an HTTP Get request with the form data appended to the URI.
User cannot easily see or edit the name and value pairs.	The name and value pairs are appended to the URI and appear in the Address field of the browser. The user can easily change these values and the changes are not processed or validated by your Web page, possibly causing problems with data validation and security.
Supports non-ASCII characters.	Prevents non-ASCII character data from being submitted to the server.
Support large amounts of data.	Is limited by the maximum length of the URI defined by the browser. To be safe, no more than one hundred characters should be submitted using get.
Does not provide bookmarking to a submission page.	Provides bookmarking to the page defined by the URI with its associated data.

Passing Data with Hidden Fields

When the user submits a form, the user-entered values or selections for elements contained within the form element tags are submitted to the server for processing. You may want to submit additional information with the form data, for example, the state of the application. One technique for submitting additional data to the Web server is to use hidden fields on the form.

Hidden fields are defined like any other input element. Since the field is not displayed to the user, you don't define a label. You simply give the hidden field a name using the name attribute and set the value attribute to the desired value. The name and value pair is submitted to the server with all of the other form data.

The code below demonstrates a hidden field:

```
<input type="hidden" name="MailingListType" value="Training" />
```

This input element can be inserted anywhere within the form element tags. By convention, hidden fields are placed immediately after the <form> tag to ensure they can be found easily for editing and other maintenance activities.

 CAUTION   *Even though the field is hidden, the user can still see the value of the field by viewing the source of the page. Don't use this for confidential or otherwise protected information, such as a password.*

Try It 6-4.

Adding a Hidden Field to a Form

Try It 6-4 adds the form method and action attributes and a hidden field to the Mailing List page from Try It 6-3.

1. Open the TrainingMailingList.htm from Try It 6-3 in your HTML editing tool.

2. Add method and action attributes for the form element.

3. Add an input element for a hidden field.

4. Save the file.

5. Open the TrainingMailingList.htm file in your browser.

   Setting the method and action attributes and adding the hidden field has no impact on the visual display of the form.

6. With the method attribute set to get, click on the Save button. You should be able to see the name and value pairs of all of the data-entry fields, including the hidden field, appended to the URI in the Address box of your browser.

7. With the method attribute set to post, and the action attribute set to post via e-mail, click on the Save button. The name and value pairs of all of the data-entry fields, including the hidden field, should appear in an e-mail message. See below for more information on the code for this technique.

The snippet of code needed to post to an e-mail address and the hidden field code is as follows:

```
<form name="MailingList" method="post" enctype="text/plain"
    action="mailto:youraddress@yoursite.com">
<input type="hidden" name="MailingListType" value="Training">
```

CAUTION   *Please note the warnings about using this e-mail technique provided in the "Submitting HTML Form Data" section of this chapter.*

The snippet of code needed for the form element and hidden field using the get attribute value is as follows:

```
<form name="MailingList" method="get" action="">
<input type="hidden" name="MailingListType" value="Training">
```

Form Layout with Absolute Positioning

In the previous sections of this chapter, you used tables to give your data-entry form a nicer appearance. But if you look closely at the result, you can see that the elements are lined up quite rigidly. You may want to have more control of the placement of each element on the form. For this, you need to use absolute positioning of your form elements.

Absolute positioning involves defining style properties that specify the exact location for each element on a page. You can define the precise placement of each text element, input element, graphic element, and any other elements on the page. The result could look like Figure 6-5. Notice that the placement of the elements is no longer restricted to specific rows and columns.

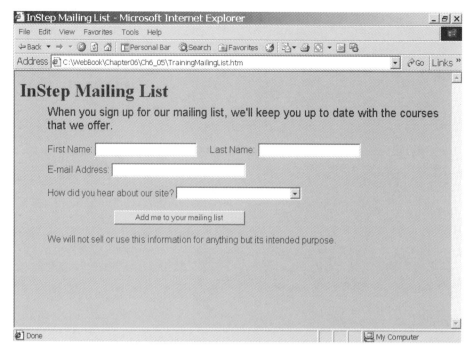

Figure 6-5. Absolute positioning gives you precise control over the location of every element on the page.

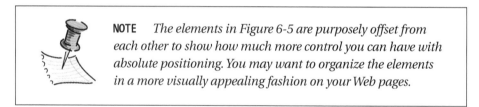

NOTE   *The elements in Figure 6-5 are purposely offset from each other to show how much more control you can have with absolute positioning. You may want to organize the elements in a more visually appealing fashion on your Web pages.*

There are some down sides to using absolute positioning:

- You need to figure out the appropriate coordinates for each element. Some tools, like Macromedia Dreamweaver, provide a user-friendly interface for positioning elements on the page and then create the style properties automatically.

- Care must be taken if using absolute positioning for only some elements on the Web page. Other elements on the page that are not absolutely positioned are displayed without regard to the absolutely positioned elements.

This may cause these elements to be positioned behind or on top of the absolutely positioned elements, especially if the user changes the size of their browser window. If this is not clear, try removing the absolute positioning of some of the elements in Try It 6-5, presented later in this section, and review the results.

- Absolute positioning requires an absolute font size. Otherwise, the positions do not appear correctly. This impacts the user's ability to define fonts and can make your Web page less accessible to users with disabilities.

- Absolute positioning requires definition of a specific screen size. For example, if you define elements to fit within 800 × 600 and the user wants to use a smaller or larger size, the elements do not adjust their position. This gives the user much less control over the look of the information. (However, depending on what you want, this may be a good thing.)

- Not all browsers and browser versions support absolute positioning.

You can define absolute positioning inline as a `style` attribute in the element's tag or as part of an embedded style within the `style` element. Specify absolute positioning by setting the style `position` property to `absolute` for each element to be positioned on the page. Then specify the `top` and `left` positional coordinates of each element.

TIP   *Using the* `style` *element instead of inline styles makes it easier to find and modify the coordinate positions of each element.*

The following code uses the `style` element in the header section of the page to define absolute positioning and the top and left coordinates of every element on the page:

```
❶   <style type="text/css">
❷   <!--
❸   div, input {font-family:arial; font-size:12pt; color:navy}
❹   #Intro {position:absolute; top:58px; left:60px; font-size:15pt}
```

⑤ `#FirstNameLabel {position:absolute; top:125px; left:60px}`

⑥ `#FirstName {position:absolute; top:123px; left:145px}`

⑦ `#LastNameLabel {position:absolute; top:125px; left:350px}`

⑧ `#LastName {position:absolute; top:123px; left:435px}`

⑨ `#EmailLabel {position:absolute; top:160px; left:60px}`

⑩ `#Email {position:absolute; top:158px; left:145px}`

⑪ `#ReferralLabel {position:absolute; top:200px; left:60px}`

⑫ `#Referral {position:absolute; top:198px; left:290px}`

⑬ `#Save {position:absolute; top:240px; left:180px}`

⑭ `#Footer {position:absolute; top:280px; left:60px}`

⑮ `-->`

⑯ `</style>`

The styles are defined within the `style` element tags (lines **❶** and **⑯**) in the header section of the Web page. The style rules (lines **❹** through **⑭**) specify the absolute positioning of each element on the page. The pound sign (#) syntax was used to associate each of these style rules with a particular element by the element's `id` attribute.

NOTE   *If you don't include the units (px for pixel in this example) for the positional properties, the absolute positioning does not work under Netscape. Netscape is also case-sensitive with regard to the value of the `id` elements.*

These styles are automatically applied to the elements on the page with the defined `id` attributes. For example, the introductory text on the page is:

```
<div id="Intro">When you sign up for our mailing list, we'll keep you up to date
    with the courses that we offer.</div>
```

This line is displayed at the coordinates specified by the style rule defined for #Intro.

Try It 6-5.

Building a Form Using Absolute Positioning

Try It 6-5 removes the table from the Mailing List page from Try It 6-4. It then adds the necessary styles to achieve absolute positioning of the elements on the form.

> **CAUTION** *Save a copy of the TrainingMailingList.htm from Try It 6-4 that uses the table for positioning before beginning this Try It. Future Try Its will use the table positioned form and not the form that uses absolute positioning.*

1. Open a copy of the TrainingMailingList.htm from Try It 6-4.

2. Remove the table element tags and table styles from the page and add div element tags around the form elements. Take care not to remove the labels, input elements, or other elements you may have.

3. Be sure every element on the page that is to be positioned has an id attribute defined.

4. Add style rules in the header section of the page to define the absolute positioning for each element on the page using the element's id attribute.

5. Save the file.

6. Open the TrainingMailingList.htm file in your browser.

The resulting page could appear similar to Figure 6-5. If the fields do not appear in the desired locations, adjust the style properties.

Listing 6-4 displays the code to position the form on the page using absolute positioning as shown in Figure 6-5.

Listing 6-4. The TrainingMailingList.htm file displays the form elements using absolute positioning to specify the exact location of each element on the page.

```
<!DOCTYPE html PUBLIC "-//W3C//DTD XHTML 1.0 Strict//EN" "DTD/xhtml1-strict.dtd">
<html>
<!--
    Try It   6-5
    Title:   Mailing List
    Author:  InStep Technologies
             www.insteptech.com
    Purpose:To demonstrate absolute positioning
 -->
<head>
<title>InStep Mailing List</title>
<link rel="stylesheet" type="text/css" href="TrainingStyle.css" />
<style type="text/css">
<!--
div, input {font-family:arial; font-size:12pt; color:navy}
#Intro {position:absolute; top:58px; left:60px; font-size:15pt}
#FirstNameLabel {position:absolute; top:125px; left:60px}
#FirstName {position:absolute; top:123px; left:145px}
#LastNameLabel {position:absolute; top:125px; left:350px}
#LastName {position:absolute; top:123px; left:435px}
#EmailLabel {position:absolute; top:160px; left:60px}
#Email {position:absolute; top:158px; left:145px}
#ReferralLabel {position:absolute; top:200px; left:60px}
#Referral {position:absolute; top:198px; left:290px}
#Save {position:absolute; top:240px; left:180px}
#Footer {position:absolute; top:280px; left:60px}
-->
</style>
</head>
<body>
<h1>InStep Mailing List</h1>
```

```
<div id="Intro">
   When you sign up for our mailing list, we'll keep you up to date with the
      courses that we offer.
</div>
<form id="MailingList" method="get" action="">
<div>
   <label id="FirstNameLabel" for="FirstName">First Name:</label>
   <input type="text" id="FirstName" name="FirstName" size="20" maxlength="40" />
   <label id="LastNameLabel" for="LastName">Last Name:</label>
   <input type="text" id="LastName" name="LastName" size="20" maxlength="40" />
   <label id="EmailLabel" for="Email">E-mail Address:</label>
   <input type="text" id="Email" name="Email" size="28" />
   <label id="ReferralLabel" for="Referral">
      How did you hear about our site?
   </label>
   <select id="Referral" name="Referral">
      <option value="<Empty>" />
      <option value="Surfing">I found it while surfing the Web</option>
      <option value="Conference">It was mentioned at a conference</option>
      <option value="Person">I heard about it from a friend</option>
   </select>
   <button type="submit" id="Save" name="Save" value="Save">
      Add me to your mailing list
   </button>
</div>
</form>
<div id="Footer">
   We will not sell or use this information for anything
   but its intended purpose.
</div>
</body>
</html>
```

HTML Form Element and Attribute Reference

Form elements provide the basic definition of the form. They include the elements needed to display text boxes, select boxes, radio buttons, command buttons and other data-entry controls to the user.

To build forms using HTML, you need to know the basic HTML form elements and attributes. These are presented in Table 6-2.

159

Table 6-2. Commonly Used HTML Form *Elements and Attributes*

ELEMENT	MEANING, USE AND COMMON ATTRIBUTES	EXAMPLE
button	Button. Used for a submit, reset, or push button on a form. Common attributes: **accesskey** - Defines an Alt key combination that can access the button using the keyboard. **disabled** - Marks the button as disabled so the user cannot push it. The button's value is not submitted to the Web server. Valid value is: `disabled`. **id** - The unique identifier of the control. **name** - The name of the button. This is sent to the Web server with the `value` attribute. If the name is not defined, the name and value of this button won't be submitted to the server. **type** - The type of button. Valid values are: `submit`, `reset`, and `button` (default). `Submit` submits the form to the Web server. `Reset` resets the form to its default values. `Button` displays a normal push button. **value** - The value representing the user's choice. This is sent to the Web server with the `name` attribute.	`<button type="submit" name="Save" value="Save">` Add me to your mailing list`</button>`

form	Form. Defines a data-entry form containing controls through which the user can review, enter, or update data. Common attributes:
	
	action - The URI to the CGI script, ASP page, or other component that will process the form when it is submitted to the Web server.
	
	id - The unique identifier of the form.
	
	method - Defines the HTTP technique used to submit the data to the server. Valid values are: `post` and `get` (default).
		`<form id="login" method="post" action="Login.asp" >`
		 . . .
		`</form>`

Table 6-2. Commonly Used HTML Form Elements and Attributes (continued)

ELEMENT	MEANING, USE AND COMMON ATTRIBUTES	EXAMPLE
input type="checkbox"	Checkbox. Used for Boolean (yes/no) options. Common attributes:	`<input type="checkbox" id="MoreInfo"`
	accesskey - Defines an Alt key combination that can access the checkbox using the keyboard.	`name="MoreInfo" checked="checked" value="Y" />Yes, send me more information.`
	checked - Marks the checkbox as checked when the page is displayed. Valid value is: checked.	
	disabled - Marks the checkbox as disabled so the user cannot change the value. The value is not submitted to the Web server. Valid value is: disabled.	
	id - The unique identifier of the control.	
	name - The name of the checkbox. This is sent to the Web server with the value attribute. If the name is not defined, the name and value of this checkbox won't be submitted to the server.	
	value - The value representing the user's choice. This is sent to the Web server with the name attribute.	
input type="hidden"	Hidden field. This is used to pass data between pages of your Web application. Common attributes:	`<input type="hidden" id="MailingListType" name="MailingListType" value="Training" />`
	id - The unique identifier of the control.	
	name - The name of the hidden field. This is sent to the Web server with the value attribute. If the name is not defined, the name and value of this field won't be submitted to the server.	
	value - The value assigned in the field within the HTML or with your code. This is sent to the Web server with the name attribute.	

Table 6-2. Commonly Used HTML Form *Elements and Attributes (continued)*

ELEMENT	MEANING, USE AND COMMON ATTRIBUTES	EXAMPLE
input type="image"	Image that is used as a submit button. Common attributes: **alt** - Alternative text displayed if the user does not load the image. **id** - The unique identifier of the control. **name** - The name of the image. This is sent to the Web server with the value attribute. If the name is not defined, the name and value of this image won't be submitted to the server. When the page is submitted, the x and y coordinates of the user's click on the image are appended to the name attribute: myname.x=35, myname.y=40. **src** - Path and filename of the image.	`<input type="image"` `src="../images/submit.gif" />`

input
type="password"
	Text box specifically defined for entry of a password. This input type works the same as the text type except that the user-entered value is shown with asterisks. See input type="text" for more information.	`<input type="password"`
		`id="Password" name="Password"`
		`size="10" maxlength="10" />`

input
type="radio"
	Radio button. Normally, radio buttons are used in a group to present a set of choices to the user when only one can be selected. Common attributes:
	
	accesskey - Defines an Alt key combination that can access the radio button using the keyboard.
	
	checked - Defines whether the radio button is selected when the page is displayed. Valid value is: checked.
	
	disabled - Marks the radio button as disabled so the user cannot change the value. The value is not submitted to the Web server. Valid value is: disabled.
		`<input type="radio"`
		`id="PaymentTypeCredit"`
		`name="PaymentType"`
		`value="C" />Credit Card`
		`<input type="radio"`
		`id="PaymentTypeDebit"`
		`name="PaymentType"`
		`value="D" />Debit Card`

Table 6-2. Commonly Used HTML Form *Elements and Attributes (continued)*

ELEMENT	MEANING, USE AND COMMON ATTRIBUTES	EXAMPLE
input type= "radio" *(cont.)*	**id** - The unique identifier of the control. **name** - The name of the radio button. This is sent to the Web server with the value attribute. If the name is not defined, the name and value of this button won't be submitted to the server. This is also used to link radio buttons in a set. **value** - The value representing the user's choice. This is sent to the Web server with the name attribute.	
input type="text"	Text box. Defines a text box for data entry. Common attributes: **disabled** - Marks the text box as disabled so the user cannot change the value. The value is not submitted to the Web server. Valid value is: disabled. **id** - The unique identifier of the control. **maxlength** - The maximum number of characters that can be entered into the text box. **name** - The name of the text box. This is sent to the Web server with the value attribute. If the name is not defined, the name and value of this text box won't be submitted to the server. **readonly** - Allows the user to see the text box and select it, but not modify it. The value is submitted to the Web server. Valid value is: readonly. **size** - The size of the text box in characters. Defaults to 20. **value** - The value entered into the text box by the user. If this is set when first displaying the text box, it provides a default value. This is sent to the Web server with the name attribute.	`<input type="text" id="FirstName" name="FirstName"size="20" maxlength="40" />`

Table 6-2. Commonly Used HTML Form *Elements and Attributes (continued)*

ELEMENT	MEANING, USE AND COMMON ATTRIBUTES	EXAMPLE
input type="submit"	Submit button. A button used to submit a form to the server for processing. See the button element for a common alternative to this type of input element. Common attributes:	`<input type="submit" name="Save" value="Add me to your mailing list" />`
	accesskey - Defines an Alt key combination that can access the button using the keyboard.	
	disabled - Marks the button as disabled so the user cannot push it. The button's value is not submitted to the Web server. Valid value is: disabled.	
	id - The unique identifier of the control.	
	name - The name of the button. This is sent to the Web server with the value attribute. If the name is not defined, the name and value of this button won't be submitted to the server.	
	value - The value representing the user's choice. This is sent to the Web server with the name attribute.	
label	Label for a control. Defines a textual label describing the control. Common attributes:	`<label for="FirstName"> First Name:</label>`
	accesskey - Defines an Alt key combination that can access the control associated with this label using the keyboard.	
	for - Specifies the id of the control associated with the label. This provides for improved accessibility.	
option	Option within a selection box. Defines the contents of a dropdown box presented for user selection. This is similar to a combo box in a Windows application. Common attributes:	See example in prior section.

Table 6-2. Commonly Used HTML Form *Elements and Attributes (continued)*

ELEMENT	MEANING, USE AND COMMON ATTRIBUTES	EXAMPLE
option *(cont.)*	**disabled** - Marks the option as disabled so the user cannot select the option. Valid value is: disabled.	
	selected – Used to define the choice that is selected when the selection box is first displayed. Valid value is: selected.	
	value - The value of the option. This is sent to the Web server with the select element name attribute.	
select	Selection box. Defines a dropdown box containing a set of options for user selection. This is similar to a combo box in a Windows application. Common attributes:	See example in prior section.
	disabled - Marks the selection box as disabled so the user cannot change the value. The value is not submitted to the Web server. Valid value is: disabled.	
	id - The unique identifier of the control.	
	multiple - Allows the user to select more than one choice. Valid value is: multiple.	
	name - The name of the selection box. This is sent to the Web server with the value attribute for each selected option element. If the name is not defined, the name and value of the selection won't be submitted to the server.	
	size - Number of lines in the selection box. Default is 1.	
textarea	Multi-line text box for entry of multiple lines of text. Up to 32,700 characters can be entered. Common attributes:	
	cols - Number of columns of text in the text area.	

Table 6-2. Commonly Used HTML Form Elements and Attributes (continued)

ELEMENT	MEANING, USE AND COMMON ATTRIBUTES	EXAMPLE
textarea *(cont.)*	**id** - The unique identifier of the control.	
	disabled - Marks the text area as disabled so the user cannot change the value. The value is not submitted to the Web server. Valid value is: `disabled`.	
	name - The name of the text area. This is sent to the Web server with the `value` attribute. If the name is not defined, the name and value of this text area won't be submitted to the server.	
	readonly - Allows the user to see the field and select it but not modify it. The value is submitted to the Web server. Valid value is: `readonly`.	`<textarea id="Feedback" name="Feedback" rows="4" cols="60">Type your feedback here.</textarea>`
	rows - Number of rows of text in the text area.	

For practice, try inserting each type of control defined in Table 6-2 into an HTML form.

HTML Forms Tips and Tricks

This section includes basic tips and techniques when working with HTML forms.

User-Friendly Forms

Here are some tips for creating user-friendly forms.

Use Tables and Styles

You can see by comparing Figures 6-1 and 6-2 that creating forms with tables and styles provides a much richer user experience. Use tables whenever possible to lay out the look of your forms and styles to add color and other visual properties. Alternatively, you can spend the extra time to define absolute positioning for your page elements.

Add Keyboard Shortcuts

Just as you can create hot-key combinations for fields on a Windows form, you can create keyboard shortcuts for HTML forms. Define the hot-key combination in the accesskey attribute for any of the input elements.

This is especially useful for radio buttons. For example:

```
<tr>
    <td align="right"><div>Primary job:</div></td>
    <td align="left">
            <input type="radio" checked="checked" id="jobTypeManager"
                name="JobType" value="M" accesskey="m" /><u>M</u>anager
    </td>
    <td align="left">
            <input type="radio" checked="checked" id="JobTypeDeveloper"
                name="JobType" value="D" accesskey="d" />Developer
    </td>
</tr>
```

The user can then toggle the radio button by using the Alt key plus the key defined by the accesskey attribute. For example, the user could press Alt + m to select the Manager radio button.

Set the Tab Order

By default, the tab order for a form depends on the order of the elements in the HTML document. If this is not the desired order for working with the form, set the tabindex attribute of the form elements to define the desired tab order.

Debugging Tips

Sometimes it is difficult to see why a page is not displayed or processed as you expect. Here are some tips for debugging your HTML forms.

Recognize Browser Differences

Text and layouts that appear correct under Internet Explorer may not appear the same in Netscape or vice versa. So it is important to understand the differences between the two browsers and ensure you code your HTML appropriately.

Watch for Missing Ending Tags

Internet Explorer is very forgiving of missing ending tags. Netscape is not as forgiving. So if your page appears correctly in Internet Explorer and not in Netscape, you should check your beginning and ending tags.

Watch for Case Sensitivity

Internet Explorer is very forgiving on inconsistent usage of uppercase and lowercase. Netscape is not as forgiving. For example, if you define an element with an `id` attribute of `LastName` and create a style for that element as `#lastName`, Internet Explorer correctly uses the style. Netscape does not.

Pay Attention to Positional Attributes

Internet Explorer uses default units for positional attributes. Netscape ignores many positional attributes if units are not specified. For example, if you define the `top` attribute for an element as `top:58`, Internet Explorer correctly positions the element. Netscape does not. You instead need to define the top attribute as `top:58px`.

Turn On Borders

When laying out forms with tables, it is easier to debug table placement errors if you set the `table` element's `border` attribute to a nonzero value. This allows you to see how the table is laid out on the page.

What Did This Cover?

This chapter took a big step toward building a Web application by providing the tools and techniques you need to create the user interface for your application. Prior to this chapter, you learned how to present data to the user. With the steps provided in this chapter, you can now build data-entry forms so the user can view and edit information.

The Try Its in this chapter demonstrated how easy it is to build a form and how much more work it is to build a form that looks good! A common way to lay out a form is with tables but if you want complete control over the layout, you can use absolute positioning.

However, even with all of this work, you still have basic static pages. How can you disable an element based on the user selection? Can you validate the user-entered values before submitting them to the server? What if you want your application to remember the user's preferences? For all of these things, you need to write some script code. So, on to object models and client-side scripting using JavaScript.

Additional Resources

This section provides some additional resource suggestions by way of books, articles, and links to Web resources.

The books, articles, and links all existed at the time of this writing. There is a good chance that the books and articles still exist as you read this. However, the same cannot be said of Web links. Ignore the suggested links if they no longer exist.

Books and Articles

Castro, Elizabeth. *HTML 4 for the World Wide Web.* Berkeley, CA: Peachpit Press, 2000.
This book has great form examples. It also provides some sample CGI scripts for use in processing the forms.

Links

`http://msdn.microsoft.com/workshop/server`: This is Microsoft's site describing its server-side technologies, including Active Server Pages (ASP).

`http://www.cgi-resources.com`: This site provides many examples of CGI scripts and other prebuilt and reusable server-side applications. It also contains many links to other CGI sites and books.

`http://www.w3.org/TR/REC-html40/interact/forms.html`: This is the standard site for the World Wide Web Consortium (W3C) that specifically addresses forms.

`http://www.wdvl.com/Authoring/Scripting/Tutorial/html_forms_intro.html`: This provides an extensive tutorial on creating forms.

Understanding Object Models

So far in this book you have seen how to create a user interface for a Web application that is laid out well and has some nice style. But the Web pages are still *static*—the elements don't move or change as the user works with the page. You can breath life into Web pages by making them more reactive to the user.

There are many ways a Web page can react to the user's actions. You can dynamically change the look of a Web page as the user works with the page. You can change an element's color or content as the user moves the mouse over the element. You can add text or other elements based on user selections. You can display other browser windows, such as a help window, when the user clicks a help button.

In order to make a Web page react to the user's actions, you need a way to access the Web browser's capabilities and reference the HTML document's elements. With access to the browser's features, you can control the browser—defining when and where browser windows are opened and specifying which HTML document is displayed in each window. By referencing the HTML document's elements, you can dynamically change the look of a Web page. You access the Web browser's capabilities and the HTML document's elements through their object models.

This chapter describes what an object model is. It then details the browser object model for controlling the browser and the document object model for accessing the HTML document's elements and attributes. The next chapter presents a scripting language you can use to work with these object models and breathe life into the user interface of your Web application.

What Will This Cover?

This chapter covers the following object model concepts:

- Understanding the basics of object models

- Viewing an object model as a tree structure

- Learning the browser object model

- Discovering the Document Object Model (DOM)

- Introducing Dynamic HTML (DHTML)

By the end of this chapter, you'll understand what an object model is and how to work with two key object models. Most importantly, you'll learn why these object models are so important to the development of a dynamic Web application.

You will not be able to try out any of the techniques presented in this chapter without using a scripting language such as JavaScript, which is covered in the next three chapters. In those chapters you will have ample opportunities to work with the object models presented in this chapter.

Object Model Basics

An *object model* provides a hierarchical structure that describes something by decomposing it into its component parts, which are called *objects*. The object model defines the component parts and how they are related.

As a simple example, let's look at a car. A car can be decomposed into its component parts, such as a body, wheels, an engine, doors, windows, and so on. Each of these would be an object in the car's object model. These objects are related: The car has a body, wheels, and an engine; the body has doors and windows; and so on. The object model would look like the hierarchy shown in Figure 7-1.

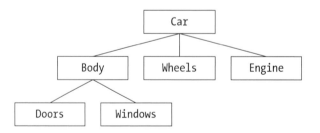

Figure 7-1. An object model breaks something complex down into its component parts, such as this overly simplified object model of a car.

Object models have a top-most object that defines the domain of the entire model. This top-most object is called a *root* because all of the other objects stem from it. In Figure 7-1, the car object is the root of the object model.

Some of the objects in the object model are not single objects but *collections* of objects. For example, a car does not have one wheel; it has a collection of four wheels. In Figure 7-1, the car object is comprised of a body, a collection of wheels, and an engine. The body is comprised of a collection of doors and a collection of windows.

Objects in an object model have properties and methods. A *property* defines the attributes of an object. For example, the body object has properties such as color, style, and metalContent. A *method* describes the actions or behaviors that the object has. For example, the windows objects could have moveUp and moveDown methods.

The object model provides a mechanism for navigating through and working with the objects within the domain. You can define or request the properties and you can execute the methods. For example, you could use the car object model to set the tinting property of the windows to true.

You navigate to any object in the object model using a dot (.) syntax. For example, to navigate from the root down to the collection of windows, you would use the following syntax:

```
Car.Body.Windows
```

You can reference a particular entry in a collection of objects using array-style syntax. In some programming languages, you use parentheses (( )) to access an entry in a collection. In other programming languages you use square brackets ([ ]). JavaScript, the language presented in the next chapter, uses square brackets, so these examples use that syntax:

```
Car.Body.Windows[0]
```

Most collections are zero-based, meaning they begin with zero. So the first window in the collection is entry 0, the second window is entry 1, and so on.

Reference an object's properties and methods using a similar dot (.) syntax. You can set a property as follows:

```
Car.Body.Windows[0].tinting = true
```

This statement sets the `tinting` property of the first `window` to `true`. To execute a method, use this syntax:

```
Car.Body.Windows[1].moveUp
```

This statement calls the `moveUp` method for the second `window`.

Tree Structures

When navigating and working with an object model, it is sometimes useful to think of the object model as a tree structure. You can move from branch to branch to navigate to a particular object.

As in genealogy, the root of the tree is presented at the top of the structure, as shown in Figure 7-1. Each object that stems from the root is a branch of the tree, called a *node*. The body object in Figure 7-1 is an example of a node. Any set of objects in the tree is called a *node list*. The objects in a node list can all be the same type, such as the `wheels` collection in Figure 7-1, or of different types, such as the set of all objects under the root node.

It is common to use genealogy terms when working with a tree structure. Above each node in the tree is the node's *parent node*. The `car` node in Figure 7-1 is the parent node of the `body`, `wheels`, and `engine` nodes. The nodes below a parent node are the *child nodes*, so the `body`, `wheels`, and `engine` nodes are the child nodes of the `car` node. Each child node can also be a parent node and have child nodes. For example, the `body` node in Figure 7-1 is a child node of the `car`, and it is also a parent node that has two child nodes: the `doors` and `windows`.

Unsurprisingly, nodes at the same level in the tree structure are called *siblings*. From Figure 7-1, `body`, `wheels`, and `engine` are siblings; `doors` and `windows` are siblings.

Object Models and the Web

By now you may be asking, "What does any of this have to do with building Web applications?" To make your Web applications respond to a user's actions, you need to work with either the browser's object model or the Web page's document object model. The rest of this chapter presents those two object models.

Browser Object Model

The *browser object model* describes the objects that most browsers, such as Internet Explorer and Netscape, provide to give your Web application control over how the browser reacts to the user.

The browser object model defines an object hierarchy as shown in Figure 7-2. The root of the browser object model is the window object. The window object defines the browser window in which the Web page is displayed.

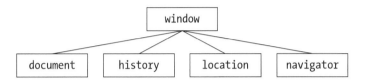

Figure 7-2. The browser object model provides objects you can use to access the browser's features.

You can access any of the properties and methods of the window object or any other object in the object hierarchy using the standard object model syntax. For example:

```
window.alert("Hello World")
```

This statement calls the alert method of the window object and displays an alert box containing the "Hello World" text.

The document object, shown in Figure 7-2, represents the HTML document associated with the Web page displayed in the browser window. You can use this object to access all of the elements and attributes of the HTML document and modify the display of the Web page as the user works with it. This document object is the root of the document object model presented later in this chapter.

The history object in Figure 7-2 references the list of URIs that the user has navigated from the browser window. This is the same history list that the user can access using the history features such as the Back and Forward buttons in the browser toolbar.

> **NOTE** *Because the user's history information could be considered private, many of the properties of the* history *object are not accessible unless you are using a signed script and obtain the user's approval. See the "Additional Resources" section for a link to more information on signed scripts.*

The location object in the browser object model defines the location of the HTML document displayed in the browser. You can use the location object to select a different HTML document for display in the browser window.

The navigator object shown in Figure 7-2 provides access to basic information about the browser itself, such as the browser's name and version. You can use this information to determine the type and version of browser the user is using and adjust the Web page accordingly, as explained in Chapter 8, "Using JavaScript."

Browser Object Model Reference

Table 7-1 describes the most common properties and methods of the objects within the browser object model shown in Figure 7-2.

Table 7-1. Primary Objects in the Browser Object Model

OBJECT	MEANING AND USE	EXAMPLE
history	The object that maintains the list of URIs visited by the user.	
	Common properties:	
	length - Read-only property that defines the number of entries in this browser window's history list.	history.length
	Common methods:	
	back() - Navigates to the previous page as defined by the history object. This has the same behavior as if the user had selected the Back button in the browser.	history.back()
	forward() - Navigates to the next page as defined by the history object. This has the same behavior as if the user had selected the Next button in the browser.	history.forward()
	go(n) - Navigates to the nth page as defined by the history object.	history.go(2)
location	The object that provides all of the information regarding the URI of the current document.	
	Common properties:	
	href - Navigates to a defined location (URI).	location.href = "http://www.insteptech.com"

Table 7-1. Primary Objects in the Browser Object Model (continued)

OBJECT	MEANING AND USE	EXAMPLE
navigator	The object defining the basic browser information.	
	Common properties:	
	appVersion - Read-only property that defines the browser's version name.	navigator.appVersion
window	The current browser window (or frame).	
	Common properties:	
	closed - Read-only property that returns true if the window is closed, false if the window is open.	If (window.closed)
	document - Read-only reference to the document displayed in the window. Each window can only contain a single document object. See the "Document Object Model" section of this chapter for details on the properties and methods of the document object.	
	history - Read-only reference to the history object. See the history object entry in this table for more information.	
	location - Read-only reference to the location object. See the location object entry in this table for more information.	
	name - Name of the window.	window.name
	navigator - Read-only reference to the navigator object for the window. See the navigator object entry in this table for more information.	
	self - Read-only reference to the current window.	
	status - Sets the text in the status bar area of the window.	window.status = "... Calculating"

Table 7-1. Primary Objects in the Browser Object Model (continued)

OBJECT	MEANING AND USE	EXAMPLE
window *(cont.)*	**Common methods:**	
	alert(sText) - Displays a message box containing the text defined by sText.	window.alert ("Hello World")
	clearInterval() - Cancels an interval timer set with the setInterval method.	window.clearInterval()
	clearTimeout() - Cancels a timer set with the setTimeOut method.	window.clearTimeout()
	close() - Closes a window.	window.close()
	open(sURI,sName,sFeatures) - Opens a new browser window and navigates to the defined URI. The name of the window is defined by sName and the specific attributes of the window are defined by an optional list of features.	See Chapter 8, "Using JavaScript," for a detailed example.
	setInterval(sScriptName,iCount) - Creates a timer that goes off in iCount milliseconds (5000 milliseconds is 5 seconds), executes the function defined by sScriptName, and then repeats. Timers are useful for animations and other interactions that are time based or repeat over time.	window.setInterval ("myTimeScript",5000)
	setTimeout(sScriptName,iCount) - Creates a timer that goes off in iCount milliseconds (5000 milliseconds is 5 seconds) and then executes the function defined by sScriptName. This does not repeat once it has gone off.	window.setTimeout ("myTimerScript",5000)

See the "Additional Resources" section of this chapter for a reference to a complete listing of valid browser objects, properties, and methods.

Document Object Model

The browser object model provides access to the browser so you can display browser windows and change window contents. But for control over how a Web page changes based on user actions, you need to access the HTML document's elements and attributes. You do that with a document object model.

A *Document Object Model* (DOM) is a platform- and language-neutral object model that allows dynamic access to the content, structure, and style of a document. It is based on an object hierarchy that closely resembles the structure of each document it models.

When working with a Web page, the HTML document itself is the document modeled with the DOM. You can use the DOM to access any of the elements or attributes of the HTML document. For example, you can use the DOM to reference the color of text on the page and change that color as the user moves the mouse over the text.

There was a basic document object model for HTML documents, known as DOM Level 0, in older versions of the browsers, such as Netscape Navigator 3 and Internet Explorer 3. This DOM exposed form elements for form input validation and other elements to provide simple dynamic features.

Newer versions of Netscape Navigator and Internet Explorer provided additional dynamic behavior by adding proprietary and incompatible extensions to the DOM. These extensions included document.layers in Netscape Navigator and document.all in Internet Explorer. These incompatible extensions made it difficult to build cross-browser Web applications.

The W3C then defined DOM Level 1 to merge the proprietary features into one industry-standard DOM for all browsers. Internet Explorer supports most of the DOM Level 1 features. Netscape 6 is hailed as the first browser to fully support DOM Level 1.

Using objects in the DOM, you can manipulate the appearance of your Web page by accessing the elements, attributes, and style properties of the HTML document. The DOM of an HTML document is shown in Figure 7-3.

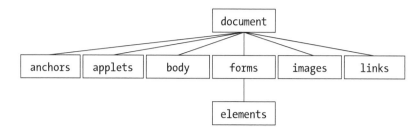

Figure 7-3. The DOM provides objects you can use to access the HTML document associated with the Web page displayed in the browser window.

The root of the DOM is the document object, which in the case of your Web page is the HTML document. This is the same document object defined in the browser object model.

You can update properties and call methods of the document object following object model syntax. For example:

```
document.title="New title"
document.write("Hello World")
```

The first statement uses the title property of the document object to update the HTML document's title element. When used in script code, this statement actually changes the title displayed in the title bar of the browser window. The second statement calls the write method of the document object to write additional text onto the Web page. This causes the text to appear on the page.

The objects below the document object are described in Table 7-2, later in this chapter. Most of these objects represent collections of objects, hence the plural of their names. These collections provide access to specific elements in the HTML document. For example, the images collection provides access to the set of img elements in the HTML document. You may recognize many of these elements from the introduction to HTML in Chapter 3, "Using HTML."

Let's look at a specific scenario for using the DOM: You want to change the src attribute of one of the img elements on your page when the user moves the mouse over the img element. This common effect is called an *image rollover* because the image changes as the user rolls over it.

To accomplish this objective, you need to locate the img element in the HTML document and then change its src attribute.

There are three ways to locate and work with elements in an HTML document using the DOM:

- Working with the DOM as objects, you can reference elements through the collections defined by the DOM.

- Working with the DOM as nodes, you can walk through the hierarchical tree structure of your HTML document.

- Working with the DOM using an id attribute, you can reference a specific element.

Each of these techniques is discussed in the following sections.

Working with the DOM as Objects

The collections of objects under the document object in the DOM provide access to the elements of an HTML document. You can navigate through the DOM to find a specific element.

How you reference any particular element within a collection is based on its position in the HTML document, parsing the HTML document from top to bottom.

For example, the forms collection, shown in Figure 7-3, provides access to any form in the HTML document. The following syntax references the first form in the document:

```
document.forms[0]
```

To find the second data-entry element on the first form, you could use:

```
document.forms[0].elements[1]
```

This locates the second data-entry element within the form element tags in the HTML document. If there is a hidden data-entry element on the form, the second data-entry element may actually be the first visible data-entry element on the form.

Let's go back to the image rollover scenario from the prior section. You can use the images collection to locate a particular img element in the HTML document. You can then change its src attribute using the DOM as follows:

```
document.images[0].src="newImage.jpg"
```

This locates the first image in the HTML document and changes the source of the image to another file, thus changing the image that is displayed.

Finding a particular element in an HTML document by using its position in a DOM collection basically involves specifying the element's sequential location within the HTML document.

This technique of locating a specific element using its position in a collection is not a generally recommended technique because it is too closely tied to the location of the element's entry in the HTML document. If you later add an image at the top of the HTML document, you would need to change all of the numerical position values within the collection. So referencing a specific element using its sequential position within one of the DOM collections does not provide a very robust solution.

In the image rollover scenario, if a graphics artist added a company logo by inserting an img element in the HTML document sequentially above your img element, images[0] references that new image instead of your image. You would need to find every place you referenced images[0] and change it to images[1].

Using the DOM collections to navigate through your HTML document is most useful if you want access to the entire set of objects provided by one of the document object's collections. For example, you may want to access all of the images in the images collection to preload them. Or, you can use a form's elements collection to iterate through all of the data-entry elements on the form and validate the data. These examples are presented in detail in Chapter 8, "Using JavaScript," and Chapter 9, "Validating Form Data," respectively.

Working with the DOM as Nodes

As described in the prior section, you can work with your HTML document as collections of different types of elements. Your HTML document may have several img elements in the DOM's images collection and a form element in the forms collection, and so on. But there is not a collection for every type of element. For example, there is no div elements collection or p elements collection.

The DOM provides an alternative view of your HTML document that allows you to access any element within the document. For this view, the DOM sequentially parses every element in the HTML document and builds a tree structure. You can then reference any node within the tree using the terminology described in the "Tree Structures" section earlier in this chapter.

You can navigate through the elements of your HTML document by walking through the nodes of the tree structure. You can get specific nodes, change node values, and add your own nodes to the tree.

To see how to navigate the DOM as nodes, let's look at a specific HTML document. Listing 7-1 is the TrainingWelcome.htm file created in the Try It sections of the preceding chapters.

Listing 7-1. TrainingWelcome.htm is a simple HTML document that welcomes users to the application and provides links to other application features.

```
<!DOCTYPE html PUBLIC "-//W3C//DTD XHTML 1.0 Strict//EN" "DTD/xhtml1-strict.dtd">
<html>
<!--
    Try It  4-5
    Title:  Welcome Page
    Author: InStep Technologies
            www.insteptech.com
    Purpose:To demonstrate style classes
            using an external style sheet
 -->
<head>
<title>InStep Training Welcome Page</title>
<link rel="stylesheet" type="text/css" href="TrainingStyle.css" />
</head>
<body>
<div class="shadow">inStep</div>
<div class="foreground">inStep</div>
<h1 class="margin">Welcome to the InStep Training Page</h1>
<p class="key">
    <br />
    Our training courses are the best in the industry.
</p>
<p class="normal">
    Sign up for one of our courses today and receive $50 off of a future course.
</p>
<div class="margin">
<br />
<a href="TrainingCourseList.htm">View a list of our courses</a>
<br />
<br />
<a href="TrainingMailingList.htm">
    <img src="MailingList.gif" alt="Mailing List" />
    Sign up for our mailing list
</a>
</div>
</body>
</html>
```

Starting from the top of the HTML document, the DOM maps the elements into the hierarchical tree structure shown in Figure 7-4.

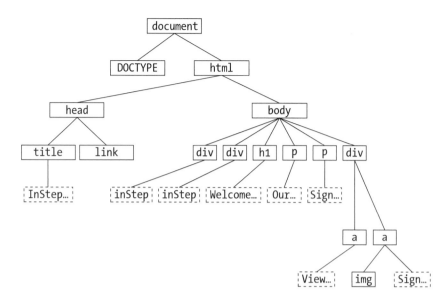

Figure 7-4. This is an approximation of the hierarchical tree structure for the HTML document in Listing 7-1, ignoring the comments and br *elements.*

TIP   *If you plan to try this particular example using scripting code, be sure to take into account the* br *elements not shown in Figure 7-4.*

The root node of this model is the document object. The document object has two child nodes: DOCTYPE and html. These child nodes are accessed using a childNodes collection. The html element is the second child node of the document object and is accessed using the following syntax:

```
document.childNodes[1]
```

The html element is also a parent node that has children of its own. These children are also accessed using a childNodes collection. The head element is the first child node of the html element, so it is accessed using the following syntax:

```
document.childNodes[1].childNodes[0]
```

You can continue to access each node's children until you reach the node you want to access. Following the example down to the title element, the syntax is as follows:

```
document.childNodes[1].childNodes[0].childNodes[0]
```

Every element within the HTML document is accessible through a `childNodes` collection within this hierarchy.

The child nodes for some of the nodes, such as the `title`, are text nodes. A *text node* represents specific text associated with an element, shown with dashed lines in Figure 7-4. Using HTML terminology from Chapter 3, "Using HTML," this text is the *content* of the element. For example, the text node under the `title` element node represents the text between the `title` element tags. You can access a text node using the `text` property:

```
document.childNodes[1].childNodes[0].childNodes[0].text = "New title"
```

Let's review what this syntax means. The first reference to `childNodes` in this statement references the child nodes under the `document` object. In Figure 7-4, the 0th node is the `DOCTYPE` declaration and the 1st node is the `html` node.

Using the `html` node as the parent, its `childNodes` collection contains the head and body elements. The first child (entry 0) of the `html` node is the head node.

The children of the head node are the `title` and `link` elements. In this case, the `childNodes` collection is referencing the first child node of the head node, which is the `title` node. The `text` property of the `title` node references the text of that node, which is the title text.

This is much more complex than accessing the document's `title` property directly using the object model:

```
document.title="New title"
```

NOTE   *The DOM also defines the concept of attribute nodes, which represent the attributes of a particular element. However, not all browsers support this. Specifically, Internet Explorer does not recognize attributes as nodes.*

Knowing the exact tree structure of your HTML document, you can navigate through the nodes to find a specific element.

Let's go back to the image rollover scenario. Before you look at the next line of code, look at Figure 7-4 and see if you can start at the `document` object on top and navigate through the set of child nodes you need to reference the `img` element. The answer is shown in Figure 7-5.

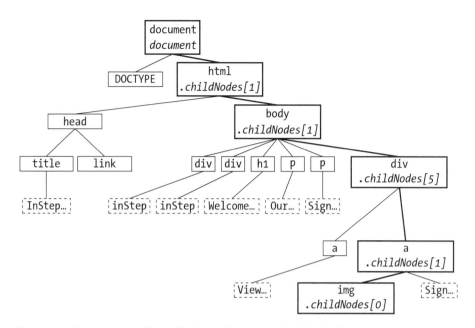

Figure 7-5. To navigate through the nodes, map the HTML document to a tree structure.

```
document.childNodes[1].childNodes[1].childNodes[5].childNodes[1].childNodes[0].src=
"newImage.jpg"
```

Node walking is not the recommended approach when you want a specific node. Finding a specific node requires that you know the exact structure of the entire HTML document. It is also prone to errors because the representation of the HTML document is not consistent between different browsers. For example, Netscape counted some of the comments as additional nodes and Internet Explorer did not. And if you add an element, you have to reevaluate all of your node navigation.

Working with your HTML document as nodes allows you to easily navigate between the elements without knowing what type of element you are navigating through. This allows you to process large sets of elements.

One of the best things about working with nodes is adding and removing them. This capability lets you add elements, text nodes, and attributes to the page without regenerating the page. For example:

```
newElement = document.createElement("p")
```

This statement creates a new p (paragraph) element. You can then append this element anywhere in the DOM structure:

```
document.childNodes[1].childNodes[1].appendChild(newElement)
```

This statement appends the new p element to the defined node. Working with the structure defined in Figure 7-5, the new child element is appended as the last child element under the body element node. This statement could also have been written as:

```
document.body.appendChild(newElement)
```

Adding a p element doesn't really do anything unless it has some text. You can create a text node using:

```
newTextNode = document.createTextNode("Testing 123")
```

This statement creates a new text node. You can then append this text node to the newly created p element node. New nodes are appended as the last child, so you can use the lastChild property to reference the newly created p element. To add the text element to the new node, you need the following statement:

```
document.childNodes[1].childNodes[1].lastChild.appendChild(newTextNode)
```

In addition to creating nodes, you can move or remove nodes. Moving nodes allows you to move sets of elements from one location on the page to another without regenerating the page, providing drag and drop and other interesting interactive effects.

Working with the DOM Using IDs

Locating a particular element within an HTML document using the DOM object collection approach or the tree nodes approach is difficult and prone to errors. This is because the specific location of any particular element moves as the HTML document is modified.

The preferred approach to locating particular elements in an HTML document is to add an id attribute to each element in the HTML document that you plan to reference. You can then locate a specific element in the HTML document by the element's id.

For example, if you want to reference a paragraph in your HTML document, set the id attribute of that element:

```
<p id="deal" class="normal">
    Sign up for one of our courses today and receive $50 off
    of a future course.
</p>
```

NOTE   *Following XHTML standards, every ID used in an HTML document must be unique.*

You can use the `getElementById` method of the DOM `document` object to reference the element with the defined `id` attribute. Once you have the reference, you can access any of the element's attributes. For example:

```
document.getElementById("deal").setAttribute("align","center")
```

This locates the element with the `id` attribute set to `"deal"` and sets its `align` attribute to center the text. This is comparable to:

```
document.getElementById("deal").align="center"
```

You can find an element using this approach and then work with the element as a node. For example:

```
document.getElementById("deal").firstChild.nodeValue="This is new text"
```

This locates the element by its `id` and then references the first child, which is the text node. The `nodeValue` property of that text node is changed to the new value. This basically replaces any text defined for the element with the new text. This is useful if you want to update text on the Web page based on a user action.

Let's take one more look at the image rollover scenario. To use the ID approach, you need to add an `id` attribute to the `img` element in Listing 7-1:

```
<img id="orgImage" src="MailingList.gif" alt="Mailing List" />
```

You can then update the `src` attribute of that element using:

```
document.getElementById("orgImage").src="newImage.jpg"
```

This is by far the easiest and most reliable approach when referencing a particular element within the HTML document.

DOM Reference

Unlike the browser object model, the DOM has a specification controlled by the World Wide Web Consortium (W3C). This means there is a defined standard set of objects, properties, and methods. As a W3C specification, one important objective for the DOM is to provide a standard programming interface that can be used in a wide variety of environments and applications and with any programming language.

In theory, the DOM defines a standardized model so that your Web pages react the same under any browser. In practice, the browsers do not all support the DOM consistently. The hope is that, over time, all browsers will support all appropriate features of the DOM, making it easier for Web developers to ensure browser compatibility. In the meantime, you need to be aware of browser differences as described in Chapter 8, "Using JavaScript."

NOTE *As of this writing, Netscape 6 provides the best support of the DOM.*

Table 7-2 describes the primary DOM objects and their key properties and methods. Additional examples are presented in the next several chapters.

Table 7-2. Primary Objects in the DOM

OBJECT	MEANING AND USE	EXAMPLE
document	The currently displayed Web page.	
	Common properties:	
	`childNodes` - Read-only reference to the collection of all nodes at the top level of the HTML document. This normally includes the `DOCTYPE` and the `html` element.	`document.childNodes.length`
	`documentElement` - Node representing the root element of a document. For HTML documents, this is the `html` element. This is the successor of the `document.all` syntax.	`document.documentElement`
	Common properties (HTML documents only):	
	`anchors` - Read-only reference to the collection of `a` elements defined on the page. Only the `a` elements with a `name` attribute are included in this collection.	

Table 7-2. Primary Objects in the DOM (continued)

OBJECT	MEANING AND USE	EXAMPLE
document *(cont.)*	applets - Read-only reference to the collection of object elements that define applets on the page. See the "Additional Resources" section at the end of this chapter for more information.	
	body - Content of the document as defined by the body element.	document.body
	cookie - Property used to read and write cookies.	See Chapter 10, "Saving Data with Cookies," for a detailed example.
	forms - Read-only reference to the collection of form elements defined on the page. See the forms object entry in this table for more information.	
	images - Read-only reference to the collection of img elements defined on the page. See the images object entry in this table for more information.	
	links - Read-only reference to the collection of a and area elements defined on the page. Only those elements with an href attribute are included in this collection.	
	referrer - The URI of the page the user was on prior to the current page.	sFrom=document.referrer
	title - Title of the Web page as specified by the title element. This title appears in the title bar of the browser.	document.title="New title"
	URL - Read-only URI of the HTML document.	document.URL
	Common methods:	
	createAttribute(sName) - Creates a new attribute with a name defined by sName.	document.createAttribute ("required")
	createElement(sTag) - Creates a new element of the type defined by sTag.	document.createElement ("p")
	createTextNode(sText) - Creates a new text node and assigns it the text defined by sText.	document.createTextNode ("New text")

Table 7-2. Primary Objects in the DOM (continued)

OBJECT	MEANING AND USE	EXAMPLE
document *(cont.)*	getElementById(sID) - Returns the element whose id attribute is sID. This id attribute is expected to be unique within a document.	document.getElementById ("InsertInfo")
	getElementsByTagName(sTag) - Returns the collection of elements of the type defined by sTag. Returns all elements if sTag is an asterisk (*).	document.getElements ByTagName("p")
	Common methods (HTML documents only):	
	getElementsByName(sName) - Returns the collection of elements whose name attribute is sName. With Internet Explorer, this only works on some of the elements, primarily the form-related tags.	document.getElementsByName ("JobType")
	open( ) - Opens a new browser window.	document.open
	write(sText) - Writes the text defined by sText to the page. Note that you cannot write to a page once it has been fully rendered.	document.write ("Confirmed")
	writeln(sText) - Writes the text defined by sText followed by a newline character.	document.writeln ("Confirmed")
forms	Collection of HTML forms on the page.	See Chapter 9, "Validating Form Data," for a detailed example.
	Common properties:	
	action - Name of the application that is executed when a form is submitted.	myForm.action="myApp.cgi"
	elements - Read-only reference to the collection of nodes representing the data-entry elements defined on the form. See the node object entry in this table for more information.	
	length - Number of data-entry elements defined on the form.	myForm.length

Table 7-2. Primary Objects in the DOM (continued)

OBJECT	MEANING AND USE	EXAMPLE
forms *(cont.)*	**Common methods:**	
	reset() - Resets the form to its default values.	myForm.reset()
	submit() - Submits the form.	myForm.submit()
images	Collection of image objects on the Web page.	
	Common properties:	
	src - URI defining the location of the image file.	document.images[0].src = "mygraphic.gif"
node	A single node in the document tree structure. For clarity, it is represented by myNode in the examples below.	
	Common properties:	
	attributes - Read-only reference to the collection of all attributes for an element node. In Internet Explorer 5.0 each attribute is a value. In Netscape 6 each attribute is an object.	myNode.attributes
	childNodes - Read-only reference to the collection of all nodes immediately under this node.	myNode.childNodes
	firstChild - Read-only reference to the first child node immediately under this node. This is determined by the sequential location of the node within the HTML document.	myNode.firstChild
	lastChild - Read-only reference to the last child node immediately under this node. This is determined by the sequential location of the node within the HTML document.	myNode.lastChild
	nodeName - Read-only property providing the name of the node. This is the element or attribute name. If the node is a text node, it returns #text.	myNode.nodeName
	nodeType - Read-only property providing the type of the node. Returns a numeric value indicating whether the node is an element (1), attribute (2), text node (3), and so on.	myNode.nodeType

Table 7-2. Primary Objects in the DOM (continued)

OBJECT	MEANING AND USE	EXAMPLE
node *(cont.)*	nodeValue - Value of the node. The text and attribute nodes have values. Many of the other nodes, such as element nodes have no value.	myNode.nodeValue
	ownerDocument - Read-only reference to the document object associated with this node.	myNode.ownerDocument
	parentNode - Read-only reference to the node immediately above this node.	myNode.parentNode
	Common properties (element nodes only):	
	tagName - Read-only property defining the name of the element.	myNode.tagName
	Common properties (HTML elements only):	
	className - Value of the class attribute for the node.	myNode.className="normal"
	id - Value of the id attribute for the node. The value of the id attribute for each element should be unique in the HTML document.	myNode.id
	innerHTML - The node's html.	myNode. innerHTML= "<p>New Text</p>"
	innerText - The node's text. This is the older style DHTML syntax - use nodeValue instead. This is not supported by Netscape.	myNode. innerText= "New Text"
	offsetHeight - Read-only property defining the height of the element in pixels as it appears in the user's browser. Can be updated with style.height.	myNode.offsetHeight
	offsetLeft - Read-only property defining the left offset of the element in pixels as it appears in the user's browser. This is normally with respect to the left of the document. Can be updated with style.left.	myNode.offsetLeft
	offsetTop - Read-only property defining the top offset of the element in pixels as it appears in the user's browser. This is normally with respect to the top of the document. Can be updated with style.top.	myNode.offsetTop

Table 7-2. Primary Objects in the DOM (continued)

OBJECT	MEANING AND USE	EXAMPLE
	offsetWidth - Read-only property defining the width of the element in pixels as it appears in the user's browser. Can be updated with style.width.	myNode.offsetWidth
	style - Provides access to the style properties of the node. This is the older style DHTML syntax - use attributes and styles instead.	myNode.style.color="blue"
	text - Value of the text attribute for this node. Undefined if there is no text attribute for this node.	myNode.text
	title - Value of the title attribute for this node. Undefined if there is no title attribute for this node.	myNode.title
	type - Value of the type attribute for this node. Undefined if there is no type attribute for this node.	myNode.type
	value - Value of the value attribute for this node. Undefined if there is no value attribute for this node.	myNode.value
	Common methods:	
	appendChild(nChild) - Appends the child node defined by nChild as the last child node of the current node. If the node already exists in the document, it is moved to the new position.	myNode.appendChild(nChild)
	hasChildNodes() - Read-only property that returns true if the current node has child nodes, otherwise returns false.	myNode.hasChildNodes()
	removeChild(nChild) - Removes the node defined by nChild.	myNode.removeChild(nChild)
	removeNode(bDoChildren) - Removes the node. If bDoChildren is true, it also removes the child nodes.	myNode.removeNode(true)
	replaceChild(newNode,nChild) - Replaces the child node of the current node, defined by nChild, with the node defined by newNode.	myNode.replaceChild (newNode,nChild)
	replaceNode(newNode) - Replaces the current node with the node defined by newNode.	myNode.replaceNode (newNode)
	swapNode(newNode) - Swaps the location of the current node with the location of the newNode.	myNode.swapNode(newNode)

Table 7-2. Primary Objects in the DOM (continued)

OBJECT	MEANING AND USE	EXAMPLE
node *(cont.)*	**Common methods (element nodes only):**	
	getAttribute(sAttribute) - Gets the value of the attribute defined by sAttribute.	myNode.getAttribute ("align")
	removeAttribute(sAttribute) - Removes the attribute defined by sAttribute.	myNode.removeAttribute ("align")
	setAttribute(sAttribute,sValue) - Sets the value of the attribute defined with the name of sAttribute to the value defined by sValue.	myNode.setAttribute ("align","center")
	Common methods (HTML element nodes only):	
	focus() - Sets focus to the element on the form defined by the node.	myNode.focus()

See the "Additional Resources" section of this chapter for a reference to a complete listing of valid objects, properties, and methods.

DOM Level 2, the newest W3C specification, also supports styleSheets objects. These objects are accessible from Netscape 6 and Internet Explorer 5.5, though Internet Explorer 5.5 does not support all of the styleSheets object features. For example, Netscape provides access to CSS rules as follows:

```
document.styleSheets[0].cssRules.length
```

This statement defines the number of style rules within a style sheet. See the "Additional Resources" section of this chapter for a link to a description of these newer features.

A Word on DHTML

Dynamic Hypertext Markup Language (DHTML) refers to the set of technologies needed to achieve dynamic behavior in your Web application.

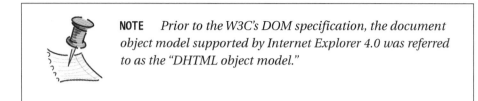

NOTE *Prior to the W3C's DOM specification, the document object model supported by Internet Explorer 4.0 was referred to as the "DHTML object model."*

The set of technologies that are normally included in DHTML are:

- **HTML**. To create the Web page. See Chapter 3, "Using HTML."

- **Cascading Style Sheets (CSS)**. To give the Web page some style. See Chapter 4, "Using Style Sheets."

- **Browser object model**. To control the browser. See the "Browser Object Model" section earlier in this chapter.

- **DOM**. To access the elements and attributes of the HTML document after it has been displayed in the browser. See the "Document Object Model" section earlier in this chapter.

- **JavaScript**. To write scripts that access the browser object model and DOM. These scripts can be executed based on a user action. As the user moves over an image on a Web page, for example, a script can be executed that uses the DOM to change the image. See Chapter 8, "Using JavaScript," for more information on writing and executing scripts.

So far, we have covered all but one of these technologies. JavaScript pulls all of these technologies together to build dynamic Web applications. The next several chapters explore how to use JavaScript to access the object models covered in this chapter.

What Did This Cover?

The browser object model provides access to the browser so you can control the display of windows and obtain information about the browser such as the browser name and version.

The DOM offers an amazing amount of flexibility and control over what you can change in an HTML document. Just about anything in an HTML document can be accessed, changed, deleted, or added using the DOM.

Since this chapter presented the object models without a programming language by which to use them, there were no Try Its in this chapter.

The next chapter presents a scripting language that can be used to access these object models. Then you will be able to see the browser object model and the DOM in action.

Additional Resources

This section provides some additional resource suggestions by way of books, articles, and links to Web resources.

The books, articles, and links all existed at the time of this writing. There is a good chance that the books and articles still exist as you read this. However, the same cannot be said of Web links. Ignore the suggested links if they no longer exist.

Books and Articles

World Wide Web Consortium. *Document Object Model Level 1 Specification.* Open Document Standards Library, 2000.
Get it from the source. I have not seen this book, but understand that it is similar to their Web page content.

Links

`http://developer.netscape.com/docs/manuals/signedobj/trust/owp.htm/`: This portion of Netscape's site provides information on object signing.

`http://developer.netscape.com/tech/dom/`: Netscape's site describing its support of the DOM in Netscape. This site has lots of links to other information on the DOM.

`http://msdn.microsoft.com/workshop/Author/dom/domoverview.asp`: Microsoft's site describing its support of the DOM in Internet Explorer. This site has several examples on using the DOM to create, move, and manipulate nodes.

`http://www.w3.org/DOM/`: The W3C site presents standards information on the DOM. Unlike most of the W3C pages, this one is much more challenging to read.

`http://www.webdevelopersjournal.com/articles/dhtml3/dhtml3.html`: This article is entitled "DHTML Part 3: Browser Object Model."

`http://www.webstandards.org/`: This site is maintained by a group of Web developers and users who are pushing for browser standardization. It includes the latest news on standardization and links to other sites on topics such as the DOM.

`http://www.xs4all.nl/~ppk/js/index.html?version5.html`: This is the most complete vender independent site that I found on the DOM. It includes a lot of details on browser compatibility.

`http://www.zvon.org/`: This site also has good reference information on the DOM.

Using JavaScript

"In the beginning, there was HTML.
And the hordes used HTML to produce Web pages.
And they looked at the Web pages, and saw that they were good.
But after a time, visitors to the Web sites grew restless and bored
with the Web sites.
They clamored for more.
They wanted the page to interact with them.
They wanted dynamic content.
The hordes were also restless.
They wanted to be able to provide different content in different contexts.
Thus, the notion of scripting was born."
   —Nancy Winnick Cluts
   MSDN Online Web Workshop
   October 27, 1997

HTML LACKS ONE IMPORTANT FEATURE: logic. There is no way to calculate a value, exe-cute a loop, or even perform simple "if" logic with HTML. There is no way to move a button, change colors, hide and show elements, or build dynamic con-tent. To add logic to HTML, you need a *scripting language*.

A scripting language lets you program your Web pages to perform calcu-lations and business logic, validate user input, reactively modify the look of the page, generate dynamic content, and control the browser's behavior. Scripting allows you to build an active user interface for your Web application.

The purpose of this chapter is to provide you with an introduction to one of the most popular scripting languages for use in Web applications: JavaScript. Later chapters expand on these basics to cover more advanced JavaScript topics such as validating user-entered values and storing and retrieving data from the user's machine using cookies.

What Will This Cover?

This chapter covers the following key JavaScript concepts:

- Understanding the basics of JavaScript

- Examining how JavaScript is processed

- Using JavaScript to respond to user actions

- Adding text to a page with JavaScript

- Hiding and showing elements with JavaScript

- Performing image rollovers with JavaScript

- Building scripts in an external file

- Understanding JavaScript syntax

By the end of this chapter, you will have a general understanding of the JavaScript language and its syntax. You will also know how to use JavaScript to respond to user actions on a Web page.

JavaScript Basics

A scripting language provides for the development of little programs called *scripts*. You can write scripts within your HTML document to add logic and reactivity to your Web page.

JavaScript is the most popular client-side scripting language for Web applications. It was designed specifically to add logic to HTML and is supported by the major browsers including Internet Explorer and Netscape. There are other scripting languages you could use for client-side scripting such as Visual Basic Scripting Edition (VBScript) and JScript. VBScript is a Microsoft scripting language that can be used for client-side or server-side scripting in Web applications or within Microsoft products such as Word and Excel. JScript is Microsoft's implementation of JavaScript.

An important thing to understand is that JavaScript is not Java. JavaScript is a scripting language; Java is a full-blown, general-purpose application language. You can write complete stand-alone applications with Java just as you can with Visual Basic or C++. You can only use JavaScript to write scripts that execute within another application. Client-side scripts in an HTML document run within the user's browser.

One of the most common reasons to add scripts to your HTML document is to react to something the user does. For example, you can use a script to perform an image rollover, which is a special effect that changes an image on a Web page as a user moves the mouse over the image. Scripts are also commonly used to execute basic logic and write additional HTML into the Web page. For example, a script could determine the current date and time and write it as part of the Web page text.

Scripts are useful when working with data-entry forms. A script can add or hide elements on the form based on the user's selection. When the user submits the form, a script can validate the entered values before submitting the data to the server.

Creating and executing scripts is easy. You simply type the JavaScript directly into your HTML document using any editor. No special tools, compilers, debuggers, or utilities are required. The hard part is knowing the correct JavaScript syntax required to create the scripts.

Basic JavaScript Syntax

With JavaScript you can define variables, create objects, call functions, and respond to events. You can perform basic operations and use basic control statements such as `if`, `for`, and `while`. A few syntax rules will help you get up to speed quickly with JavaScript.

JavaScript is case sensitive. If you define a variable in lowercase and attempt to use it as uppercase, JavaScript does not recognize it. This is true for objects, functions, and event handlers as well.

Each JavaScript statement ends with a semicolon (`;`). For example:

```
x = 4;
y = 5;
z = x + y;
```

CAUTION *Some browsers allow you to write some JavaScript statements without semicolons. Leaving off the semicolons can introduce obscure errors because the JavaScript interpreter may not interpret each statement as you intended. It is good programming practice to end every JavaScript statement with a semicolon.*

Declare your variables before you use them with the var keyword. You can initialize the variable when it is declared by assigning it the initial value as part of the var syntax:

```
var x = 1;
```

CAUTION   *Always declare your variables before you use them. Some browsers generate an error if an undeclared variable is encountered in a script.*

Variables in JavaScript are loosely typed, meaning that you cannot declare a variable to be of a specific type such as a string or integer. Rather, JavaScript determines the type when the variable is used. JavaScript has three basic variable types: numeric (integer or floating-point), string, and Boolean (true or false).

JavaScript supports the standard operators such as addition (+), subtraction (-), assignment (=), and shortcut operators such as:

```
x ++; // This increments the variable by one
x += 5; // This adds 5 to the value of the variable
```

JavaScript also supports comparison operators such as:

```
x == 1; //This compares x to 1. If x is equal to 1 this is true, otherwise it
is false.
```

Use curly braces ({ }) to combine multiple JavaScript statements into a statement block. Statement blocks are used to define the body of a function. They are also used by control statements such as if, for, or while. For example:

```
if (credit==true)
{
    i = AddTwo(i);
}
else
{
    i = SubtractTwo(i);
}
```

If you only have one statement in the statement block, you could forgo the curly braces. However, good programming practice dictates using curly braces for all statement blocks regardless of the number of statements. This aids with maintenance if more statements are added later.

All good code, including JavaScript, should be commented for clarity and ease of maintenance. However, all of the JavaScript code, including the comments, is downloaded to the client to be executed. The user can view the source of the script and read all of your comments. This means you don't want to say anything in your comments that you don't want the world to see!

To add single-line comments to your JavaScript code, use slashes (//). For example:

```
// This script validates the user-entered values
```

For multiline comments you can use the /* comment */ construct. For example:

```
/* This script validates the user-entered values
   and returns true or false */
```

The most common JavaScript operators, objects, and statements are summarized in the "JavaScript Reference" section toward the end of this chapter.

JavaScript Functions

Code structure is as important in an HTML document as in an application program. In some respects, code structure may be more important in an HTML document because of its potential complexity. A single HTML document can contain HTML, styles, and JavaScript. If the code does not have some structure, then reading, writing, and maintaining that code may become difficult.

One of the easiest ways to simplify the structure of your HTML document is to write your JavaScript code as functions. A *function* is a logical set of statements that performs a specific task. Functions help you to organize your scripts by grouping and encapsulating script statements into logical and manageable units.

To create a JavaScript function, use the function keyword and give the function a logical name. You can follow the name of the function with a list of *parameters*. The parameters allow you to pass data into the function. By passing parameters to the function, your code can perform operations based on that data. To return a value from the function, use the return keyword. For example:

```
//This function increments a value by 2
function AddTwo(x)
{
  x += 2;
  return x;
}
```

This function has one parameter, x. The function increments x by 2 and returns the new value.

JavaScript functions are normally defined in the header section of an HTML document, though they can be defined within the body section. Code you put within a function is only executed when the function is called. Any code outside of a function is executed as the HTML document is parsed.

TIP   *Adding your JavaScript functions to the header section of the HTML document is a good general practice to ensure that the function has been parsed before the page is displayed. See the "How JavaScript Works" section later in this chapter for more information.*

You can declare variables in a function if those variables are only used within the function. If you want to access a variable anywhere on the page, declare the variable outside of a function.

You can call a function anywhere within the HTML document. When you call the function, you must pass required parameters. For example:

```
i = AddTwo(7);
```

This statement calls the AddTwo function and passes in 7. The result is returned and assigned to the variable i, so i is set to 9.

Use functions wherever possible to encapsulate logically related sets of code. More meaningful function examples are presented throughout this chapter.

JavaScript and Events

To make your Web application more reactive to the user, you can write JavaScript code that is executed when the user performs an action, such as moving the mouse over an image or clicking on a button.

When a user performs an action on a Web page the browser generates an *event* for the element associated with that action. For example, if the user moves the mouse over an image, the HTML img element associated with that image generates a mouseover event.

You can write an *event handler* to recognize an event for an element. The event handler can execute JavaScript statements or call a JavaScript function to respond to that event. For example, you can write an onmouseover event handler for the img element to recognize the mouseover event. The onmouseover event handler could call a JavaScript function to change the source of the graphic associated with the image, basically causing the image on the page to change as the user moves the mouse over the image.

You define an event handler for an element by specifying the event handler name as an attribute of the element. The JavaScript statements or function are defined as the value of that attribute:

```
<img onmouseover="changeImage();">
```

In this example, an onmouseover event handler is specified for the img element. This event handler calls the changeImage() function. When the user moves the mouse over this image, the defined function is called to change the source of the image.

There is a predefined set of intrinsic event handlers for HTML elements such as onload when a Web page is loaded and onfocus when an element receives input focus. See "JavaScript Reference" toward the end of this chapter for a list of these intrinsic event handlers. Additional event examples are provided throughout this chapter.

NOTE *The description of events in this chapter follows the HTML 4 and DOM Level 1 specifications because this is what most browsers currently support. The event model has changed for DOM Level 2. See the DOM references in "Additional Resources" at the end of this chapter for links to the DOM Level 2 specification and for more information on the new event model.*

JavaScript and Object Models

You can use JavaScript to access an object model using the standard object model syntax described in Chapter 7, "Understanding Object Models."

When building Web applications, you can use JavaScript to access browser information using the browser object model. For example, when a user accesses your Web application, a script can use the browser object model to check the type or version of the user's browser to adjust the page accordingly:

```
if (navigator.appName=="Netscape")
{
    //Do some Netscape-specific scripting
}
```

You can use JavaScript with the Document Object Model (DOM) to access and modify the elements and attributes of the Web page displayed in the browser. For example, as a user moves the mouse over an element on the Web page, JavaScript code can use the DOM to change the color of the element:

```
<span onmouseover="style.color='red';">
   Watch for mouse movement over this text
</span>
```

Notice that the DOM syntax used in this example did not need to specify the affected element because the syntax is within the element's tag.

Additional object model examples are provided throughout this chapter.

How JavaScript Works

To best understand the effect of your scripts, it is useful to know a little about what actually goes on behind the scenes as the user's browser interprets your script.

JavaScript can be inserted into an HTML document as client-side scripting, meaning that the Web browser (not the Web server) executes the JavaScript code. One of the primary benefits of client-side scripting is performance. Client-side scripting responds to user actions almost instantly, optimizing response time and improving the user's experience. If your logic is on the Web server, the Web page must be submitted through a network to the shared Web server to perform the processing, which reduces response time.

JavaScript code is not compiled. JavaScript is an interpreted language, meaning that each line of script is processed as the script is executed.

When an HTML document containing client-side JavaScript code is downloaded to the user's browser, the browser interprets the script code using the browser's JavaScript parsing engine. Each line in the HTML document is sequentially parsed. The header section of the HTML document is parsed first, so any scripting in the header section of the HTML document is interpreted first, before any text is displayed on the page. Each line in the body section of the HTML document is then parsed. Any scripting in the body section of the HTML document is interpreted as it is parsed.

Any JavaScript code defined within the HTML document is executed as it is interpreted. This means that the code is run before the page is displayed. This allows you to adjust the look of the Web page before it is displayed to the user. Script code within a function is not executed until the function is called somewhere on the page, normally in response to a user action.

If you want to see how this works, add the following script to the header section of an HTML document:

```
<script type="text/javascript">
<!--
   window.alert("hello");
//-->
</script>
```

This code displays a message box before it displays any of the Web page contents. Then move this script to the body section of the HTML document between some of the page's text. The first part of the text is displayed and then the message box appears. Notice how the message box prevents any other text on the page from displaying until you close the message box. (The syntax of this script is described in detail in the next sections of this chapter.)

It is important to note that JavaScript code associated with an event handler is invoked asynchronously. This means that it is possible for the user to cause an event before the body section of the HTML document is fully parsed. For example, the user could click on some of the Web page text before the entire page is displayed. If the JavaScript function called by that event has not yet been parsed, the function is not found and an error may occur. This happens most frequently if the functions are at the end of the script. If the functions are instead in the header section of the HTML document, they are parsed before the body section of the HTML document is parsed preventing this potential error.

Another important note is that once the page is fully displayed, you can no longer write to the Web page using the write method of the document object:

```
document.write("Add some text");
```

Using this method after the page is fully displayed causes the new text to appear on a new, empty page. To add text to the page after it has been displayed, use the techniques for inserting text on a page as described in the section "Using Functions to Hide and Show Elements" later in this chapter.

Because the user's browser runs the client-side script, JavaScript must be safe for the Web. That is, JavaScript must not perform an operation that could cause harm to the user's system. You cannot, for example, use JavaScript to read directory structures, call client-side applications, or format a hard disk. Imagine the viruses users could get if JavaScript did not have these limitations!

Defining Scripts

There are three basic techniques for defining scripts in your HTML document. These are similar to the techniques used to define styles in Chapter 4, "Using Style Sheets."

- **Inline**. Specify the script directly within an HTML element. This is useful to associate an event that the element generates with an event handler that reacts to the event.

- **Embedded**. Specify the script within the HTML document. This is useful if you have logic that is required by a particular Web page.

- **External**. Specify the script in an external file. This is the recommended technique for defining script that is reused by multiple Web pages.

These techniques are discussed in detail in the sections that follow. In many cases, you may want to combine inline, embedded, and external scripts within one HTML document.

Before you use any scripting on a page, you need to specify the scripting language that you plan to use by defining a `meta` element in the header section of your HTML document:

```
<meta http-equiv="Content-Script-Type" content="text/javascript" />
```

The `http-equiv` and `content` attributes of the `meta` element set the scripting language for scripts to JavaScript.

Using Inline Scripts to React to Events

One of the reasons you want to add JavaScript to your HTML document is to provide some reactivity to the user's actions. You may want to change the look of the Web page as the user moves the mouse. You may want to perform a calculation as the user leaves a particular element.

When a user performs an action on an element of a Web page, the browser generates an event for that element. You can write an event handler for an element to recognize the event and execute JavaScript code in response to the event. For example, when the user displays a Web page, the body of the page is loaded and you can write an `onload` event handler for the `body` element to execute code immediately after the page is loaded. When the user moves over an image, a mouseover event is generated and you can write an `onmouseover` event handler for the `img` element to execute code when the mouse is moved over the image.

In all of these cases, you follow the same basic set of steps when writing scripts to react to an action:

1. Identify an action.

2. Define the element that generates an event in response to the action.

3. Determine the appropriate event handler. (See the "JavaScript Reference" section toward the end of this chapter for the list of event handlers.)

4. Assign script to that event handler for that element.

Let's try these steps using a simple example:

Step 1: You want to change the color of some of the text on your page when the user moves the mouse over the text and change it back when the user moves the mouse off of the text; this is the action.

Step 2: You don't want the entire p (paragraph) element to change, only a portion of it, so you can add a span element to demarcate the desired text. This is the element that generates the event.

Step 3: The event handlers are onmouseover and onmouseout.

Step 4: You can then add script to the event handlers for the span element. The code would look like this:

```
❶   <p class="normal">
❷       Sign up for one of our courses today and receive
❸       <span onmouseover="style.color='red';" onmouseout="style.color='navy';">
❹           $50 off
❺       </span>
❻       of a future course.
❼   </p>
```

The text resides within p element tags (lines ❶ and ❼). The span element tags (lines ❸ and ❺) are added to isolate the desired text. The two event handlers, onmouseover and onmouseout, are defined as attributes of the span element.

The value of the event handler attribute is set to the script that is executed when the event occurs (line ❸). This script can contain inline script statements, as shown in this example, or call a JavaScript function, as shown later in this chapter. In this case the inline script statements change the style color of the span element text to red when the user moves the mouse over the text and navy when the mouse is moved away from the text.

Notice the single quotes (' ') around the color value. They are used in place of double-quotes (" ") because of the double-quotes around the entire script. Notice also that each script statement terminates with a semicolon (;).

Another thing to notice about the inline script in this example is that it did not specify the element to use. The document and element are implied because the script is inline within the element's tag.

If this script were not inline within the tag of the element to modify, the script would need to specify the element using the syntax shown in Chapter 7, "Understanding Object Models." In the following example, the desired element has an id attribute set to "deal":

```
document.getElementById("deal").style.color="red";
```

Ready to try one?

Try It 8-1.

Adding Reactivity to a Web Page

Try It 8-1 adds reactivity to the Welcome page from Try It 4-5. The Welcome page reacts by changing the color of some of the text when the user moves over it.

1. Open the TrainingWelcome.htm file from Try It 4-5 in your HTML editing tool.

2. Add the meta element to define JavaScript as your scripting language.

3. Add a span element around several words of text on the page to define which text changes as the user moves the mouse.

4. Add the onmouseover and onmouseout event handlers as attributes for the span element.

5. Assign JavaScript code to the onmouseover and onmouseout event handlers. You can add any JavaScript code, such as changing the color of the text.

6. Save the file.

7. Open the TrainingWelcome.htm file in your browser. Move the mouse over the text and see if it changes. When you move the mouse off of the text, it should change again.

If your page does not work as you expect, check your quotes and your use of uppercase and lowercase. Missing or incorrect quotes and incorrect use of capitalization are a common source of scripting errors.

Listing 8-1 presents the code used to generate the page.

Listing 8-1. The TrainingWelcome.htm file uses an inline script to change the color of text as the user moves the cursor over the text.

```
<!DOCTYPE html PUBLIC "-//W3C//DTD XHTML 1.0 Strict//EN" "DTD/xhtml1-strict.dtd">
<html>
<!--
    Try It   8-1
    Title:  Welcome Page
    Author: InStep Technologies
            www.insteptech.com
    Purpose:To demonstrate simple inline JavaScript
 -->
<head>
<title>InStep Training Welcome Page</title>
<meta http-equiv="Content-Script-Type" content="text/javascript" />
<link rel="stylesheet" type="text/css" href="TrainingStyle.css" />
</head>
<body>
<div class="shadow">inStep</div>
<div class="foreground">inStep</div>
<h1 class="margin">Welcome to the InStep Training Page</h1>
<p class="key">
    <br />
    Our training courses are the best in the industry.
</p>
<p class="normal">
    Sign up for one of our courses today and receive
    <span onmouseover="style.color='red';" onmouseout="style.color='navy';">
       $50 off
    </span>
    of a future course.
</p>
<div class="margin">
<br />
<a href="TrainingCourseList.htm">View a list of our courses</a>
<br />
<br />
<a href="TrainingMailingList.htm">
    <img src="MailingList.gif" alt="Mailing List"/>
    Sign up for our mailing list
</a>
</div>
</body>
</html>
```

Using Embedded Scripts to Add Text to Your Page

Most scripts are written to react to something that the user has done on the Web page, but you can also write scripts that are executed immediately when the HTML document for the Web page is parsed. This is useful for performing operations or adding text to the page as the page is being loaded.

In this case, the script is not tied to an event or an element on the page. Rather, the script is simply a bit of programming logic within the HTML document.

Here is a simple script that adds the date and time to the Web page:

```
❶  <script type="text/javascript">
❷  <!--
❸     document.write("<p style='color:navy'>" + Date() + "</p>");
❹  //-->
❺  </script>
```

The `script` element tags (lines ❶ and ❺) define the beginning and ending of the script. The `type` attribute of the script element defines the scripting language, in this case JavaScript.

NOTE   *You may see a* language *attribute within a* script *element tag. The* language *attribute has been deprecated in favor of the* type *attribute.*

CAUTION   *You can mix JavaScript and VBScript on a single page, but be aware that Netscape browsers do not parse VBScript.*

The comment marks (lines ❷ and ❹) hide the script from the browser's display. This ensures that any browser that cannot process the script won't display the script contents as text on the page. Older versions of browsers, such as Internet Explorer before version 3 and Netscape before version 2, don't support scripting. By convention, the HTML comment marks are added around all scripts to ensure the script itself is not parsed as HTML in these older browsers. The JavaScript parser understands the HTML start comment mark (<!--) and ignores everything on that line. The JavaScript comment mark (//) hides the HTML end comment mark (-->) from the JavaScript parser.

This script contains one line of code (line ❸). The write method of the DOM document object writes the defined string to the Web page. In this case, it uses the JavaScript Date() function and writes a paragraph that contains the date and time.

NOTE *JavaScript is case sensitive. If you specify* date() *instead of* Date() *you get a scripting error or just no date.*

Notice the quotation marks used when defining the string to write to the Web page. Each string constant within the write method is enclosed within double-quotes (" "). For any quotes that would normally be defined within the HTML, such as the quotes around attributes, single quotes (' ') are used.

The semicolon (;) at the end of the document.write statement is the standard statement terminator for JavaScript. This identifies the end of a code line. Many browsers are forgiving about the semicolon and accept lines without it, but it can cause obscure scripting errors. Good programming practice is to include semicolons at the end of each statement.

This script is executed when the browser parses the HTML document. The date and time would appear in different locations on the page, depending on where this script is inserted into the HTML document. If this script is added to the end of the HTML document, the date and time appears at the bottom of the page, as shown in Figure 8-1.

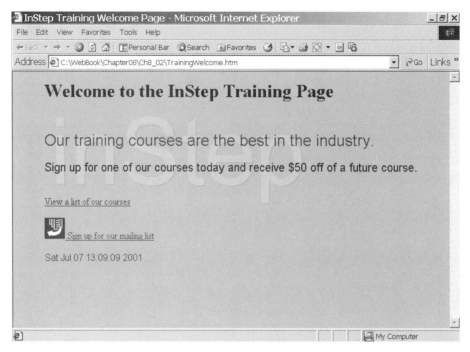

Figure 8-1. Give your page a little life by adding the date and time using JavaScript.

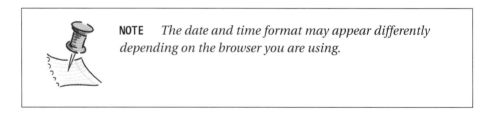

NOTE *The date and time format may appear differently depending on the browser you are using.*

Try It 8-2.

Using an Embedded Script to Display the Date and Time

Try It 8-2 adds the date and time to the Welcome page from Try It 8-1.

1. Open the TrainingWelcome.htm file from Try It 8-1 in your HTML editing tool.

2. Add a `script` element to define the script at the location in the HTML document where you want to display the date and time.

3. Write JavaScript code to display the date and time within the `script` element tags.

4. Save the file.

5. Open the TrainingWelcome.htm file in your browser.

6. Experiment with moving the script to different locations within the HTML document and with writing other text into your browser with JavaScript.

The resulting page will appear similar to Figure 8-1. If your page does not appear as you expect, check your quotes and your use of uppercase and lowercase. Missing or incorrect quotes and incorrect use of capitalization are common sources of scripting errors.

The code used to generate the page shown in Figure 8-1 is presented in Listing 8-2.

Listing 8-2. The TrainingWelcome.htm file displays the date and time on the Welcome page to give it a sense of freshness.

```
<!DOCTYPE html PUBLIC "-//W3C//DTD XHTML 1.0 Strict//EN" "DTD/xhtml1-strict.dtd">
<html>
<!--
    Try It  8-2
    Title:  Welcome Page
    Author: InStep Technologies
            www.insteptech.com
    Purpose:To demonstrate embedded JavaScript
 -->
<head>
<title>InStep Training Welcome Page</title>
<meta http-equiv="Content-Script-Type" content="text/javascript" />
<link rel="stylesheet" type="text/css" href="TrainingStyle.css" />
</head>
<body>
```

```
<div class="shadow">inStep</div>
<div class="foreground">inStep</div>
<h1 class="margin">Welcome to the InStep Training Page</h1>
<p class="key">
    <br />
    Our training courses are the best in the industry.
</p>
<p class="normal">
    Sign up for one of our courses today and receive
    <span onmouseover="style.color='red';" onmouseout="style.color='navy';">
        $50 off
    </span>
    of a future course.
</p>
<div class="margin">
<br />
<a href="TrainingCourseList.htm">View a list of our courses</a>
<br />
<br />
<a href="TrainingMailingList.htm">
    <img src="MailingList.gif" alt="Mailing List" />
    Sign up for our mailing list
</a>
</div>
<script type="text/javascript">
<!--
    document.write("<p style='color:navy'>" + Date() + "</p>");
//-->
</script>
</body>
</html>
```

Using Functions to Hide and Show Elements

There are many useful and fun things you can do if you know how to hide and show elements on your page. You may want to provide detail, such as help text, which is shown or hidden when the user clicks. If you are displaying a form, you may want to hide or show particular controls based on the user's selection in other controls. You can provide this interactivity using JavaScript functions.

Earlier in this chapter, you saw how to react to a user's action by assigning a single code statement to an event handler in an element. This works great if you have one line of code, but how often can you accomplish a specific coding objective with one or two lines of code? Adding many lines of code within the HTML element tag is not only messy, it makes the code more difficult to maintain and ties the code to a visual element.

For any nontrivial tasks, it is better to write the JavaScript code in a function. You can then call the function from within an element's tag or from anywhere else on the page.

Let's look at an example that displays additional text if the user clicks on specific text on the page. If the user clicks again, the additional text is hidden. The JavaScript function is as follows:

```
①  <script type="text/javascript">
②  <!--
③     var isHidden = true;
④     function DisplayInfo()
⑤     {
⑥        if (isHidden==true)
⑦        {
⑧           document.getElementById("InsertInfo").style.display = "block";
⑨           isHidden = false;
⑩        }
⑪        else {
⑫          document.getElementById("InsertInfo").style.display="none";
⑬           isHidden = true;
⑭        }
⑮     }
⑯  //-->
⑰  </script>
```

If you have not seen much JavaScript before, this may look a little scary. But it gets easier if you look at it one line at a time. The script element (lines ① and ⑰) defines the beginning and ending of the script. The comment marks (lines ② and ⑯) hide the script from browsers that don't support scripting.

The script begins by declaring a variable and assigning it the Boolean true value (line ③). This variable is used as a toggle to define when the text is shown and when it is hidden. It starts out hidden. This statement exists outside of the function, so this code is executed when the HTML on the page is first parsed.

NOTE *JavaScript is case sensitive. The value of true must be* true *and not* True.

The function, `DisplayInfo`, is declared next (line ❹). The body of the function is defined with curly braces (lines ❺ and ❶❺). It is good practice to document your functions with comments on the lines above the function declaration. The documentation should contain a description of the general purpose of the function and information about the function's parameters and any return values. (Not shown in this example.)

The `DisplayInfo` function begins by checking the value of the Boolean variable that was initialized outside of the function. If the variable is `true` (line ❻), the code within curly braces (lines ❼ and ❶❶) is executed.

In this example, the DOM is used to locate the element to hide or show by its id attribute (line ❽). The `style.display` method of the element shows the element as a block. This causes the element to be shown on the Web page.

 CAUTION *You cannot use* `document.write` *here because the Web page is already displayed. See "How JavaScript Works" earlier in this chapter for more information.*

The Boolean variable is then set to `false` (line ❾). This provides a toggle indicating that the text is no longer hidden.

When the user clicks a second time, the Boolean variable is `false` and the `else` case (line ❶❶) is executed. In this example, the `style.display` method is set to `none` to hide the element (line ❶❷) and the Boolean variable is set back to `true` (line ❶❸). If the user clicks again, the text is shown again and so on.

You could extend this concept to build tree-view style content on your Web pages with HTML and JavaScript. When a user clicks on a parent, the child nodes of the tree can appear. When the user clicks again, the child nodes disappear.

There are two things missing from this example: the code that calls this function and the text to display. Functions are most frequently called from event handlers or from other functions. In this example, the function is called from an element's event handler:

```
❶  <p class="normal" onclick="DisplayInfo();">
❷      Click here for more information.
❸  </p>
❹  <div id="InsertInfo" style="display:none">
❺      <p class="key">
❻      Yes, we will give you a credit toward your next class with us! ...
❼      </p>
❽  </div>
```

When the user clicks on the defined paragraph (lines ❶ through ❸), the onclick event handler calls the DisplayInfo function. The div element with an id attribute set to InsertInfo (lines ❹ through ❽) defines the new text to appear. The style attribute sets the display to none, effectively hiding the element until it is shown in the DisplayInfo function. When the user clicks on the text, the result will be similar to Figure 8-2.

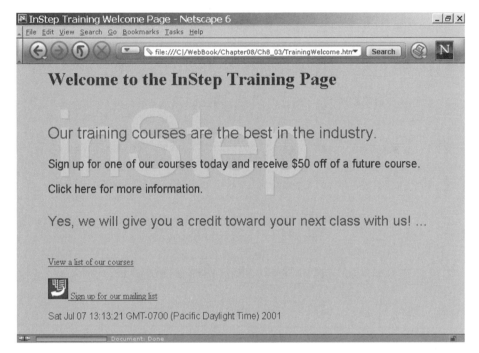

Figure 8-2. Hide and show elements on the page using JavaScript.

Try It 8-3.

Creating a JavaScript Function to Hide and Show Text

Try It 8-3 adds a JavaScript function to the Welcome page from Try It 8-2. This function hides and shows text on the page.

1. Open the TrainingWelcome.htm file from Try It 8-2 in your HTML editing tool.

2. Define a div element in the body of the HTML document where you want the new text to appear, set the id attribute to a descriptive identifier, and set the style attribute display to hide the element.

3. Define text within the div element. This is the text that will appear when the user clicks on other text on the page.

4. Add a `script` element for the function that will hide and show the element. By convention, this is normally in the header section of the HTML document.

5. Within the `script` element, write JavaScript to declare and initialize a Boolean variable to use as a hide/show toggle.

6. Also within the `script` element, create a function to modify the style of the `div` element created in step 2 to hide or show the element.

7. Add text, a button, or other element that the user can click. Call the function created in the prior step from the `onclick` event handler of this new element.

8. Save the file.

9. Open the TrainingWelcome.htm file in your browser.

10. Experiment with hiding and showing other elements with JavaScript.

The resulting page will appear similar to Figure 8-2. If your page does not work as you expect, check your quotes and your use of uppercase and lowercase. Missing or incorrect quotes and incorrect use of capitalization are a common source of scripting errors.

The code used to generate the page shown in Figure 8-2 is presented in Listing 8-3.

Listing 8-3. The TrainingWelcome.htm file hides and shows text on the page to make the best use of the screen real estate.

```
<!DOCTYPE html PUBLIC "-//W3C//DTD XHTML 1.0 Strict//EN" "DTD/xhtml1-strict.dtd">
<html>
<!--
    Try It  8-3
    Title:  Welcome Page
    Author: InStep Technologies
            www.insteptech.com
    Purpose:To demonstrate hiding and showing elements with JavaScript
 -->
<head>
<title>InStep Training Welcome Page</title>
<meta http-equiv="Content-Script-Type" content="text/javascript" />
<link rel="stylesheet" type="text/css" href="TrainingStyle.css" />
<script type="text/javascript">
<!--
    var isHidden = true;
```

```
    function DisplayInfo()
    {
        if (isHidden ==true)
        {
            document.getElementById("InsertInfo").style.display = "block";
            isHidden = false;
        }
        else
        {
            document.getElementById("InsertInfo").style.display = "none";
            isHidden = true;
        }
    }
//-->
</script>
</head>
<body>
<div class="shadow">inStep</div>
<div class="foreground">inStep</div>
<h1 class="margin">Welcome to the InStep Training Page</h1>
<p class="key">
    <br />
    Our training courses are the best in the industry.
</p>
<p class="normal">
    Sign up for one of our courses today and receive
    <span onmouseover="style.color='red';" onmouseout="style.color='navy';">
        $50 off
    </span>
    of a future course.
</p>
<p class="normal" onclick="DisplayInfo();">
    Click here for more information.
</p>
<div id="InsertInfo" style="display:none">
    <p class="key">
    Yes, we will give you a credit toward your next class with us! ...
    </p>
</div>
<div class="margin">
<br />
<a href="TrainingCourseList.htm">View a list of our courses</a>
<br />
<br />
<a href="TrainingMailingList.htm">
    <img src="MailingList.gif" alt="Mailing List"/>
```

```
    Sign up for our mailing list
</a>
</div>
<script type="text/javascript">
<!--
    document.write("<p style='color:navy'>" + Date() + "</p>");
//-->
</script>
</body>
</html>
```

Performing Image Rollovers

One of the most common effects you see on a Web page is an image rollover. With this effect, an image changes when the user moves the mouse over the image. It then changes back to its original image when the user moves the mouse out of the image. This is used most often on images that represent buttons on the form, but any images can have a rollover effect.

There are two basic steps to the image rollover effect. First preload the images that you are using for the effect. Then write JavaScript code for the `onmouseover` and `onmouseout` event handlers to display the appropriate image.

When an HTML document is downloaded, any images that are displayed are downloaded as well. With an image rollover effect there are some images defined in the HTML document that won't be displayed until the user actually rolls over the image. These images won't be downloaded until they are actually displayed. You can preload images so that they are downloaded and ready when they are needed. This is especially important for image rollovers because you don't want the user to wait for images to download as the user moves the mouse around the page.

TIP   *You can use this technique to preload all of the images for a page even if you are not planning to use the rollover effect.*

The code required to preload images is as follows:

```
❶  if (document.images)
❷  {
❸      MailingListN = new Image(140,80); // normal
❹      MailingListN.src = "MailingList.gif";
❺      MailingListHL = new Image(140,80); // highlight
❻      MailingListHL.src = "MailingListHL.gif";
❼  }
```

The first line of code ensures that the browser provides support for image objects. Check this by referencing the images collection of the document object (line ❶). If this evaluates as true, the browser supports image objects and the code preloads them. Otherwise this code is ignored.

TIP *It is recommended that you determine support for image objects before referencing the images, as in this example.*

You then need to create an Image object using the new keyword (line ❸). This example creates a new Image object of the defined height (140) and width (80). The variable name for this object (MailingListN) provides a logical name for use in referencing the Image object.

The desired image is then preloaded into this Image object by assigning the object's src (source) property to the absolute or relative path to the image (line ❹). In this line of code the normal image is preloaded.

This image preloading code is repeated (lines ❺ and ❻) for the highlighted image that is to appear as the mouse is moved over the normal image. You can repeat these two lines of lines for every image that you want to preload.

Once the images are preloaded, you are ready for the rollover effect. You need to change the image as the mouse moves over it.

If you are adding the affect to a simple image on the Web page, add onmouseover and onmouseout event handlers for the img element associated with the Web page. For links, define an img (image) element within the a (anchor) element and then add the onmouseover and onmouseout event handlers for the a element (not for the img element).

The code for this is as follows:

```
❶  <a href="TrainingMailingList.htm"
❷      onmouseover="document.getElementById('MailingList').src=MailingListHL.src;"
❸      onmouseout="document.getElementById('MailingList').src=MailingListN.src;">
❹      <img src="MailingList.gif" id="MailingList" alt="Mailing List"/>
```

❺   `Sign up for our mailing list`
❻   `</a>`

In this example, the image with the rollover effect is part of an a element (lines **❶** through **❻**), so the script must first locate the img element to change. This is done by setting the id attribute of the desired img element (line **❹**) and using the getElementById method of the DOM document object (line **❷** and **❸**). If this effect was defined for an img element instead of an a element, the event handler would be simplified as follows:

```
onmouseover="src=MailingListHL.src;"
```

The src attribute of that img element is then set to the src attribute of the highlighted Image object (line **❷**). This replaces the img element image with the image defined by the MailingListHL Image object. As the mouse moves out of the image, the img element is found again and reset to the src attribute of the normal Image object (line **❸**).

Want to give it a try? First find two images that you can use for the effect. Then try it!

Try It 8-4.

Adding an Image Rollover Effect

Try It 8-4 adds an image rollover effect to the Welcome page from Try It 8-3. This effect changes an image as the user moves the mouse over the image.

1. Find at least two images you can use for this effect. You can find images by searching your system for files with GIF extensions or by locating any image on a Web page and selecting Save Picture As. (If you use the second approach, be careful of image copyrights.)

2. Open the TrainingWelcome.htm file from Try It 8-3 in your HTML editing tool.

3. Add a script element, or use the script element created in Try It 8-3. By convention, this is normally in the header section of the HTML document.

4. Add JavaScript code to the script element to preload the images you found in step 1.

5. Add an img element to the page or use the img element previously defined for an a element on this page.

6. In the onmouseover event handler for this img element (or the a element if you are using a link), set the src attribute of the img element to the src attribute of one of the Image objects.

7. In the onmouseout event handler for this img element (or the a element if you are using a link), set the src attribute of the img element to the src attribute of the other Image object.

8. If you define the event handlers for the a element and not the img element, be sure the associated img element has an id attribute value.

9. Save the file.

10. Open the TrainingWelcome.htm file in your browser.

11. Experiment with other image effects with JavaScript.

If your image does not appear as you expect, check your quotes and your use of uppercase and lowercase. Missing or incorrect quotes and incorrect use of capitalization are common sources of scripting errors.

The code used to demonstrate this effect is shown in Listing 8-4.

Listing 8-4. The TrainingWelcome.htm files demonstrates an image rollover, a common effect whereby the image changes as the user moves the mouse over the image.

```
<!DOCTYPE html PUBLIC "-//W3C//DTD XHTML 1.0 Strict//EN" "DTD/xhtml1-strict.dtd">
<html>
<!--
    Try It   8-4
    Title:  Welcome Page
    Author: InStep Technologies
            www.insteptech.com
    Purpose:To demonstrate image rollovers
 -->
<head>
<title>InStep Training Welcome Page</title>
<meta http-equiv="Content-Script-Type" content="text/javascript" />
<link rel="stylesheet" type="text/css" href="TrainingStyle.css" />
<script type="text/javascript">
<!--
    if (document.images)
    {
        MailingListN = new Image(140,80); // normal
        MailingListN.src = "MailingList.gif";
        MailingListHL = new Image(140,80); // highlight
        MailingListHL.src = "MailingListHL.gif";
    }
    var isHidden = true;
    function DisplayInfo()
    {
```

```
        if (isHidden==true)
        {
            document.getElementById("InsertInfo").style.display = "block";
            isHidden = false;
        }
        else
        {
            document.getElementById("InsertInfo").style.display = "none";
            isHidden = true;
        }
    }
//-->
</script>
</head>
<body>
<div class="shadow">inStep</div>
<div class="foreground">inStep</div>
<h1 class="margin">Welcome to the InStep Training Page</h1>
<p class="key">
    <br />
    Our training courses are the best in the industry.
</p>
<p class="normal">
    Sign up for one of our courses today and receive
    <span onmouseover="style.color='red';" onmouseout="style.color='navy';">
        $50 off
    </span>
    of a future course.
</p>
<p class="normal" onclick="DisplayInfo();">
    Click here for more information.
</p>
<div id="InsertInfo" style="display:none">
    <p class="key">
    Yes, we will give you a credit toward your next class with us! ...
    </p>
</div>
<div class="margin">
<br />
<a href="TrainingCourseList.htm">View a list of our courses</a>
```

```
<br />
<br />
<a href="TrainingMailingList.htm"
    onmouseover="document.getElementById('MailingList').src=MailingListHL.src;"
    onmouseout="document.getElementById('MailingList').src=MailingListN.src;">
    <img src="MailingList.gif" id="MailingList" alt="Mailing List" />
    Sign up for our mailing list
</a>
</div>
<script type="text/javascript">
<!--
    document.write("<p style='color:navy'>" + Date() + "</p>");
//-->
</script>
</body>
</html>
```

Reusing JavaScript Files

You've written some great JavaScript code and now you want to reuse it in all of your Web pages. You can reuse your code by copying and pasting it into each HTML document. But that makes the code hard to maintain. If you find an error in that code, you would have to make the change to every HTML document in which the code was pasted.

It would be better if you could create the script in an external file and then just include it in each HTML document that needs it. You can more easily reuse the script in any HTML document. If you find an error in the code, you only need to change it in the external file.

To create the external file, simply create a text file and include any JavaScript code in the file. You can include any number of functions or other code in the text file. Do not include the script element tags in the text file. By convention, the extension for JavaScript files is .js.

To reference the external file in your HTML page, use the src attribute of the script element. This defines the source of the script.

```
<script language="javascript" src="Images.js">
</script>
```

An important side effect of using an external file is the ability to "hide" the JavaScript code. Normally, if the user views the source, the user sees the JavaScript. If you reference your external file instead, you can prevent the JavaScript from appearing in the source. However, if the user has any technical savvy, the user can see the code within the browser's cache files.

JavaScript Reference

As with any programming language, JavaScript requires that you learn specific language syntax. This syntax defines the valid set of statements, commands, and operators that you can use to write your scripts. This section provides a reference to the most commonly used event handlers, operators, functions, objects, and statements.

Event Handlers

Event handlers are used to respond to user actions on a Web page. When the event occurs, script associated with the event handler is executed. Table 8-1 provides a list of the intrinsic HTML event handlers as defined by the World Wide Web Consortium (W3C). Notice that the event handlers are lowercase and have an on prefix.

Table 8-1. The Standard Set of Intrinsic HTML Event Handlers

EVENT HANDLER	EVENT OCCURS WHEN . . .	APPLIES TO. . .
onblur	An element loses focus. This is the opposite of the onfocus event handler.	a, button, label, input, select, and textarea elements
onchange	The user changes the value of an element and the control loses the input focus. This is used to perform field-by-field validation or to modify other parts of the form based on changes to a particular element.	input, select, and textarea elements
onclick	The user clicks on an element. This is used to perform an operation, such as enabling elements, when a particular element is clicked.	Most elements
ondblclick	The user double-clicks on an element.	Most elements
onfocus	An element receives the focus either by mouse action or the keyboard.	a, button, label, input, select, and textarea elements
onkeydown	A key is pressed down over an element.	Most elements
onkeypress	A key is pressed and released over an element.	Most elements
onkeyup	A key is released over an element.	Most elements
onload	The browser finishes loading a browser window. This is useful for preprocessing the page immediately of after it is loaded into the browser window.	body element
onmousedown	The user presses the mouse button on an element.	Most elements
onmousemove	The user moves the mouse while it is over an element.	Most elements
onmouseout	The user moves the mouse out of an element. This is used to turn off a visual effect as the user moves the mouse off a specific element.	Most elements

Table 8-1. The Standard Set of Intrinsic HTML Event Handlers (continued)

EVENT HANDLER	EVENT OCCURS WHEN . . .	APPLIES TO. . .
onmouseover	The user moves the mouse over an element. This is used to perform image rollovers and other visual effects as the user moves the mouse over an element.	Most elements
onmouseup	The user releases the mouse button on an element.	Most elements
onreset	A form is reset.	form element
onselect	The user selects the contents of an element such as text.	input and textarea elements
onsubmit	A form is about to be submitted to the server. This is used to perform validation prior to submitting the form. See Chapter 9, "Validating Form Data," for more information.	form element
onunload	The browser begins unloading a browser window. Used to perform any cleanup processing of the page immediately before it is unloaded.	body element

After looking at Table 8-1, you may think of many different ways to use these event handlers in your Web application. You may want to automatically select the text when a user enters an element (onfocus). You may want to perform a calculation as the user leaves an element (onblur). You may want to change an image as the user moves the mouse over the image (onmouseover), and so on.

See "Using Inline Scripts to React to Events" earlier in this chapter for an event handler example.

Operators, Assignments, and Comparisons

JavaScript provides a rich set of operators as shown in Table 8-2. It provides basic operators to manipulate values, assignment operators to assign values to variables, and comparison operators to compare values. It also has some convenient shortcut operators.

Table 8-2. Common JavaScript Operators

OPERATOR	MEANING	EXAMPLE

+	Addition.	x = 4;
		y = 5;
		z = x + y; // Result is 9.

+	Concatenation. Used to concatenate strings.	x = "sand"; y = "wich"; z = x + y; // Result is "sandwich"

++	Incremental addition. If defined as a prefix to a variable, the variable is incremented by one and then assigned. If defined after a variable, the variable is assigned first and then incremented by one.	a = 4;
		b = 4;
		x = ++a; // Result: x = 5, a=5
		y = b++; // Result: y = 4, b=5

-	Subtraction.	x = 4;
		y = 5;
		z = y - x; // Result is 1

--	Incremental subtraction. If defined as a prefix to a variable, the variable is decremented by one and then assigned. If defined after a variable, the variable is assigned first and then decremented by one.	a = 4;
		b = 4;
		x = --a; // Result: x = 3, a=3
		y = b--; // Result: y = 4, b=3

*	Multiplication.	x = 4;
		y = 5;
		z = x * y; // Result is 20

/	Division.	x = 4;
		y = 5;
		z = x / y; // Result is .8

Many languages support the basic assignment operator (=). JavaScript also provides convenient shortcut assignments as presented in Table 8-3.

Table 8-3. Common JavaScript Assignment Operators

ASSIGNMENT	MEANING	EXAMPLE
=	Assignment.	`x = 5;    // Result is 5`

+=	Increment and assign.	`x = 4;`
		`y = 2;`
		`x += y; // Result is 6`
		`// This is equivalent to x = x + y`

-=	Decrement and assign.	`x = 4;`
		`y = 2;`
		`x -= y; // Result is 2`
		`// This is equivalent to x = x - y`

*=	Multiply and assign.	`x = 4;`
		`y = 2;`
		`x *= y; // Result is 8`
		`// This is equivalent to x = x * y`

/=	Divide and assign.	`x = 4;`
		`y = 2;`
		`x /= y; // Result is 2`
		`// This is equivalent to x = x / y`

In some languages, the comparison operator is the same as the assignment operator. So x = 5 could mean "assign 5 to x" or it could mean "does x = 5?" JavaScript makes the meaning clearer by using a separate set of comparison operators as shown in Table 8-4.

Table 8-4. Common JavaScript Comparison Operators

COMPARISON	MEANING	EXAMPLE

==	Comparison. The resulting expression evaluates to true or false.	`x = 4; // Assignment`
		`x == 5; // Comparison whose result is false`

!	Not. Returns true if the expression is not true. Returns false if the expression is true.	`x = 4;` `y = !(x==5);  // Result is true`

!=	Not equal. Returns true if the values are not equal.	`x = 4;`
		`y = 5;`
		`z = (x != y); // Result is true`

>	Greater than. Returns true if the left value is greater than the right value.	`x = 4;`
		`y = 5;`
		`z = (y > x); // Result is true`

>=	Greater than or equal to. Returns true if the left value is greater than or equal to the right value.	`x = 4;`
		`y = 5;`
		`z = (y >= x); // Result is true`

<	Less than. Returns true if the left value is less than the right value.	`x = 4;`
		`y = 5;`
		`z = (y < x); // Result is false`

<=	Less than or equal to. Returns true if the left value is less than or equal to the right value.	`x = 4;`
		`y = 5;`
		`z = (y <= x); // Result is false`

&&	And. Returns true if the left value and the right value are true. If either are false, returns false.	`x = 4;`
		`y = 5;`
		`z = (x==5) && (y==5); // Result is false`

||	Or. Returns true if the left value or the right value are true. If both values are false, returns false.	`x = 4;`
		`y = 5;`
		`z = (x=5) || (y=5); // Result is true`

Built-in JavaScript Functions

JavaScript provides a set of built-in functions that you can use. These functions are independent from any particular DOM object and perform a variety of operations such as converting variables from one data type to another. The most commonly used JavaScript functions are described in Table 8-5.

Table 8-5. Common Built-in JavaScript Functions

FUNCTION	MEANING AND USE	EXAMPLE
eval()	Evaluates a string of JavaScript code and returns the result. This is useful for dynamically performing calculations based on user-entered values.	`var strExp = "4 + 5";` `z = eval(strExp); // Result is 9`
isNaN()	Evaluates an argument to determine whether it is not a number (NaN). Returns true if the argument is not a number and false if the argument is a number. This is frequently used in conjunction with parseFloat or parseInt for validating user-entered values.	See Chapter 9, "Validating Form Data," for an example.
parseFloat()	Converts a string to a floating point number. Returns NaN if the first character of the string cannot be converted to a number.	`fTotal = parseFloat(strMyTotal);`
parseInt()	Converts a string to an integer number. Returns NaN if the first character of the string cannot be converted into an integer.	`iTotal = parseInt(strMyTotal);`

Working with Objects and Collections

You can declare and use objects in JavaScript. You can use existing objects, like the browser object model window object, the DOM document object, or the JavaScript Array object. You can also create your own objects.

When working with JavaScript objects, you create an instance of the object using the new keyword. For example:

```
arr = new Array();
```

This code creates a new instance of an Array object. You can then access the object's properties and methods. In the case of an array, you can add values to each entry in the array. Continuing the example:

```
arr[0] = "Eggs";
arr[1] = "Cheese";
arr[2] = "Milk";
size = arr.length;
arr.sort();
```

You can access the length property of the Array object to determine the number of entries in the array. The result is 3 because there are three elements in the array, 0–2. You can access methods on the array, such as the sort method, to perform operations on the array.

When working with objects, you can use JavaScript's this keyword. The this keyword refers to the current object. This keyword is useful when an object wants to pass itself to a function. Using this allows you to write generic functions that can be reused by many different types of elements. For example, this function changes the color of an any element to red:

```
function ChangeToRed(e)
{
e.style.color="red";
}
```

This function can be called from an element as follows:

```
<p onmouseover="ChangeToRed(this);">
    We'll keep you up to date with the courses that we offer.
</p>
```

When the user moves the mouse over this element, the onmouseover event handler is executed. The function is called and passes a reference to this, which defines the current paragraph in this case.

JavaScript Objects

In addition to the DOM objects, JavaScript can work with its own objects. The most commonly used JavaScript objects and their associated properties and methods are presented in Table 8-6.

Table 8-6. Other Common JavaScript Objects

OBJECT	MEANING AND USE	EXAMPLE
Array	An array of values or objects. The array is 0 based.	
	Common properties:	
	length - Returns the number of elements in the array.	`document.write(arr.length);`
	Common methods:	
	sort() - Sorts an array.	`arr.sort();`
Date	An object for creating and manipulating dates.	
	Common methods:	

	getDate() - Returns the day of the monthfor the specified date.	`dt = new Date("July 4, 2001 8:22);`
		`dt.getDate();`
		`//Returns 4`

	getDay() - Returns the day of the week for the specified date.	`dt = new Date("July 4, 2001 8:22);`
		`dt.getDay();`
		`//Returns 3 (Wednesday)`

	getFullYear() - Returns the year of the specified date.	`dt = new Date("July 4, 2001 8:22);`
		`dt.getFullYear();`
		`//Returns 2001`

	getHours() - Returns the hour in the specified date.	`dt = new Date("July 4, 2001 8:22);`
		`dt.getHours();`
		`//Returns 8`

	getMinutes() - Returns the minutes in the specified date.	`dt = new Date("July 4, 2001 8:22);`
		`dt.getMinutes();`
		`//Returns 22`

Table 8-6. Other Common JavaScript Objects (continued)

OBJECT	MEANING AND USE	EXAMPLE
Date *(cont.)*	**getMonth()** - Returns the month in the specified date.	`dt = new Date("July 4, 2001 8:22");` `dt.getMonth();//Returns 6`
	getSeconds() - Returns the seconds in the defined date.	`dt = new Date("July 4, 2001 8:22");` `dt.getSeconds();//Returns 0`

	getTime() - Returns the numeric value corresponding to the time for the specified date.	`dt = new Date("July 4, 2001 8:22");`
		`dt.getTime();`
		`//Returns 994260120000`

	getYear() - Returns the year in the specified date. See also getFullYear.	`dt = new Date("July 4, 2001 8:22");`
		`dt.getYear();`
		`//Returns 2001 in Internet Explorer`
		`//Returns 101 in Netscape`

	toGMTString() - Converts the date to Greenwich Mean Time (GMT), the base of international time zones.	`dt = new Date("July 4, 2001 8:22");`
		`dt.toGMT();`
		`//Returns Wed, 4 Jul 2001 15:22:00`
		`UTC in Internet Explorer`
		`//Returns Wed, 04 Jul 2001 15:22:00`
		`GMT in Netscape`

	toString() - Converts the date to a string.	`dt = new Date("July 4, 2001 8:22");`
		`dt.toString();//Returns Wed Jul 4 08:22:00`
		`PDT 2001 in Internet Explorer`
		`//Returns Wed Jul 4 08:22:00`
		`GMT-0700 (Pacific Daylight Time)`
		`2001 in Netscape`

Number	An object for manipulating and formatting numbers.	
	Common properties:	
	NaN - Not a Number.	`parseFloat("Hello");//Returns NaN`
	Common methods:	

	toString - Converts the number into a string.	`myNum=15;`
		`myNum.toString;`
		`//Returns "15"`

Table 8-6. Other Common JavaScript Objects (continued)

OBJECT	MEANING AND USE	EXAMPLE
String	An object for manipulating and formatting strings.	
	Common properties:	
	length - Returns the length of the string.	myString="This is a string" myString.length;//Returns 16
	Common methods:	

	replace(regEx,newStr) - Replaces the string matched by the regular expression, regEx, with the string defined by newStr. See Chapter 9, "Validating Form Data," for more information on regular expressions.	myString="This is a string";
		myString.replace(/ is /," was ");
		//Returns "This was a string"

	slice(begin,end) - Slices a piece of a string starting at the character defined by begin and optionally ending with the character defined by end.	myString="This is a string";
		myString.slice(5,7);
		//Returns is

	split(sSep) - Splits a string into an array of strings based on a passed in separator, sSep.	monthString="Jan,Feb,Mar,Apr,May,
		Jun,Jul,Aug,Sep,Oct,Nov,Dec";
		arrMonths = monthString.split(",");
		arrMonths[8];
		
		//Returns Sep because
		the array is 0-based

Control Statements

JavaScript allows you to build complex control statements using variables, objects, operators, expressions, and functions. These control statements include while loops, for loops, and if conditionals.

A while loop is a simple control statement that repeats execution of a statement block while a particular condition is true. For example:

```
var count = 0;
var numberLine = "";
while (count < 10)
{
    numberLine = numberLine + count.toString();
    ++count;
}
```

This code builds a number line string of the numbers from 0 to 9. The toString method of the count number object converts a number to a string. The string is concatenated to the number line string. The count is then incremented and this process is repeated while the count is less than 10.

The for control statement repeats execution of a statement block based on more complex parameters. The format is:

```
for (initialize expression ; continuation condition ; update expression)
```

The *initialize expression* declares and initializes the loop counter. The loop continues while the *continuation condition* is true. The *update expression* provides a convenient way to increment the loop counter.

The code in the while statement example can be rewritten using a for statement as follows:

```
var numberLine = "";
for (var count = 0; count < 10; count++)
{
    numberLine = numberLine + count.toString();
}
```

In this example, the count variable is initialized to 0. The continuation condition is then checked to determine if the loop should continue. If so, the statements within the statement block are executed. Then the update expression is executed. This process repeats as the continuation condition is checked again. As soon as the continuation condition expression is evaluated as false, the loop terminates.

An if control statement defines an if statement block that is executed if a specific condition is true and an optional else statement block that is executed if the specific condition is not true. For example:

```
if (numberLine.length==0)
{
    newNumberLine = "0123456789";
}
else
{
    newNumberLine = numberLine;
}
```

This example checks the length of the number line string. If the length is 0, the new number line is built with a string. Otherwise the new number line is built using the original number line.

For simple if statements, there is a short-hand syntax:

```
(NumberLine.length) ? newNumberLine = "0123456789" : newNumberLine = numberLine;
```

This statement is comparable to the prior if statement. This statement evaluates the first expression. If it is true, the first statement after the question mark (?) is executed. If it is false, the second statement is executed.

Some of these control statements were used in examples in this chapter. Other examples are presented in Chapter 9, "Validating Form Data," and Chapter 10, "Saving Data with Cookies."

JavaScript Tips and Tricks

This section includes basic tips and techniques when working with JavaScript.

User-Friendly Pages

Here are some tips for creating user-friendly pages.

Display Secondary Windows

You may want to allow a user to view some additional information without leaving the page that they are on. For example, you may want to display the current window and show some help text in a new window. Or you may want to display the concert ticket order page and allow the user to view the seating chart for the arena in a new window.

Though you can display a new window with HTML, doing it with JavaScript gives you more control over the window. To create a window with JavaScript, use the following code:

```
<script type="text/javascript">
<!--
    var winNew
    function OpenWindow(sURL,sName)
    {
        winNew = window.open(sURL,sName);
    }
//-->
</script>
```

With JavaScript, you have control over the location and size of the window and whether to include the toolbar, location, scrollbars, and so on. Add the desired attributes to the open command to achieve your desired look:

```
winNew = window.open(sURL, sName,
    "toolbar=no, location=no, scrollbars=yes, width=600, height=300, top=400, left=300");
```

Notice that all of window attributes are in one string parameter.

To link to a new window, call the `OpenWindow` function in the a (anchor) element as follows:

```
<a href="javascript:OpenWindow('TrainingCourseList.htm','CourseList');">
    View a list of our courses
</a>
```

To be a good citizen, close the new window when you no longer need it. Here is a function that closes the window:

```
function CloseWindow()
{
    if (winNew && !winNew.closed)
    {
        winNew.close()
    }
}
```

This code only closes the window if a new window exists and it is not already closed. This type of coding prevents errors in your JavaScript.

You may want to call this function from a button that the user can select, or from the unload event for the page so the new window is closed when the user leaves the page:

```
<body onunload="CloseWindow()">
```

Debugging Tips

If you are using Visual Interdev with client-side debugging, Microsoft's Script Debugger, or the Netscape JavaScript Debugger, you have some help debugging your JavaScript. If you are using a simple text editor, you don't have much debugging help. Here are some tips for debugging your JavaScript code.

Watch Your Case

JavaScript is case sensitive, so you must take care to use the correct uppercase and lowercase. For your functions, define a standard convention for defining the case (all upper, all lower, or mixed case) and stick to it. You will be very glad you did.

Watch Your Quotation Marks

When you call a JavaScript function from an event attribute, the entire function call must be in quotation marks (" "). Any quoted string within the function call must be within single quotes (' '). Alternatively, you can use single quotes around the entire function call and quotation marks around any quoted string within the function. Whichever you choose, be consistent and be sure that you have matching sets of quotation marks.

TIP *If you need single quotes within the single quotes, use a forward slash (/). For example:* `'Today/'s date'`.

Don't Call an Object Before Its Time

Script in a Web page is interpreted following a set of rules:

- Any script in the header section of the HTML document is interpreted first. The script is executed as it is interpreted unless the script is inside a function.

- Any script in the body section of the HTML document is interpreted when it is parsed with the rest of the HTML in the HTML document. The script is executed as it is interpreted unless the script is inside a function.

- Any script inside a function is executed when the function is called.

Any objects referenced in JavaScript, such as an `input` element on a form, must exist before it is referenced. This means that JavaScript code in the header section of the HTML document and outside of any function must not reference elements that have not yet been created.

The most common message you may see is "Object required" because the HTML element you are referencing does not yet exist.

Write Out Debug Messages

Write messages to the status bar using `window.status` while you are debugging. This gives you information without impacting the flow, as the `window.alert` would do.

Alternatively, one of the prior tips demonstrated how to open a secondary window. You can write to the secondary window to display debugging or other information as part of your testing.

Recognize Browser Differences

Internet Explorer and Netscape do not have identical implementations of the browser object model, the DOM, or JavaScript itself. This can cause errors that are reported by users with older or different versions of the browser. It is important to recognize and code for browser differences and, most importantly, test with each browser that you expect to support.

For example, Internet Explorer 4.0 and above and Netscape 6 and above allow you to change style properties at any time. Netscape 4 cannot change style properties after the page has loaded.

You have several choices for dealing with the browser differences. One choice is to write code at the top of each HTML document that determines which type of browser that the user has. Code within the HTML document can use that information to adjust accordingly.

The following code uses the differences in the DOM for Internet Explorer 4.0 and Netscape 4 to determine if the browser is Netscape or Internet Explorer:

```
var verIE4up = (document.all)? true: false
var verN4up = (document.layers)? true: false
```

However, this approach does not help you handle the individual differences in the browser capabilities. It also does not help your page support future versions of browsers. Interestingly, neither of the statements in the previous script is true for Netscape 6. So this code does not provide any useful version information when used in a page displayed by Netscape 6.

Another approach is to specifically check for the browser name and version. These have some of the same problems as the prior approach plus they rely on the exact browser names:

```
var browserVer = navigator.appVersion;
var browserName = navigator.appName;
```

The result of browserName for Internet Explorer for example is "Microsoft Internet Explorer."

A better approach is to use *support detection*. Support detection requires checking for specific support of a feature instead of checking for browser versions.

For example, before you use the DOM image object, you would check for support of an image object using:

```
If (document.images)
```

Before you use the DOM, you could check for DOM support:

```
If (document.getElementById)
```

The support detection technique allows you to focus on the features that you need without worrying about which browser versions support these features.

What Did This Cover?

This chapter took the plunge into the depths of scripting. Though one chapter could not begin to tell you everything about JavaScript, the information provided in this chapter described how scripting works and provided a reference to basic JavaScript syntax.

Throughout this chapter, you worked with JavaScript. You learned how to use inline scripts to add reactivity to your Web applications. You saw how to use embedded scripts to add text to a page, hide and show elements, and generate image rollover effects. You also learned how to write your JavaScript in an external file and reference it from all of the pages of your Web application.

In the tips section, you learned about creating external windows, detecting browser features, and debugging your scripts.

The Try Its in this chapter provided some practice with simple scripts. You changed the color of text as the user moved over that text. You added text to the page as the page was loaded to display the current date and time. You worked with some simple effects such as hiding and showing elements and performing image rollovers.

The next two chapters expand on this knowledge and use JavaScript to validate forms and store data on the user's computer using cookies.

Additional Resources

This section provides some additional resource suggestions by way of books, articles, and links to Web resources.

The books, articles, and links all existed at the time of this writing. There is a good chance that the books and articles still exist as you read this. However, the same cannot be said of Web links. Ignore the suggested links if they no longer exist.

Books and Articles

Flanagan, David. *JavaScript: The Definitive Reference.* **Cambridge: O'Reilly & Associates, 1997.**
This is an excellent reference book. It takes a complete tour of JavaScript in reference fashion.

Negrino, Tom and Smith, Dori. *JavaScript for the World Wide Web.* **Berkeley, CA: Peachpit Press, 1999.**
As with the HTML book by the same publisher, this book is easy to read. It is formatted as a task-oriented book instead of as a reference book, allowing you to get started quickly toward building some great JavaScript functions.

Links

`http://www.builder.com/Programming/JsTips/ss06.html`: This site provides links to several JavaScript tips with their source code.

`http://www.w3.org/DOM/`: This is the site for the W3C that presents standards information on the DOM. The DOM Level 2 specification at this site includes information on the new event model.

`http://www.w3.org/TR/html4/interact/scripts.html`: This is the site for the W3C that specifically addresses scripting.

`http://www.w3schools.com/js/`: This site provides tutorials and allows you to work through those tutorials online. The site also has extensive links to other JavaScript reference material.

`http://www.wdvl.com/Authoring/JavaScript/`: This provides an extensive set of links to references on JavaScript, including a tutorial.

`http://www.webcoder.com/scriptorium/index.html`: This site describes itself as "a compendium of code." It contains sample and demo scripts to help get you started.

`http://www.webreference.com/javascript/`: This site has an archive of JavaScript tips to help you find the answer to many JavaScript questions.

`http://www.webreference.com/js/tips/`: This is the "Doc JavaScript" site that contains tips and links to JavaScript articles.

Validating Form Data

PICTURE THIS SCENARIO: You are using a Web application to register for a course. You enter all of the requested data and click on the submit button. The page is submitted to the Web server (which may take a bit of time) and then redisplayed with a message stating that your e-mail address is not formatted correctly. You correct your mistake and click on the submit button again. The page is submitted to the server (again with a wait) and then redisplayed with a message stating that your home phone number cannot be blank. Repeat ad nauseam, and you can get very frustrated!

It would be much better if all of the data entries were validated *before* they were submitted to the server. This would save the time in waiting for the server to receive, process, and return the request. It would also be nice to get the entire list of errors at once, instead of one at a time.

JavaScript is well suited for this validation logic. You can write JavaScript functions to ensure that a user-entered value is numeric, falls within a particular range, is a valid e-mail address, and so on.

The purpose of this chapter is to provide you with the basics you need to validate user-entered values in your HTML forms before they are submitted to the Web server. This chapter applies many of the JavaScript techniques demonstrated in the previous chapter.

What Will This Cover?

This section covers the following key validation concepts:

- Understanding the basics of validation

- Writing validation functions with JavaScript

- Performing field-level validation

- Performing form-level validation

- Adding validation attributes to HTML elements

- Notifying the user of invalid entries

- Handling required fields

- Checking for a range of values

- Learning the basic set of regular expression patterns you can use
  for validation

By the end of this chapter, you'll know how to use JavaScript to validate user-entered values on a form and provide feedback to the user regarding any invalid entries—all without hitting the Web server.

Validation Basics

Validation is a key part of a Web application. When you present a form to the user for entry or update of information, you want to ensure that the data the user enters is what you expect. Otherwise, the Web server application that receives the data, such as a CGI or ASP application, could have difficulty processing that data.

When you validate data, you want to ensure that a date is a date, a number is a number, and so on. For example, if your form asks, "How many people will attend?" you want to ensure that the user did not press the e key instead of the 3 key, which are close to each other on the keyboard, or enter "three."

There are three basic ways to validate data in a Web application:

- Add validation code to the Web server application and validate after sub-mission to the Web server.

- Validate as the user leaves each data-entry field on the form, called *field-level validation.*

- Validate all of the fields on the form before the form data is submitted to the Web server, called *form-level validation.*

Performing the validation in the Web server application means that the user has to enter the data, submit it, and wait for a response before knowing whether there were any data-entry errors. This works, but this technique is not as user friendly as the other two choices. For more information on Web server applications, see Chapter 15, "Web Application Architectures."

Validating on the client side, before submitting to the server, gives the user more immediate feedback on the validity of the entered data. It also ensures that the user-entered values are correct before the responses are submitted to the server for processing. Client-side validation of data-entry forms is one of the most common uses of JavaScript.

The first step for both field-level and form-level validation is to decide what you need to validate in your Web application. Common types of validation include:

- **Numeric**. A field is expecting a number. For example, the number of people that will attend a course must be a number.

- **Required**. A field must be entered and cannot be left blank or empty. For example, a password may be a required field.

- **Range**. A field has a predefined range of valid values. For example, the number of people that will attend the course must be at least 1 and no more than 12.

- **Phone number**. A field is a properly entered phone number. This may not check for existence of the number, just that it is correctly formatted.

- **Zip code**. A field is a properly entered zip code. This may or may not check for the existence of the entered zip code.

NOTE *Some Web applications validate phone numbers and zip codes assuming valid U.S. formats. If you want your site to be accessible to other locations, consider international formats as you develop your validation.*

The next step for both field-level and form-level validation is to create a JavaScript function to perform each type of validation. For field-level validation, you call the appropriate validation function as you leave each field of the form. To validate all of the fields at once using form-level validation, you can iterate through each field on the form and call the appropriate validation function.

The remainder of this chapter details both field-level and form-level validation techniques.

Writing Validation Functions

Validation is normally accomplished by writing a set of JavaScript functions, one for each type of validation you want to perform. Since these functions can be generic and not specific to any particular Web page, you can create this validation logic once and put it into an external JavaScript file for use throughout your Web application.

For example, you can write a function to ensure that an entered value is a number:

```
❶   function isNumeric(e)
❷   {
❸     if (e.value=="") return true;
❹     var v = parseFloat(e.value);
❺     if (isNaN(v))
❻     {
❼       alert("The entry in " + e.name + " must be numeric");
❽       return false;
❾     }else{
❿       return true;
⓫     }
⓬   }
```

This function checks the value of an element to ensure that it is numeric. It returns a Boolean (true or false) value, so the function is named as a true/false question: isNumeric?

The function takes an HTML element object as the parameter (line ❶). This element is a data-entry field on the form. You can pass any element to this function that has a value attribute, such as an input element. The curly braces (lines ❷ and ⓬) identify the body of the function. Instead of using an element as the parameter, you could pass the actual value of the element as the parameter to this function. Passing the element itself instead of the element's value gives you more flexibility. For example, by passing the element you can use the element's name in an alert message (line ❼).

If the value of the element passed into this function is empty, the value does not need to be validated, so this function returns true (line ❸). This makes the assumption that it is valid for the user to leave this data-entry element empty.

JavaScript has a built-in function, parseFloat, that converts any text to a floating-point number (line ❹). JavaScript also has a parseInt function if you want to validate for integers only. If the first character of the element's value cannot be converted into a number, the parseFloat (and parseInt) function returns Not a Number (NaN).

You can use the JavaScript isNaN function to check the result (line ❺). If the result is not a number, the function displays an alert box (line ❼) and the isNumeric function returns false (line ❽) because the value is not a number. Otherwise, the else case (line ❾) returns true (line ❿).

Both the parseFloat and parseInt functions attempt to convert a value into a floating point or integer, respectively. These functions start with the first character of the value and if that can be converted to a number, the rest of the value is converted up until the function reaches a non-numeric value.

For example:

```
parseFloat(""); //Result is NaN
parseFloat("test"); //Result is NaN
parseFloat("123"); //Result is 123
parseFloat("3px"); //Result is 3
```

In the last case, the value started with a 3 so the value was converted to a 3, ignoring the remaining characters. This can be a good thing if the user adds text, such as units, to a response.

> **NOTE**   *Watch out for strings with preceding zeros when using* parseInt, *such as in this statement:* var v = parseInt("000010"). *You may expect that this returns a numeric value of 10; instead, it returns 8. This is because* parseInt *assumes that if the first digit of the value is 0 that you are providing an octal number. To ensure you get the correct result, use* parseFloat("000010") *or* parseInt("000010",10) *to define base 10.*

If you want to ensure that all of the characters are numeric, you can use a loop to check each character of the element. Alternatively, you can use regular expressions to validate the entire string.

A *regular expression* is simply a pattern that has special meaning. You can use a regular expression to ensure that a user-entered value conforms to a particular pattern. For example, the following regular expression checks an entire string to ensure it is numeric:

```
/^\d+$/
```

The slashes (/ /) delimit the regular expression, defining the beginning and the ending of the pattern. The caret (^) defines that the pattern matching should begin with the first character of the user-entered value. The \d defines a digit (0–9). The plus sign (+) requires that the preceding character occurs one or more times, in this case this means one or more digits. The dollar sign ($) specifies that the pattern matching should end with the last character of the user-entered value. See "Regular Expression Reference" later in this chapter for additional details on regular expressions.

The function to validate that all characters of a user-entered value are numeric using regular expressions is as follows:

```
① function isAllNumeric(e)
② {
③    if (e.value=="") return true;
④    var numericExp=/^\d+$/;
⑤    if (numericExp.test(e.value))
⑥    {
⑦        return true;
⑧    }else{
⑨        alert("The entry in " + e.name + " must be numeric");
⑩        return false;
⑪    }
⑫ }
```

This function is similar to the isNumeric function, but it returns a Boolean defining whether the entire string is numeric, not just the first character(s) of the string.

The regular expression (line ④) defines the pattern that the user-entered value should match. In this case, the pattern defines that the user-entered value should begin with a digit and consist of one or more digits until the end of the value.

The other key difference between this function and the isNumeric function is the test condition (line ⑤). The test method of a regular expression tests the user-entered value against the regular expression defined in line ④. If the expression matches the pattern then the user-entered value is numeric, the test method returns true, and isAllNumeric returns true (line ⑦). Otherwise (line ⑧), the alert method is used to notify the user of the error (line ⑨) and isAllNumeric returns false (line ⑩).

Performing Field-Level Validation

Field-level validation allows you to notify the user of an invalid entry immediately as the user leaves the field. This can be useful if you want the user to correct each entry while moving through the form. However, this may be disruptive because it interrupts the user's work. The alternative form-level validation approach is shown later in this chapter.

To perform field-level validation, you need to call one of your JavaScript validation routines as the user leaves the field. This is done using the `onblur` event handler of each field that needs to be validated:

```
<input type="text" id="Attendees" name="Attendees" size="2"
    maxlength="2" onblur="isAllNumeric(this);" />
```

In this example, `this` is passed to the `isAllNumeric` function. `this` references the current object, in this case, the `input` element object. So the `Attendees input` element is validated as the user leaves the element.

The field-level validation validates the user-entered value as the user leaves the field and notifies the user about any errors. However, it does not require that the user make the correction. The user can still submit the form with invalid values in any of the form fields.

An example can illustrate this important point: If the user enters an invalid value into the Attendees text box and clicks on the submit button, the text box loses focus, the `onblur` event handler is executed, the validation is performed, and the alert box displays the error message. After dismissing the alert box, the submit button has focus. If the user clicks on the submit button again, the text box does not lose focus so the `onblur` event handler is not executed, the value is not validated, and the form is submitted with invalid data. (You can try this yourself in Try It 9-1.)

To prevent sending invalid values to the Web server, you need to revalidate all of the fields before the form is submitted using the `onsubmit` event handler as you would for form-level validation. A form-level validation example is presented in detail later in this chapter. Alternatively, when an error is found you can explicitly set the focus back to the field that is in error. This prevents the user from leaving a field until its value is valid.

The basic steps for adding field-level validation for your forms are:

1. Define the types of validation that your Web application must perform.

2. Write JavaScript functions to perform the desired validation and insert them in an external JavaScript file.

3. Ensure that a `meta` element specifying JavaScript as your scripting language is inserted in the header section of each HTML document that must be validated.

4. Add the `script` element tags in the header section of the HTML document and reference the JavaScript file containing your validation code.

5. For each element that you want to validate, call the appropriate validation function in the `onblur` event handler.

Let's try one of these.

Try It 9-1.

This Try It adds field-level validation to the Mailing List page from Try It 6-4.

1. Create a new text file.

2. In this file, write a JavaScript function to determine if the value of an element is numeric. You can use either the isNumeric or isAllNumeric function examples from the prior section.

3. Save the file as Validate.js.

4. Open the TrainingMailingList.htm file from Try It 6-4 in your HTML editing tool.

5. Add a `meta` element to define JavaScript as your scripting language.

6. Add a script element to the header section of the Mailing List page and set the src attribute to the location of the JavaScript file you just created. You can use relative or absolute paths.

7. Add an input element in the body of the form to request a numeric value, such as the number of people who might be interested in attending a course.

8. Call the JavaScript validation function using the onblur event handler of the input element.

9. Save the file.

10. Open the TrainingMailingList.htm file in your browser. Try entering a nonnumeric value. Try a numeric value. Try combination values. Notice that an entry such as "8a" is validated as numeric if you used the isNumeric function, and it won't be valid if you used the isAllNumeric function.

11. Experiment with writing other validation functions using JavaScript.

If your validation is not working, check your use of uppercase and lowercase, = vs ==, and missing semicolons. These are the most common errors in JavaScript code.

The JavaScript file with both the `isNumeric` and `isAllNumeric` functions is shown in Listing 9-1. Notice that both functions have detailed comments that define the function name, description, parameters, and possible return values. The revised HTML document is shown in Listing 9-2.

Listing 9-1. The Validate.js file can include all of your validation functions.

```
// ***********************************************************************
// isNumeric
// Determines whether the first character of an element's value is numeric
// Parameters:
//    e         Element to validate
// Returns:
//    true      If element is numeric
//    false     If the element is not a valid number
function isNumeric(e)
{
   // blank is valid
   if (e.value=="") return true;
   var v = parseFloat(e.value);
   // If not a number, generate an error
   if (isNaN(v))
   {
      alert("The entry in " + e.name + " must be numeric");
      return false;
   }else{
      return true;
   }
}


// ***********************************************************************
// isAllNumeric
// Determines whether every character of an element's value is numeric
// Parameters:
//    e         Element to validate
// Returns:
//    true      If element is numeric
//    false     If the element is not a valid number
function isAllNumeric(e)
{
   // blank is valid
   if (e.value=="") return true;
   var numericExp=/^\d+$/;
   if (numericExp.test(e.value))
   {
      return true;
   }else{
```

```
            alert("The entry in " + e.name + " must be numeric");
            return false;
        }
    }
}
```

Listing 9-2. The input element in the TrainingMailingList.htm calls the validation function as the user leaves the field.

```
<!DOCTYPE html PUBLIC "-//W3C//DTD XHTML 1.0 Strict//EN" "DTD/xhtml1-strict.dtd">
<html>
<!--
    Try It   9-1
    Title:   Mailing List
    Author: InStep Technologies
            www.insteptech.com
    Purpose:To demonstrate field-level validation
 -->
<head>
<title>InStep Mailing List</title>
<meta http-equiv="Content-Script-Type" content="text/javascript" />
<link rel="stylesheet" type="text/css" href="TrainingStyle.css" />
<style type="text/css">
<!--
input {
    font-size:12pt;
    color:navy
    }
tr {
    font-size:12pt;
    color:navy;
    height:30px
    }
tr.rowButton {
    height:50px
    }
button.rowButton {
    font-size:14pt;
    color:navy;
    height:40px
    }
-->
</style>
<script type="text/javascript" src="Validate.js">
</script>
```

```
</head>
<body>
<h1>InStep Mailing List</h1>
<p class="normal">
    When you sign up for our mailing list, we'll keep you up to date with the
     courses that we offer.
</p>
<form id="MailingList" method="get" action="">
    <table>
      <tr>
         <td align="right">
            <label for="FirstName">First Name:</label>
         </td>
         <td align="left">
            <input type="text" id="FirstName"  name="FirstName" size="20"
               maxlength="40" />
         </td>
         <td align="right">
            <label for="LastName">Last Name:</label>
         </td>
         <td align="left">
            <input type="text" id="LastName" name="LastName" size="20"
               maxlength="40" />
         </td>
      </tr>
      <tr>
         <td align="right">
            <label for="Email">E-mail Address:</label>
         </td>
         <td align="left">
            <input type="text" id="Email"  name="Email" size="28" />
         </td>
         <td> </td>
         <td> </td>
      </tr>
      <tr>
         <td align="right">
            <label for="Referral">How did you hear about our site?</label>
         </td>
         <td align="left">
            <select id="Referral" name="Referral">
               <option value="Empty" />
               <option value="Surfing">I found it while surfing the Web</option>
               <option value="Conference">It was mentioned at a conference</option>
```

```
                <option value="Person">I heard about it from a friend</option>
              </select>
          </td>
          <td> </td>
          <td> </td>
        </tr>
        <tr>
          <td align="right" colspan="3">
            <label for="Attendees">
                Number of people at your location that may want training:
            </label>
          </td>
          <td align="left">
            <input type="text" id="Attendees" name="Attendees" size="2"
                maxlength="2" onblur="isAllNumeric(this);" />
          </td>
        </tr>
        <tr class="rowButton">
          <td> </td>
          <td colspan="3" align="center">
              <button class="rowButton" type="submit" name="Save" value="Save">
                Add me to your mailing list
              </button>
          </td>
        </tr>
    </table>
</form>
<p class="normal">
  We will not sell or use this information for anything
   but its intended purpose.
</p>
</body>
</html>
```

Performing Form-Level Validation

Instead of validating each value as the user leaves the field, you may want to validate all of the fields at one time. You can then notify the user once about all of the data-entry validation errors instead of presenting the errors one at a time.

There are many different ways to perform form-level validation. You can write a function that calls the correct validation function for each field on the form. You can add a specific keyword to the end of each field's name or ID and then iterate through the fields looking for that keyword. You can get really complex and create your own JavaScript objects, giving them new properties and methods to support validation. The script code for many of these techniques is available from the links listed in the "Additional Resources" section of this chapter.

The form-level validation technique presented in this chapter adds validation attributes to each field and then iterates through each field on the form and validates it.

Iterating through the Elements on a Form

Many of the techniques used to perform form-level validation require that you iterate or loop through all of the fields of the form.

The Document Object Model (DOM), presented in Chapter 7, "Understanding Object Models," provides an easy way to iterate through a form's fields. The DOM form object has an elements property that defines the collection of elements on a form. This collection defines all of the data-entry elements defined within the form element tags. These elements are referred to as the *controls* or *fields* on the form. You can iterate through the collection of these elements to validate each field within one routine.

NOTE *Internet Explorer includes all data-entry elements in the* elements *collection, including hidden fields. Netscape includes all data-entry elements, hidden fields, and all labels in the* elements *collection.*

For example, the following code iterates through all of the elements on a form and displays each element's name and type in an alert box:

```
1   function validate(f)
2   {
3       // Check each element on the form
4       var str="";
5       for (var i=0; i<f.length; i++)
6       {
7           var e = f.elements[i];
8           str += "Element name is: " + e.name + " Type is: " + e.type + "\n";
9       }
10      window.alert(str);
11  }
```

The function in this case is called `validate` because ultimately it will be the function that validates the elements on the form (line ❶). Currently, however, it only iterates through the form elements and displays their values in an alert box for debugging purposes.

The function parameter is the form itself. Every element in the `elements` collection for this form will ultimately be validated in this function.

The first line of the body of this function is a comment that provides documentation. A variable is then declared and initialized (line ❹) to hold the string that will be displayed in the alert box.

The `for` loop (❺ through ❾) uses the `length` property of the form to determine the number of elements in the `elements` collection. This loop repeats for each element on the form.

Each form element is individually retrieved from the form's `elements` collection (line ❼). The element name and type are then concatenated onto a string to be displayed in the alert box (line ❽). The `\n` syntax inserts a new line after each element. After the loop is complete, the resulting string is displayed in the alert box (line ❿).

This code loops through the elements on the form, but does not validate any of them. To validate the elements, the code needs to call the correct validate function depending on the validation required by the particular element. For example, a name field may not require validation, but a field for the number of people attending a course should have numeric validation. To complete this code, you need some way to associate a particular field on the form with the desired validation for that field.

Associating Validation with a Field

When iterating through all of a form's fields for form-level validation, the `validate` function needs to know which type of validation to perform for each field. You need a way to associate the desired validation with each field on the form.

Browsing through JavaScript Web sites (using the links from the "Additional Resources" section of this chapter), you will find many different ways to associate validation with a field on the form.

One way to associate the type of validation with a particular field on the form is to define a keyword for each type of validation and then concatenate the keyword onto the field element's `name` or `id` attribute, such as:

```
<input type="text" id="AttendeesNumeric" name="Attendees" size="2"
   maxlength="2" />
```

The `validate` function can then parse the `id` attribute of each field to extract the keyword and call the appropriate validation function. This technique is relatively easy but may not be clear to someone maintaining the Web application.

It also ties the validation logic to HTML code that may be created by a visual designer. This becomes even more complex if you want to perform multiple types of validation on a single field:

```
<input type="text" id="AttendeesRequiredNumericRange" name="Attendees" size="2"
   maxlength="2" />
```

A similar but more straightforward technique for associating validation with a field on the form is to explicitly add attributes to the field's element in the HTML document. You can define your own attributes for any HTML elements. For example, you can add a `numeric` attribute for an `input` element to define the element as numeric. You can add a `required` attribute to any field's element to identify the field as required. You can add your own `min` and `max` attributes to an `input` element to define the smallest and largest possible value for a numeric entry.

To add your own attributes to an HTML element, simply type the attribute into the element's beginning tag, just like any other attribute:

```
<input type="text" id="Attendees" name="Attendees" size="2"
   maxlength="2" required="true" numeric="true" />
```

This technique makes the `validate` function simple; the function can refer to any attribute of the element using syntax such as `e.numeric`. However, this technique is not XHMTL-compliant against the strict Document Type Definition (DTD) as discussed in Chapter 3, "Using HTML."

The form-level validation technique presented in this chapter uses the DOM to add attributes to the elements. Using JavaScript and the DOM to add your own validation attributes rather than adding them into the HTML ensures that the HTML itself remains XHTML compliant against the strict DTD. This technique also separates the validation logic from the HTML code that a visual designer may create.

The DOM provides a `setAttribute` method that adds attributes to any element in an HTML document. You can use the `setAttribute` method to add your own validation attributes to any field elements on the form. For example:

```
❶  function doValidation(f)
❷  {
❸     document.getElementById("Attendees").setAttribute("numeric","true");
❹     var result = validate(f);
❺     return result;
❻  }
```

This function sets the desired validation attributes for each field on the form that needs to be validated. This function is unique to a form, so it would reside within the HTML document, not within the generic JavaScript validate file.

In this example, only the field with the element id of `Attendees` needs validation. This adds a `numeric` attribute to the Attendees field and sets the value of that attribute to `true` (line ❸). If other fields require validation or if this field requires additional validation, additional `setAttribute` statements would be added here.

The `doValidation` function then calls the generic `validate` function to validate the fields (line ❹).

So far, the `validate` function simply loops through the elements and displays an alert box. This function needs to be changed to use the new attributes and call the appropriate validation function:

```
❶  function validate(f)
❷  {
❸     for (var i=0; i<f.length; i++)
❹     {
❺        var e = f.elements[i];
❻        var numeric = e.getAttribute("numeric");
❼        if (numeric)
❽        {
❾            if (!isAllNumeric(e)) return false;
❿        }
⓫     }
⓬     return true;
⓭  }
```

This function loops through all of the elements in the `elements` collection on a form (line ❸). Each data-entry element is retrieved from the `elements` collection (line ❺) and checked for the custom `numeric` attribute (line ❻). If this attribute is set to `true`, this function calls the `isAllNumeric` function (line ❾) that was defined earlier in this chapter. If the value was not all numeric, this function returns `false`. Otherwise it returns `true` (line ⓬).

This function works with any form, so you can insert this code into the JavaScript file containing your other generic validation functions.

Putting It All Together

So far, you created JavaScript functions to perform the specific validation, defined attributes for the validation types, and used those attributes to call the correct validation functions. Now you need to put all of these techniques together to validate a form.

The basic steps for adding form-level validation for your forms are:

1. Define the types of validation that your Web application must perform. Define a name for each type of validation that you can use as the validation attribute name; for example, `required` and `numeric`.

2. Write JavaScript functions to perform the desired validation and insert them in an external JavaScript file.

3. Add a `validate` function to the JavaScript validation file that iterates through all of the elements of a form and calls the appropriate validation function.

4. Ensure that a `meta` element specifying JavaScript as your scripting language is inserted in the header section of each HTML document that must be validated.

5. Add the `script` element tags in the header section of the HTML document and reference the JavaScript file containing your validation code.

6. Add a `doValidation` function in the header section of the HTML document that associates the appropriate validation attributes with the elements on the form and calls the `validate` function.

7. Call the `doValidation` function from the `form` element's `onsubmit` event handler.

This section has covered all but the last step:

```
<form id="MailingList" method="get" action=""
    onsubmit="return doValidation(this);">
```

The `form` element's `onsubmit` event handler attribute calls the `doValidation` function and passes `this`, which is always the current object. The event handler in this case is in the `form` element, so `this` represents the `form`. The `doValidation` function returns `true` if all of the elements on the form are valid and `false` if any element on the form fails any of the validation tests.

The `return` statement before the call to the `doValidation` function takes the return value of the `doValidation` function and returns it to the `onsubmit` event handler. If the `doValidation` function returns `true`, the submit occurs as usual. If the `doValidation` function returns `false`, the submit is automatically cancelled. This is desirable behavior because the goal of client-side validation is to prevent the submission to the Web server until the fields on the form are valid.

Try It 9-2.

This Try It replaces the field-level validation in the Mailing List page from Try It 9-1 with form-level validation.

1. Open the Validate.js file from Try It 9-1 in a text editor.

2. Add a validate function that loops through the elements on the form and calls the appropriate validation function based on the validation attributes.

3. Save the file.

4. Open the TrainingMailingList.htm file from Try It 9-1 in your HTML editing tool.

5. Add a script element to the header section of the Mailing List page and create a doValidation function within this element. This function should set appropriate validation attributes for elements on the form.

6. Call the doValidation function using the onsubmit event handler of the form element.

7. Remove the validation function call from the onblur event handler of the input element. This removes the field-level validation added in Try It 9-1.

8. Save the file.

9. Open the TrainingMailingList.htm file in your browser. Try entering a nonnumeric value. Try a numeric value. Try combination values.

10. Experiment with defining other validation attributes and functions using JavaScript.

If your validation is not working, check your use of uppercase and lowercase, = vs ==, and missing semicolons. These are the most common errors in JavaScript code.

The new function in the JavaScript file is shown in Listing 9-3. Since the other functions in that file were not changed, they are not included in this listing. The revised HTML document is shown in Listing 9-4.

Listing 9-3. This code snippet from the Validate.js file presents the code required to iterate through and validate all of the elements of a form.

```
// **********************************************************************
// validate
// Validation for elements in a form
```

```
// Parameters:
//   f       Form being validated. Normally passed as (this)
// Returns:
//   true    If all elements on the form are valid
//   false   If any element fails validation
function validate(f)
{
   // Check each element on the form
   for (var i=0; i<f.length; i++)
   {
      var e = f.elements[i];
      var numeric = e.getAttribute("numeric");
      if (numeric)
      {
         if (!isAllNumeric(e)) return false;
      }
   }
   return true;
}
```

Listing 9-4. The validation required for this form is defined in one routine in TrainingMailingList.htm. This routine is called when the form is submitted.

```
<!DOCTYPE html PUBLIC "-//W3C//DTD XHTML 1.0 Strict//EN" "DTD/xhtml1-strict.dtd">
<html>
<!--
   Try It  9-2
   Title:  Mailing List
   Author: InStep Technologies
           www.insteptech.com
   Purpose:To demonstrate validating all of the elements on a form
 -->
<head>
<title>InStep Mailing List</title>
<meta http-equiv="Content-Script-Type" content="text/javascript" />
<link rel="stylesheet" type="text/css" href="TrainingStyle.css" />
<style type="text/css">
<!--
input {
   font-size:12pt;
   color:navy
   }
```

```
tr {
   font-size:12pt;
   color:navy;
   height:30px
   }
tr.rowButton {
   height:50px
   }
button.rowButton {
   font-size:14pt;
   color:navy;
   height:40px
   }
-->
</style>
<script type="text/javascript" src="Validate.js">
</script>
<script type="text/javascript">
   // Any fields requiring special validation have their validation defined here
   function doValidation(f)
   {
      document.getElementById("Attendees").setAttribute("numeric","true");
      var result = validate(f);
      return result;
   }
</script>
</head>
<body>
<h1>InStep Mailing List</h1>
<p class="normal">
   When you sign up for our mailing list, we'll keep you up to date with the
     courses that we offer.
</p>
<form id="MailingList" method="get" action=""
   onsubmit="return doValidation(this);">
   <table>
      <tr>
         <td align="right">
            <label for="FirstName">First Name:</label>
         </td>
         <td align="left">
            <input type="text" id="FirstName"  name="FirstName" size="20"
               maxlength="40" />
         </td>
```

```
   <td align="right">
      <label for="LastName">Last Name:</label>
   </td>
   <td align="left">
      <input type="text" id="LastName" name="LastName" size="20"
         maxlength="40" />
   </td>
</tr>
<tr>
   <td align="right">
      <label for="Email">E-mail Address:</label>
   </td>
   <td align="left">
      <input type="text" id="Email"  name="Email" size="28" />
   </td>
   <td> </td>
   <td> </td>
</tr>
<tr>
   <td align="right">
      <label for="Referral">How did you hear about our site?</label>
   </td>
   <td align="left">
      <select id="Referral" name="Referral">
         <option value="Empty" />
         <option value="Surfing">I found it while surfing the Web</option>
         <option value="Conference">It was mentioned at a conference</option>
         <option value="Person">I heard about it from a friend</option>
      </select>
   </td>
   <td> </td>
   <td> </td>
</tr>
<tr>
   <td align="right" colspan="3">
     <label for="Attendees">
        Number of people at your location that may want training:
      </label>
  </td>
   <td align="left">
     <input type="text" id="Attendees" name="Attendees" size="2"
        maxlength="2" />
  </td>
</tr>
```

```
        <tr class="rowButton">
           <td> </td>
           <td colspan="3" align="center">
              <button class="rowButton" type="submit" name="Save" value="Save">
                 Add me to your mailing list
              </button>
           </td>
        </tr>
     </table>
</form>
<p class="normal">
   We will not sell or use this information for anything
    but its intended purpose.
</p>
</body>
</html>
```

Notifying the User When an Element Is Invalid

Part of the purpose of validation is notifying the user that something is wrong. There are lots of different ways to do this, with pros and cons for each.

One common option is to display a message box. There are several reasons why this is *not* your best choice. First, it interrupts the flow of the application by requiring that the user stop to read the message. Second, users are so used to being annoyed by message boxes, they may dismiss it without even reading it. But more importantly, the user cannot make corrections while the box is displayed. So if the user has made more than one error, there is no way to see the list of errors while making the changes.

A better option is to provide a visual clue on the page regarding any errors. You can do this by changing the color of the label or of the background of the element itself. You can add a generic function to add this visual clue as part of your generic JavaScript validation file:

```
❶  function generateErrorMessage(e,str)
❷  {
❸     e.style.backgroundColor = "orangered";
❹     return ("* " + e.name + str + "\n");
❺  }
```

This function has two parameters (line ❶), the element being validated and the desired message string. This function changes the background color of the invalid element to an orange-red color (line ❸), but you could use any color. It then returns the formatted error message string (line ❹).

By encapsulating this code within a function, you can easily change how you are handling the visual clue or the error messages without having to rewrite a lot of code.

Each validation function no longer needs to display a message to the user. Instead, the validate function handles the error messages. This is a better technique because the error messages are handled in one function instead of in each validation function, making the messages easier to review and modify.

The validate function handles the error messages by creating one large string with all of the message contents:

```
❶   function validate(f)
❷   {
❸     var msg = "";
❹     for (var i=0; i<f.length; i++)
❺     {
❻       var e = f.elements[i];
❼       // Ensure the background starts out as white
❽       if (e.style.backgroundColor) e.style.backgroundColor = "white";
❾       var numeric = e.getAttribute("numeric");
❿       if (numeric)
⓫       {
⓬         if (!isNumeric(e))
⓭         {
⓮             msg += generateErrorMessage(e, " must be a number.");
⓯             continue;
⓰         }
⓱       }
⓲     }
⓳     if (!msg) return true;
⓴     return msg;
㉑   }
```

The msg variable (line ❸) will contain any of the error messages. As this function iterates through each element on the form (line ❹), the background color is first changed to white (line ❽). This is to ensure any elements changed to orange-red are changed back before they are validated, allowing the user to correct a problem and resubmit.

If the field has the numeric attribute set (line ❾), the field is validated to ensure it is numeric (line ⓬). If the field is not numeric (line ⓬), the generic generateErrorMessage function is called and the error text for the field is appended to the msg variable (line ⓮). The continue statement causes the loop to continue with its next iteration (line ⓯). When all of the elements are validated, the function returns `true` if all fields were valid (line ⓲) or the message text if there was any error (line ⓳).

The `validate` function returns the error message if there is an error. So the JavaScript code within the HTML document that calls this `validate` function needs to display this message. This message could be shown in an alert box, but it is nicer to have a place on the form to report the messages.

In this example, the messages are reported at the bottom of the Web page as shown in Figure 9-1.

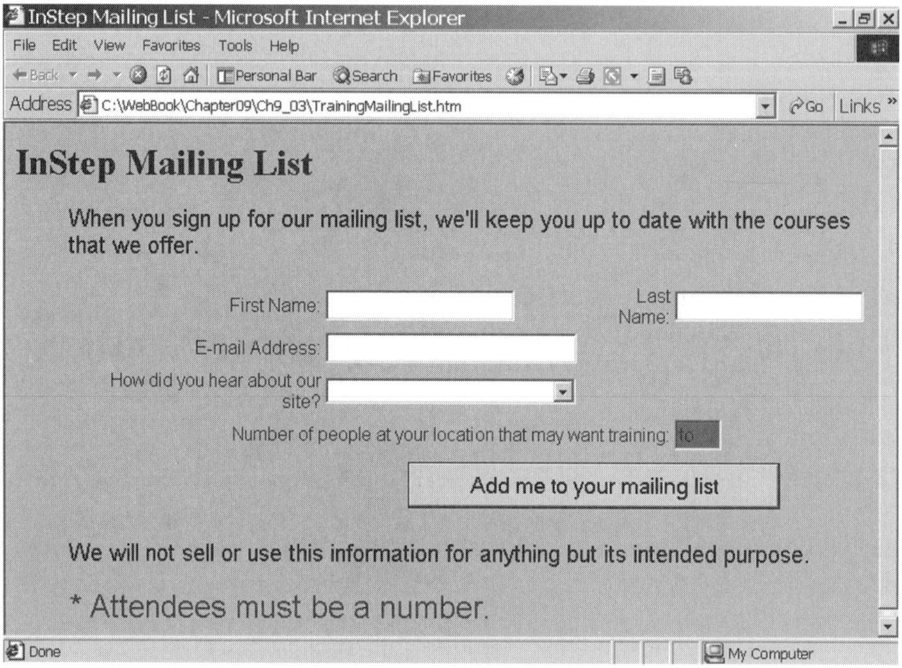

Figure 9-1. When the user has entered something incorrectly, the fields are highlighted and the error message(s) appears on the bottom of the form.

To display the message, you first need to add an element to the Web page for the message text:

```
<p id="Error" class="key"></p>
```

This element must have an `id` attribute so it can be referenced by the JavaScript code that inserts the error text into this element:

```
❶   function doValidation(f)
❷   {
❸       document.getElementById("Attendees").setAttribute("numeric","true");
❹       var result = validate(f);
❺       if (result==true) return true;
❻       document.getElementById("Error").innerHTML = result;
❼       return false;
❽   }
```

The `validate` function now returns a result that is `true` if all of the fields are valid or the error string if there is an error (line ❹). If the result is `true`, there was no error so the `validate` function returns `true` (line ❺). Otherwise, the error string is assigned to the paragraph with the `id` attribute set to `"Error"` (line ❻) and this function returns `false` (line ❼).

Try It 9-3.

Adding Error Text to Form-Level Validation

This Try It adds error text to the Mailing List page from Try It 9-2 to display the errors resulting from the form-level validation.

1. Open the Validate.js file from Try It 9-2 in a text editor.

2. Add a JavaScript function that handles an error by setting the background color of an invalid element and building an error string.

3. Modify the validate function to call the function created in step 2.

4. Remove the alert boxes from the other validation functions.

5. Save the file.

6. Open the TrainingMailingList.htm file from Try It 9-2 in your HTML editing tool.

7. Add an element to the form that displays the error text. Either p or div elements are the most common to use for this purpose. Be sure to set the id attribute of this element.

8. Modify the doValidation function to display the error text if there is an error.

9. Save the file.

10. Open the TrainingMailingList.htm file in your browser. Try entering a nonnumeric value and clicking on the submit button. Your error text should appear at the bottom of the form.

If your validation is not working, check your use of uppercase and lowercase, = vs ==, and missing semicolons. These are the most common errors in JavaScript code.

The entire JavaScript file is shown in Listing 9-5 because of the numerous changes to this file. The entire HTML document is shown in Listing 9-6.

Listing 9-5. The Validate.js file contains all of the generic validation code for your Web applications. You can add any other validation routines you need to this file.

```
// ***********************************************************************
// validate
// Validation for elements in a form
// Parameters:
// f        Form being validated. Normally passed as (this)
// Returns:
//   true    If all elements on the form are valid
//   false   If any element fails validation
function validate(f)
{
   var msg = "";
   // Check each element on the form
   for (var i=0; i<f.length; i++)
   {
      var e = f.elements[i];
      // Ensure the background starts out as white
      if (e.style.backgroundColor) e.style.backgroundColor = "white";
      var numeric = e.getAttribute("numeric");
      if (numeric)
      {
           if (!isNumeric(e))
           {
              msg += generateErrorMessage(e, " must be a number.");
              continue;
           }
      }
   }
   if (!msg) return true;
   return msg;
}
// ***********************************************************************
```

```javascript
// isNumeric
// Determines whether the first character of an element's value is numeric
// Parameters:
//   e          Element to validate
// Returns:
//   true       If element is numeric
//   false      If the element is not a valid number
function isNumeric(e)
{
    // blank is valid
    if (e.value=="") return true;
    var v = parseFloat(e.value);
    // If not a number, generate an error
    if (isNaN(v)) return false;
    return true;
}
// ***********************************************************************
// isAllNumeric
// Determines whether every character of an element's value is numeric
// Parameters:
//   e          Element to validate
// Returns:
//   true       If element is numeric
//   false      If the element is not a valid number
function isAllNumeric(e)
{
    // blank is valid
    if (e.value=="") return true;
    var numericExp=/^\d+$/;
    if (numericExp.test(e.value)) return true;
    return false;
}
// ***********************************************************************
// generateErrorMessage
// Marks an element as an error and defines an error message
// Parameters:
//   e          Element to set
//   str        Message string
// Returns:
//     Message string
function generateErrorMessage(e,str)
{
    e.style.backgroundColor = "orangered";
    return ("* " + e.name + str + "\n");
}
```

Listing 9-6. The TrainingMailingList.htm file displays any validation error messages at the bottom of the form.

```
<!DOCTYPE html PUBLIC "-//W3C//DTD XHTML 1.0 Strict//EN" "DTD/xhtml1-strict.dtd">
<html>
<!--
   Try It  9-3
   Title:  Mailing List
   Author: InStep Technologies
           www.insteptech.com
   Purpose:To demonstrate adding error text to the page
 -->
<head>
<title>InStep Mailing List</title>
<meta http-equiv="Content-Script-Type" content="text/javascript" />
<link rel="stylesheet" type="text/css" href="TrainingStyle.css" />
<style type="text/css">
<!--
input {
   font-size:12pt;
   color:navy
   }
tr {
   font-size:12pt;
   color:navy;
   height:30px
   }
tr.rowButton {
   height:50px
   }
button.rowButton {
   font-size:14pt;
   color:navy;
   height:40px
   }
-->
</style>
<script type="text/javascript" src="Validate.js">
</script>
<script type="text/javascript">
   // Any fields requiring special validation have their validation defined here
```

```
    function doValidation(f)
    {
        document.getElementById("Attendees").setAttribute("numeric","true");
        var result = validate(f);
        if (result==true) return true;
        document.getElementById("Error").innerHTML = result;
        return false;
    }
</script>
</head>
<body>
<h1>InStep Mailing List</h1>
<p class="normal">
    When you sign up for our mailing list, we'll keep you up to date with the
     courses that we offer.
</p>
<form id="MailingList" method="get" action=""
    onsubmit="return doValidation(this);">
    <table>
        <tr>
            <td align="right">
                <label for="FirstName">First Name:</label>
            </td>
            <td align="left">
                <input type="text" id="FirstName"  name="FirstName" size="20"
                    maxlength="40" />
            </td>
            <td align="right">
                <label for="LastName">Last Name:</label>
            </td>
            <td align="left">
                <input type="text" id="LastName" name="LastName" size="20"
                    maxlength="40" />
            </td>
        </tr>
        <tr>
            <td align="right">
                <label for="Email">E-mail Address:</label>
            </td>
            <td align="left">
                <input type="text" id="Email"  name="Email" size="28" />
            </td>
            <td> </td>
            <td> </td>
        </tr>
```

```
        <tr>
          <td align="right">
            <label for="Referral">How did you hear about our site?</label>
          </td>
          <td align="left">
            <select id="Referral" name="Referral">
              <option value="Empty" />
              <option value="Surfing">I found it while surfing the Web</option>
              <option value="Conference">It was mentioned at a conference</option>
              <option value="Person">I heard about it from a friend</option>
            </select>
          </td>
          <td> </td>
          <td> </td>
        </tr>
        <tr>
          <td align="right" colspan="3">
            <label for="Attendees">
                Number of people at your location that may want training:
            </label>
          </td>
          <td align="left">
            <input type="text" id="Attendees" name="Attendees" size="2"
                maxlength="2" />
          </td>
        </tr>
        <tr class="rowButton">
          <td> </td>
          <td colspan="3" align="center">
            <button class="rowButton" type="submit" name="Save" value="Save">
                Add me to your mailing list
            </button>
          </td>
        </tr>
      </table>
  </form>
  <p class="normal">
    We will not sell or use this information for anything
     but its intended purpose.
  </p>
  <p id="Error" class="key"></p>
  </body>
  </html>
```

Adding Additional Validation Types

Once you have the basic structure of your validation code in place, adding additional validation logic is easy. Just follow these steps:

- Define the type of validation you need to perform; for example, validating for required fields.

- Add a JavaScript function that contains the validation logic; for example, an isEntry function.

- Add a validation attribute for this validation type; for example, required.

- Add code in the validate function to check for this attribute type and call the appropriate validation function.

- Modify any HTML document that needs the validation to set this attribute for each field to be validated.

The order of these steps does not matter, but each step must be performed to ensure that the validation is fully implemented.

Let's follow these steps for required fields and then let you try adding range validation.

Validating Required Fields

Your Web application may require that the user enter values into several of the fields on a form. For example, you may require that the user enter a value into the password field on a login form. In that case, you want a required field validation type to ensure that a value was entered into the required field.

Once the validation type is defined, the next step is to create the isEntry function in the generic JavaScript validation file:

```
function isEntry(e)
{
    var entryExp=/./;
    if (entryExp.test(e.value)) return true;
    return false;
}
```

This uses regular expression pattern matching. The period (.) matches any character. So if the field contains any character, this returns true.

You can define a validation attribute name to be any name that does not conflict with existing attribute names. For required fields, you may want to use a simple name such as `required`. You can then add code to the `validate` function to check for the `required` attribute and call the `isEntry` function:

```
1   var required = e.getAttribute("required");
2   if (required)
3   {
4       (!isEntry(e))
5       {
6           msg+=generateErrorMessage(e," must be entered");
7           continue;
8       }
9   }
```

This code checks the new `required` attribute (line ❶) and if it exists (line ❷) it calls the `isEntry` function (line ❹). If the field does not contain a value, the `isEntry` function returns `false` and the error message is generated (line ❻).

To use this new type of validation, you can set the `required` attribute for any element on any form:

```
document.getElementById("Email").setAttribute("required","true");
```

That's all there is to it.

Try It 9-4.

Adding Range Validation

This Try It adds range validation to the Mailing List page from Try It 9-3.

1. Open the Validate.js file from Try It 9-3 in a text editor.

2. Add a JavaScript function that performs the numeric range validation. This code should ensure that a value is numerically between two other values. The element, min value, and max value can be passed to this function.

3. Modify the `validate` function to call the function created in step 2. Be sure to include a message to display to the user if the value is not within the range.

4. Save the file.

5. Open the TrainingMailingList.htm file from Try It 9-3 in your HTML editing tool.

6. Modify the `doValidation` function to set min and max attributes for the Attendees input field.

7. Save the file.

8. Open the TrainingMailingList.htm file in your browser. Try entering a value outside of the range and clicking on the submit button. Your error text should appear at the bottom of the form.

If your validation is not working, check your use of uppercase and lowercase, = vs ==, and missing semicolons. These are the most common errors in JavaScript code.

The function to perform the range validation and the revised validate function are shown in Listing 9-7. The revised doValidation function in the HTML document is presented in Listing 9-8.

Listing 9-7. Any new validation routines can be added to the Validate.js file as shown in this snippet.

```
// ***************************************************************************
// validate
// Validation for elements in a form
// Parameters:
//   f          Form being validated. Normally passed as (this)
// Returns:
//   true       If all elements on the form are valid
//   false      If any element fails validation
function validate(f)
{
   var msg = "";
   // Check each element on the form
   for (var i=0; i<f.length; i++)
   {
      var e = f.elements[i];
      // Ensure the background starts out as white
      if (e.style.backgroundColor) e.style.backgroundColor = "white";
      // Numeric validation
      var numeric = e.getAttribute("numeric");
      if (numeric)
      {
         if (!isNumeric(e))
         {
            msg+=generateErrorMessage(e, " must be a number.");
            continue;
         }
      }
      // Required field validation
      var required = e.getAttribute("required");
```

```
        if (required)
        {
           if (!isEntry(e))
           {
              msg+=generateErrorMessage(e," must be entered");
              continue;
           }
        }
        // Range validation
        var min=e.getAttribute("min");
        var max=e.getAttribute("max");
        if (min || max)
        {
           if (!isInRange(e,min,max))
           {
              msg+=generateErrorMessage(e,
              " must be between " + min + " and " + max + ".");
              continue;
           }
        }
     }
     if (!msg) return true;
     return msg;
  }
  // ************************************************************************
  // isInRange
  // Determines whether a numeric value
  // is within a given min and max range
  // Parameters:
  //   e          Element to check
  // Returns:
  //   true       If element is in the defined range
  //   false      If the element is not in the defined range
  function isInRange(e,min,max)
  {
     // Convert the value to a number
     var v = parseFloat(e.value);
     // If not a number, generate an error
     if (isNaN(v)) return false;
     if ((min != null) && (v < min))
     {
        return false;
     }
     if ((max != null) && (v > max))
```

```
    {
        return false;
    }
    return true;
}
```

Listing 9-8. None of the HTML code needs to be changed to support new validation types. Only the doValidation function in the TrainingMailingList.htm file needs to be modified.

```
function doValidation(f)
{
    document.getElementById("Email").setAttribute("required","true");
    document.getElementById("Attendees").setAttribute("numeric","true");
    document.getElementById("Attendees").setAttribute("min","1");
    document.getElementById("Attendees").setAttribute("max","12");
    var result = validate(f);
    if (result==true) return true;
    document.getElementById("Error").innerHTML = result;
    return false;
}
```

Regular Expression Reference

As presented earlier in this chapter, a *regular expression* is a pattern of special characters that you can use to manipulate or validate a string. You can use regular expressions to ensure that a phone number is ten digits long or that a Social Security Number is three digits, a dash, two digits, a dash, and four digits.

Table 9-1 lists the most common characters used in regular expressions. Table 9-2 presents the two key flags used with regular expressions.

Table 9-1. Common Regular Expression Characters

CHARACTER	MATCHES	EXAMPLE
\b	Word boundary	\bon matches "on" if it is found at the beginning of a word, such as "Come here **on**ce." on\b matches "on" if it is found at the end of a word, such as "I am a pers**on**." \bon\b matches "on" only if a word in the string is "on" such as "I am **on** top of things."
\B	Non-word boundary	\Bon matches "on" if it is found anywhere but at the beginning of a word, such as "This c**on**tains that."
\d	Digits, 0 through 9	\d matches the first digit in a string, such as "**4**44B Privet Drive."
\D	Non-digit	\D matches the first non-digit anywhere in a string, such as "444**B** Privet Drive."
\s	Space	\s matches the first space, such as "444B▪ Privet Drive."
\S	Non-space	\S matches the first non-space, such as "**4**44B Privet Drive."
\w	Any alphanumeric character, including an under score	\w matches the first alphanumeric or underscore character, such as "**4**44B Privet Drive."
\W	Non-word character	\W matches the first non-alphanumeric or under-score character, such as "444B ▪ Privet Drive."
.	Any character except newline. This is frequently used to determine if the user entered something in a required field.	. matches any character, such as "**4**44B Privet Drive."
[...]	Set of valid characters	[ABC] matches the first occurrence of A, B or C, such as "444**B** Privet Drive."
[^...]	Set of invalid characters	[^ABC] matches the first occurrence of any character except A, B or C, such as "**4**44B Privet Drive."
*	Last character occurs zero or more consecutive times	\d* matches all occurrences of digits, such as "**444**B Privet Drive."
+	Last character occurs one or more times	\d+ matches all occurrences of digits, such as "**444**B Privet Drive."
?	Last character occurs zero or one time	\d? matches zero or 1 occurrences of digits, such as "**4**44B Privet Drive."

Table 9-1. *Common Regular Expression Characters (continued)*

CHARACTER	MATCHES	EXAMPLE
{n}	Last character occurs exactly *n* times	\d{2} matches the first two occurrences of digits, such as "**44**4B Privet Drive."
{n,}	Last character occurs *n* or more times	\d{2,} matches the first two or more occurrences of digits, such as "**444**B Privet Drive."
{n,m}	Last character occurs at least *n*, at most *m* times	\d{1,3} matches the first occurrence and up to three occurrences, such as "**444**B Privet Drive."
^	Pattern occurs at the beginning of the string	^4 matches the number "4" if it is the first character in the string, such as "**4**44B Privet Drive."
$	Pattern occurs at the end of the string	Drive$ matches the word "Drive" if it is at the end of the string, such as "444B Privet **Drive**."
a|b	a OR b	P | Q matches "P" or "Q" such as "444B **P**rivet Drive."

Table 9-2. *Regular Expression Flags*

FLAG	MEANING	EXAMPLE
g	Globally, matches all occurrences of the pattern	/[v]/g globally matches all occurrences of v, such as "444B Pri**v**et Dri**v**e."
i	Is case insensitive	/[p]/i matches both "p" and "P" such as "444B **P**rivet Drive."

See the "Additional Resources" section at the end of this chapter for a reference to a complete list of valid regular expression characters.

You can combine these regular expression characters to define specific matching criteria. For example, for a Social Security Number you would define the following pattern:

```
/^\d{3}-\d{2}-\d{4}$/
```

This pattern starts matching at the beginning of the pattern (^), matches to three digits (\d{3}), a dash (-), two digits (\d{2}), a dash (-), and four digits (\d{4}) to complete the match at the end of the string ($). See "Validation Patterns" later in this chapter for more information on working with patterns.

Validation Tips and Tricks

This section includes basic tips and techniques when working with JavaScript, forms, and validation.

User-Friendly Pages

Here are some tips for creating user-friendly forms with JavaScript.

Use Size and Maxlength Attributes

Several elements on a form, such as text boxes, have size and maxlength attributes. For example:

```
<input type="text" id="Attendees" name="Attendees" size="2"
    maxlength="2" onblur="isAllNumeric(this);" />
```

The size attribute defines how large the data-entry area should be, in this case two characters wide. The maxlength attribute defines how many characters that the user can enter into the field, in this case, two characters.

The size and maxlength attributes can be used to help with validation. The size attribute defines the visual size of the field. This gives the user some visual concept of how large the field entry might be. The maxlength attribute ensures the user does not enter more characters than you are expecting.

Set Focus to an Element

When you display a Web page containing a form, focus is not given to an element on that page. You can try this by loading the TrainingMailingList.htm page in your browser. If you start to type, the characters do not appear in any of the text boxes. It would make it more efficient for the user if focus was set to the first element on the page. You can do that with the following code:

```
<body onload="MailingList.FirstName.focus();">
```

After the form is loaded, the focus is set to the FirstName element on the MailingList form.

 CAUTION *Be careful if you try to put this code into a function. The function must be called after the form and elements on the form are parsed.*

Validation Patterns

This chapter touched on the use of regular expressions to validate user entry. Here are some additional patterns that you may find useful.

Generic Pattern Validation

You may find that you want to validate with many different patterns. You could repeat the pattern validation code in every function that needs it, or simply create a function to validate against a pattern.

The code for a generic pattern matching routine is:

```
function isMatch(str,pattern)
{
    if (pattern.test(str)) return true;
    return false;
}
```

If the provided string matches the defined pattern, the test method of the pattern returns true. Otherwise it is false.

Validating a Phone Number

You can validate that the user has entered a valid phone number. This is not to say that you are verifying the existence of the phone number, but rather that the phone number is in the correct format.

There are two steps to validate information such as a phone number. First, you need to remove any special characters that the user may have entered, parentheses or dashes in a phone number, for example.

The function can then use a regular expression pattern to validate the numbers. The code for a U.S. standard phone number is:

```
❶  // Phone validation
❷  var phone=e.getAttribute("phone");
❸  if (phone)
❹  {
❺      var phonePattern = /^\d{10}$/;
❻      var newPhone = e.value.replace(/[^0-9]/g,"");
```

```
⑦    if (!isMatch(newPhone,phonePattern))
⑧    {
⑨        msg+=generateErrorMessage(e, " must be a phone number with area code.");
⑩      continue;
⑪    }
⑫ }
```

This function assumes you defined a new attribute called phone (line ②). If a particular element has a phone attribute (line ③), the function uses a regular expression to define a pattern for a valid phone number (line ⑤). The pattern defines that the phone number must be 10 digits. The caret (^) and dollar sign ($) define that the entire value must match the pattern and the \d{10} syntax specifies that the pattern is expecting ten digits.

The user may enter other characters into the phone number, such as parentheses or dashes. To ignore these extra characters, this function removes any character that is not a digit using the string object replace method (line ⑥). The [^0-9] syntax replaces any character that is not a digit. The g in this replacement pattern defines that the replacement occurs globally throughout the pattern, replacing every non-digit character. The second parameter to the replace method defines what the non-digit characters are replaced with. In this case, the value is an empty string to remove all non-digit characters.

After the non-digits are removed from the user-entered string, the string is compared with the pattern using the isMatch function (line ⑦) created earlier in this section. If there is not a match, an error is generated (line ⑨).

You can use this same basic technique to validate any types of patterns.

What Did This Cover?

This chapter provided details on validating a form using JavaScript. It demonstrated a simple field-level validation example. It then presented a basic framework for performing all of your form-level validation.

Several validation routines were presented including a numeric check and checking for required fields.

The Try Its in this chapter modified the Mailing List example to use the JavaScript validation code.

The next chapter presents how to save the user-entered values onto the user's computer using JavaScript.

Additional Resources

This section provides some additional resource suggestions by way of books, articles, and links to Web resources.

The books, articles, and links all existed at the time of this writing. There is a good chance that the books and articles still exist as you read this. However, the same cannot be said of Web links. Ignore the suggested links if they no longer exist.

Books and Articles

Negrino, Tom and Smith, Dori. *JavaScript for the World Wide Web*. Berkeley, CA: Peachpit Press, 1999.

There is an entire section of this book devoted to verifying forms. These techniques build upon the techniques presented here.

Links

`http://javascript.internet.com/forms/`: This site provides many pre-built scripts that you can use with forms. These scripts handle validation and other form-based processing such as adding commas to numeric entries, converting entries to uppercase, and so on.

`http://msdn.microsoft.com/library/periodic/period99/valid.htm`: This article provides a good description and examples of using regular expressions for validation.

CHAPTER 10

Saving Data
with Cookies

MOST WEB APPLICATIONS store data in a database that resides on a Web server. This allows multiple users to process and share that data. For example, a course registration application would store the list of courses and the people enrolled in those courses in a database on the Web server. However, there may be times when you want to save user-specific data on the user's computer. Instead of a database, you can store user-specific data in cookies.

You can use cookies to store a user's ID and password for automatic login to your application. You can use cookies to save how the user has configured a particular page of your application. You can use cookies to track all of the items the user has selected to purchase or download. You can store and retrieve user preferences such as frequently used selection criteria or defined report formats.

The purpose of this chapter is to provide you with the basics you need to store information in and retrieve information from cookies on the user's computer. This chapter builds upon the JavaScript techniques presented in the prior two chapters to first create the cookies and then reference them within your Web application.

What Will This Cover?

This chapter covers the following key cookie concepts:

- Understanding the basics of using cookies

- Storing data in cookies

- Retrieving data from cookies

- Managing state with cookies

- Using cookies to share data between pages

- Understanding security issues regarding cookies

- Alternatives to cookies for managing state

By the end of this chapter, you'll know how to use JavaScript to store data in and retrieve data from cookies. You will also learn how to use cookies to share data between the pages of your application.

Cookie Basics

With a technology term like "cookies" to work with, how can you help but to have some fun? Shall we bake our first cookies? How about some java with those cookies? Before we take our first bite, let's look at what cookies are in this context.

Cookies are the mechanism provided by the Web browser that allows scripting, such as JavaScript, to store and retrieve information on the user's computer.

> **NOTE**   *The term "cookie" is a short version of the phrase "magic cookie," which is an old computer term meaning a small set of data with a "magical" purpose. The term primarily refers to little bits of data that an application may create and later reference to remember a setting or prior selection. This is considered "magical" because it is hidden from the user (and often from the maintenance programmers!).*

The purpose of cookies is to allow your Web application to store information on the user's computer. That information can then be read from the user's computer by your Web application as the user accesses other pages of your Web application. It can be stored and read again whenever that user accesses that same application or another application in the same domain.

Cookies are frequently used to store specific user settings and preferences. For example, your Web application may want to provide a feature to optionally remember the user's ID and password. If the user selects this feature, the ID and password can be saved in cookies. The next time the user accesses your Web application, the ID and password can be retrieved from the cookies and used to automatically log the user into the application.

> **CAUTION**   *Storing cookies with IDs and passwords can pose a security issue. See "Cookies and Security" later in this chapter for more information.*

As another example, your Web application could allow the user to select date ranges and sort criteria for a Web page that displays report information. You could save the user's selections in a cookie so the same dates and criteria are used the next time the user accesses that same report page.

There are tools you can use to view the cookies that are stored on your computer. In Internet Explorer you can view cookies choosing Tools and then Internet Options, and then clicking on the Settings button and then on the View Files button. You can see all of the temporary Internet files. Each cookie file has `cookie:` as the first part of the Internet Address. To view the contents of the cookie file, double-click on the filename, and the file appears as shown in Figure 10-1. Alternatively, you can find the cookies in a directory such as: `Documents and Settings\`*username*`\Cookies` where *username* is the name used to log into the computer.

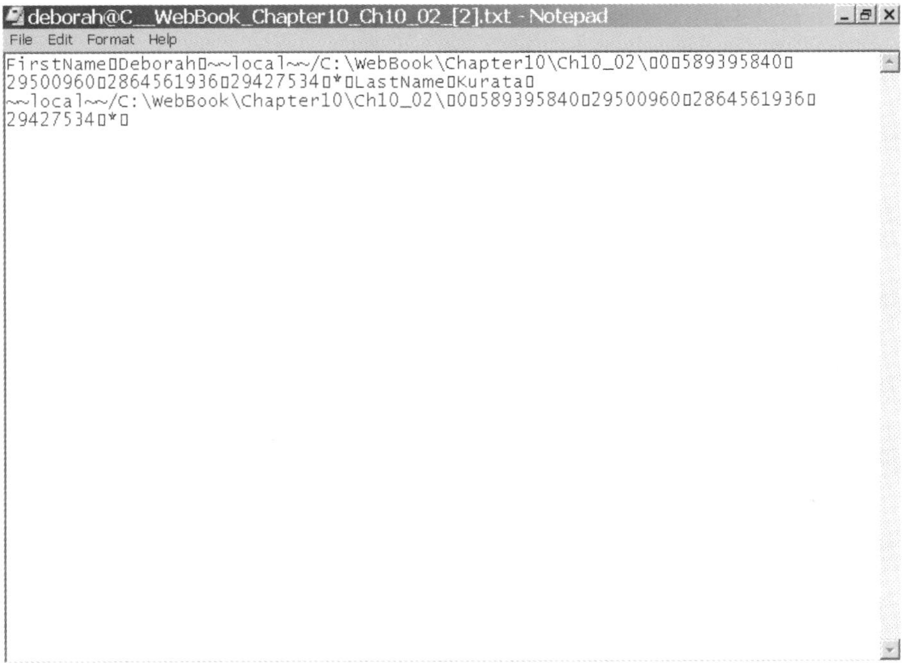

Figure 10-1. The cookie file presented in Internet Explorer contains recognizable text but much of the file is not human readable in this format.

Netscape 6 provides a more user-friendly display of your cookies and their contents, as shown in Figure 10-2. To see these cookies, choose Tasks, then Privacy and Security, then Cookie Manager, and View Stored Cookies.

Cookie Manager ☒

Stored Cookies	Cookie Sites

View and Remove Cookies that are stored on your computer.

Site	Cookie Name
	FirstName
	LastName
bcentral.com	MC1
cnet.com	aid
cnet.com	s_cur_1_0
exnedia.com	MC1

Information about the selected Cookie

Name:	FirstName
Information:	Deborah
Host:	
Path:	/C|/WebBook/Chapter
Server Secure:	No
Expires:	Sun Jul 07 18:41:24 2

[Remove Cookie]   [Remove All Cookies]

☐ Don't allow removed cookies to be reaccepted later

[OK]   [Cancel]

Figure 10-2. Click on any cookie to see the details. The cookie information provided by Netscape is much more user friendly than looking at the cookie file in Internet Explorer.

As you can see from Figure 10-2, every cookie has a name. To better remember the name of the cookie when you need to retrieve it, the name should be descriptive of the cookie contents. For example, you could use FirstName for the first name of the user.

The data associated with the cookie is the cookie value, called *Information* in Figure 10-2. If you have multiple pieces of data to store, such as a set of report criteria, you can store each piece of data in a separate cookie, each with a unique name. Alternatively, you can concatenate all of the pieces of data into one string and assign that string to a single cookie.

NOTE   *Cookie values cannot contain special characters such as semicolons, commas, or spaces. If the value contains any of these characters, you must encode the value to convert these special characters. JavaScript provides a function you can use to perform this conversion as shown later in this chapter.*

Optionally, a cookie can have an expiration date (see *Expires* in Figure 10-2). The expiration date defines how long the cookie resides on the user's computer. The cookie is automatically deleted when it expires. This expiration date is normally defined in Greenwich Mean Time (GMT), the base of international time zones. If the cookie does not have an expiration date, it is temporary and expires when the browser is closed. Temporary cookies are not written to the user's computer but are stored in memory during the session. Temporary cookies are most commonly used to share data between pages of a Web application when that data does not need to persist after the user exits the application.

For example, when the user logs in you could store the user's name in a temporary cookie, that is, a cookie with no expiration date. Any other page in the Web application could retrieve the name from the cookie and use it where needed. So a later page in the application could display text such as: "Welcome, Dave" or "Thank you for your order, Dave." If the user exits the browser and later returns to the application, the user would need to log in again because the login information was temporary and not stored on the user's computer.

A cookie can explicitly define how it shares its data. If you specify a domain when you create the cookie (for example, `insteptech.com`), a cookie can share its data with any page on any server in that domain. This is called *Site* in Figure 10-2. Note that you cannot specify a domain other than the domain of the Web server running the Web application.

NOTE   *No Site was listed in Figure 10-2 for the* `FirstName` *and* `LastName` *cookies because these cookies were created using a Web application running on the client without a Web server. The code to create these cookies is presented later in this chapter.*

If you set a path when you create a cookie (see *Path* in Figure 10-2), the cookie shares its data with any other pages on the same path and any subfolders of that path. If you want your cookies visible to all pages within your Web application (assuming they are all part of the same directory structure), set the path to /, which is the default if you do not specify a path.

NOTE   *A cookie is only accessible to the Web page that created it and any other Web pages in the same domain, same directory, or any subdirectories. This provides a level of security for using cookies in an application.*

You can require that a cookie only be accessed from a secure environment by specifying the secure keyword in the cookie (see *Server Secure* in Figure 10-2). In this case, the cookie can only be transmitted over a Secure Sockets Layer (SSL) connection. The SSL encrypts the cookie data.

All of the information about the cookie including its name, value, expiration date, domain and path specification, and security are stored in a single string:

```
UserName=JessK;expires=Sat, 22 Apr 2002 23:59:59 GMT;domain=Insteptech.com;path=/;secure;
```

When a page of your Web application requests a cookie from the user's computer, you get a single string containing the name and value pairs for all of the cookies that the page has access to based on the domain and path specified in the cookie. Your code then needs to parse the string to find a particular cookie.

You can use a scripting language, such as JavaScript, to store information in and retrieve information from cookies.

Storing Data in Cookies

You can store many different types of data in cookies. You can store the user's identification or preferences. You can keep a count of the number of times the user accessed a particular page of your Web application. You can track the date that the user last accessed your Web application. You can store any information that you need to share between the pages of your application or that you want to persist between uses of your application.

To store data in cookies, you can use the cookie property of the document object. The cookie property is a string that contains the names and values of cookies. Your Web application can set this cookie property using JavaScript.

The following JavaScript code defines a cookie named FirstName with a value of Jessica:

```
document.cookie = "FirstName=Jessica";
```

In this example, the cookie is hard-coded to a particular value. More commonly, the cookie value will be determined as the user works with your Web application. For example, after the user logs into your Web application, your application could store the user-entered ID as a cookie.

The JavaScript required to store any data in a cookie is the same, so you can write a generic function in an external JavaScript file and include a reference to this file in any page that needs to store data in cookies.

The following JavaScript function creates a cookie with the defined name and value. It automatically sets the expiration date to one year from the current date:

```
❶  function setCookie(sName, sValue)
❷  {
❸      var expireDate = new Date;
❹      expireDate.setYear(expireDate.getFullYear() + 1);
❺      document.cookie = sName + "=" + escape(sValue) +
            ";expires=" + expireDate.toGMTString();
❻  }
```

The setCookie function (line ❶) has two parameters: the name of the cookie and the value of the cookie. A Date object is created (line ❸) and set to the current date plus one year (line ❹). This date is the cookie's expiration date.

> **NOTE** *The* getFullYear *function was used instead of the* getYear *function because of a feature of Netscape that incorrectly subtracts 1900 from the date when using* getYear.

The cookie property of the document object is then used to set the cookie (line ❺). The cookie's name and value are obtained from the parameters passed into this function. The built-in JavaScript escape function is used to encode any special characters in the value, such as semicolons, commas, and spaces. The expiration date, set in line ❹, is converted to GMT using the built-in toGMTString function.

Any page in the Web application that needs to set a cookie can use this setCookie function. You can call this function any number of times to create multiple cookies for a page.

If you want to store the user's first name in a cookie when the user enters it, you could call the setCookie function as the user leaves the FirstName field on the form, like this:

```
<input type="text" name="FirstName" size="20" maxlength="40"
onBlur="setCookie('FirstName',FirstName.value);" />
```

This code creates a cookie with the name defined by the first parameter and a value defined by the second parameter, in this case for the user's first name. If you want to store both the first and last name, you can use similar onBlur event handler code in the input element for the LastName.

Just setting cookies doesn't do much unless you are also going to retrieve them. Accessing the cookies once you have stored them is covered in the next topic.

Try It 10-1.

Storing Data in Cookies

Try It 10-1 uses cookies to store the user-entered first and last name from the Mailing List page from Try It 9-4.

1. Create a new text file.

2. In this file, write a JavaScript function to store data in cookies. You can use the setCookie function example from this section.

3. Save the file as Cookies.js.

4. Open the TrainingMailingList.htm file from Try It 9-4 in your HTML editing tool.

5. Add a script element to the header section of the Mailing List page and set the src attribute to the location of the JavaScript file you just created. You can use relative or absolute paths.

6. Call the JavaScript function from the onblur event of the input elements for the first and last name.

7. Save the file.

8. Open the TrainingMailingList.htm file in your browser. Enter the first and last name and then exit the browser.

9. Use the cookie viewing features of your browser to view the cookies that you created (see Figures 10-1 and 10-2).

If the cookies were not created, check your use of uppercase and lowercase letters because JavaScript is case sensitive.

Once the cookies are created, any page of the Web application can retrieve and use them. Since the cookies are given an expiration date, they are stored on the end-user's computer, so you can access them every time the user uses your Web application.

Listing 10-1 displays the contents of the JavaScript file. Listing 10-2 shows the three modifications to the TrainingMailingList.htm file.

Listing 10-1. The Cookies.js file can include all of your cookie functions.

```
// ************************************************************************
// setCookie
// Sets a cookie onto the user's computer
// Parameters:
//      sName    Name of the cookie
//      sValue   Value of the cookie
// Return value:
//      none
function setCookie(sName, sValue)
{
    var expireDate = new Date;
    expireDate.setYear(expireDate.getFullYear() + 1);
    document.cookie = sName + "=" + escape(sValue) +
        ";expires=" + expireDate.toGMTString();
}
```

Listing 10-2. The TrainingMailingList.htm file required three minor changes to create the cookies as shown in these code snippets.

```
. . .
<script language="javascript" src="Cookies.js">
</script>
. . .
<input type="text" name="FirstName" size="20" maxlength="40"
onBlur="setCookie('FirstName',FirstName.value);" />
. . .
<input type="text" name="LastName" size="20" maxlength="40"
onBlur="setCookie('LastName',LastName.value);" />
```

Retrieving Data from Cookies

Once you create some cookies, you may want to retrieve them. You can then use the cookies to provide defaults, adjust the browser based on user preferences, or return the Web application to a specific state. But whatever you do, don't lose your cookies! (Ha-Ha.)

In the prior section, you saw how to use `document.cookie` to store information in cookies. You can also use `document.cookie` to retrieve the cookies. The `cookie` property of the document object returns all of the cookies you created in one long string. For example:

```
FirstName=Jessica; LastName=Jorkins
```

There are no built-in methods for accessing a particular cookie from this string. However, the JavaScript string object has a useful split method that can help you parse the cookies. The split method converts the string containing all of your cookies into an array. You can then iterate through the array to find a particular cookie.

The JavaScript required to retrieve any data from a cookie is generic, so you can write a generic function in an external JavaScript file and include a reference to this file in any page that needs to retrieve data from cookies.

The following function retrieves the cookies, converts them into an array, and iterates through the array until it finds the cookie with the defined name:

```
❶ function getCookie(sName)
❷ {
❸    var arrCookies = document.cookie.split("; ");
❹    for(var i = 0; i < arrCookies.length; i++)
❺    {
❻        if(sName == arrCookies[i].split("=")[0])
❼        {
❽            return unescape(arrCookies[i].split("=")[1]);
❾        }
❿    }
⓫    return ""
⓬ }
```

The getCookie function (line ❶) has one parameter: the name of the cookie to retrieve. The cookie property of the document object returns a single string containing all of the cookies for your Web application, separated by a semicolon and space (;). For example:

```
FirstName=Jessica; LastName=Jorkins
```

The split method converts the string of cookies into an array, using the semicolon and space (;) between the cookies as the delimiter (line ❸). Using the split method on the cookie string above results in two array elements:

ARRAY ELEMENT	CONTENTS
arrCookies[0]	FirstName=Jessica
arrCookies[1]	LastName=Jorkins

The for structure (lines ❹ through ❿) loops through each cookie in the array. For each cookie in the array, the cookie name passed in to this function is compared with the name of the cookie from the array (line ❻). This code also uses the split method, this time splitting the cookie name from the cookie value using the equal sign (=) as the parameter. This creates another array within the arrCookies array, for example:

ARRAY ELEMENT	CONTENTS
arrCookies[0][0]	FirstName
arrCookies[0][1]	Jessica
arrCookies[1][0]	LastName
arrCookies[1][1]	Jorkins

If the cookie name matches one of the names in the array, the value of the cookie is retrieved and returned (line ❽). The built-in JavaScript unescape function is used to decode the value since it was encoded with the escape function when writing the cookie.

If the function did not find a cookie with the defined name, an empty string is returned (line ⓫).

You can use the value of the cookie as a default value for a data-entry field or to define specific user preferences. In the following example, the cookie values are used to set a default on the Mailing List page as follows:

```
❶ <script type="text/javascript">
❷   //Get names from the cookie
❸   function getName()
❹   {
❺       first = getCookie("FirstName");
❻       if (first)
❼       {
❽           document.getElementById("FirstName").value=first;
❾       }
❿       last = getCookie("LastName");
⓫       if (last)
⓬       {
⓭           document.getElementById("LastName").value=last;
⓮       }
⓯   }
⓰ </script>
```

This code directly references elements on this specific page, so the getName function (line ❸) is contained within the Mailing List page and not in a generic JavaScript file. This local getName function calls the generic getCookie function to retrieve the first name from a cookie (line ❺). If the first name is found (line ❻), the getElementById method of the document is used to find the FirstName element and assign its value to the first name from the cookie (line ❽). This code is repeated for the last name (lines ❿ through ⓮).

The getName function is called from the onload event of the form:

```
<body onload="javascript:getName();">
```

This ensures that the default values appear as soon as the form is loaded.

Try It 10-2.

Retrieving Data from Cookies

Try It 10-2 retrieves data from cookies to add default values to the Mailing List page from Try It 10-1.

1. Open the Cookies.js file from Try It 10-1.

2. In this file, write a JavaScript function to locate a particular cookie and return its value. You can use the getCookie function example from this section.

3. Save the file.

4. Open the TrainingMailingList.htm file from Try It 10-1 in your HTML editing tool.

5. Add a script element to the header section of the Mailing List page and write a JavaScript function to call the getCookie function for the first and last name. You can use the getName function example from this section.

6. Call the JavaScript getName function from the onload event of the body element.

7. Save the file.

8. Open the TrainingMailingList.htm file in your browser. The first and last name you entered when testing Try It 10-1 should appear as defaults.

9. Optionally, add a setName function in the same script element as the getName function. The setName function calls setCookie for the first and last name. The setName function is called when the form is unloaded instead of creating the cookies as the user leaves each field.

10. Experiment with writing other cookies.

If the default values do not appear, ensure the cookies were created using the techniques demonstrated in Figure 10-1 and 10-2. If the cookies were created but are not appearing as defaults, check your use of uppercase and lowercase because JavaScript is case sensitive.

Listing 10-3 shows the new functions in the JavaScript file. Listing 10-4 shows the modifications to the TrainingMailingList.htm file.

Listing 10-3. The addition of the getCookie *function completes the Cookies.js file. You could also add a function to this file to delete cookies.*

```
// ***********************************************************************
// getCookie
// Gets a cookie from the user's computer
// Parameters:
//     sName     Name of the cookie
// Return value:
//     sValue    Value of the cookie
//     ""        If the cookie is not found
function getCookie(sName)
{
    var arrCookies = document.cookie.split("; ");
    for(var i = 0; i < arrCookies.length; i++)
    {
        if(sName == arrCookies[i].split("=")[0])
        {
            return unescape(arrCookies[i].split("=")[1]);
        }
    }
    return ""
}
```

Listing 10-4. To retrieve the cookies, the TrainingMailingList.htm file needs a new function and one minor change as shown in this code snippet. This snippet also shows an optional setName *function for setting the values for the cookies.*

```
. . .
<script type="text/javascript">
    //Get name
    function getName()
    {
        first = getCookie("FirstName");
        if (first)
        {
```

```
            document.getElementById("FirstName").value=first;
        }
        last = getCookie("LastName");
        if (last)
        {
            document.getElementById("LastName").value=last;
        }
    }
    function setName()
    {
        setCookie("FirstName",document.getElementById("FirstName").value);
        setCookie("LastName",document.getElementById("LastName").value);
    }
</script>
</head>
<body onload="javascript:getName();" onunload="javascript:setName();">
...
```

Cookies and State Management

The Web is fundamentally *stateless*; it has no innate ability to track any information about its state. Each time the user accesses a page of your Web application, the user appears as a stranger. The Web application cannot remember who the user is or what they have done. You can use cookies to store state information and then retrieve this information from any page of the Web application, thereby providing state management.

For example, one page of your Web application can request the user's name. Any other page can then use the name to personalize the page.

State management is important to your Web application. If your Web application requires that the user log in, you would not want the user to have to log in on every page. Rather, you want the user to log in upon entry into the Web application. Once the login is validated, your application can write a cookie with the login ID. Each subsequent page can then check this cookie to ensure that the user was logged in.

 CAUTION *Doing this can pose a security issue. See "Cookies and Security" later in this chapter for more information.*

State management is also important to ensure your application tracks the user's preferences, habits, and history. For example, if the user leaves at a particular page of your Web application, you may want to return the user to that page when the user returns.

You can minimize the amount of information stored in a cookie by storing state information in a database record on the Web server. You can then simply store the ID of the record in a cookie. For example, you could store your user's preferences in a record in a user-preferences database on the Web server. When the user logs in, you could find this record and store the ID of the record in a cookie. Any other page that needs preference information can then access the record using the ID from the cookie.

This technique has the added benefit of "following" the user. By looking up the user's preferences in a database, the user can access the Web application from any computer and the preference information is still available. For example, the user can set report parameters for a particular Web page at the office and then see that report again with those specific parameters from a different computer at home.

If this information were all stored in a cookie on the user's computer instead of in a database, any other computer the user accessed would not have the user's preferences.

Cookies and Security

There are some security issues you need to consider when using cookies, though not nearly as many as you might think.

A cookie is really no more threatening than handing the user a ticket stub at a movie theater. If the user leaves the theater (for example, to get popcorn) and then returns you can check the ticket stub to verify the movie for which the user had paid. Security only becomes an issue when someone else gets a hold of that ticket stub and uses it to enter the movie theater.

Cookies have some real and some imagined security issues. Let's look at the imagined issues first. Many of the concerns about cookies came from wild rumors and bad press:

- **Contrary to some popular fears, a cookie cannot contain a virus.**
  A cookie is simply a text file and is not executed. In order to pass along a virus, a file needs to be executed.

- **Cookies cannot steal data or access private information from the user's hard drive.** Cookies cannot interact with or access any other data on the user's hard drive. Cookies can only store information provided by the Web application or the user.

- **Cookies cannot read or extract information from cookies belonging to other sites.** For example, cookies written by your Web application cannot be read by any other application. A cookie can only be read by the site domain that created it.

Cookies are simply a scratch pad (like a Post-It note) that can be used by Web applications for storing bits of information. They are basically benevolent. However, there are some real security issues when working with cookies. If your Web application saves the user's ID and password in a cookie on the user's computer, anyone with access to the user's computer can get into the Web application.

But even though most of the real security issues are rumors and not reality, there are some things you can do to minimize the user's concerns over cookies:

- **Don't define an expiration date**. If you don't define an expiration date with the cookie, the cookie is only stored in memory for the duration of the browser session. This is useful if you want to store information or state, such as the user's ID, only during the session itself. Because the cookie is not stored on the user's hard disk, there is less concern about the impact of the cookie on the user's computer.

- **Provide a privacy policy.** Rumors spread when the user does not know how the cookie will be used. You can provide a privacy policy regarding cookies, stating that you won't sell any information about them and so on. Otherwise cookies are sometimes seen as an invasion of privacy.

- **Don't store private information.** Sometimes the appearance of security is as important as the security itself. So, don't save any information that is sensitive. For example, don't put credit card numbers into cookies.

As benign as cookies are by design, some enterprising organizations, such as DoubleClick, have come up with very clever ways to use cookies to gather more information about users. Using a combination of quirks in the Web, cookie design and user culpability, it is sometimes possible to link a specific user with personal information.

See "Additional Resources" at the end of this chapter for links to more information on cookies and security, including the DoubleClick story.

Alternatives to Cookies

There are certain times when you just cannot use cookies. Or, you could use cookies, but the user has them turned off. For these situations, there are alternatives to cookies for maintaining state information between the pages of your Web application.

Using Hidden Fields

You can transmit data between the pages of your application using hidden fields on a form as shown in Chapter 3, "Using HTML." These hidden fields are similar to other fields on an HTML form, but they are not visible to the user. You can put any value you want into a hidden field.

The down side of this approach is that you must then process every page by submitting it. Even if the page is a report, you need to submit the page in order to pass any hidden fields along to the next page.

Another thing to consider if you choose to use this approach is that the user can view the contents of the hidden fields by viewing the source of the Web page. So this technique should not be used for sensitive information.

Appending to the URI

You can append any information to the URI passed between the pages of your application. You may have seen this approach when accessing other pages on the Web. Try accessing a few Web sites and watch the Address field. Most search sites, for example, add information to the URI:

```
http://search.msn.com/results.asp?RS=CHECKED&FORM=MSNH&v=1&q=%22Lone+gunmen%22
```

The first part of the string up to the question mark (?) character is the URI that links to the search results page. The information after the question mark is information that was appended to the URI for use by the search results page. The string is comprised of encoded name and value pairs separated by amper-sands (&). The encoding replaces each space in the name and value pairs with a plus sign (+) and quotation marks with %22. The decoded name and value pairs in the URI string above are:

```
RS=CHECKED
FORM=MSNH
v=1
q="Lone gunmen"
```

These name and value pairs can then be extracted from the URI and used in the search results page to find the defined value and generate the search results.

If you want to use the URI approach, you can append a question mark (?) character and the encoded name and value pairs after the URI on the link to another page. The linked page can then access the values after the question mark using location.search. Alternatively, you can append a hash (#) character instead of the question mark. You can then access the name and value pairs after the hash using `location.hash`.

The down side of using the URI to pass data between pages is that the user can view, and potentially modify, the information attached to the URI. The length of the URI is also limited, so this alternative does not work with long strings.

Using a Database

It's a much better idea to save sensitive information in a server-side database. Assign your customer an ID number, and use a cookie to store that number on their computer. Then, whenever the customer visits, retrieve their ID number from the cookie and use it to look up other user-preference information in the database.

This is not technically an alternative to cookies because you still need a small cookie to store the customer ID. But this technique can dramatically reduce the amount of information you need to store in a cookie.

Using the Server

You can maintain state information on the server. See Chapter 15, "Web Application Architectures" for more information on server-side technologies.

Cookie Tips and Tricks

This section includes basic tips and techniques when working with JavaScript and cookies.

Cookie Tips

These tips are specifically for working with cookies.

Check for Turned Off Cookies

If any of your users have listened to the negative hype about cookies, they may have turned cookies off in their browser. One way to check for this is to try to read the cookie immediately after writing it using the `getCookie` function described in this chapter. If you cannot read the cookie you could assume that the user has them turned off and either display an alert box or work without cookies.

Watch Browser Compatibility Issues

Cookies created with Internet Explorer cannot be accessed by Netscape and vice versa. Sometimes even cookies created with an older version of a browser cannot be accessed by a newer version of the same browser.

Any user-preference information stored when the user accessed your Web application with Internet Explorer can be retrieved if the user accesses your Web application again with Internet Explorer. If the user later accesses your Web application with Netscape, any user-preference settings are not available.

This may not be an issue with your Web application if you expect the user to use one browser. If you want the user to be able to interchangeably use Internet Explorer and Netscape, then you may want to store user-preference information in a database on the Web server.

Your Web application can then look up the user-preference information when the user logs into the system. The application can create a temporary cookie by setting no expiration date. The temporary cookie can contain the user-preference information from the database record or the ID of the record containing this information.

This solution also works well if the user changes computers, such as between a desktop machine and a laptop.

Cookie Tricks

If you want to see the value of any cookies that a site is writing and you don't want to use one of the tools provided by the browser to see them, you can get them another way.

Try going to a site that uses cookies, such as `www.amazon.com`, or you can use the Mailing List page used in this chapter. After the page is displayed, type the following into the address box of your browser:

```
Javascript:alert("Cookie: "+document.cookie)
```

This code displays an alert message containing the cookie information for the site you are visiting, if there is any.

This works in both Netscape and Internet Explorer.

What Did This Cover?

This chapter discussed the purpose and use of cookies and how to store and access them with JavaScript.

The Try Its in this chapter used cookies to store and retrieve default values for data-entry forms. The cookies created in Try It 10-1 could be used in other pages of the Web application to display the user's name on the page.

The next chapter shifts gears and introduces XML.

Additional Resources

This section provides some additional resource suggestions by way of books, articles, and links to Web resources.

The books, articles, and links all existed at the time of this writing. There is a good chance that the books and articles still exist as you read this. However, the same cannot be said of Web links. Ignore the suggested links if they no longer exist.

Books and Articles

Negrino, Tom and Smith, Dori. *JavaScript for the World Wide Web.* Berkeley, CA: Peachpit Press, 1999.
There is an entire section of this book devoted to JavaScript and cookies.

Links

`http://ciac.llnl.gov/ciac/bulletins/i-034.shtml`: This is a link to the U.S. Department of Energy Computer Incident Advisory Center information bulletin on Internet cookies. This notice provides a vulnerability assessment that basically states that cookies do not pose a threat.

`http://www.cookiecentral.com`: This site is devoted entirely to cookies and includes information on privacy issues.

`http://www.usatoday.com/life/cyber/tech/cth211.htm`: This article from USA Today is entitled "Activists charge DoubleClick double cross" with a subtitle of "Web users have lost privacy with the drop of a cookie, they say." The article describes how DoubleClick uses cookies to store information about a user's Web surfing and participating retailers to request name and address information to profile Web users for marketing purposes.

`http://www.w3.org/P3P/`: This site presents the Platform for Privacy Preferences Project (P3P), developed by the World Wide Web Consortium (W3C). The P3P is emerging as an industry standard providing a simple, automated way for users to gain more control over the use of personal information on Web sites they visit. Though this does not directly address cookies, it covers many concerns users may have regarding privacy.

CHAPTER 11

Introduction to XML

SO FAR, ALL OF THE DATA displayed by the Web pages presented in this book has been static. The Course List Web page from Chapter 5, "Building Tables," for example, contained a hard-coded set of offered courses. Someone has to manually update the HTML to remove past courses, update course dates or locations, and add new courses. Wouldn't it be nice if you could separate the HTML used for the presentation of the data from the data itself? Then you could update the contents of the page without having to modify the HTML. That is where the Extensible Markup Language (XML) can help.

XML provides a standardized syntax for defining data. You can use XML in the Course List Web page example to define all of the offered courses. You can then use HTML to define how the courses will be displayed.

The purpose of this chapter is to provide you with an introduction to XML and how to use it to define the data for your Web applications. Later chapters expand on these basics, combining HTML and XML for display of the data and adding schemas for data validation.

What Will This Cover?

This chapter covers the following key XML concepts:

- Understanding XML basics

- Examining the anatomy of an XML document

- Attribute-based vs. element-based XML documents

- Defining a well-formed XML document

- Parsing an XML document

- Creating an XML file

- Viewing XML in a browser

- Understanding namespaces

- Exploring the many uses of XML

By the end of this chapter, you will know how to define data for your Web applications using XML. You will be able to create well-formed XML documents and display them in your browser.

XML Basics

XML is an extensible markup language. As HTML defines a standard syntax for marking up a document for display, XML defines a standard syntax for marking up a document that specifies data structures. HTML has a predefined set of markup elements that browsers understand, such as p (paragraph) and a (anchor); XML is called an *extensible* markup language because anyone can define a set of markup elements to use for any particular XML document.

You can use XML to define the data in your application, such as a list of courses your company offers or the list of invoices that have been paid. You can also use XML to define data relationships. For example, you can define that courses have a name, date, and location; invoices have a customer and a set of line items. Since you can create any markup elements you need, you can give the elements meaningful names and structure the data in a way that makes sense to your Web application. This makes XML a descriptive markup tool.

You can also include data about your data, called *metadata*, in your XML. For example, you can define the data type, data format, or any other information that describes the data in the XML. This makes the XML self-describing.

You might think that with all of this power and flexibility that XML is complex. Actually, XML is text similar to HTML. The text can be stored in a file, called an XML file, or in memory as a text string. In either case, the XML is referred to as an *XML document*. Because XML is just text, XML documents are human readable.

XML documents are comprised of elements and attributes. With XML, you define your own elements and attributes based on the data structures needed by your application.

Defining Elements

Elements define the structure of the data in an XML document. The syntax for defining XML elements is similar to that used for HTML elements with a few differences. Let's look at the differences first.

In HTML, the browser interprets the element tags to determine how an HTML document should be displayed. To ensure all browsers treat these elements consistently, the set of valid elements is predefined. So the p element always displays a new paragraph, regardless of the browser that parses it. The World Wide Web Consortium (W3C) has the responsibility for standardizing these elements.

Unlike HTML, XML elements are extensible and not predefined. *You* define the XML elements appropriate for your Web application data. For example, a course catalog could define XML elements such as `course` and `instructor`. An invoicing application could define XML elements such as `customer` and `invoice`.

You can name an XML element anything you choose as long as it follows some basic naming rules:

- Names can contain letters, numbers, and other characters such as underscores (_).

- Names can be uppercase, lowercase, or mixed case.

 CAUTION *Element names are case sensitive, so be consistent with your use of case.*

- Names cannot start with a number.

- Names cannot contain spaces.

 TIP *Use an underscore (_) character to provide space between words in an element name; for example:* `<start_date>`.

- Names cannot contain a colon (:). A colon defines a namespace as discussed later in this chapter.

 TIP *Give your elements descriptive names, so your XML is easier to read. If your XML contains data fields from a database, you may want to make the element name the same as the database field name.*

The syntax of an XML element is the same as an HTML element: beginning tag, content, and ending tag. The beginning tag consists of a left angle bracket (<), the element name, and a right angle bracket (>) with no spaces between the angle bracket and the element name. The ending tag consists of a left angle bracket (<), a forward slash (/), the element name, and a right angle bracket (>). For example:

```
<course></course>
```

The information between an element's beginning and ending tag is the element's *content*. Element content types are:

- **Elements**. An element can contain other elements. For example, a course could have multiple instructors:

```
<course>
    <instructor></instructor>
    <instructor></instructor>
</course>
```

- **Text**. An element can contain text, such as this example:

```
<instructor>Jessica</instructor>
```

- **Attributes**. An element can contain attributes as detailed in the next section. The attributes must be within the beginning tag of the element. If an element contains only attributes and no elements or text, you can combine the beginning and ending tag by appending the forward slash (/) before the right angle bracket (>). The following defines an element that contains only an attribute and an element that contains an attribute and another element:

```
<course id="42"/>
<course id="57">
    <instructor>Jessica</instructor>
</course>
```

- **Empty**. An element has no contents. When an element is empty, you can combine the beginning and ending tag:

```
<instructor />
```

When an element contains one or more other elements, the elements must be correctly nested. This means that you must insert the beginning and ending tags of the other elements between the beginning and ending tags of the original element. For example, you can define two instructor elements within a course element as follows:

```
<course>
    <instructor>Jessica</instructor>
    <instructor>Krysta</instructor>
</course>
```

TIP   *Indenting your XML can help you to see the nesting of the elements. Any extra spaces or tabs are ignored when the XML is processed.*

Notice how both of the instructor element tags are nested entirely within the course element tags. Because of this structure, the course element is called the *parent* element, and the instructor elements are called *child* elements. This capability to nest elements allows you to define relationships between data. Courses can have instructors; invoices can have line items, and so on.

Be careful as you nest elements because the element tags must not overlap. That is, if a tag begins within another tag, it must also end within that tag. For example, the following is not correctly formatted XML:

```
<course>
<instructor>
</course>
</instructor>
```

In this example, the instructor beginning tag resides within the course beginning tag, but the instructor ending tag appears after the course ending tag. These tags are overlapping and are therefore not correctly formatted.

Defining Attributes

Attributes define the properties of elements, such as the color attribute of an HTML font element. Attributes also define the properties of XML elements. For example, the course element could have name, date, and location attributes. The customer element could have name, address, and phone number attributes.

An attribute is defined by an attribute name, followed by an equal sign (=) and a value. The attribute value must be enclosed in quotation marks, usually with double-quotes (" "). Single quotes can also be used (' ') and are required if the attribute itself contains double-quotes. For example:

```
name="Object-Oriented Design"
name='XML for "XPerts" - Part 1'
```

Attribute name and value pairs are defined within the beginning tag for the element, after the element name and before the right angle bracket (>). You can specify multiple attributes for an element by separating the attributes with a space. For example, the course element has name, date, and location attributes:

```
<course name="Object-Oriented Design" date="June 25-28, 2002"
    location="Hiltonian, Pleasanton, CA"/>
```

Each attribute for an element must be unique; you cannot specify multiple attributes of the same name for one element. For example, the following XML is not correct because it has two date attributes:

```
<course name="Object-Oriented Design" date="June 25, 2002" date="June 26, 2002"
    location="Hiltonian, Pleasanton, CA"/>
```

Attributes often define information that is not actually a part of the data itself but rather describe the data. This descriptive metadata can be used by the Web application to manage and process the data. For example:

```
<instructor read-only="true">Jessica</instructor>
```

In this case, the attribute defines how the data is handled.

Benefits of XML

There are many benefits to using XML for defining the data structures needed by your Web application:

- **XML is not owned by a single vendor**. XML is not a Microsoft or Sun technology. XML standards are defined by the W3C. This ensures XML is vendor independent.

- **XML is a standard**. Because XML is defined by the W3C, it follows a standard syntax. This standardization makes it easier to work consistently with XML.

- **XML is platform independent**. Because XML is text, it can easily be transported and shared between disparate systems. For example, you can create XML on a Windows system to collect purchase-order data, provide it to a Unix system to process the purchase order and then to a mainframe system to update accounting information based on the purchase order.

- **XML is application independent**. You can create XML to share with any applications, including applications provided by outside vendors. Companies that develop software, such as accounting and automatic bill paying applications, are now providing imports and exports from their systems using XML.

- **XML is self-describing**. You can give your XML elements meaningful names and add metadata to the XML that describes the data.

Now that you have a general idea of the benefits of XML, let's look further at XML documents and how you create them.

The Anatomy of an XML Document

An XML document is the text string containing your XML elements and attributes. The structure of the document describes the relationships between the data needed by your Web application. For example, a course catalog contains a set of courses. Each course has a name, date, and location. You define these relationships by nesting elements and defining attributes.

An XML document can be structured in many different ways, as long as it follows the basic XML syntax. However, most XML documents follow one of two basic structures: attribute-based or element-based.

Attribute-Based XML

An attribute-based XML document uses elements for the basic data entities and attributes for the data fields associated with those entities. This is comparable to a record-based structure where each element is a record and each attribute is a field in that record. For example:

```
❶   <?xml version="1.0"?>
❷   <!-- Course XML -->
❸   <courses>
```

④   `<course name="Object-Oriented Design" date="June 25-28, 2002"`
             `location="Hiltonian, Pleasanton, CA"/>`

⑤   `<course name="Web Application Development" date="August 5-8, 2002"`
             `location="Hiltonian, Phoenix, AZ"/>`

⑥ `</courses>`

The XML declaration (line **❶**) is a processing instruction that defines the XML version of the document. In this case the document conforms to the 1.0 specification of XML.

NOTE   *This declaration is not an element, so it does not require an ending tag.*

A comment (line **❷**) can exist anywhere within an XML document. Any text between the beginning comment marker (`<!--`) and the ending comment marker (`-->`) is considered to be a comment and is ignored when the XML document is parsed.

Every XML document must have a single root element (lines **❸** and **❻**), called the *document element*, which is the top-level element in the document. All other elements of the XML document must be nested within this single root element. The name of this document element normally defines the contents of the XML document. In this example, the plural of the XML contents, `courses`, was used as the element name because this XML document describes the list of courses. There is nothing special about this name; we could have used `catalog` or `course_offerings`.

This particular XML document contains one type of element: `course`. Each course element (lines **❹** and **❺**) has three attributes: `name`, `date`, and `location`. The actual data associated with each course is defined as values of these attributes, hence the reason this is called an attribute-based structure.

Element-Based XML

The other common XML document structure, called an element-based structure, uses elements for the basic data entities and sub-elements for the data fields associated with those entities. Attributes are reserved for the metadata, such as a data type or validation information. For example:

```
①  <?xml version="1.0"?>
②  <!-- Course XML -->
③  <courses>
④    <course>
⑤      <name>Object-Oriented Design</name>
⑥      <date>June 25-28, 2002</date>
⑦      <location>Hiltonian, Pleasanton, CA</location>
⑧    </course>
⑨    <course>
⑩      <name>Web Application Development</name>
⑪      <date>August 5-8, 2002</date>
⑫      <location>Hiltonian, Phoenix, AZ</location>
⑬    </course>
⑭  </courses>
```

Notice how much more verbose this structure is than the prior attribute-based structure. This can be a drawback of element-based structures.

As with the prior example, this example begins with the XML declaration (line ①), a comment (line ②) and a single root element (lines ③ and ⑭).

The courses root element has two children that are course elements (lines ④ through ⑧ and ⑨ through ⑬). Each course element has three child sub-elements: name (lines ⑤ and ⑩), date (lines ⑥ and ⑪), and location (lines ⑦ and ⑫). Child elements that have the same parent are *siblings*. Figure 11-1 shows the tree structure for this XML document.

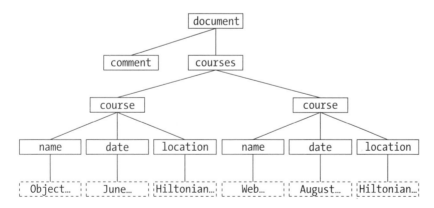

Figure 11-1. An XML document can be represented as a tree structure. Notice the similarities between this figure and the figures in Chapter 7, "Understanding Object Models."

317

Each of the sub-elements in this example contains text. For example, the text associated with the name element of the first course element is "Object-Oriented Design." This text is sometimes referred to as a *text node* or simply as *character data* and is shown as dashed boxes in Figure 11-1.

When you create your XML document, you can use the attribute-based structures, element-based structures, or a combination of the two. There are no specific rules regarding when to use attributes and when to use sub-elements.

One of the benefits of using elements to define all of your data is that elements can have sub-elements. For example, if you define a date as an attribute, it is just an attribute. If you define the date as an element, you can later decide to break the date into its sub-elements:

```
<date>
    <startDate>June 25, 2002</startDate>
    <endDate>June 28, 2002</endDate>
</date>
```

This makes elements more evolvable for future changes to your data.

 **TIP**   *A good practice is to use elements and sub-elements to define the XML data, and use attributes to define the information about the data, the metadata. Examples of metadata include the data type, whether the data is read-only, and the unique ID for the data.*

A Well-Formed XML Document

You determine the appropriate structure, elements, and attributes of your XML document depending on the data needed by your application. However, an XML document must follow specific syntactical rules. When an XML document follows these rules, it is said to be *well-formed*.

Ensuring that all XML documents follow specific syntactical rules allows the XML documents to be processed consistently, regardless of the application processing it. This is one of the key benefits of XML. It is also why the current version of HTML applied XML syntactical rules to form XHTML as described in Chapter 3, "Using HTML."

A well-formed XML document has the following characteristics:

- The XML document should begin with the XML declaration.

- There must be one and only one root element.

- All of the other elements must be nested within the root element.

- Every element must have beginning and ending tags.

- Element tags must not overlap.

- Attribute values must be within quotation marks.

- No attribute name may appear more than once in the same beginning tag.

- Text nodes cannot contain less than (<) or ampersand (&) characters. You must replace them with the character entities defined in Chapter 3, "Using HTML." See the next section, "Parsing XML," for an example.

These rules are important to remember when defining your XML. XML that is not well-formed is not even considered to be an XML document. Both the attribute-based and element-based XML documents presented in the prior section are well-formed.

Parsing XML

When an XML document is well-formed, it has a predictable syntax that can easily be parsed. This parsing is done with an *XML parser*. An XML parser verifies that an XML document is well-formed. If the XML document is well-formed, the parser can read the document without any knowledge of its contents.

The W3C specification states that if an XML document is not well-formed, any application that accesses it should throw an exception and not attempt to continue. This is quite different from HTML, which frequently ignores everything it cannot understand.

There are many XML parsers available to verify that your XML is well-formed. You can get XML parsers on many different platforms including Windows, Unix, and MVS. The "Additional Resources" section at the end of this chapter provides a link to several XML parsers.

Both Internet Explorer (version 4 and above) and Netscape (version 6 and above) provide XML parsers as part of the browser. These parsers are discussed later in this chapter.

When an XML document is parsed, the elements, attributes, and text contents of the elements are parsed. This can cause difficulty if the text contains characters that the parser recognizes. For example:

```
<date>June 25, 2002 < June 28, 2002</date>
```

The parser incorrectly recognizes the less than character (<) as a part of a tag and then assumes that the XML document containing this element is not well-formed. To prevent this, you need to replace these XML characters with character entities as defined in Chapter 3, "Using HTML." The previous example would be changed as follows:

```
<date>June 25, 2002 &lt; June 28, 2002</date>
```

If the text associated with an element in your XML document contains a lot of special characters that you don't want parsed, you can embed the text within a character data (CDATA) section:

```
<date><![CDATA[June 25, 2002 &lt; June 28, 2002]]></date>
```

The CDATA section begins with `<![CDATA[` and ends with `]]>`. (The W3C probably wanted to pick something that had no chance of being valid XML contents.) The parser ignores everything within the CDATA section. This is especially useful if your element text contains programming code or HTML.

In addition to parsing the XML document, some XML parsers provide programmatic access to the XML document's elements and attributes. You can then write application or script code to access the elements and attributes. A detailed example of this is shown in Chapter 14, "Reading XML with JavaScript."

Creating an XML File

You can manually create XML files because they are just text files. You can then check the syntax of the files using an XML parser. Alternatively, and more commonly, you can build XML files from databases or from an application.

You can create an XML file using a basic text editor, such as Notepad or WordPad for Windows and Emacs or vi for Unix. Using a simple tool has the benefit of simplicity, but it requires you spend the time typing in all of the data with the correct syntax.

Several tools are available to help you create your XML file. Tools such as XML Spy allow you to view and edit your XML. Most of these tools have an XML parser that parses your XML and ensures that it is well-formed. See the "Additional Resources" section at the end of this chapter for links to information on XML tools.

Frequently, you may have much more data than you want to type into a text file. In many cases, the data you need in the XML file is already in a database. Some database products, such as Microsoft SQL Server, can produce data in an XML file format. You can also write a program using C or Visual Basic to read data from a database (or other sources) and reformat it as an XML file.

For the purposes of this chapter, create the XML file manually:

1. Create a text file and save it with an .xml extension.

2. Add the XML declaration.

3. Add a root element.

4. Add other elements and attributes as required for your data.

5. Ensure your XML is well-formed.

Follow these steps to get started with XML.

Try It 11-1.

Building an XML File

Try It 11-1 builds an XML file that contains course information. The Try Its in Chapter 12, "Using XSL," will use this XML file to display the courses on the Course List page.

1. Using Notepad or your tool of choice, create a new text file.

2. Insert the XML declaration.

3. Add a root element, such as courses.

4. Add elements within the root element to define course data. Use the element-based structure.

5. Save the file as course.xml.

 CAUTION *Be sure to save the file as text-only. The default file type may not be text-only in the tool you are using.*

6. Optionally, add elements to include character entities or a CDATA section.

7. Optionally, try creating the XML file again using the attribute-based approach and save it under a different name.

Listing 11-1 shows the element-based course.xml file.

Listing 11-1. The course.xml file contains all of the information for the courses.

```
<?xml version="1.0"?>
<!--
    Try It  11-1
    Title:  Course XML in element-based structure
    Author: InStep Technologies
            www.insteptech.com
    Purpose:To demonstrate XML
 -->
<courses>
    <course>
        <name>Object-Oriented Design</name>
        <date>June 25-28, 2002</date>
        <location>Hiltonian, Pleasanton, CA</location>
    </course>
    <course>
        <name>Web Application Development</name>
        <date>August 5-8, 2002</date>
        <location>Hiltonian, Phoenix, AZ</location>
    </course>
</courses>
```

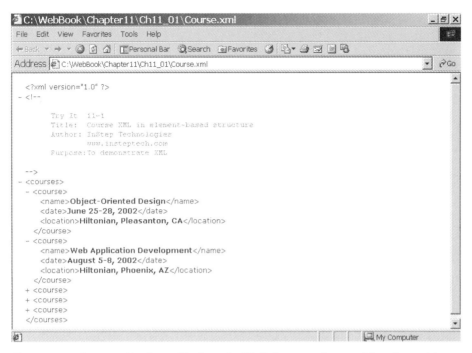

Figure 11-2. Internet Explorer displays the XML in a tree format. The pluses (+) allow you to expand the branches and the minus (-) signs collapse the branches.

Viewing an XML File with a Browser

Both Internet Explorer (version 4 and higher) and Netscape (version 6 and higher) include an XML parser. You can open an XML file with either browser, and the data in the file is displayed within the browser.

Internet Explorer displays the XML in a tree structure with expanding and collapsing branches, as shown in Figure 11-2. This is a great structure for developers to review the XML, but it is not meant to be used to display data to users.

Internet Explorer also provides assistance in debugging your XML. If the XML is not well-formed, Internet Explorer displays a detailed error message, as shown in Figure 11-3.

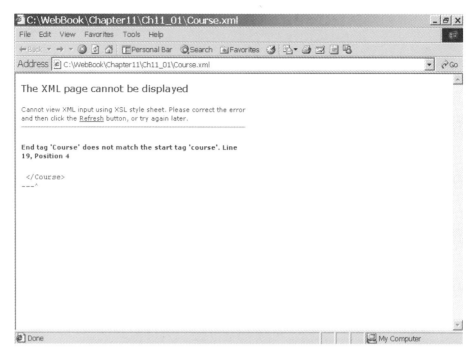

Figure 11-3. The XML in this example is not well-formed because the capitalization used in one of the ending tags, Course, *did not match the capitalization used in the associated beginning tag,* course.

The parser provided with Internet Explorer is a *nonvalidating* parser. This means that it ensures the XML is well-formed, but it won't validate the XML. See Chapter 13, "Defining Schemas and DTDs," for more information on validating XML.

Netscape displays the XML in a single string as shown in Figure 11-4. It also displays a detailed error message if the XML is not well-formed, as shown in Figure 11-5.

In all of these examples you did not have any control over the presentation of the data. The XML document does not contain any information about how to display the data. To associate display information with XML, you need to use the Extensible StyleSheet Language (XSL) as described in Chapter 12, "Using XSL."

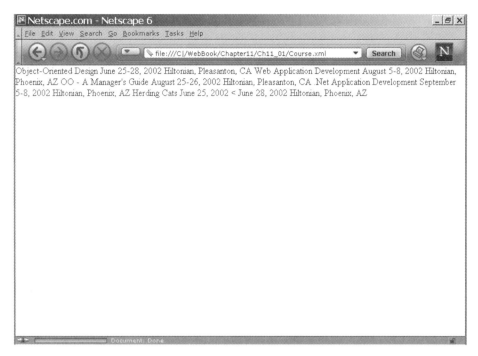

Figure 11-4. Netscape displays the XML as a single string.

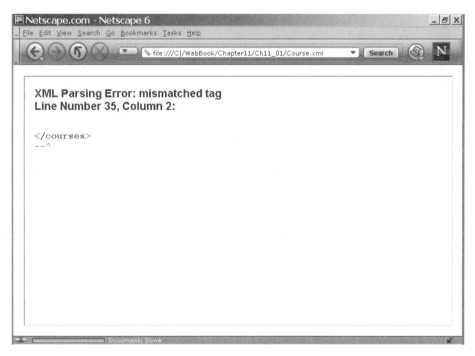

Figure 11-5. The XML in this example was missing an ending tag, so Netscape displays an error message.

Try It 11-2.

Viewing an XML File

Try It 11-2 uses a browser to view the XML file created in Try It 11-1.

1. Open the course.xml file in Internet Explorer (version 4 or higher) or Netscape (version 6 or higher). If you have an association set up for the .xml extension and you are using Windows, you can double-click on the page in Windows Explorer, and it will appear in your browser.

2. Optionally, open the attribute-based XML file you created in Try It 11-1.

The element-based XML file appears similar to Figure 11-2 or Figure 11-4, depending on the browser you are using.

Namespaces

Every language has a vocabulary that defines the set of established words. This vocabulary is often published in a dictionary, which contains and describes the set of words in the vocabulary. To use a language effectively, you need to learn the language's vocabulary.

Markup languages also have a *vocabulary* that defines the set of valid elements and attributes. For example, HTML has a specific vocabulary that includes elements such as p, a, and table. This vocabulary is defined in a *namespace*, which is basically the dictionary of unique element and attribute names. Technically speaking, a namespace is a logically related set of names in which each name must be unique.

As you have seen in this chapter, *you* select the element and attribute names that are appropriate for your XML document, thereby defining the document's vocabulary. This vocabulary identifies the set of element and attribute names available for use in your XML document.

Namespaces are normally identified using a unique Uniform Resource Identifier (URI). For example, the HTML namespace is defined with:

```
http://www.w3.org/TR/REC-html40
```

Using the URI to define the namespace can be somewhat confusing because it implies there is a file or other reference located at that URI. This is not the case. Rather, the namespace URI is simply a unique string selected to identify the namespace.

There is no standard syntax for the actual definition of the namespace contents. The W3C simply uses a written specification for its namespaces that is posted to its Web site: www.w3.org. If you create your own namespace, you are free to document the contents of the namespace in any way that helps you track the set of names and ensure uniqueness.

The primary purpose of a namespace is to prevent name conflicts. For example, the following XML document uses the element name for two different purposes, as the course name and as the location name:

```
<courses>
    <course>
        <name>Object-Oriented Design</name>
        <date>June 25-28, 2002</date>
        <location>
            <name>Hiltonian</name>
            <address>123 Main, Pleasanton, CA</address>
        </location>
    </course>
</courses>
```

You can remove this ambiguity by defining separate namespaces for courses and locations. Let's define the location namespace.

As per standard practice, the namespace is identified using a URI to ensure uniqueness. The URI is comprised of the domain name and any qualifier to ensure uniqueness within the domain name. For example:

```
http://www.insteptech.com/location
```

Each element and attribute within the XML document that refers to names in this namespace must somehow be associated with the namespace. Referencing this long URI in each element and attribute name is not practical, so the W3C provides syntax for defining an abbreviation for the namespace. The syntax is as follows:

```
xmlns:loc='http://www.insteptech.com/location'
```

The first part of this syntax, xmlns, identifies this statement as the definition of an XML namespace. The letters following the colon (:) defines the abbreviation for the namespace, in this case loc. The remaining syntax defines the namespace URI.

The namespace abbreviation is then used as a prefix on each element and attribute within the XML document that refers to names in this namespace. The complete XML is then:

```
<courses xmlns:loc='http://www.insteptech.com/location'>
    <course>
        <name>Object-Oriented Design</name>
```

```
        <date>June 25-28, 2002</date>
      <loc:location>
          <loc:name>Hiltonian</loc:name>
          <loc:address>123 Main, Pleasanton, CA</loc:address>
      </loc:location>
   </course>
</courses>
```

A schema, and to some extent a Document Type Definition (DTD), can provide a syntax for defining a namespace. The schema or DTD defines the set of valid elements and attributes for your XML document for purposes of validating the content of your XML document. See Chapter 13, "Defining Schemas and DTDs," for more information.

The Many Uses of XML

XML is simple in concept, but it is powerful in its simplicity. Because XML is just text, it is platform- and operating system–independent. It can be used for everything from a data communication protocol to a database.

These many uses of XML are sometimes associated with the definition of XML, causing confusion on what XML really is. You may see an article stating that XML is the next generation communication protocol between companies and their suppliers. Then you may see another article stating that XML is the database of the future. Well, which is it? Using these definitions for XML is like defining a computer as an electronic mail carrier. Yes, a computer can deliver mail, but it can also do a whole lot more.

Let's start by looking at how you can use XML as a client-side technology:

- **Populating lists.** Instead of hard-coding list values into your HTML pages, such as the selection box on the Mailing List page example in Chapter 6, "Building Forms," an XML document could be used to define this data. The HTML page can read the XML document and build the list contents. This simplifies maintenance of the list as the list values change over time.

- **Dynamic data.** If you hard-code data into your HTML page, like the Course List page example in Chapter 5, "Building Tables," someone must update this page every time a new course is added. Instead, XML could be used to define this data. The HTML page can read the XML document and build the table dynamically. This simplifies the maintenance of the Web pages in your Web application. An example of this is provided in Chapter 14, "Reading XML with JavaScript."

- **Dynamic data, another option.** Instead of having an HTML page that reads an XML document, you can format the XML document for display using XSL as shown in Chapter 12, "Using XSL." This prevents the need to write code in your HTML page to read the XML document.

- **Preventing round-trips.** If the data you need for a particular Web page is on the server, the application needs to return to the server each time it needs to reformat that data. By using XML, you can allow the user to sort or filter data in an HTML table without returning to the server. This is discussed further in Chapter 12, "Using XSL."

XML is not, however, just for Web applications. You can also use XML for the following:

- **Communication protocol between corporations (a.k.a. business-to-business or B2B).** XML is seen as a potential replacement for Electronic Data Interchange (EDI). EDI allows a company to share data with its strategic partners. However, EDI requires that both companies support the defined EDI file format. XML provides a simpler way to transfer data between the corporations. For example, a company can send its order via XML, and the supplier can import that XML directly into its order-processing system.

- **Communication between applications within a corporation.** Most mid- to large-sized companies support numerous computer systems, software, and databases. The information in these systems is usually stored and provided in incompatible formats. XML provides a mechanism for transferring data between these disparate systems. For example, a mainframe accounting system could generate an XML document containing the day's customer data changes for use by the sales department's Unix system and the customer support department's Windows-based system.

- **Information reuse**. Since XML separates the data from the display, you can define the data once and then create as many user interface options as necessary. A course XML document could be used by an application that generates a printed course catalog. That same XML document could be used by a Web application to display an online catalog. The same XML document could be used again by an internal software system that provides phone-based student enrollment.

- **Storing temporary local copies of data.** Some job functions require time away from the office but also require access to corporate information. Data required for the job could be collected from a database and copied to a laptop or palmtop computer as XML, thus preventing the need for connectivity. If changes are made to the local copy of the data, the XML changes can be merged back when the person returns to the office. For example, a sales person plans to meet with a set of customers. All of the relevant information for those customers, such as contact information and past purchase history, could be pulled from corporate systems and stored on the salesperson's laptop as an XML document. The salesperson can then review and update the customer information as required using an application that parsed that XML document. When the salesperson returns from the customer meetings, the updated data can be merged back into the corporate systems.

- **Application logs.** XML works well for use in building application log documents because it is easy to read, easy to change over time, and easy to format.

To fully understand what XML is, it may also be useful to look at what XML is not:

- **Formatting or display.** XML defines data with no information on the formatting or display of that data. This separates the data from the visual display, making your Web application more flexible and easier to maintain.

- **Relational database.** XML is not a fully relational database nor does it provide the management tools that a robust database provides.

- **Efficiently stored.** As you have seen, XML is verbose. It requires more bandwidth than smaller, binary formats. But its verboseness provides several benefits: It is platform independent, an open standard, self-describing, and human-readable.

The bottom line is that XML does not change the way your Web application looks. Rather, it redefines how you define and share data in both Web and non-Web applications.

XML Tips and Tricks

This section includes basic tips and techniques when working with XML.

Define Your Directories and Files

If you plan to store information in an XML file, the file needs to reside somewhere on your Web server. Here are several tips on defining the structure of your Web application source directories.

Create Logical Filenames

Give each XML file a logical name. You may define hundreds of Web pages, graphics, and other files in your application, so the more logical the filenames, the easier it is to remember which file is which.

Set Up a Logical Directory Structure

Define your working directory structure so that all of the files for your application are in one directory and its subdirectories. Normally, you can put all of your XML files into the application's directory containing the HTML files.

Use Relative Paths Where Possible

If you follow the suggested directory structure, you can define the location of the XML files using relative paths.

Debugging Tips

Here are some tips for debugging your XML documents.

Watch for Missing Ending Tags

A common source of error is missing ending tags. If you receive an error like the one shown in Figure 11-5, you may be missing an ending tag.

Watch Case Sensitivity

As stated earlier, XML is case sensitive. This could lead to a missing ending tag error if the element name case in the beginning and ending tags don't match.

For example, the element course is not the same as the element Course. If you have XML document that uses case inconsistently, such as the following, you get an error when the XML is parsed as shown in Figure 11-3.

```
<course>
    <name>Object-Oriented Design</name>
    <date>June 25-28, 2002</date>
    <location>Hiltonian, Pleasanton, CA</location>
</course>
```

Watching your case is even more important when you read through the XML document, as shown in Chapter 12, "Using XSL." If you search through the XML document to find all course elements, the search ignores all Course elements and the application would not show all of the courses.

Use a Parser

There are several XML parsers available that can ensure your XML document is well-formed. If you have Internet Explorer (version 4 or higher) or Netscape (version 6 or higher) you already have an XML parser.

Open your XML document in Internet Explorer or Netscape, and the browser gives you error messages if the XML is not well-formed. See the "Links" section at the end of this chapter for links to several other parsing tools.

What Did This Cover?

XML provides a way for you to define data, the structure of that data, and the metadata. You have complete control over the elements and attributes of the XML, as long as you ensure that your XML document is well-formed.

The Try Its in this chapter demonstrated how to build an XML document and view it in a browser.

XML is very much a part of future Web development. Over the past year, it seemed like every technology magazine had XML broadly emblazoned on the cover. The better you understand XML, the better you can cut through the hype and leverage XML for your Web applications.

This chapter provided a basic introduction to XML. But there are entire 1,000-page books dedicated to XML, so there is more to it than this, as presented in the next several chapters.

Additional Resources

One chapter could not begin to cover everything there is to know about basic XML. This section provides some additional resource suggestions by way of books, articles, and links to Web resources.

This section was harder than I expected, not because there weren't many references, but because there were so many. Quite a few of these references began with topics beyond the scope of this chapter. It was hard to pick a few good introductory books, but I browsed my company's internal library and found a few on par with this introductory material.

The books, articles, and links all existed at the time of this writing. There is a good chance that the books and articles still exist as you read this. However, the same cannot be said of Web links. Ignore the suggested links if they no longer exist.

Books and Articles

Chandak, Ramesh, Norbert Mikula, and Ed Tittel. *XML for Dummies.* **Foster City, CA: IDG Books, 1998.**
I skimmed through some of the material here and found it to be a good introduction to many of the concepts presented in this chapter.

Pardi, William. *XML in Action: Web Technology.* **Redmond, WA: Microsoft Press, 1999.**
This was the first XML book that I read *way* back in 1999. As you may guess from the publisher, it has a very Microsoft-centric view of XML.

Links

http://hotwired.lycos.com/webmonkey/98/41/index1a.html: This article is a fun introduction to XML.

http://msdn.microsoft.com/xml: Microsoft's XML Developer Center provides technical papers, documentation, specifications, and other information on XML. It also provides access to newsgroups to discuss XML issues.

http://www.extensinet.com/: This Web site provides links to a full range of XML topics including lists of XML editors and tools, tutorials, and specifications.

http://www.ibm.com/developer/xml/: IBM's XML Zone provides articles, tool information, and tutorials. It even contains case studies if you need some help convincing your boss that XML is the way to go.

`http://www.w3.org/XML/`: This site contains the specification for XML.

`http://www.webreference.com/xml/column8/`: This site provides a review of XML editing tools.

`http://www.xml.com/`: This site provides tutorials and other XML news. It is focused on keeping up-to-date with all of the XML standards. Because it is not supported by a major vendor such as Microsoft, Sun, or IBM, it provides a less biased view of XML.

`http://www.xmlspy.com/`: This site provides an integrated development environment tool for XML. This tool edits and validates your XML syntax. You can download a demo version to try it out.

Using XSL

IN THE PREVIOUS CHAPTER you learned how to create an XML document that contains data needed by your Web application. An XML document does not, however, define a way to display that data in any user-friendly format. Transforming an XML document into another format, such as a user-friendly HTML page, is the primary purpose of the Extensible Stylesheet Language (XSL).

You can use XSL to transform your XML document in many different ways. For example, you could use XSL to transform an XML document containing course information into HTML for presentation on a course list Web page. You could use XSL to transform that same XML document into a format needed for printing a course catalog. You could use XSL to transform that same XML document in a format to be e-mailed to perspective students.

You can also use XSL to transform an XML document into another XML document. This makes it easy to accept an XML document from another system and transform it into the XML needed by your system. Or you can export XML from your system and transform it into an XML document needed by another system. This simplifies communication between different systems.

The purpose of this chapter is to provide you with an introduction to XSL and how to use it to transform your XML documents into HTML for display to the users.

What Will This Cover?

This chapter covers the following key XSL concepts:

- Understanding XSL basics

- Exploring the difference between XSL and XSLT

- Envisioning XML documents as nodes

- Examining the anatomy of an XSLT stylesheet

- Creating an XSLT stylesheet

- Associating an XSLT stylesheet with an XML document

- Understanding transformations

- Setting selection criteria with XPath

- Using XSLT templates

- Understanding the effects of the built-in templates

- Using XSLT structures

- Learning the basic set of XSLT elements and attributes

By the end of this chapter, you will know how to leverage XSL to transform your XML documents.

XSL Basics

XSL transforms the data in an XML document into a format that is useful for a particular purpose. The result can be HTML, another XML document, or any other text-based output format.

The XSL transformation can do a lot more than simply format XML document data. You can extract information from an XML document in any order and rearrange it. You can evaluate and calculate information, such as totaling amounts. You can modify values, converting from one numbering scheme to another, for example. You can sort. You can add any information to the output.

XSL is powerful, and it can be quite complex. To manage this complexity, we'll start with a simple example of transforming XML document data into HTML for display in a browser.

Figures 11-2 and 11-4 from Chapter 11, "Using XML," depict how an XML document is presented in a browser. As you can see from these figures, XML documents have no real style or formatting making them impractical for display to the users. Figure 12-1 shows that same XML document after transforming it into HTML using XSL. Notice the significant difference in the result.

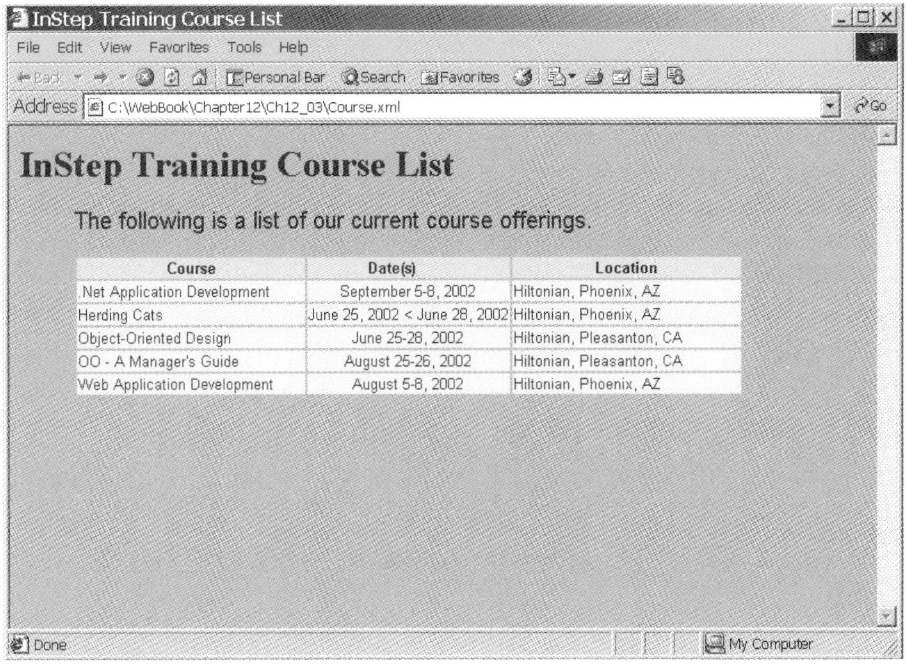

Figure 12-1. XSL can transform your XML document into HTML for display in your Web application.

Before going into the details of how you perform these transformations, let's take a closer look at what XSL is.

XSL, XSLT, and XSL-FO

XSL is a language for transforming and formatting XML documents. It is comprised of two parts: a language for transforming an XML document, called XSL Transformations (XSLT), and syntax for formatting the result of that transformation, called XSL Formatting Objects (XSL-FO).

The XSL specification is a World Wide Web Consortium (W3C) recommendation and includes a specification for XSLT and XSL-FO. The XSLT specification is a W3C recommendation and is therefore fully defined and implemented in several XSL processors, such as Internet Explorer. As of this writing, the XSL-FO specification is a candidate recommendation and is not yet finalized.

You can use XSLT alone to transform an XML document into HTML or another XML document. XSL-FO adds the ability to generate high-quality typographical output, like that needed for printed materials such as newspapers, magazines, and books. XSL-FO is a large topic and is beyond the scope of this book. See the "Additional Resources" section of this chapter for a link to the XSL specification for more information on XSL-FO.

The remainder of this chapter focuses on XSLT, with an emphasis on transforming XML documents into HTML for display to the users.

XSLT Stylesheets

To use XSLT, you create an XSLT stylesheet. A *stylesheet* details the selection, filtering, sorting, reordering and desired layout of data from an XML document.

XSLT is sometimes referred to as "transformation by example" because an XSLT stylesheet describes the output desired as the result of the transformation. The stylesheet does not define *how* to transform an XML document into another format, just *what* the new format should be. It is up to the XSL processor to figure out how to perform the transformation to achieve that result.

An XSLT stylesheet contains a set of *templates* that define the desired output and *patterns* that define how to match the templates with the information in the XML document. You can define multiple templates in one stylesheet to identify different layouts for different types of data within the XML document.

Depending on the output you want as a result of the transformation, a stylesheet could include:

- XSLT elements that select data from the XML document

- HTML elements that build an HTML page

- XML elements that build an XML document

One XML document can be formatted many different ways by simply applying different stylesheets. Figure 12-2 presents the same XML document as Figure 12-1, but with a different XSLT stylesheet.

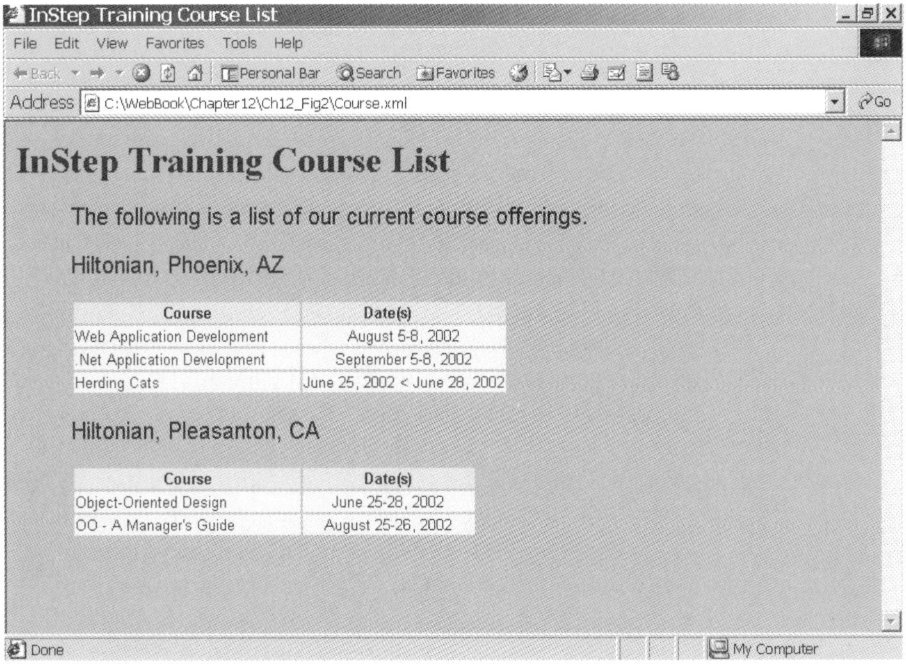

Figure 12-2. The same XML document transformed with an XSLT stylesheet in Figure 12-1 can be transformed differently using a different XSLT stylesheet.

XML Documents as Nodes

To use an XSLT stylesheet, you need an XML document to transform. The XML document from Chapter 11, "Using XML," is used for the majority of examples presented in this chapter. Listing 12-1 provides the original XML document for your reference.

Listing 12-1. The course XML document defines the name, date, and location for a set of courses.

```
<?xml version="1.0"?>
<!-- Course XML -->
<courses>
   <course>
      <name>Object-Oriented Design</name>
      <date>June 25-28, 2002</date>
      <location>Hiltonian, Pleasanton, CA</location>
   </course>
   <course>
      <name>Web Application Development</name>
```

```
        <date>August 5-8, 2002</date>
        <location>Hiltonian, Phoenix, AZ</location>
    </course>
</courses>
```

 **NOTE** *Additional* course *elements were added to this XML document to generate the figures in this chapter. This was needed to provide more interesting examples. Feel free to add your own* course *elements to this XML document for your use in the Try It sections of this chapter.*

An *XSL processor* parses through an XML document, matching the patterns and using the templates in the XSLT stylesheet to generate the output.

The XSL processor internally represents the XML document as a tree structure. Every element in the XML document is represented as a *node* in the tree. Figure 12-3 shows the tree structure for the course XML document presented in Listing 12-1. See Chapter 7, "Understanding Object Models," for more information on tree structures and nodes.

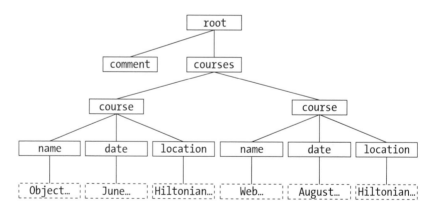

Figure 12-3. Every XML document can be represented as a tree structure with each element represented as a node. This tree structure is the representation of the XML document in Listing 12-1.

The Anatomy of an XSLT Stylesheet

An XSLT stylesheet defines the desired output of an XML document transformation. It contains the set of patterns that specify the data to select from an XML document and templates that specify how that data should appear in the output.

There are two basic approaches for selecting data from an XML document. With the *declarative* approach, sometimes referred to as the push model, the XSL processor parses through every node in the XML document. When a node matches one of the patterns the XSL processor pushes the data to the output following the template in the XSLT stylesheet. The *procedural* approach, sometimes referred to as the pull model, uses flow of control and looping constructs such as for-each to pull the desired data from the XML document and then output it. These two approaches can be combined within an XSLT stylesheet.

The declarative approach is the most common and will be covered in detail in this section. See the "Iterating Through XML Nodes" section for information on the procedural approach.

NOTE *Most anything you can do with the procedural approach you can also do with the declarative approach. Some developers say that "real programmers" don't use the procedural approach and that all XSLT stylesheets should be developed using the declarative approach.*

Most XSLT stylesheets that use the declarative approach follow the same basic structure. They contain the following:

- A template with a pattern to match the root node.

- Elements or text within the template to define the output for the root node.

- XSLT syntax to process the templates for the child nodes of the root node.

- One or more templates with a pattern to match child nodes of the root node.

- Elements or text within each template to define the output for the child nodes of the root node.

- XSLT syntax to process the templates for the child nodes for each child node, basically all of the grandchild nodes.

- One or more templates with a pattern to match grandchild nodes.

- Elements or text within each template to define the output for the grandchild nodes.

This repeats down through the XML document tree structure.

Let's start with a simple example and transform the XML document in Listing 12-1 into HTML as shown in Figure 12-4. We'll work our way up to more sophisticated transformations as shown in Figures 12-1 and 12-2.

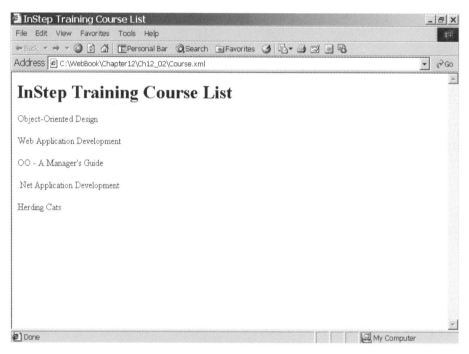

Figure 12-4. A simple stylesheet retrieves and presents the course names.

The stylesheet used to generate Figure 12-4 is as follows:

```
❶  <xsl:stylesheet version="1.0" xmlns:xsl="http://www.w3.org/1999/XSL/Transform">
❷  <!-- Course.xsl  -->
❸  <xsl:template match="/">
❹     <xsl:apply-templates />
❺  </xsl:template>
❻  <xsl:template match="courses">
❼     <html>
❽       <head>
❾         <title>InStep Training Course List</title>
❿       </head>
⓫       <body>
⓬         <h1>InStep Training Course List</h1>
⓭         <xsl:apply-templates />
⓮       </body>
⓯     </html>
⓰  </xsl:template>
⓱  <xsl:template match="course">
⓲     <p><xsl:value-of select="name"/></p>
⓳  </xsl:template>
⓴  </xsl:stylesheet>
```

Notice how the XSLT stylesheet is formatted like an XML document. Actually, an XSLT stylesheet is itself an XML document and must be well-formed with a root element, beginning and ending tags, and so on. Any HTML or XML within the stylesheet must also be well-formed. See Chapter 11, "Using XML," for more information on the requirements for a well-formed XML document. See "XHTML" in Chapter 3, "Using HTML," for more information on well-formed HTML.

The XSLT stylesheet begins with a root stylesheet element (lines ❶ and ⓴) that defines it as an XSLT stylesheet.

NOTE transform *is allowed as a synonym for* stylesheet, *but* stylesheet *is more commonly used.*

The version attribute of the stylesheet element is required to specify the XSLT version. The xmlns attribute identifies the XML namespace used by the stylesheet. This namespace defines the set of XSLT element names that can be used in the stylesheet. See Chapter 11, "Using XML," for more information on namespaces.

To distinguish between the XSLT elements and any other HTML or XML elements in the stylesheet, the XSLT elements must be prefixed with the namespace abbreviation. This ensures that the XSLT element names don't conflict with any other element names. In this example, xsl is used as the abbreviation. You can use any prefix for a namespace, but xsl is most commonly used when referring to the XSLT namespace.

Whatever abbreviation you define, you must append it as a prefix to each XSLT element name. For example, xsl:template defines the template element from the XSLT namespace.

Comments (line ❷) can be inserted anywhere in the XSLT stylesheet. Notice that the comments conform to the XML convention.

The XSLT template element tags (lines ❸ and ❺) identify the beginning and ending of a template. The match attribute specifies the pattern that defines when the template should be applied. A pattern of "/" indicates that this template should be applied as soon as the root node of the XML document is processed. The elements within this template (between lines ❸ and ❺) define the output that should be generated when the template is applied, if any.

Because the root node of the XML document is processed first, any information that you want to appear in the output before any XML document data should be defined within the XSLT template element matching the root node.

In this example, there is no output required when the root node is processed. This template only contains the XSLT apply-templates element (line ❹). This element applies any template defined for the child nodes of the current, or *context*, node. Since the match attribute for this template was the root node, the context node is the root node and the apply-templates element applies the templates for all of the child nodes of the root node.

Looking at the XML document in Listing 12-1 and Figure 12-3, the child nodes of the root node are the comment and the courses nodes. The comment has no defined template in this stylesheet, but there is a template defined for the courses node.

The courses node template (lines ❻ through ⓰) defines the information that should be output when a courses node is processed in the XML document. In this example, the template consists of HTML syntax because this stylesheet is transforming an XML document into HTML output. Notice the standard html element (lines ❼ and ⓯), head element (lines ❽ and ❿), and so on. These elements are simply passed through to the output. Any elements or other text within the template that is not identified as belonging to the XSLT namespace is written directly to the output.

The XSLT apply-templates element (line ⓭) again applies any templates defined for the child nodes of the context node. This time the context node is the courses node so this applies any template defined for the child nodes of the courses node, or any course node template.

The course node template (lines ⓱ through ⓳) defines the information output when a course node is processed. In this example, the XSLT value-of element selects the name attribute of the XML document's course node and outputs it as part of an HTML p (paragraph) element. This template is processed for each child resulting in the output shown in Figure 12-4.

This simple stylesheet only gives you basic output. As you can see from Figures 12-1 and 12-2, you can do much more. The stylesheets needed to produce the HTML presented in those figures are shown later in this chapter.

Creating an XSLT Stylesheet

You can manually create your stylesheets because they are just text files. You can then check the syntax of the stylesheet and verify the result of the transformation using an XSL processor.

You can create an XSLT stylesheet using a basic text editor, such as Notepad or WordPad for Windows and Emacs or vi for Unix. Using a simple tool has the benefit of simplicity, but it requires that you spend the time typing in XSLT elements with the correct syntax.

Several tools are available to help you create your stylesheet. Tools such as XML Spy allow you to view and edit your stylesheet. Most of these tools have an XSL processor that transforms an XML document using your stylesheet so you can verify the result of the transformation.

Internet Explorer also provides an XSL processor, so you can see the results of your transformation.

For the purposes of this chapter, create the XSLT stylesheet manually:

1. Create a text file and save it with an .xsl extension.

2. Add the `stylesheet` root element.

3. Define a template that matches to the root node. Within this template, add any elements that should be written to the beginning of the output.

4. Define one or more additional templates including elements and attributes as required for your data and your desired output.

5. Ensure your XSLT stylesheet is well-formed.

6. Ensure that your stylesheet transforms your XML document as you intended.

Follow these steps to get started with XSLT stylesheets.

Try It 12-1.

Creating an XSLT Stylesheet

Try It 12-1 builds a simple XSLT stylesheet that can transform the Course XML document shown in Listing 12-1, into an HTML page for display in a Web application.

1. Using Notepad or your tool of choice, create a new text file.

2. Insert the XSLT stylesheet element. Be sure to specify the appropriate XML namespace for XSLT. If you want to ensure that the HTML within the stylesheet is XHTML compliant, you can also add the strict DTD namespace, as defined in Chapter 3, "Using HTML."

3. Insert a `template` element and define a match to the root node of the XML document.

4. Insert an `apply-templates` element to apply the templates for the child nodes of the root node.

5. Insert a `template` element and define a match to the `courses` node of the XML document.

6. Add HTML to give the output a title and a heading.

7. Insert an apply-templates element to apply the templates for the child nodes of the courses node.

8. Insert a `template` element and define a match to the `course` nodes of the XML document.

9. Add HTML and XSLT elements to display each course name in a paragraph.

10. Save the file as course.xsl.

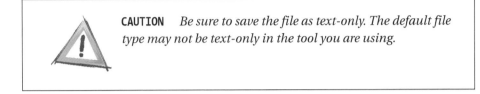

CAUTION *Be sure to save the file as text-only. The default file type may not be text-only in the tool you are using.*

Listing 12-2 shows the resulting course.xsl stylesheet. See the next section for information on using this stylesheet to transform the course.xml file.

Listing 12-2. The course.xsl stylesheet contains the HTML and XSLT needed to display the list of courses.

```
<xsl:stylesheet version="1.0"
    xmlns:xsl="http://www.w3.org/1999/XSL/Transform"
    xmlns="http://www.w3.org/TR/xhtml1/strict">
<!--
   Try It  12-1
   Title:  Course XSL
   Author: InStep Technologies
           www.insteptech.com
   Purpose:To demonstrate XSL transformation to HTML
 -->
 <xsl:template match="/">
   <xsl:apply-templates />
</xsl:template>

<xsl:template match="courses">
  <html>
     <head>
        <title>InStep Training Course List</title>
     </head>
```

```
      <body>
         <h1>InStep Training Course List</h1>
         <xsl:apply-templates />
      </body>
   </html>
</xsl:template>

<xsl:template match="course">
   <p><xsl:value-of select="name" /></p>
</xsl:template>
</xsl:stylesheet>
```

Associating an XSLT Stylesheet

The XSLT stylesheet does not do anything by itself. You need to associate the XSLT stylesheet with an XML document to transform the XML document.

There are several ways to associate an XSLT stylesheet with an XML document. One way is to add a line to your XML document defining the desired stylesheet. For the course.xsl file, this line is:

```
<?xml-stylesheet type="text/xsl" href="Course.xsl"?>
```

This declaration defines the type of stylesheet and the filename of the stylesheet using either absolute or relative paths. This statement associates a specific XSLT stylesheet with the XML document.

Alternatively, you can associate an XSLT stylesheet with an XML document within an XSL processor such as XML Spy or LotusXSL. Options within these tools allow you to associate an XSLT stylesheet with an XML document.

Try It 12-2.

Associating a Stylesheet with an XML Document

Try It 12-2 associates the XSLT stylesheet created in Try It 12-1 with the Course XML document created in Chapter 11, "Using XML," and shown in Listing 12-1.

1. Open the course.xml file from Try It 11-1 in your text editor.

2. Add the `xml-stylesheet` declaration as shown in this section.

3. Open the course.xml file in Internet Explorer (version 5 or higher). When you load the XML document into Internet Explorer, the XML is transformed into HTML using the XSLT stylesheet and displayed in the browser window.

NOTE   *The Microsoft XML Parser (MSXML) included in Internet Explorer 5 and 5.5 has an implementation of XSL that was based on a working draft of the XSL specification and is not fully compatible with the final XSL specification. To use all of the XSL features, you need to download and install MSXML 3.0 or above. See* msdn.microsoft.com/xml *for more information and to download the latest version of MSXML.*

NOTE   *Netscape does not transform an XML document. You need to use a tool such as XML Spy or LotusXSL to perform the transformation (see the "Additional Resources" section of this chapter for links to these products). You can then display the resulting HTML in Netscape.*

The XSLT transforms the XML document to HTML and displays the HTML similar to Figure 12-4. If the data is not transformed as you would expect, check your code against the prior Try It. Remember that an XSLT stylesheet is itself an XML document and must follow the XML rules, such as matching beginning and ending tags and quoting attributes.

TIP *You may receive an "Unspecified Error" message if you do not use the correct case for XSLT elements. For example, using* `Template` *instead of the correct* `template` *can produce an error. Ensure you are using the correct uppercase and lowercase.*

Iterating through XML Nodes

The stylesheet created in Try It 12-1 used a declarative approach for selecting data and transforming the XML document into HTML. This section presents a procedural approach that selectively processes desired nodes.

In this example, the XML document data is transformed into an HTML table. This provides the result shown in Figure 12-1. The XSLT stylesheet needed for this transformation is shown next.

```
❶  <xsl:stylesheet version="1.0" xmlns:xsl="http://www.w3.org/1999/XSL/Transform">
❷  <!-- Course.xsl  -->
❸  <xsl:template match="/">
❹    <html>
❺      <head>
❻        <title>InStep Training Course List</title>
❼      </head>
❽      <body>
❾        <h1>InStep Training Course List</h1>
❿        <table>
⓫         <xsl:for-each select="courses/course">
⓬         <tr>
⓭            <td><xsl:value-of select="name" /></td>
⓮            <td><xsl:value-of select="date" /></td>
⓯            <td><xsl:value-of select="location" /></td>
⓰         </tr>
```

17   `</xsl:for-each>`
18   `</table>`
19 `</body>`
20 `</html>`
21 `</xsl:template>`
22 `</xsl:stylesheet>`

  The first thing to notice in this example is that there is only one template. All of the syntax to transform the XML document into HTML output is within the one template.

  The XSLT stylesheet begins with a `stylesheet` element (lines **1** and **22**). This statement is followed by a comment (line **2**).

  The XSLT `template` element tags (line **3** and **21**) identify the beginning and ending of the only template. The `match` attribute specifies a pattern of "/" indicating that this template should be applied as soon as the root node of the XML document is processed.

  The basic HTML elements (lines **4** through **9**) are passed directly through to the output, creating the start of an HTML document. The HTML `table` element (line **10**) begins the definition of the table that lists the course name, dates, and location.

  To display each course in a row in the table, each `course` node must be retrieved from the XML document. This is done using the XSLT `for-each` element (lines **11** and **17**). The XSLT `for-each` element defines its own template. The pattern for this template is defined by the `select` attribute. In this case, each `course` node within the `courses` node is selected from the XML document. This select syntax is discussed further in the "Setting Selection Criteria Using XPath" section later in this chapter.

  The template is comprised of the elements within the XSLT `for-each` element (lines **12** through **16**). For each `course` node extracted from the XML document, HTML elements are generated in the output to create a new row in the table (lines **12** and **16**).

  The XSLT `value-of` element retrieves the value of a specific element or attribute from the XML document as defined by the `select` attribute value. In this case, the `name` node from the XML document is output into the first table column (line **13**), the `date` node from the XML document is output into the second table column (line **14**) and the `location` node from the XML document is output into the third table column (line **15**).

NOTE *To use* value-of *to select an attribute instead of an element, prefix the attribute name with an at sign (@); for example:* `<xsl:value-of select="@room"/>`.

The remaining basic HTML elements (lines ❶❽ through ❷⓿) are passed directly through to the output, completing the HTML document.

The result of this transformation, with the addition of CSS, is a nicely format-ted table as shown in Figure 12-1.

Try It 12-3.

Creating a Table with an XSLT Stylesheet

Try It 12-3 creates a new XSLT stylesheet that presents the Course XML docu-ment from Listing 12-1 in a table.

1. Save the stylesheet from Try It 12-1 in a different directory. That stylesheet will be used again in a later Try It.

2. Using Notepad or your tool of choice, create a new text file.

3. Insert the XSLT stylesheet element. Be sure to specify the appropriate XML namespace for XSLT. If you want to ensure that the HTML within the stylesheet is XHTML compliant, you can also add the strict DTD name-space, as defined in Chapter 3, "Using HTML."

4. Insert a template element and define a match to the root node of the XML document.

5. Add HTML elements to define the basic structure of an HTML document, including the html, head, and body elements.

6. Add HTML elements to define a table. If desired, add HTML elements to define column headings.

7. After the table element, insert the XSLT for-each element and select each XML document course node within the courses node.

8. Add a tr element to define a row and td elements to define each column of data. Insert the XSLT value-of element to select the appropriate data for each column of the table.

9. Save the file as course.xsl.

10. Optionally, add a reference to the CSS style sheet created in Chapter 4, "Using Style Sheets" and the XSLT sort element to sort the courses by name or location.

11. Open the course.xml file in Internet Explorer (version 5 or higher). When you load the XML document into Internet Explorer, the XML is transformed into HTML using the XSLT stylesheet and displayed in the browser window.

Listing 12-3 shows the course.xsl stylesheet, and Figure 12-1 shows the result of the transformation.

Listing 12-3. The course.xsl stylesheet contains the HTML needed to display XML data in a table.

```
<xsl:stylesheet version="1.0"
    xmlns:xsl="http://www.w3.org/1999/XSL/Transform"
    xmlns="http://www.w3.org/TR/xhtml1/strict">
<!--
   Try It  12-3
   Title:  Course XSL
   Author: InStep Technologies
           www.insteptech.com
   Purpose:To demonstrate XSL transformation to HTML
 -->
<xsl:template match="/">
   <html>
   <head>
      <title>InStep Training Course List</title>
      <link rel="stylesheet" type="text/css" href="TrainingStyle.css" />
   </head>
   <body>
      <h1>InStep Training Course List</h1>
      <p class="normal">The following is a list of our current course offerings.</p>
      <table>
         <tr class="even">
            <th class="wide">Course</th>
            <th class="narrow">Date(s)</th>
            <th class="wide">Location</th>
         </tr>
         <xsl:for-each select="courses/course">
            <xsl:sort select="name" />
            <tr class="odd">
               <td><xsl:value-of select="name" /></td>
               <td align="center"><xsl:value-of select="date" /></td>
               <td><xsl:value-of select="location" /></td>
            </tr>
```

```
        </xsl:for-each>
    </table>
  </body>
  </html>
</xsl:template>
</xsl:stylesheet>
```

Understanding the Transformation

How did that XML document get transformed into an HTML page? How does the XSL processor work? Figure 12-5 shows a simplistic view of the transformation process.

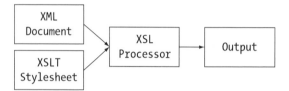

Figure 12-5. An XSL processor reads in the XML document and transforms it following the output specification in the XSLT stylesheet.

The XML document contains the data. The XSLT stylesheet contains the templates that define the desired output.

The XSL processor processes each node of the XML document tree structure. For each node, the XSLT stylesheet template patterns are checked. If that node matches a pattern in one of the templates, the template is applied. The template normally adds specific content to the output. When all of the nodes of the tree structure have been processed, the output is complete.

Let's take this process step by step.

The XSL processor begins by loading the XML document into memory, internally representing the XML document as a tree structure. Every element in the XML document is represented as a node on the tree. Figure 12-3 shows the tree structure for the course XML document listed in Listing 12-1 and presented in Figures 12-1, 12-2, and 12-4.

The second step of the transformation is to process each node of the XML document tree and apply the templates defined within the stylesheet.

An XML document is processed from top to bottom. Using the XML document shown in Listing 12-1 as an example, the courses node is processed, then the first course node is processed, then the name, the text for the name, the date, the text for the date, the location, and the text for the location for that course are processed. Then the second course node is processed, then the name, the text for the name, the date, the text for the date, the location, and the text for the location for that course are processed. This is repeated until all of the course nodes are processed.

When that XML document is represented in a tree structure, the processing stays the same: the courses node is processed, then the first course node is processed, then the name, the text for the name, the date, the text for the date, the location, and the text for the location for that course are processed. Then the second course node is processed and so on.

Follow this processing on Figure 12-3 and you can see that the tree is navigated from the left down to the bottom of the tree to reach every node below a node before moving to the next node at the same level. This is called *document* or *depth-first* order. This concept is much less confusing if you think of the XML document as in Listing 12-1, processed from the top and navigating down through each element and all of its sub-elements, then the next element and its sub-element until reaching the bottom of the document.

Each node in the XML document is processed using this depth-first order. The node currently being processed is called the current, or *context node.*

As each node is processed, the template patterns in the XSLT stylesheet are checked. If one of the patterns matches the context node, the associated template is applied. The template frequently contains elements that select an additional set of nodes for processing. This continues recursively until all of the nodes of the XML document have been processed.

For example, the XML document in Listing 12-1 and shown in Figure 12-3 can be transformed using the XSLT stylesheet from Listing 12-3. As soon as the root node of the XML document is processed, the following template from the XSLT stylesheet is matched:

```
<xsl:template match="/">
```

The elements within this template element are then processed. The majority of these elements are HTML elements that are written directly to the output, thereby creating the resultant HTML page.

When an XSLT for-each element is processed, the XSL processor finds all elements that are children of the context node and match the select attribute. In the example from Listing 12-3, the XSL processor retrieves each course node within the courses node from the XML document tree structure and applies the template defined within the for-each element:

```
<xsl:for-each select="courses/course">
  <tr class="odd">
    <td><xsl:value-of select="name" /></td>
    <td align="center"><xsl:value-of select="date" /></td>
    <td><xsl:value-of select="location" /></td>
  </tr>
</xsl:for-each>
```

The XSLT value-of element locates the node defined by the select attribute within the context node. It then extracts the text node of that node and writes it to the output.

The final result is an HTML page containing the introductory text and a table displaying the details for each course in the XML document.

Setting Selection Criteria Using XPath

To transform an XML document into different formats, you need a way to reference and navigate to the parts of the XML document. This is done using specific syntax called the XML Path Language (XPath).

XPath provides a mechanism for defining specific nodes in the XML document tree structure. It also provides basic programmatic functionality.

XPath can be used to:

- Reference a node or set of nodes in the XML document

- Specify the matching criteria for a template pattern

- Perform numerical calculations

- Manipulate strings

- Call functions

- Test conditions

XPath can be used to identify a specific node or set of nodes relative to the current, or *context node* of the XML document tree structure. This is used in XSLT attributes such as the match attribute of a template element or the select attribute of a for-each element.

Table 12-1 presents examples of XPath selections using the XML document example from Listing 12-1. For clarity, node names from the XML document are shown in bold. Other syntax and keywords are shown without bold.

 NOTE *To illustrate selection of an attribute from the XML document, the examples in Table 12-1 assume a* room *attribute as part of the* location *node in the XML document that is not included in Listing 12-1.*

Table 12-1. Common XPath Expressions

XPATH EXPRESSION	SELECTION
/	Selects the root node.
.	Selects the context node itself.
..	Selects the parent of the context node.
*	Selects all element nodes that are children of the context node.
	If the context node is the root node, this syntax selects the courses node from Listing 12-1.
text()	Selects all text nodes that are children of the context node.
node()	Selects all nodes that are children of the context node, regardless of its type. This selects element, attribute, or text nodes.
	If the context node is the root node, this syntax selects the xml-stylesheet, comment, and courses nodes from Listing 12-1.
name()	Selects the name of the context node.
courses	Selects all courses nodes that are children of the context node.
	If the context node is the root node, this syntax will select the courses node from Listing 12-1.
courses/course	Selects all course nodes that are children of a courses node that is a child of the context node.
	If the context node is the root node, this syntax selects each course node from Listing 12-1.
courses/course/name	Selects all name nodes that are children of course nodes that are children of a courses node that is a child of the context node.
	If the context node is the root node, this syntax selects each name node from Listing 12-1.
courses/ /name	Selects all name nodes that are descendents of a courses node that is a child of the context node. This is sometimes referred to as *arbitrary descendants*.
	This syntax selects each name node anywhere under the courses node. This is different from courses/course/name, which only selects name nodes that are children of the course node. In this example using Listing 12-1, the results are the same because there are no name nodes other than those under the course node.

Table 12-1. Common XPath Expressions (continued)

XPATH EXPRESSION	SELECTION
`//name`	Selects all name nodes anywhere within the current XML document.
`courses/course[name]`	Selects all course nodes that have a name child node and are children of a courses node that is a child of the context node.
	You can think of the [ ] syntax as a *where clause*. In this case: Where the course has a name child node.
`courses/course[name|location]`	Selects all course nodes that have a name or location node and are children of a courses node that is a child of the context node.
	Where clause: Where the course has a name or location child node.
`courses/course` `[name='Herding Cats']`	Selects all course nodes that have a name node whose value is Herding Cats and are children of a courses node that is a child of the context node.
	Where clause: Where the course has a name node with a value of Herding Cats.
`courses/course/` `location[@room]`	Selects all location nodes that have a room attribute and are children of course nodes that are children of a courses node that is a child of the context node.
	Where clause: Where the location has a room attribute.
	If the context node is the root node, this syntax selects all of the location nodes that have a room attribute.
`courses/course/location` `[@room='Rm 17']`	Selects all location nodes that have a room attribute equal to the defined value (Rm 17) and are children of course nodes that are children of a courses node that is a child of the context node.
	Where clause: Where the location has a room attribute with a value of Rm 17.
	If the context node is the root node, this syntax selects all of the location nodes that have a room attribute set to Rm 17.
`@*`	Selects all attributes of the context node.

Table 12-1. Common XPath Expressions (continued)

XPATH EXPRESSION	SELECTION
courses/course/location/@*	Selects all attributes of the location nodes that are children of course nodes that are children of a courses node that is a child of the context node. If the context node is the root node, this syntax selects all of the location node attributes.
@room	Selects the room attribute of the context node.
courses/course/location/ @room	Selects the room attribute of the location nodes that are children of course nodes that are children of a courses node that is a child of the context node. If the context node is the root node, this syntax selects the room attribute for each of the location nodes.
courses/course[1]	Selects the first course node that is a child of a courses node that is a child of the context node. This is a short-cut syntax for: courses/course[position()=1]. Where clause: Where the course is not the first one. If the context node is the root node, this syntax selects the course named "Object-Oriented Design" in Listing 12-1.
courses/course[position()!=1]	Selects all course nodes except the first course node that is a child of a courses node that is a child of the context node. If the context node is the root node, this syntax selects all of the courses except the one named "Object-Oriented Design" in Listing 12-1.
courses/course[position() < 2]	Selects all course nodes that are in positions less than position 2 that are children of a courses node that is a child of the context node. Where clause: Where the course is in a position less than the second position. If the context node is the root node, this syntax selects the course named "Object-Oriented Design" in Listing 12-1.
courses/course[position() > 2]	Selects all course nodes that are in positions greater than 2 that are children of a courses node that is a child of the context node. Where clause: Where the course is in a position greater than the second position. If the context node is the root node, this syntax will not select any courses in Listing 12-1 because there are only two courses.

Table 12-1. Common XPath Expressions (continued)

XPATH EXPRESSION	SELECTION
courses/course[position() mod 2 = 1]	Selects all course nodes that are in odd positions that are children of a courses node that is a child of the context node. Where clause: Where the course is in an odd position. The mod operator performs a division and determines the remainder. In this example, mod 2 is dividing the position by two and checking for a remainder of 1, thereby looking for nodes that are in the first position, third position, and so on. This is useful for formatting tables where you want to format odd and even rows differently. See "Using XSLT Structures" and Figure 12-7 for an example.

CAUTION   *XPath is case sensitive. For example, you will not find a* course *node if you use* courses/Course.

CAUTION   *XSLT* position() *values are 1-based, not 0-based. The first node is in position 1, the second in position 2, and so on.*

See the "Additional Resources" section of this chapter for a reference to a complete listing of valid XPath syntax.

Try It 12-4.

Working with XPath

Try It 12-4 provides a simple stylesheet that accesses the Course XML document to practice XPath syntax.

1. Using Notepad or your tool of choice, create a new text file.

2. Insert the XSLT stylesheet element. Be sure to specify the appropriate XML namespace for XSLT.

3. Insert an XSLT template element and define a match to the root node of the XML document.

4. Add an XSLT for-each element and set the select attribute to the XPath expression that you want to test.

5. Add an XSLT value-of element and set the select attribute to name() to display the name or . to display the content of the nodes returned by the for-each in step 4. If desired, put this information into a table with any other information you want to view.

6. Save the file as courseXPath.xsl.

7. Copy the course.xml file from Try It 12-2 to a new name such as courseXPath.xml.

8. Open the courseXPath.xml file in your text editor and updated the xml-stylesheet declaration to specify the courseXPath.xsl file.

9. Open the courseXPath.xml file in Internet Explorer (version 5 or higher). When you load the XML document into Internet Explorer, the result of the XPath expression is displayed.

The result shows you the nodes that are selected based on the XPath expression that you defined. This gives you an idea of what you are selecting as you work with XPath syntax.

Listing 12-4 presents an XSLT stylesheet that demonstrates two XPath expressions. You can change these expressions or add others to display a table of XPath syntax.

Listing 12-4. This XSLT stylesheet tests XPath expressions by setting different selection criteria.

```
<xsl:stylesheet version="1.0"
    xmlns:xsl="http://www.w3.org/1999/XSL/Transform">
<!--
   Try It  12-4
   Title:  Course XSL
   Author: InStep Technologies
           www.insteptech.com
   Purpose:To demonstrate XPath
 -->
<xsl:template match="/">
   <html>
     <head>
        <title>XPath Test</title>
        <link rel="stylesheet" type="text/css" href="TrainingStyle.css" />
     </head>
     <body>
        <table border="1">
           <xsl:for-each select=".">
              <tr>
                 <td>.</td>
```

```
                        <td><xsl:value-of select="name()" /></td>
                        <td><xsl:value-of select="." /></td>
                    </tr>
                </xsl:for-each>
                <xsl:for-each select="node()">
                    <tr>
                        <td>node()</td>
                        <td><xsl:value-of select="name()" /></td>
                        <td><xsl:value-of select="." /></td>
                    </tr>
                </xsl:for-each>
            </table>
        </body>
    </html>
</xsl:template>
</xsl:stylesheet>
```

Working with XSLT Templates

Now that you know how to build XSLT stylesheets using both a declarative and procedural approach and know the basics of XPath, you are ready to create more complex XSLT templates.

Using Multiple XSLT Templates

Using multiple templates within one stylesheet allows you to format header information separately from detail and format detail information using differing templates for differing types of detail. For example, course name information could be formatted with one style, course dates with another, and course location with yet another style, as shown in Figure 12-6.

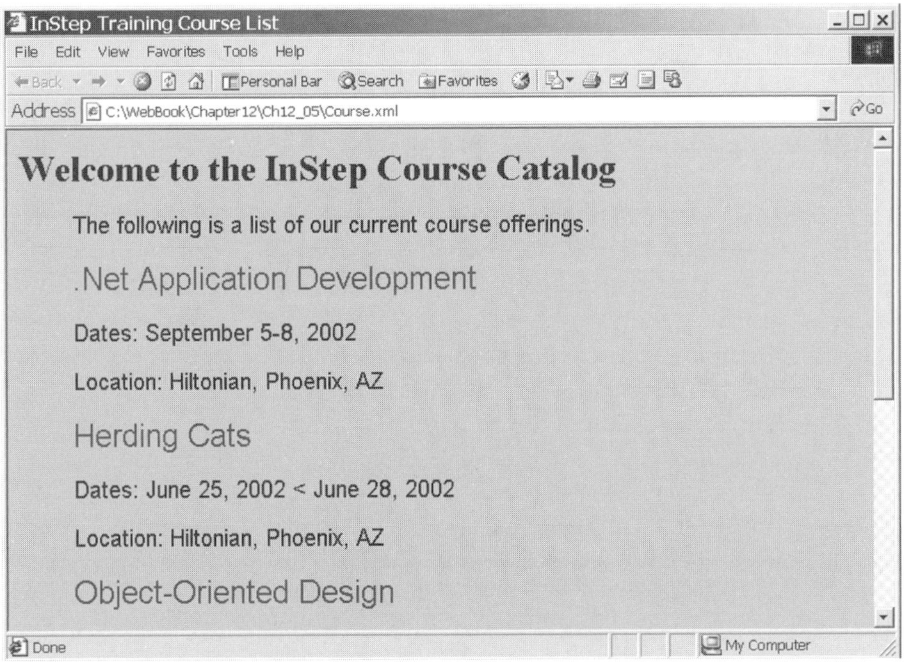

Figure 12-6. Different parts of the XML document can be formatted differently using multiple templates.

The basic structure of the XSLT stylesheet used to generate the HTML for this figure is as follows:

```
❶  <xsl:stylesheet version="1.0"
❷      xmlns:xsl="http://www.w3.org/1999/XSL/Transform">
❸  <xsl:template match="/">
❹    <xsl:apply-templates />
❺  </xsl:template>
❻  <xsl:template match="courses">
❼    <xsl:apply-templates>
❽        <xsl:sort select="name" />
❾    </xsl:apply-templates>
❿  </xsl:template>
⓫  <xsl:template match="name">
⓬      <p><xsl:value-of select="." /></p>
⓭  </xsl:template>
⓮  <xsl:template match="location">
⓯      <p>Location: <xsl:value-of select="." /></p>
⓰  </xsl:template>
⓱  <xsl:template match="date">
```

⑱   `<p>Dates: <xsl:value-of select="." /></p>`
⑲   `</xsl:template>`
⑳   `</xsl:stylesheet>`

This XSLT stylesheet begins with the `stylesheet` element identifying the XSLT version and namespace. As stated previously, all XSLT stylesheets should begin with this syntax as the root node.

The first template (line **❸**) is applied as soon as the root of the XML document is processed. The elements within this `template` element (lines **❸** through **❺**) are processed immediately.

The only statement within this first template is an XSLT `apply-templates` element (line **❹**). The `apply-templates` element applies any templates defined for the child nodes of the context node. At this point in this example, the context node is the root node of the XML document. The children of the root node for the XML document in Listing 12-1 are the comment and the `courses` node.

Without the `apply-templates` element, you would not transform any nodes beyond the root of the XML document. None of the other nodes of that document would be written to the output. By adding the `apply-templates` element the XSL processor checks other templates as it processes the XML document tree structure.

The `courses` node template (lines **❻** through **❿**), is applied when the `courses` node is processed. The `apply-templates` element within this template applies any template defined for child nodes of the context node, which in this case is the `courses` node. The children of the `courses` node are `course` nodes. So the `apply-templates` element in this example processes each `course` node. The `sort` (line **❽**) sorts the `course` nodes by the defined selection criteria before processing the nodes.

The `name` node template (lines **⓫** through **⓭**) is applied when a `name` node from the XML document is processed. This template uses the XSLT `value-of` element (line **⓬**) to output the value of the context node, in this case the `name` node, which writes the name of the course from the XML document into the output.

A `location` node template (lines **⓮** through **⓰**) is applied when a `location` node from the XML document is processed. When a `location` node is processed, a label is output along with the text for the context node, which is the `location` node text.

A `date` node template (lines **⓱** through **⓳**) is applied when a `date` node is processed. When a `date` node is processed, a label is output along with the text for the context node, which is the `date` node text.

By using multiple templates within your XSLT stylesheets, you can format any data from your XML document in any way you desire.

Try It 12-5.

Working with XSLT Templates

Try It 12-5 builds a more complex XSLT template for use with the Course XML document shown in Listing 12-1.

1. Open the course.xsl file from Try It 12-1.

2. Add an XSLT sort element to the courses node template. Be sure to add the sort as a sub-element of the XSLT `apply-templates` element.

3. Add HTML to display a page similar to Figure 12-6.

4. Remove the `course` node template.

5. Add templates for `name`, `location`, and `date` similar to those shown in this section.

7. Open the course.xml file in Internet Explorer (version 5 or higher). When you load the XML document into Internet Explorer, the results are displayed.

8. Optionally, add the CSS file and associated styles that have been used throughout the prior Try Its.

The resulting XSLT stylesheet, presented in Listing 12-5, transforms your course XML document into an HTML page similar to that shown in Figure 12-6.

Listing 12-5. The course.xsl stylesheet in this example demonstrates use of multiple XSLT templates.

```
<xsl:stylesheet version="1.0"
    xmlns:xsl="http://www.w3.org/1999/XSL/Transform"
    xmlns="http://www.w3.org/TR/xhtml1/strict">
<!--
   Try It  12-5
   Title:  Course XSL
   Author: InStep Technologies
           www.insteptech.com
   Purpose:To demonstrate XSLT templates
 -->
<xsl:template match="/">
   <xsl:apply-templates />
</xsl:template>

<xsl:template match="courses">
   <html>
      <head>
```

```
            <title>InStep Training Course List</title>
            <link rel="stylesheet" type="text/css" href="TrainingStyle.css" ></link>
        </head>
        <body>
            <h1>Welcome to the InStep Course Catalog</h1>
            <p class="normal">
                The following is a list of our current course offerings.
            </p>
            <xsl:apply-templates>
                <xsl:sort select="name" />
            </xsl:apply-templates>
        </body>
    </html>
</xsl:template>

<xsl:template match="name">
    <p class="key"><xsl:value-of select="." /></p>
</xsl:template>

<xsl:template match="location">
    <p class="normal">Location: <xsl:value-of select="." /></p>
</xsl:template>

<xsl:template match="date">
    <p class="normal">Dates: <xsl:value-of select="." /></p>
</xsl:template>
</xsl:stylesheet>
```

Built-in Templates

The XSLT specification defines several built-in, or default, templates. These built-in templates provide output specifications for elements, attributes, and text nodes that are not matched anywhere in your templates. These built-in templates are not added to your XSLT file, but the XSL processor assumes they exist. This section covers two of these built-in templates.

The first built-in template ensures that the entire XML document is processed. This template is as follows:

```
<xsl:template match="*|/">
    <xsl:apply-templates />
</xsl:template>
```

This template matches the all element nodes that are children of the context node or the root node and applies any other templates. This allows recursive processing to continue in the absence of a successful pattern match by a template in the stylesheet. This default template does not write anything to the output.

The example presented in Listing 12-5 would not have provided the expected results without this built-in template. The first template in Listing 12-5 matched to the root node (/). The second template matched the courses node. There was no template for the course nodes. The remaining templates were for the name, location, and date nodes. Without the built-in template, processing would have stopped when no template for the course nodes was found. Instead, the built-in template was applied and the XSLT apply-templates element in the built-in template applied the templates for the children of the course nodes.

A second built-in template ensures that something is written to the output. This template is as follows:

```
<xsl:template match="text()|@*">
   <xsl:value-of select="." />
</xsl:template>
```

This template matches all text or attribute nodes and writes their values to the output.

NOTE *The documentation for the Microsoft XSL Parser defines this built-in template using* match="text()", *ignoring the attribute nodes. So only the text nodes are output, not text and attribute nodes, when using the Microsoft XSL Parser.*

You can see the effect of these built-in templates if you develop an XSLT stylesheet with no templates of your own. For example, the following stylesheet contains no templates:

```
<xsl:stylesheet version="1.0"
     xmlns:xsl="http://www.w3.org/1999/XSL/Transform">
</xsl:stylesheet>
```

If you associate this stylesheet with an XML document, all of the text or attribute elements are displayed.

By knowing about the built-in templates, you can understand why the XSLT stylesheet above displays all of the text from your XML document. Using the default template like the previous example during debugging can help you understand the depth-first ordering that the XSL processor uses.

The built-in templates do not provide much in the way of formatting, however, so normally you write your own templates. The main reason this section covers the built-in templates is because of their side effects.

In order to ensure that the built-in templates are not used, you need to override each of these built-in templates. If you define templates that don't process all of the child nodes, for example, you may find that the built-in templates process the other child nodes for you and adds unexpected nodes to your output.

Understanding the actions of the built-in templates helps you to debug your templates and understand why you sometimes get unexpected data in your output.

Try It 12-6.

Working with Built-in Templates

Try It 12-6 works with the built-in templates and the Course XML document shown in Listing 12-1.

1. Using Notepad or your tool of choice, create a new text file.

2. Insert the XSLT stylesheet element. Be sure to specify the appropriate XML namespace for XSLT.

3. Save the file as courseBuiltIn.xsl.

4. Copy the course.xml file from Try It 12-5 to a new name such as course-BuiltIn.xml.

5. Open the courseBuiltIn.xml file in your text editor and updated the xml-stylesheet declaration to specify the courseBuiltIn.xsl file.

6. Open the courseBuiltIn.xml file in Internet Explorer (version 5 or higher). When you load the XML document into Internet Explorer, the data is displayed, even though you have no templates or other formatting in the courseBuiltIn.xsl file. This is the work of the built-in templates.

7. Optionally, remove one of the templates from the course.xsl file created in Try It 12-5 to see what the built-in templates do when you do not override them.

The resulting XSLT stylesheet, presented in Listing 12-6, displays the data from your XML document using the default template.

Listing 12-6. This stylesheet does not contain any templates, so it uses the built-in templates to process and display all of the data from the XML document.

```
<xsl:stylesheet version="1.0"
    xmlns:xsl="http://www.w3.org/1999/XSL/Transform">
</xsl:stylesheet>
```

Using XSLT Structures

XSLT stylesheets can contain basic programming structures. These include variables, if statements, and choose statements.

Using XSLT structures you can add more logic to your stylesheets. For example, you may want to change the formatting of even and odd lines in a table as shown in Figure 12-7.

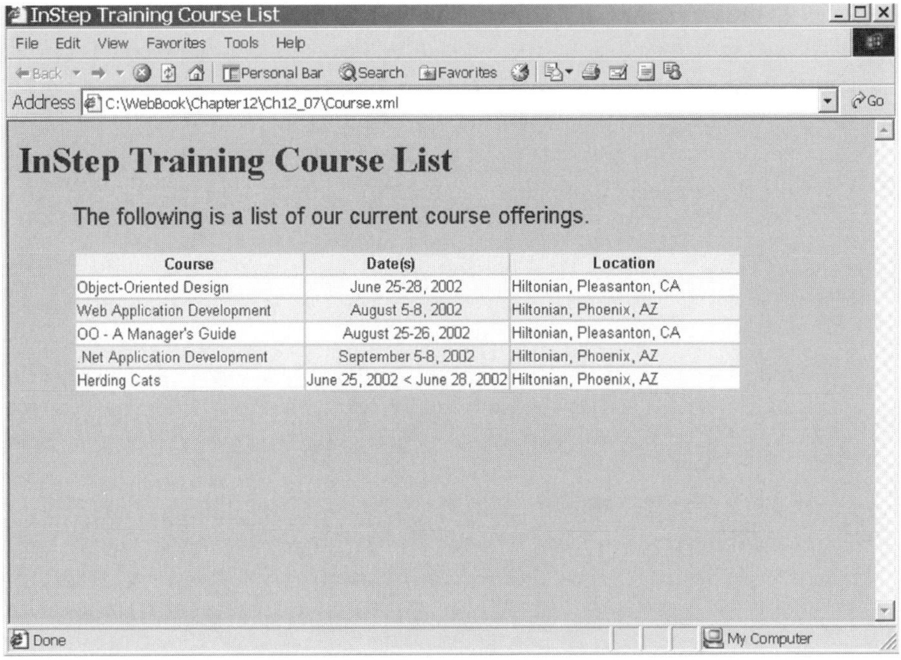

Figure 12-7. Using XSLT structures you can define more complex logic, such as setting the colors of the even and odd lines of the table.

The XSLT template required to perform this logic is as follows:

```
❶  <xsl:template match="course">
❷    <tr id="tableLayout">
❸      <xsl:attribute name="class">
❹        <xsl:choose>
❺          <xsl:when test="position() mod 2 = 1">odd</xsl:when>
❻          <xsl:otherwise>even</xsl:otherwise>
❼        </xsl:choose>
❽      </xsl:attribute>
❾      <td><xsl:value-of select="name" /></td>
```

⑪   `<td align="center"><xsl:value-of select="date" /></td>`
⑫   `<td><xsl:value-of select="location" /></td>`
⑬   `</tr>`
⑭ `</xsl:template>`

This template (line ❶) is applied for each course node in the XML document. For each course node, a tr (table row) element is first added to the output (line ❷).

The color of the row is set using a class attribute to define the style class from a CSS file. If the row is an odd number, the row should use the style class called odd. If the row is an even number, the row should use the style class called even.

Since the class attribute of the tr element had to be determined based on the row position, it could not be hard-coded like the other HTML elements. Rather, the attribute needed to be added using the XSLT attribute element (lines ❸ and ❻). The XSLT attribute element normally is defined as follows:

```
<xsl:attribute name="class">
    odd
</xsl:attribute>
```

This would add class="odd" to the tr element in the output. In this case, however, the value assigned to this class attribute needs to be adjusted based on whether the row is even or odd.

This logic is accomplished with the XSLT choose element (lines ❹ and ❺). The choose element contains one or more when elements and optionally an otherwise element. Each when element includes a test attribute. If the statement defined in the test attribute is true, the when element is processed. If none of the when element tests are true, the otherwise element is processed.

In this example, the when element (line ❹) test attribute uses the mod function to divide the node's position, defined with the position function, by 2. If the remainder is 1, the value of the class attribute is odd. Otherwise, the position is even and the class attribute is set to even (line ❺).

The remaining lines (lines ❺ through ❸) define the data to be included in the cells of the row.

Try It 12-7.

Working with XSLT Structures

Try It 12-7 adds a more complex XSLT structure to the XSLT template created in Try It 12-3.

1. Open the course XSLT stylesheet from Try It 12-3 in your editing tool.

2. Remove the XSLT for-each element from the HTML table element.

3. Insert the XSLT apply-templates element following the table header in the HTML table element.

4. Insert the course node template containing the XSLT choose element as shown in this section.

5. Save the file.

6. Open the course.xml file in Internet Explorer (version 5 or higher). When you load the XML document into Internet Explorer, the results are displayed.

The resulting XSLT stylesheet, presented in Listing 12-7, transforms your course XML document into an HTML page similar to that shown in Figure 12-7.

Listing 12-7. This stylesheet demonstrates use of an XSLT choose element.

```
<xsl:stylesheet version="1.0"
    xmlns:xsl="http://www.w3.org/1999/XSL/Transform"
    xmlns="http://www.w3.org/TR/xhtml1/strict">
<!--
   Try It  12-7
   Title:  Course XSL
   Author: InStep Technologies
           www.insteptech.com
   Purpose:To demonstrate XSLT structures
 -->
<xsl:template match="/">
<html>
<head>
   <title>InStep Training Course List</title>
   <link rel="stylesheet" type="text/css" href="TrainingStyle.css" />
</head>
<body>
   <h1>InStep Training Course List</h1>
   <p class="normal">The following is a list of our current course offerings.</p>
   <table>
      <tr class="even">
         <th class="wide">Course</th>
         <th class="narrow">Date(s)</th>
         <th class="wide">Location</th>
      </tr>
      <xsl:apply-templates />
   </table>
</body>
</html>
```

```
    </xsl:template>
    <xsl:template match="course">
       <tr id="tableLayout">
          <xsl:attribute name="class">
             <xsl:choose>
                <xsl:when test="position() mod 2 = 1">odd</xsl:when>
                <xsl:otherwise>even</xsl:otherwise>
             </xsl:choose>
          </xsl:attribute>
          <td><xsl:value-of select="name" /></td>
          <td align="center"><xsl:value-of select="date" /></td>
          <td><xsl:value-of select="location" /></td>
       </tr>
    </xsl:template>
</xsl:stylesheet>
```

XSLT Element and Attribute Reference

XSLT is the vocabulary for transforming an XML document into the format defined in the XSLT stylesheet. There are many XSLT elements and attributes a subset of which is defined in Table 12-2.

Table 12-2. Common XSLT Elements and Attributes

ELEMENT	MEANING, USE, AND COMMON ATTRIBUTES	EXAMPLE
apply-templates	Recursively applies a template to the child nodes of the context node. **Common attributes:** select - XPath expression defining the set of child nodes to be processed. If there is no select clause, all child nodes are processed.	`<xsl:apply-templates select="/" />` See "Working with XSLT Templates" in this chapter for a detailed example.
attribute	Adds an attribute to an element. **Common attributes:** name - Name of the attribute.	`<xsl:attribute name="room" />` See "Using XSLT Structures" in this chapter for a detailed example.
choose	Defines a mechanism to choose between a set of alternatives.	See "Using XSLT Structures" in this chapter for a detailed example.

Table 12-2. Common XSLT Elements and Attributes (continued)

ELEMENT	MEANING, USE, AND COMMON ATTRIBUTES	EXAMPLE
element	Writes an element to the output. **Common attributes:** **name** - Name of the element.	`<xsl:element name="instructor" />`
for-each	Creates a loop so you can select and process multiple nodes from the XML document. **Common attributes:** **select** - XPath expression defining the nodes to be processed within the loop.	`<xsl:for-each` `select="courses/course" />`

if	Defines a conditional branch.
	Common attributes:
	test - An expression to test. If the expression is true, the statements within the if element are processed.
		`<xsl:if`
		`test="not(position()=last())">`
		`,`
		`</xsl:if>`
		This code inserts a comma if processing any node except the last node.

otherwise	Part of the choose element. The statements within the otherwise element are executed if none of the when elements were true.	See "Using XSLT Structures" in this chapter for a detailed example.

param	Defines a parameter.
	Common attributes:
	name - Name of the parameter.
		`<xsl:param name="sortorder">`
		`name`
		`</xsl:param>`

sort	Defines sort criteria. The sort element must be a child of the apply-templates or for-each elements. **Common attributes:** **select** - Defines the sort key. **order** - Defines the sort order. Valid values are: ascending and descending.	`<xsl:sort select="name"` `order="ascending"/>`

Table 12-2. Common XSLT Elements and Attributes (continued)

ELEMENT	MEANING, USE, AND COMMON ATTRIBUTES	EXAMPLE

stylesheet	Root element for the XSLT stylesheet.
	Common attributes:
	xmlns - Namespaces associated with the stylesheet.
	version - Version of XSLT.
		`<xsl:stylesheet version="1.0"`
		`xmlns:xsl="http://www.w3.org`
		`/1999/XSL/Transform">`

template	Defines an output specification to be applied to a specified set of nodes. **Common attributes:** **match** - XPath expression defining the nodes for which this template is applied.	`<xsl:template match="/">`
text	Writes text to the output.	`<xsl:text> </xsl:text>` This code inserts a space in the output.
value-of	Writes the value of the defined element or attribute node to the output. **Common attributes:** **select** - XPath expression defining the node whose value you wish to select. Use "." for the context node.	`<xsl:value-of select="name" />`

variable	Defines a variable that can be associated with a particular value.
	Common attributes:
	name - Name of the variable.
	select - XPath expression defining the node whose value you wish to assign to the variable.
		`<xsl:variable name="bestcourse">`
		OOP
		`</xsl:variable>`
		See "Using Variables to Locate Specific Nodes" later in this chapter for a detailed example.

when	Part of the choose element. **Common attributes:** **test** - Defines a condition to test. If this condition is true, the statements within this when element are processed.	See "Using XSLT Structures" in this chapter for a detailed example.

Table 12-2. Common XSLT Elements and Attributes (continued)

ELEMENT	MEANING, USE, AND COMMON ATTRIBUTES	EXAMPLE
with-param	Provides a way to pass parameters to templates. **Common attributes:** **name** - Name of the parameter.	`<xsl:with-param name="sortorder">`

See the "Additional Resources" section of this chapter for a reference to a complete listing of valid XSLT commands.

XSL Tips and Tricks

This section includes basic tips and techniques when working with XSL.

More Advanced XSLT Template

The HTML shown in Figure 12-2 radically reorders the information in the XML document. The XML document lists each course along with the course name, dates, and location. Figure 12-2 displays each location and lists the courses and dates.

Much of the XSLT stylesheet required to produce this HTML output uses the standard techniques presented in this chapter. However, several advanced XSLT techniques were required to ensure that the display did not show duplicate locations and that all of the courses at a particular location were included in the display.

Testing for Uniqueness

If you are collecting information from child nodes and reordering that information, you may need to ensure there is no duplication.

In Figure 12-2, the output lists all of the locations. Because several courses were at the same location, simply collecting the list of locations would display those locations several times.

There are three steps required to ensure uniqueness in this type of situation. First, you need to collect the nodes to use. In this case, we are collecting the set of course nodes. This was done using an XSLT for-each element:

```
<xsl:for-each select="courses/course">
```

Next, you need to sort these elements by the field that is to be unique. In this example, the location needed to be unique:

```
<xsl:sort select="location"/>
```

This ensures the course nodes are then in location order.

The final step is to check the location node of each course node against the prior course node's location node. If the location is the same as the prior location, it is a duplicate and should be skipped. Otherwise, it is processed.

```
<xsl:when test="preceding-sibling::course[location=current()/location]" />
```

The preceding-sibling syntax accesses the prior course node. The current() syntax represents the current course node. The test attribute of this XSLT when element can be read as: "When the location of the preceding course node is equal to the current course node's location."

Using Variables to Locate Specific Nodes

You may need to retrieve a value from the XML document and use that value to locate other nodes within that XML document. To do this, you can use XSLT variables.

You define a variable using the XSLT variable element:

```
<xsl:variable name="locname" select="." />
```

This element defines a variable named locname and assigns the value of the variable to the context node's value.

You can use the variable anywhere you can define selection or matching criteria. You identify a string as a variable by prefixing it with a dollar sign ($). For example, to apply a template to any course with a location value equal to the value in the locname variable, you would use the following syntax:

```
<xsl:apply-templates select ="/courses/course[location=$locname]" />
```

This locates all of the course nodes that have a particular location.

Result

Listing 12-8 presents the XSLT stylesheet required to produce the result shown in Figure 12-2.

Listing 12-8. This stylesheet transforms the XML document into the HTML shown in Figure 12-2.

```
<xsl:stylesheet version="1.0"
     xmlns:xsl="http://www.w3.org/1999/XSL/Transform"
     xmlns="http://www.w3.org/TR/xhtml1/strict">
<!--
   Try It  None
   Title:  Course XSL
   Author: InStep Technologies
           www.insteptech.com
   Purpose:To demonstrate alternative XSL transformation to HTML
 -->
<xsl:template match="/">
   <html>
      <head>
         <title>InStep Training Course List</title>
         <link rel="stylesheet" type="text/css" href="TrainingStyle.css" />
      </head>
      <body>
         <h1>InStep Training Course List</h1>
         <p class="normal">The following is a list of our current course offerings.</p>
         <xsl:for-each select="courses/course">
            <xsl:sort select="location" />
            <xsl:choose>
               <xsl:when test="preceding-sibling::course[location=current()/location]" />
               <xsl:otherwise >
                  <xsl:apply-templates select ="location" />
               </xsl:otherwise>
            </xsl:choose>
         </xsl:for-each>
      </body>
   </html>
</xsl:template>

<xsl:template match="location">
   <p class="normal"><xsl:value-of select="." /></p>
   <table>
      <tr class="even">
            <th class="wide">Course</th>
            <th class="narrow">Date(s)</th>
      </tr>
```

```
        <xsl:variable name="locname" select="." />
        <xsl:apply-templates select ="/courses/course[location=$locname]" />
    </table>
</xsl:template>
<xsl:template match = "/courses/course">
    <tr class="odd">
        <xsl:apply-templates select="name | date" />
    </tr>
</xsl:template>
<xsl:template match ="name">
    <td><xsl:value-of select="." /></td>
</xsl:template>
<xsl:template match ="date">
    <td align="center"><xsl:value-of select="." /></td>
</xsl:template>
</xsl:stylesheet>
```

Debugging Tips

Here are some tips for debugging your XSLT stylesheets.

Watch Case Sensitivity

XSLT stylesheets and XPath are case sensitive. This could lead to errors or invalid data appearing in the output.

For example, the course node is not the same as the Course node. If you are using XPath to find a Course node, it does not find course.

Watch for Missing Ending Tags

A common source of error is missing ending tags. If you receive an error when processing your stylesheet, check for matching beginning and ending tags. Most XSL processors produce a useful message helping you find this problem.

Watch for Extra Elements in the Output

If your output contains more elements than you expect, you may not be overriding all of the built-in templates. See the "Build-in Templates" section for details on these built-in templates and how they can adversely affect the output of your transformations.

Use an XSL Processor

There are several XSL processors available that ensure your XSLT stylesheet is well-formed and your transformation produced the desired output.

You can use Internet Explorer (version 5 or higher) to verify your XSLT stylesheet if you download and install the updated Microsoft XSL processor. Otherwise, there are other tools such as XML Spy that include an XSL processor. See the "Additional Resources" section at the end of this chapter for links to the Microsoft XSL processor and several other XSL tools.

Use XSL on the Server

XSL is powerful and can be quite useful for transforming XML documents. You can use XSL to transform XML documents into HTML directly for display in the browser as shown in this chapter. However, the current browsers don't support XSL very well. Users would need to use Internet Explorer with the most recent XSL parser, which must be downloaded and installed. They could not use Netscape.

For these reasons, you may want to consider doing the XSL transformations on the Web server or on an application server. You can then use XSL to transform the XML document into HTML before downloading it to the client so the resulting HTML could be displayed in any browser. You can also use XSL to transform the XML document into other formats for communication with other systems.

We have even successfully used XSL to transform an XML document created from our database tables into retrieve and update stored procedures, effectively providing a stored procedure generator. The usefulness of XSL is bounded only by your imagination.

Using XSL with ASP

If you are using Active Server Pages (ASP) on the server, your ASP code can read an XML document and transform it into HTML using the Microsoft XML parser, MSXML. See "Additional Resources" at the end of this chapter for links to ASP and XSL samples.

Using XSL with Java

If you are using Java on the server, your Java code can read an XML document and transform it using any number of XSL processor products. See "Additional Resources" at the end of this chapter for links to Java and XSL samples.

What Did This Cover?

XSL transforms the data in an XML document into a format that is useful for a particular purpose. The resulting format may be an HTML page for display in a browser, a different HTML output for handheld devices, a paginated output for printing, spoken word for a text-to-speech device, another XML document for export to another application, or even a text file for communication with applications that don't understand XML.

This chapter provided a basic introduction to using XSL. It examined the anatomy of an XSLT stylesheet and demonstrated both the declarative and procedural approach to building stylesheets. It also presented several advanced techniques such as applying multiple templates, using variables, and ensuring uniqueness.

The Try Its in this chapter worked through several XSLT examples, all using the XML document from Chapter 11, "Introduction to XML."

Displaying the data from an XML document in a user-friendly way is important, but how do you know if that data is valid? The next chapter defines how to validate the data in your XML document.

Additional Resources

One chapter could not begin to cover everything there is to know about XSL. This section provides some additional resource suggestions by way of books, articles, and links to Web resources.

The books, articles, and links all existed at the time of this writing. There is a good chance that the books and articles still exist as you read this. However, the same cannot be said of Web links. Ignore the suggested links if they no longer exist.

Books and Articles

Cagle, Kurt, et al. *Professional XSL.* **Birmingham, UK: Wrox Press, 2001.**
This is a new book that I have not yet seen, but the description of this book expands on all of the topics discussed in this chapter.

Kay, Michael. *XSLT Programmer's Reference 2nd Edition.* **Birmingham, UK: Wrox Press, 2001.**
This is a reference book on XSLT.

Links

`http://msdn.microsoft.com/library/periodic/period00/beyondasp.htm`: This is an article regarding ASP and XSL with links to other ASP/XSL resources.

`http://msdn.microsoft.com/xml/general/xmlparser.asp`: This site provides the link to the new MSXML3 parser.

`http://technet.oracle.com/tech/xml/`: This Oracle site provides a set of XSL parsers and processors.

`http://www.4guysfromrolla.com/webtech/xml.shtml`: This site provides a set of links to articles on XSL including articles on using XSL with ASP.

`http://www.alphaworks.ibm.com`: This site provides a wealth of tools and technologies. It includes an XSL processor called LotusXSL that transforms an XML document into HTML using XSL. You need to install a Java Runtime Environment to use this program.

`http://www.javaworld.com/javaworld/topicalindex/jw-ti-javaxml.html`: This site provides a set of *JavaWorld* articles on XML and XSL.

`http://www.vbxml.com/xsl/XSLTRef.asp`: This site provides a detailed XSLT reference.

`http://www.w3.org`: The standard site for the World Wide Web Consortium (W3C) that is responsible for setting standards for the Web.

`http://www.w3.org/Style/XSL/`: This site contains the specification for XSL, including XSLT and XSL-FO.

`http://www.w3.org/TR/xml-stylesheet/`: This site specifically covers the standards regarding associating a stylesheet with an XML document.

`http://www.xmlspy.com/`: This site provides an integrated development environment tool for XML and an XSL processor. This tool edits and validates your XML and XSL syntax and performs XSL transformations. You can download a demo version to try it out.

`http://xml.apache.org/`: This site provides access to the Apache XML project. This project includes XML and XSL processors and tools.

CHAPTER 13

Defining
Schemas and DTDs

XML ALLOWS YOU TO CREATE your own elements and attributes to define data for your Web application. You can basically create your own vocabulary for describing your data. But how do you communicate that vocabulary? How do you validate that the elements and attributes in the XML document conform to the defined vocabulary? This is the purpose of Document Type Definitions (DTDs) and schemas.

Both DTDs and schemas provide a way for you to define the valid structure and content of your XML document. The DTD or schema is the dictionary for your vocabulary, providing documentation for the elements and attributes used in your XML document.

Because the DTD or schema defines the valid structure and content of an XML document, you can use it to validate your XML. This is particularly useful if you are receiving XML from another source, such as another application, and want to ensure that the data is valid.

The purpose of this chapter is to provide you with an introduction to DTDs and schemas. Because schemas are now recommended by the World Wide Web Consortium (W3C) instead of DTDs, the focus of this chapter is on schemas.

What Will This Cover?

This chapter covers the following key DTD and schema concepts:

- Understanding schemas

- Looking at schemas vs. DTDs

- Examining the anatomy of a schema file

- Creating a schema

- Using a schema to validate your XML

By the end of this chapter, you will know how to use schemas to validate your XML.

Schema Basics

When creating an XML document, you define your own vocabulary based on the requirements of the data within the XML document. Schemas are the current W3C recommendation for documenting that vocabulary. They provide the formal description of the structure and content of your XML documents.

For example, an XML document containing a list of courses could have a vocabulary that includes courses, course, name, date, and location. These words have special meaning within the context of that XML document.

The schema for the course XML document would define a `courses` element that consists of one or more `course` elements, a `course` element that consists of a set of `name`, `date`, and `location` elements, a `name` element that is a string, a `date` element that is a string (or a date), and a `location` element that is a string.

The schema provides the documentation of your XML data structures and includes the following information:

- The complete list of elements used in the XML document

- The complete list of attributes for each element, including default values

- The structure and hierarchy of the XML document in terms of elements and sub-elements

- The order or sequence of elements within the XML document

Because the schema defines the valid set of elements and attributes required for the XML document, you can use the schema to validate the contents of the XML document. After your XML document has been validated using a schema, it is called a *valid* XML document.

For example, if you produce or receive a course XML document that is missing a `name` element, the schema can evaluate that XML document and determine it is not valid.

An XML document can be well-formed without being valid. A discussion of well-formed versus valid XML documents is often the first topic in books devoted to XML. A well-formed XML document is one that follows the correct XML syntax as defined in Chapter 11, "Introduction to XML." A valid XML document is one that contains valid data based on a schema or DTD.

You don't have to have a schema (or DTD) for your XML document. They are optional but recommended if you are sharing your XML document with other applications or other developers. The schema provides the documentation of the vocabulary to aid in understanding and correctly working with your XML document.

Schema vs. DTD

The purpose of a DTD is the same as that of a schema, to provide a description of an XML document's vocabulary. DTDs were the original W3C standard for documenting the content of an XML document.

DTDs use a syntax different from the standard XML syntax. This makes DTDs more difficult to learn and understand. When schemas were introduced with their recognizable and understandable XML structure, they quickly replaced DTDs as the standard.

DTDs did not provide much control over the type of data in the XML document, whereas schemas let you define data types, such as string, numbers, and dates. This means you can perform better validation using schemas than using DTDs.

Because DTDs were the first standard, many XML documents still use DTDs instead of schemas. For links to a description of the DTD syntax, see the "Additional Resources" section of this chapter.

DTD and Schema Standards

To more easily share XML documents between companies and applications, some industries have established a common standard vocabulary and have built standard DTDs/schemas to define that vocabulary. See the "Additional Resources" section of this chapter for links to sites describing several of these industry-specific vocabularies.

The Anatomy of a Schema

Schemas conform to XML document syntax standards, meaning that a schema is itself a well-formed XML document.

Most schemas follow the same basic structure and use a top-down approach to describing the XML document contents. They begin by defining the vocabulary for the XML document's root node, then describe the children of the root, then the grandchildren, and so on.

The schema example in this section defines the schema for the XML document from Chapter 11, "Introduction to XML." This XML document is provided for reference in Listing 13-1.

Listing 13-1. The course XML document defines the name, date, and location for a set of courses.

```xml
<?xml version="1.0"?>
<courses>
    <course>
        <name>Object-Oriented Design</name>
        <date>June 25-28, 2002</date>
        <location>Hiltonian, Pleasanton, CA</location>
    </course>
    <course>
        <name>Web Application Development</name>
        <date>August 5-8, 2002</date>
        <location>Hiltonian, Phoenix, AZ</location>
    </course>
</courses>
```

The schema for this XML document is shown below.

```xml
❶  <xsd:schema version="1.0" xmlns:xsd="http://www.w3.org/2000/10/XMLSchema">
❷      <xsd:element name="courses" type="coursesType"/>
❸      <xsd:complexType name="coursesType">
❹          <xsd:sequence>
❺            <xsd:element name="course" type="courseType" maxOccurs="unbounded"/>
❻          </xsd:sequence>
❼      </xsd:complexType>
❽      <xsd:complexType name="courseType">
❾          <xsd:sequence>
❿            <xsd:element name="name"     type="xsd:string"/>
⓫            <xsd:element name="date"     type="xsd:string"/>
⓬            <xsd:element name="location" type="xsd:string"/>
⓭          </xsd:sequence>
⓮      </xsd:complexType>
⓯  </xsd:schema>
```

The XML schema begins with a schema root element (lines ❶ and ⓯) that defines this file as an XML schema.

Because the schema is itself an XML document, the schema element has a required version attribute to specify the schema version. It also has an attribute, xmlns, which defines the schema namespace. The letters after the colon (:), xsd in this case, assigns an abbreviation to the defined namespace. This abbreviation is used as a prefix onto any schema element. This ensures that the names of the schema elements won't conflict with any other elements.

NOTE   *Though this example uses* xsd, *you can use any prefix for a namespace. However,* xsd *is most commonly used when referring to the schema namespace.*

CAUTION   *A new schema namespace has recently been identified. It was not used in the examples in this book because none of the validation tools support this new namespace as of this writing. The new namespace is* xmlns:xsd="http://www.w3.org/2001/XMLSchema".

The remainder of the schema defines the structure and valid content of the XML document it is describing, starting at the top of the XML document and progressing through each sub-element. For each element, the schema defines the element name and data type.

Some of the XML document elements contain data that is a fundamental data type, such as a string or integer. For example, a course name element is a string. See the "Schema Reference" section at the end of this chapter for the list of fundamental data types.

Other XML document elements are comprised of sub-elements. For example, the course element in Listing 13-1 is comprised of name, date, and location elements. These elements cannot be described using a fundamental data type; rather, a complex type must be defined. The schema provides a facility for defining the complex types you need to describe your XML document. You can give each of these complex types any logical name and use that name to associate the data type with the XML document element it describes.

Starting at the top of the XML document shown in Listing 13-1, the topmost element is courses. Since courses is an element, it is identified in the schema with a schema element (line ❷). A schema element defines the name and data type of an element in the XML document. The name attribute must be the element name as defined in the XML document. The type attribute is the type of data that is valid for that element. The courses element is not a fundamental data type but rather a complex type comprised of the list of course elements. You can assign any descriptive name you choose for a complex type. In this case, coursesType was used as the name of the complex type.

The complex type must then be defined using the complexType element (lines ❸ and ❼). The name attribute for this element must match the type attribute defined for the courses element (line ❷).

As shown in Listing 13-1, the XML document courses element is comprised of a sequence of course elements. The schema sequence element (lines ❹ and ❻) specifies that this complex type is a sequence of elements. The schema element defines the name and data type of the elements in the sequence, in this case course elements (line ❺). Schema element attributes can include minOccurs and maxOccurs attributes that define how many elements must be defined within the sequence. In this case, the XML document must contain a sequence of one or more course elements in a courses element.

The XML document course element is comprised of a sequence of sub-elements. The complex type describing the course element defines the sequence of those sub-elements (lines ❽ through ❹). Notice again how the name attribute of this type, courseType, matches the type attribute for the course element (line ❺).

The course element has a name sub-element that must be a string (line ❿), a date sub-element that must be a string (line ⓫), and a location sub-element that must be a string (line ⓬).

If you look at this schema again, you see that it simply states that the XML document must contain a courses element. The courses element must contain a sequence of course elements. Each course element must contain a sequence of name, date, and location elements. Each name element must be a string, each date element must be a string, and each location element must be a string.

Creating a Schema

You can manually create your schema since they are just text files. Alternatively, there are several tools available that automatically build a schema (or DTD) from your XML document.

You can add a schema for an XML document directly into that XML document. More commonly, however, schemas are defined in a separate text file, normally with an extension of .xsd.

You can create a schema using a basic text editor, such as Notepad or Word-Pad for Windows and Emacs or vi for Unix. Using a simple tool has the benefit of simplicity, but it requires that you spend the time typing in all of the definitions with the correct syntax.

Several tools are available, such as XML Spy, to automatically create your schema or DTD from your XML document. Most of these tools also have a validator that validates your XML document against the resulting schema or DTD. See the "Additional Resources" section at the end of this chapter for a link to these tools.

For the purposes of this chapter, create the schema manually:

1. Create a text file and save it with an .xsd extension.

2. Add the schema root element.

3. Insert a schema element element to define the root of the XML document. Be sure to define its data type, which is most likely a complex type that you need to define.

4. Insert a schema complexType element to define the composition of the root element.

5. Insert a schema sequence element to define the sequence of elements within the complexType element.

6. Insert a schema element element for each sub-element of the root element. Be sure to define the data type of each of these, which is also likely to be a complex type that you will need to define.

7. Continue defining sub-elements and their types until all elements within the XML document are defined.

8. Ensure your schema is well-formed.

Follow these steps to get started with schemas.

Try It 13-1.

Creating a Schema

Try It 13-1 builds a schema for the course XML document shown in Listing 13-1.

1. Using Notepad or your tool of choice, create a new text file.

2. Insert the schema root element. Be sure to specify the appropriate XML namespace for the schema.

3. Insert a schema element element to define the root of the XML document. The root element is courses for the course XML document. Be sure to provide a descriptive type name in the type attribute.

4. Insert a schema complexType element to define the contents of the courses element. Be sure to set the name attribute of this element to the same value as the type attribute from step 3.

5. Insert the schema sequence and element elements to define the complex type for the courses element to be a sequence of course elements as shown in "The Anatomy of a Schema" earlier in this chapter. Be sure to provide a descriptive type name in the type attribute.

6. Insert a schema `complexType` element to define the contents of the course element. Be sure to set the `name` attribute of this element to the same value as the `type` attribute from step 5.

7. Insert the schema `sequence` and `element` elements to define the complex type for the `course` element to be a sequence of `name`, `date`, and `location` elements as shown in "The Anatomy of a Schema" earlier in this chapter.

8. Save the file as course.xsd.

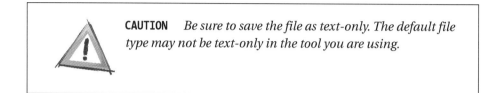

CAUTION   *Be sure to save the file as text-only. The default file type may not be text-only in the tool you are using.*

9. Optionally, use a tool such as XML Spy to validate the schema.

Listing 13-2 presents the resulting schema file.

Listing 13-2. The course.xsd file contains the schema for the course XML document.

```
<xsd:schema xmlns:xsd="http://www.w3.org/2000/10/XMLSchema" version="1.0">
  <xsd:element name="courses" type="coursesType"/>
  <xsd:complexType name="coursesType">
    <xsd:sequence>
      <xsd:element name="course" type="courseType" maxOccurs="unbounded"/>
    </xsd:sequence>
  </xsd:complexType>
  <xsd:complexType name="courseType">
    <xsd:sequence>
      <xsd:element name="name" type="xsd:string"/>
      <xsd:element name="date" type="xsd:string"/>
      <xsd:element name="location" type="xsd:string"/>
    </xsd:sequence>
  </xsd:complexType>
</xsd:schema>
```

Associating a Schema

The schema does not do anything by itself. You need to associate the schema with an XML document in order to use the schema to validate that XML document.

To associate a schema with an XML document, modify your XML document to define the desired schema. For the course.xsd file, this line is:

```
<courses xmlns:xsi="http://www.w3.org/2000/10/XMLSchema-instance"
 xsi:noNamespaceSchemaLocation="course.xsd">
```

Notice that the schema is defined using attributes of the XML document's root element, in this case the `courses` element. The `xmlns` attribute defines the schema namespace. The `noNamespaceSchemaLocation` attribute defines the location of the schema when the schema does not use a namespace. If the schema does use a namespace, use the `schemaLocation` attribute.

CAUTION   *A new schema namespace has just been identified. It was not used in this book's examples because none of the validation tools support this new namespace as of this writing. The new namespace is:*
`xmlns:xsi="http://www.w3.org/2001/XMLSchema-instance"`

Try It 13-2.

Associating a Schema with an XML Document

Try It 13-2 associates the schema created in Try It 13-1 with the Course XML document created in Chapter 11, "Introduction to XML," and shown in Listing 13-1.

1. Open the course.xml file from Try It 11-1 in your text editor.

2. Add the attributes to the `courses` element as shown in this section.

3. Use a tool such as XML Spy to validate the XML document using your schema.

Schema Reference

There are many schema elements and attributes, but most schemas use a core set. Table 13-1 defines these elements and attributes. This list should get you started with most of what you want to do with schemas.

Table 13-1. Frequently Used Schema Elements and Attributes

ELEMENT	MEANING, USE, AND COMMON ATTRIBUTES	EXAMPLE

attribute	Defines a valid attribute in the XML document.
	
	Common attributes:
	`default` - A default value to use if none is supplied.
	
	`name` - The name of the attribute in the XML document.
	
	`type` - The data type of the attribute.
	
	`use` - Constrains how the attribute can appear in the XML document. Valid types: `optional`, `prohibited`, `required`.
		`<xsd:attribute name=`
		`"CourseAbbreviation"`
		`type="xsd:string" use="optional">`

complexType	Defines a complex data type. This is the description of a data type used in the type attribute of an element when the element is comprised of sub-elements. **Common attributes:** `name` - The name of the data type described by this complex type.	`<xsd:complexType name="coursesType">`
element	Defines a valid element in the XML document. **Common attributes:** `maxOccurs` - The maximum number of times this element can occur within the XML document. By default this value is 1. Set this value to unbounded to allow any number of elements. `minOccurs` - The minimum number of times this element can occur within the XML document. By default this valueis 1. Set this value to 0 to make the element optional.	`<xsd:element name="courses"` `type="coursesType" />`

Table 13-1. Frequently Used Schema Elements and Attributes (continued)

ELEMENT	MEANING, USE, AND COMMON ATTRIBUTES	EXAMPLE
element *(cont.)*	**name** - The name of the element in the XML document.	
	type - The data type of the element. This can be a fundamental data type or a complex type.	
sequence	Defines a sequence of elements or attributes within a data type.	`<xsd:sequence>`

See the "Additional Resources" section of this chapter for a reference to a complete listing of valid schema elements and their associated attributes.

Schemas also provide a standard set of fundamental data types. Table 13-2 presents a subset of these.

Table 13-2. A Subset of the Fundamental Data Types Defined in the Schema Specification

DATA TYPE	MEANING	EXAMPLE
boolean	Value is `true` or `false`. 1 and 0 are also valid values.	`true`
date	Value is a date of the form yyyy-mm-dd.	`2001-05-19`
double	Value is a double-precision 32-bit floating point number.	`6.4`
int	Value is an integer between 2147483647 and -2147483648.	`8`
float	Value is a single-precision 32-bit floating point number.	`6.4`
long	Value is a long number.	`2147483649`
negativeInteger	Value is a negative number.	`-3`
positiveInteger	Value is a non-zero positive number	`6`
string	Value is a string of characters.	`Object-Oriented Design`

See the "Additional Resources" section for a link to the W3C specification that defines the full set of fundamental data types.

Basic Schema Tips and Tricks

This section includes basic tips and techniques when working with schemas.

Use a Tool

Creating a schema is work, especially if you have many elements and attributes in your XML document. Instead of creating the schema manually, use a tool such as XML Spy to build the schema from the XML document.

Comment Your Code

You can add documentation to a schema following the standard XML document syntax. However, to better process extra comment information, the recommended syntax for comments is as follows:

```
<xsd:annotation>
  <xsd:documentation xml:lang="en">
  Try It  13-1
  Title:  Course Schema
  Author: InStep Technologies
          www.insteptech.com
  Purpose:To demonstrate schemas
</xsd:documentation>
</xsd:annotation>
```

Documentation such as this can provide information on special conditions or other notes required to complete the specification of the schema.

What Did This Cover?

Validation is important to ensure the integrity of the data in your Web application. Schemas and DTDs provide validation of the data in an XML document.

This chapter provided a basic introduction to creating schemas for use in documenting and validating the vocabulary in your XML document.

The Try Its in this chapter worked through a simple example that built a schema to validate the course XML document from Chapter 11, "Introduction to XML." It was clear from this simple example that you may want to use a tool to create the schema from an XML document instead of manually creating the schema.

The next chapter presents the details of reading an XML document within an HTML page using JavaScript.

Additional Resources

One chapter could not begin to cover everything there is to know about basic schemas, and this chapter barely touched on DTDs. This section provides some additional resource suggestions by way of books, articles, and links to Web resources.

The books, articles, and links all existed at the time of this writing. There is a good chance that the books and articles still exist as you read this. However, the same cannot be said of Web links. Ignore the suggested links if they no longer exist.

Books and Articles

Duket, Jon, et al. *Professional XML Schemas*. Birmingham, UK: Wrox Press, 2001.
Schemas are so new that it's difficult to find any published books on the topic. The description of this book expands on all of the topics discussed in this chapter.

Links

`http://technet.oracle.com/tech/xml/`: This Oracle site provides an XML schema processor.

`http://www.ofx.net/`: Open Financial Exchange (OFX) is a vocabulary for the electronic exchange of financial data between financial institutions, businesses, and consumers. It was created by CheckFree, Intuit, and Microsoft in early 1997. It supports financial activities such as banking, bill payment, and investments.

`http://www.w3.org`: The standard site for the W3C which is responsible for setting standards for the Web.

`http://www.w3.org/2000/09/webdata/xsv`: This W3C site provides an online schema validator to validate the format of your schema.

`http://www.w3.org/Math/`: The Mathematical Markup Language (MathML) is a vocabulary that provides for mathematical expressions in Web pages.

`http://www.w3.org/TR/NOTE-XFDL`: Extensible Forms Description Language (XFDL) is an XML vocabulary describing form fields, computations, and validation rules. The proposed XFDL standard provides for associating HTML input fields with XML elements. The XFDL specification may also provide a standard for client-side input and server-side processing.

`http://www.w3.org/XML/1998/06/xmlspec-report-v21.htm`: This site contains the original specifications for DTDs.

`http://www.w3.org/XML/Schema`: This is the W3C site defining schemas.

`http://www.w3schools.com/dtd/`: If you still need to use DTDs, this site provides a tutorial on how to build a DTD.

`http://www.w3schools.com/schema/`: This site provides a similar tutorial on how to build schemas.

`http://www.xmlspy.com/`: This site provides an integrated development environment tool for XML. This tool automatically generates a schema or DTD from your XML document. It also validates XML against a schema or DTD. You can download a demo version to try it out.

`http://xml.apache.org/xerces-j/`: This site provides a Java XML parser that includes an XML schema processor.

Reading XML with JavaScript

THERE ARE MANY WAYS TO work with XML documents. You can use XSL to transform data from an XML document into HTML for display in the browser as shown in Chapter 12, "Using XSL." You can perform this transformation on the client side within the browser if the browser is Internet Explorer. Or you can perform the transformation on the Web server and send the resulting HTML to any browser as described in Chapter 15, "Web Application Architectures."

But sometimes you may need a client-side solution that works in both Internet Explorer and Netscape. In this case, you can read an XML document directly from your HTML document without using XSL.

The purpose of this chapter is to demonstrate how to read an XML document using JavaScript to display XML data on a Web page. This chapter pulls together many of the technologies covered in this book including Hypertext Markup Language (HTML), Cascading Style Sheets (CSS), HTML tables, the Document Object Model (DOM), JavaScript, and Extensible Markup Language (XML).

What Will This Cover?

This chapter covers the following key concepts:

- Reading XML documents using JavaScript

- Navigating an XML document with JavaScript

- Building HTML tables from XML data without XSL

By the end of this chapter you will know how to access an XML document from within an HTML document using JavaScript. You will also know how to build tables on the fly using the DOM.

Reading an XML Document with JavaScript

You can use an XML document to maintain data to populate lists, generate tables, or define any other content for your Web pages. In your HTML document, you can read the data from the XML document to dynamically build the content for your Web page.

The basic steps for reading an XML document with JavaScript are:

1. Define the content that will be dynamically generated.

2. Create the XML document containing the data needed for the content. See Chapter 11, "Using XML," for details on creating an XML document.

3. Create the HTML document that will use the defined content.

4. In the HTML document, load the XML document into memory.

5. In the HTML document, reference the parts of the XML document as needed to retrieve the desired data and dynamically generate the desired content.

The last two steps use JavaScript and the DOM, detailed in Chapter 7, "Understanding Object Models," to load and access the XML document. These steps are discussed in detail in the remainder of this chapter.

The JavaScript code required to load the XML document is different for Internet Explorer and for Netscape. For Internet Explorer (version 5.0 and above), the XML document is loaded using the Microsoft XML Parser. For Netscape (version 6.0 and above), the XML document is loaded directly using the DOM.

Loading XML in Internet Explorer

An HTML document displayed in Internet Explorer (version 5.0 and above) can use the Microsoft XML Parser, MSXML.DLL, to load an XML document.

This JavaScript function uses the Microsoft XML Parser to create a DOM document and load an XML file into that document:

```
❶   function readXML()
❷   {
❸      xmlDoc = new ActiveXObject("Microsoft.XMLDOM");
❹      xmlDoc.async=false;
❺      xmlDoc.load("course.xml");
❻   }
```

This function first creates an XML document object using the Microsoft XML Parser (line ❸).

Normally, the XML file is loaded asynchronously, which means it loads as your script continues to execute. If you want to access the XML document data immediately after loading it, set the `async` property of the DOM document to `false` (line ❹). This ensures the document is fully loaded before continuing to execute the script.

The `load` method of the DOM (line ❺) loads the defined XML file into the DOM document. The XML file location can be defined using a relative or absolute path. For testing purposes, you can look at the XML document that is loaded using the following:

```
window.alert(xmlDoc.xml);
```

This displays a message box containing the entire XML string. This `xml` property is only available when using the Microsoft XML parser.

Loading XML in Netscape

As you may expect, Netscape does not use the Microsoft XML Parser. An HTML document displayed in Netscape (version 6.0 and above) uses the DOM to load an XML document.

This JavaScript function uses the DOM to create a DOM document and load an XML file into that document:

```
❶  function readXML()
❷  {
❸      xmlDoc = document.implementation.createDocument("", "", null);
❹      xmlDoc.onload = "";
❺      xmlDoc.load("course.xml");
❻  }
```

This function first creates an XML document object (line ❸). It then assigns a function that should be executed when the DOM is loaded (line ❹). This function is not yet defined in this code snippet; we'll define it later in this chapter.

The `load` method of the DOM (line ❺) loads the defined XML file into the DOM document. The XML file location can be defined using a relative or absolute path. From this point on, the DOM document processing of the XML is the same for both browsers.

Try It 14-1.

Reading an XML File

Try It 14-1 adds scripting to the Course List Web page to read the Course XML file. Currently, the Course List Web page contains a hard-coded set of courses. Ultimately, these hard-coded values will be replaced with values from the Course XML file. This Try It takes the first step toward that goal.

1. Open the TrainingCourseList.htm file from Try It 5-3 in your HTML editing tool.

2. Add the meta element to define JavaScript as the scripting language.

3. Add a script element for the JavaScript function.

4. Write a function to read an XML file. You can use either the Internet Explorer code or the Netscape code shown in this section. Alternatively, you can add both sets of code and execute the appropriate code based on the available browser functionality.

5. If you are using Internet Explorer, optionally add an alert to verify that the XML file is read properly.

6. Call the function in the onload event handler of the body element.

7. Save the file.

8. Open the TrainingCourseList.htm file in your browser. If you are using Internet Explorer, you will see a message box containing the XML. If you are using Netscape, you won't be able to verify that your XML is loaded until Try It 14-2.

Listing 14-1 shows the revised Course List HTML document. Notice that the hard-coded courses are still needed because the data is not retrieved from this XML file until a later Try It.

Listing 14-1. The readXML function loads an XML file. It checks features of the browser to use the correct syntax for Internet Explorer or Netscape.

```
<!DOCTYPE html PUBLIC "-//W3C//DTD XHTML 1.0 Strict//EN" "DTD/xhtml1-strict.dtd">
<html>
<!--
    Try It  14-1
    Title:  Course List with XML
    Author: InStep Technologies
            www.insteptech.com
    Purpose:To demonstrate reading an XML file using JavaScript
  -->
```

```
<head>
<title>InStep Training Course List</title>
<meta http-equiv="Content-Script-Type" content="text/javascript" />
<link rel="stylesheet" type="text/css" href="TrainingStyle.css" />
<script type="text/javascript">
    function readXML()
    {
        var sName = "course.xml";
        if (document.implementation && document.implementation.createDocument)
        {
            xmlDoc = document.implementation.createDocument("", "", null);
            xmlDoc.onload = "";
            xmlDoc.load(sName);
        }
        else if (document.documentElement && document.documentElement.applyElement)
        {
            xmlDoc = new ActiveXObject("Microsoft.XMLDOM");
            xmlDoc.async=false;
            xmlDoc.load(sName);
            alert(xmlDoc.xml);
        }
        else
        {
            alert("Your browser can\'t display this page." +
                    "  You need IE5 or Netscape 6 or greater');
            return;
        }
    }
</script>
</head>
<body onload="readXML();">
<h1>InStep Training Course List</h1>
<p class="normal">The following is a list of our current course offerings.</p>
<div class="scroll">
<table>
    <tr class="even">
        <th class="wide">Course</th>
        <th class="narrow">Date(s)</th>
        <th class="wide">Location</th>
    </tr>
```

```
        <tr class="odd">
            <td>Object-Oriented Design</td>
            <td align="center">June 25-28, 2002</td>
            <td>Hiltonian, Pleasanton, CA</td>
        </tr>
        <tr class="even">
            <td>Web Application Development</td>
            <td align="center">August 5-8, 2002</td>
            <td>Hiltonian, Phoenix, AZ</td>
        </tr>
        <tr class="odd">
            <td>OO - A Manager's Guide</td>
            <td align="center">August 25-26, 2002</td>
            <td>Hiltonian, Pleasanton, CA</td>
        </tr>
        <tr class="even">
            <td>.Net Application Development</td>
            <td align="center">September 5-8, 2002</td>
            <td>Hiltonian, Phoenix, AZ</td>
        </tr>
</table>
</div>
</body>
</html>
```

Navigating Through an XML Document with JavaScript

After the XML file is loaded into a DOM document, you can navigate through the document to retrieve the data needed by the Web page.

In the prior section, the XML document from Chapter 11, "Using XML," is loaded into a DOM document. To navigate through that XML document, you need to know its structure. Listing 14-2 provides the original XML document for your reference, and Figure 14-1 shows the tree structure for that XML document.

Listing 14-2. The course XML document defines the name, date, and location for a set of courses.

```
<?xml version="1.0"?>
<!-- Course XML -->
<courses>
    <course>
        <name>Object-Oriented Design</name>
        <date>June 25-28, 2002</date>
```

```
        <location>Hiltonian, Pleasanton, CA</location>
    </course>
    <course>
        <name>Web Application Development</name>
        <date>August 5-8, 2002</date>
        <location>Hiltonian, Phoenix, AZ</location>
    </course>
</courses>
```

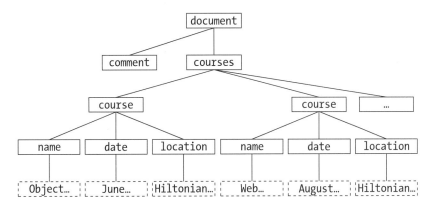

Figure 14-1. Every XML document can be represented as a tree structure with each element represented as a node. This tree structure is the represenation of the XML document in Listing 14-2.

You can work with the XML file loaded into the DOM as nodes, referencing elements using a hierarchical tree structure. You can also use DOM object properties and methods to reference specific elements. These techniques are defined in Chapter 7, "Understanding Object Models."

To locate a set of elements with a defined name in the XML document, use the getElementsByTagName method of the DOM. This method returns an array containing all of the elements with the defined name. For example, locate all of the course elements in the XML document using:

```
var ele = xmlDoc.getElementsByTagName("course");
```

This returns an array containing every course element. In DOM terms, this is the set of course *nodes*. You can access each node in the array using standard JavaScript array syntax: ele[0], ele[1], ele[2], and so on.

You can reference the sub-nodes (sub-elements) of a node using the childNodes collection of the DOM. For the course XML document example, the childNodes collection for each course element contains the name, date, and location elements.

To display the names of the nodes within the `childNodes` collection for one element in the array of elements (ele), use the following JavaScript code:

```
① for (j=0; j<ele[0].childNodes.length; j++)
② {
③     if (ele[0].childNodes[j].nodeType == 1)
④     {
⑤         window.alert(ele[0].childNodes[j].nodeName);
⑥     }
⑦ }
```

The loop starts at 0 and processes all of the child nodes (line ①) under the first element in the `ele` array (ele[0]). The number of child nodes is defined by `childNodes.length`.

The `nodeType` property is retrieved from the child node (line ③) to check the content type. Only element nodes (nodeType of 1) are processed. This ensures all attribute or text nodes are ignored. This check is required because Netscape includes text nodes in the `childNodes` collection. Internet Explorer only includes the element nodes in that collection, so this statement is not necessary in Internet Explorer. It is included to ensure this code works with either browser.

The `alert` method of the window object (line ⑤) displays a message box for each child node. The `nodeName` property of the child node is the child node's element name.

By iterating through a set of nodes, you can access the node names. This can give you names to use for column titles or field labels, for example. You can use this same type of iteration to access the node values. The node values provide the data from the XML document for use on the Web page.

Try It 14-2.

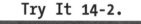
Iterating Through the XML

Try It 14-2 adds more scripting to the Course List Web page to iterate through the XML that was loaded into an XML document in Try It 14-1. This Try It takes the next step toward replacing the hard-coded set of courses in the Course List Web page with XML document data.

1. Open the TrainingCourseList.htm file from Try It 14-1 in your HTML editing tool.

2. In the same `script` tags containing the `readXML` function, write a function to iterate through the XML document, as shown in this section.

3. Modify the `readXML` function created in Try It 14-1 to call the new function. In Netscape, the function is called by assigning the function name to the `onload` method of the document. In Internet Explorer, the function is called directly after the document is loaded.

4. Save the file.

5. Open the TrainingCourseList.htm file in your browser. If your XML was correctly loaded into an XML document, you will get three message boxes that list the three child nodes: name, date, and location.

Listing 14-2 shows the revised script from the Course List HTML document. The remainder of the HTML document is unchanged and the hard-coded courses are still needed because the data is not yet retrieved from this XML file.

Listing 14-2. This snippet presents the readXML and buildTable functions. The readXML function loads an XML file and calls the buildTable function to display the elements that will be the table headers.

```
. . .
<script type="text/javascript">
    function readXML()
    {
        var sName = "course.xml";
        if (document.implementation && document.implementation.createDocument)
        {
            xmlDoc = document.implementation.createDocument("", "", null);
            xmlDoc.onload = buildTable;
            xmlDoc.load(sName);
        }
        else if (document.documentElement && document.documentElement.applyElement)
        {
            xmlDoc = new ActiveXObject("Microsoft.XMLDOM");
            xmlDoc.async=false;
            xmlDoc.load(sName);
            buildTable();
        }
        else
        {
            alert("Your browser can\'t display this page." +
                    "  You need IE5 or Netscape 6 or greater');
            return;
        }
    }
    function buildTable()
    {
        //Find all course elements
```

```
        var ele = xmlDoc.getElementsByTagName("course");
        for (j=0; j<ele[0].childNodes.length; j++)
        {
            //Only display the element nodes
            if (ele[0].childNodes[j].nodeType == 1)
            {
                window.alert(ele[0].childNodes[j].nodeName);
            }
        }
    }
</script>
. . .
```

Building a Table Using XML

With the XML document loaded into memory and the routine to iterate through the XML document, you now have all of the background information to build a table of data from the XML document within your HTML page.

Building an HTML table from XML data combines many of the techniques that were covered in this book:

- HTML to build the basic visual parts of the page

- The DOM as covered in Chapter 7, "Understanding Object Models," to build the table

- Cascading Style Sheets (CSS) as covered in Chapter 4, "Using Style Sheets," to give the new table some style

- The XML document as covered in Chapter 11, "Using XML"

- The DOM to iterate through the elements of the XML document

The code to build an HTML table from the XML document data basically creates a tree structure that represents the table with HTML table, tbody, tr, and td elements. This tree structure is then appended to the HTML document. At that point, the table (magically!) appears on the HTML page. Let's look at this code line by line:

TIP *Pay close attention to which code lines are using the XML document (*xmlDoc*) versus the HTML document (*document*).*

```
1   function buildTable()
2   {
3       var ele = xmlDoc.getElementsByTagName("course");
4       var newTable = document.createElement("table");
5       var newTableBody = document.createElement("tbody");
6       newTable.appendChild(newTableBody);
7       var row = document.createElement("tr");
8       row.setAttribute("class","even");
9       for (j=0; j<ele[0].childNodes.length; j++)
10      {
11          if (ele[0].childNodes[j].nodeType == 1)
12          {
13              var header= document.createElement("th");
14              var data = document.createTextNode(ele[0].childNodes[j].nodeName);
15              header.appendChild(data);
16              row.appendChild(header);
17          }
18      }
19      newTableBody.appendChild(row);
20      for (var i=0;i<ele.length;i++)
21      {
22          row = document.createElement("tr");
23          //Each subelement is a column
24          for (j=0;j<ele[i].childNodes.length;j++)
25          {
26              if (ele[0].childNodes[j].nodeType == 1)
27              {
28                  var column = document.createElement("td");
29                  var data =
                        document.createTextNode(ele[i].childNodes[j].firstChild.nodeValue);
30                  column.appendChild(data);
31                  row.appendChild(column);
32              }
33          }
```

```
34          newTableBody.appendChild(row);
35          row.setAttribute("class","odd");
36      }
37      document.getElementById("courseList").appendChild(newTable);
38  }
```

This function (line ❶) builds an HTML table from XML document data. It begins by using the getElementsByTagName method of the DOM to read all of the course elements into an array (line ❸). It then creates an HTML table element (line ❹) and a tbody element (line ❺) to begin building the HTML table. The tbody element is a child element of the table element, so it is appended to the table element (line ❻).

The HTML tree structure built at this point looks like Figure 14-2.

Figure 14-2. So far, the JavaScript function has created HTML table *and* tbody *elements.*

The row of the table is created with an HTML tr element (line ❼). The setAttribute method assigns a style class from the style sheet to the row (line ❽).

The first row of the table contains the table headings. In this example, the sub-element names (name, date, and location) are retrieved from the XML document and used as the column headings for the table.

The table headings are generated by iterating through the child nodes of the first course element from the XML document (line ❾). If the node is an element node (line ⓫), an HTML th element is created (line ⓭). A text element is created (line ⓮) that contains the element name. This element name is used as the column heading. The text element is appended to the th element (line ⓯) and the th element is then appended to the tr element (line ⓰).

After all th elements are defined, the tr (row) element is appended to the tbody element to add the header row elements to the table structure (line ⓳). Figure 14-3 shows the resulting HTML document tree structure.

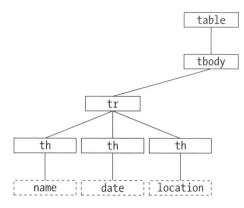

Figure 14-3. The headings for the table are defined with HTML th *elements.*

After the column headings are defined, the function iterates through all of the course elements (line **20**) to create a row in the table for the data for each course. The HTML tr element is created (line **22**) to define the row. Each sub-element of the course is then processed (line **24**).

If the node is an element node (line **26**), an HTML td (table data) element is created to define a column (line **28**). A text element is created (line **29**) that contains the actual value of the element. In the case of the course XML document, the nodeValue property is the value of the name element during the first iteration, the date element during the second iteration, and the location element during the third iteration.

After the text node is created, it is appended to the td element (line **30**). The td element is then appended to the tr element (line **31**). This adds each value from each sub-element in a course element as a column in a row of the table.

After each column of the row is created, the row is appended to the tbody element (line **34**). The attribute of the row is then set using a class from the style sheet (line **35**). This process is repeated for each course element in the ele array. Figure 14-4 shows the resulting HTML document tree structure.

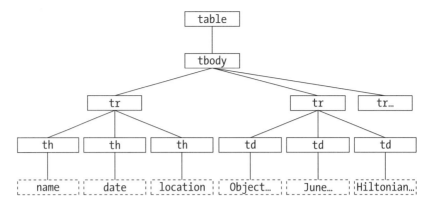

Figure 14-4. The table columns are defined with HTML td *elements. There would be one HTML* tr *element for each* course *element in the XML document, though only one* course *element is shown in this figure.*

When all rows have been created, the table element is appended to the element in the HTML page that has an id attribute set to courseList (line **㊲**). In this case, the element is a div element. This appends the entire table to the HTML page. The table then appears in the browser.

Try It 14-3.

Building a Table with XML

Try It 14-3 adds scripting to the Course List Web page to generate a table with the XML data that was loaded in Try It 14-1. This Try It completes the final step in dynamically generating the list of courses from the Course XML document using JavaScript.

1. Open the TrainingCourseList.htm file from Try It 14-2 in your HTML editing tool.

2. Modify the buildTable function created in Try It 14-2 to actually build the table. The code for this is shown in this section.

3. Remove the hard-coded table element and all of its contents.

4. Add a div element that will enclose the new table and set its id attribute to a value such as courseList.

5. Save the file.

6. Open the TrainingCourseList.htm file in your browser. If your XML was correctly loaded into an XML document, you will see the list of courses.

NOTE *If you use Internet Explorer 5.5, the styles defined using* setAttribute *are not recognized and your table does not appear with the styles. Netscape displays the styles correctly.*

7. Optionally, add additional courses to the XML document and try step 6 again. Notice how the page automatically changes to contain the new entries without needing to manually update the HTML.

Listing 14-3 shows the complete Course List HTML document. Though the JavaScript is quite long, notice how small the HTML code is.

Listing 14-3. The TrainingCousresList.htm file now separates presentation from content.

```
<!DOCTYPE html PUBLIC "-//W3C//DTD XHTML 1.0 Strict//EN" "DTD/xhtml1-strict.dtd">
<html>
<!--
    Try It   14-3
    Title:  Course List with XML
    Author: InStep Technologies
            www.insteptech.com
    Purpose:To demonstrate building a table from XML data
 -->
<head>
<title>InStep Training Course List</title>
<meta http-equiv="Content-Script-Type" content="text/javascript" />
<link rel="stylesheet" type="text/css" href="TrainingStyle.css" />
<script type="text/javascript">
    function readXML()
    {
        var sName = "course.xml";
        if (document.implementation && document.implementation.createDocument)
        {
            xmlDoc = document.implementation.createDocument("", "", null);
            xmlDoc.onload = buildTable;
            xmlDoc.load(sName);
        }
            else if (document.documentElement && document.documentElement.applyElement)
            {
```

```
            xmlDoc = new ActiveXObject("Microsoft.XMLDOM");
            xmlDoc.async=false;
            xmlDoc.load(sName);
            buildTable();
        }
        else
        {
            alert("Your browser can\'t display this page." +
                    "  You need IE5 or Netscape 6 or greater');
            return;
        }
    }
    function buildTable()
    {
        //Find all course elements
        var ele = xmlDoc.getElementsByTagName("course");
        //Create the table
        var newTable = document.createElement("table");
        var newTableBody = document.createElement("tbody");
        newTable.appendChild(newTableBody);

        //Each subelement name is a table header
        var row = document.createElement("tr");
        row.setAttribute("class","even");
        for (j=0;j<ele[0].childNodes.length;j++)
        {
            //Only display the element nodes
            if (ele[0].childNodes[j].nodeType == 1)
            {
                var header= document.createElement("th");
                var data = document.createTextNode(ele[0].childNodes[j].nodeName);
                header.appendChild(data);
                row.appendChild(header);
            }
        }
        newTableBody.appendChild(row);

        //Each course element is a row
        for (var i=0;i<ele.length;i++)
        {
            row = document.createElement("tr");
            //Each subelement is a column
            for (j=0;j<ele[i].childNodes.length;j++)
            {
```

```
            //Only display the element nodes
            if (ele[0].childNodes[j].nodeType == 1)
            {
                var column = document.createElement("td");
                var data =
                 document.createTextNode(ele[i].childNodes[j].firstChild.nodeValue);
                column.appendChild(data);
                row.appendChild(column);
            }
        }
        newTableBody.appendChild(row);
        row.setAttribute("class","odd");
    }
    document.getElementById("courseList").appendChild(newTable);
  }
</script>
</head>
<body onload="readXML();">
<h1>InStep Training Course List</h1>
<p class="normal">The following is a list of our current course offerings.</p>
<div id="courseList"></div>
</body>
</html>
```

What Did This Cover?

This chapter focused on reading an XML document using JavaScript and dynamically building HTML to display a table on a Web page. This is a useful client-side technique for building dynamic Web pages without the limitation of browser support for XSL.

The Try Its in this chapter worked through a single example demonstrating this technique. Though complex, this example was a great way to summarize HTML, CSS, DOM, and JavaScript.

The next chapter takes a look at Web application architectures to help you select the right set of technologies for your Web application.

Web Application Architectures

FROM A SOFTWARE PERSPECTIVE, the term *architecture* describes the structure and behavior of an application. It defines the individual software components that comprise the application and how they interact. The architecture defines the framework within which an application is built and all of the pieces of the application that fit into that framework.

As with any type of building project, the architecture is critical to the project's success. Imagine building a new house without a well thought-out architectural plan; there would be stairs going nowhere, doors that could not open, and windows in closets.

Without a good architectural plan for your Web application, you could end up with pages that cannot support dynamic data, forms that cannot be processed, or features that cannot easily be implemented.

The architecture for a Web application can include many different software components developed with several different technologies and residing on several computer systems. A key step in the design of your Web application is deciding how to partition the functionality of the application into the appropriate architectural components and deciding which of the many Web technologies to use for each component.

The good news is that there are some common Web application architecture patterns from which to choose. You can select one to use as a starting point for the architecture of your Web application.

The purpose of this chapter is to present several common Web application architectures. These architectures include both client-side technologies, covered in the prior chapters of this book, and server-side technologies that you may need to successfully complete your Web application.

What Will This Cover?

This chapter covers the following key concepts:

- Using only client-side technologies in an architecture

- Using only server-side technologies in an architecture

- Combining client-side and server-side technologies

- Designing a three-tiered architecture

By the end of this chapter you will have an understanding of some of the most common Web application architecture patterns and how to select the best pattern for your Web application.

Client-Side Architecture

It is possible to build an entire Web application using only client-side technologies. This may be by choice or because of limitations on your Web server. If you are using an external Web hosting company, for example, it may not allow or support server-side processing. In any case, a client-side architecture defines how client-side technologies work together to provide the functionality required by the Web application.

In a client-side architecture, the Web browser client on the user's computer performs all of the processing for the Web application. The Web server simply stores the files and downloads them to the browser as described in Chapter 1, "Introduction to the Web." Because the processing is on the client, this style of architecture is sometimes called a *thick client* or *fat client* architecture. Figure 15-1 shows a common client-side architecture pattern.

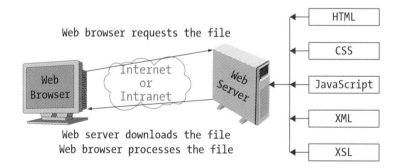

Figure 15-1. In a client-side architecture, the Web server stores the files, downloading them on request, and the Web browser performs all of the processing.

The files on the Web server are the architectural components of your Web application. These components can include the technologies shown in Figure 15-1 as well as other file types, such as graphics, audio, and video.

Web pages in a client-side architecture can be static, meaning that they do not change as the user works with the page. For static pages, the Web browser downloads the HTML file from the Web server and displays it to the user.

A client-side architecture supports interactivity, meaning a Web page can react to the user's actions. Interactivity is accomplished by adding JavaScript to the HTML. When the Web browser downloads an HTML file from the Web server that contains JavaScript or a link to a JavaScript file, the JavaScript is downloaded as well.

A client-side architecture also provides for specialized client-side applications, called *applets*, which support more advanced client-side features such as streaming video and image effects. Java applets, written in the Java programming language, can be used in both Internet Explorer and Netscape. ActiveX controls, another type of applet written in Microsoft C++ or Microsoft Visual Basic, can only be used in Internet Explorer. Both types of applets can be referenced from an HTML file, causing them to be downloaded when the HTML file is downloaded.

Common Client-Side Architecture Applications

A client-side architecture is useful for displaying static information, such as a welcome page. It also supports interactive features and is great for performing basic calculations such as summing columns of entered data or determining mortgage premiums. A client-side architecture can even support display of dynamic data, such as an online catalog.

Some common uses of a client-side architecture include:

- **Static content**. Company marketing information or simple online catalogs are examples of static content.

- **Interactive marketing**. A user can interact with a company's products on line. For example, a furniture company allows a user to design a room by dragging and dropping furniture and fabrics online or an electronics company allows a user to build a stereo system online. (However, with only a client-side architecture, there is limited facility for the user to order any of the selected furniture or stereo components.)

- **E-learning**. Online courses include everything from bread making to Web technologies to personal finance. Using JavaScript, the course can even include homework and quizzes. (However, with only a client-side architecture, there would be limited facility for a user to sign up for a course or for an instructor to monitor progress or scores.)

- **Simple games**. A checkers game where the logic is client-side JavaScript is an example of the simple types of games that can be developed using only client-side technologies.

417

With all of the processing on the client, a client-side architecture does not provide for any Web server-based processing. A client-side architecture cannot easily collect user contact information and save it in a database. It also cannot retrieve data, such as the current mortgage interest rates, from a database. For these scenarios, you need a server-side architecture, as described later in this chapter.

Client-Side Technologies

By definition, a client-side architecture requires that you partition your Web application into a set of files that can be processed by the Web browser client. The Web server simply serves up these files when requested by the Web browser.

Many different client-side technologies are available for developing these files, as shown in the sample applications and Try Its throughout this book.

Let's review some common client-side technologies and how they are used within a client-side architecture.

HTML

Hypertext Markup Language (HTML) files are used to define the user interface for a Web application with a client-side architecture. These files are downloaded to the Web browser client for display to the user.

With HTML, you can create static Web pages as described in Chapter 3, "Using HTML." For example, you could create a welcome page, a corporate information page, or a set of help system pages. You can also create tables with HTML as detailed in Chapter 5, "Building Tables." For example, you could create a schedule of courses or a frequently asked questions (FAQ) page using tables. With borderless tables you can lay out pages in a columnar fashion, such as an electronic newspaper or e-zine.

You can build forms with HTML as illustrated in Chapter 6, "Building Forms." However, with no server-side processing you cannot collect the information that the user enters on the form, though you could save user-entered information on the client using cookies as described in the upcoming "JavaScript" section. Or if the user has an e-mail system, you can e-mail the user-entered information back to yourself as shown in Chapter 6.

CSS

Cascading Style Sheet (CSS) files define the basic styles used within the HTML documents as described in Chapter 4, "Using Style Sheets." Styles include background colors, font sizes and colors, paragraph formatting, and so on.

Use CSS to define all of the basic styles for your Web application to ensure a consist look throughout all of the pages of the application. By using CSS, you can make changes to the style of the entire Web application by simply changing the CSS file. For example, if you define the style for validation error messages in a CSS style, when the user wants those messages larger you simply change the style in the CSS file and all of the messages in all of the pages are displayed with the new style.

JavaScript

JavaScript provides for client-side scripting as detailed in Chapter 8, "Using JavaScript." You can add JavaScript to your HTML document to provide for interactivity.

Any calculations, business logic, or other processing that you need in your Web application can be developed using JavaScript. For example, a search page can search by name or phone number. If the user selects to search by name, a name-entry box is displayed; otherwise a phone number entry box is displayed. You create this type of interactive response to user actions using JavaScript.

You can validate user entries with JavaScript, as described in Chapter 9, "Validating Form Data." You can save user entries on the client using cookies as illustrated in Chapter 10, "Saving Data with Cookies."

XML

Extensible Markup Language (XML) defines data that your Web application uses. This provides a mechanism for displaying Web pages based on dynamic data as presented in Chapter 11, "Using XML."

If your data is in a database, but you want to only use a client-side architecture, you could generate an XML file from the data in the database using an application on the Web server. You could then refresh this XML file weekly, daily, hourly, or as often as necessary.

You can read the resulting XML file directly from your HTML using JavaScript as detailed in Chapter 14, "Reading XML with JavaScript." Or you can use XSL, described next.

XSL

An XML file contains no formatting instructions. To display XML data within the browser, you need to read the XML file from your HTML document or you can transform the XML file directly into HTML using the Extensible Stylesheet Language (XSL). Examples of using XSL within a client-side architecture are provided in Chapter 12, "Using XSL."

XSL is much more full-featured and is significantly easier to use than JavaScript to process and format the XML file. However, only Internet Explorer supports client-side XSL. This limits its usefulness in client-side applications; its full power is in its use on the server-side, as described later in this chapter.

VBScript

Microsoft Visual Basic Scripting Edition (VBScript) is a Microsoft scripting language. You can use VBScript in place of JavaScript for client-side scripting. However, the only browser that fully supports VBScript is Internet Explorer. JavaScript is the preferred language for client-side scripting.

VBScript is more commonly used for server-side scripting. See the "ASP" section later in this chapter.

ActiveX Controls

ActiveX controls are a Microsoft technology used to build client-side applet components. ActiveX controls are downloaded from a Web server, installed on the user's computer, and executed inside the browser. Each ActiveX control provides functionality that would be difficult to accomplish with HTML and JavaScript alone such as streaming media, image effects, or complex graphics manipulation.

ActiveX controls are available for purchase from ActiveX control vendors. See the "Additional Resources" section for links to ActiveX control vendors. Alternatively, you can build your own ActiveX controls using a programming language such as Microsoft C++ or Microsoft Visual Basic.

You use an ActiveX control in your Web application by including a reference to the control in your HTML file. You can then respond to the user's actions on that control using JavaScript or VBScript.

The down side of using ActiveX controls is that they are only fully supported by Internet Explorer on Microsoft Windows systems. Don't use ActiveX controls if you need to provide cross-browser or cross-platform support.

Java Applets

Like ActiveX controls, Java applets provide specialized functionality that would be difficult to accomplish with HTML and JavaScript alone. Java applets are written using a programming language called Java, developed by Sun Microsystems, which is similar to C++. This makes Java applets better able to support cross-browser and cross-platform applications. Also like ActiveX controls, Java applets are available for purchase. You can purchase chat applets, e-mail applets, search applets, stock ticker applets, and so on. See the "Additional Resources" section for links to Java applets. Many common user interface features, such as scrolling banners, are available both as ActiveX controls and Java applets. Alternatively, you can write your own Java applets using the Java programming language.

Using a Java applet is similar to using an ActiveX control. You reference the applet in your HTML file and then respond to the user's actions on the applet using scripting such as JavaScript.

A key difference between ActiveX controls and Java applets is that ActiveX controls are compiled to machine code. This means they must be installed on the user's computer. Java applets are compiled for the Java Virtual Machine (JVM) that runs the applets. The JVM must be installed on the user's computer, but the applet itself is not installed. This difference also means that ActiveX controls may have better performance.

Flash

Macromedia's Flash is a set of technologies that allows you to build animated, vector-based content and display it on a Web page. This is most often used to create impressive welcome screens, Web-based presentations, and Web application demos. To view the content, the user must download and install the Macromedia Flash Player.

Putting It All Together

As you can see, you can use many different technologies in client-side applications. This list summarizes a common use of each technology in a client-side architecture:

- **HTML**. Build one HTML file for each Web page shown to the users.

- **CSS**. Build one CSS file to contain the common formatting styles used in the Web pages of the application. Reference this CSS file from every HTML page.

- **JavaScript**. Build one JavaScript file for each kind of common processing used by the Web pages of the application. For example, build one JavaScript file for validation, one for working with cookies, and so on. JavaScript is also common within an HTML page to perform logic unique to that page.

- **XML**. Define one XML file for each type of data needed to dynamically update the data on a Web page. Most commonly, however, dynamic data is handled using a server-side architecture, as described later in this chapter.

- **XSL**. Create one XSL file instead of an HTML file for any Web page that needs to display data from an XML file. However, this only works with Internet Explorer 5 and above and does not work with Netscape.

- **VBScript**. This is not normally used in a client-side architecture.

- **ActiveX controls**. If the Web page must perform some client-side feature that is difficult to implement with HTML and JavaScript alone, such as graphing data or manipulating images, you can build or purchase an ActiveX control. However, these work with Internet Explorer and not with Netscape.

- **Java applets**. Use these for the same reason you would use an ActiveX control but when you want to support both Internet Explorer and Netscape.

- **Flash**. Use Flash to build a fancy welcome page or a demo of the application. Flash supports both Internet Explorer and Netscape, but the user needs to download the Macromedia Flash Player to view the Flash.

Advantages of a Client-Side Architecture

The primary benefits of a client-side architecture are:

- It is relatively easy to build a Web application using a client-side architecture, compared with server-side architectures.

- Processing is performed on the client, offloading the Web server.

- Web designers without extensive programming knowledge can build client-side Web applications if they are not highly interactive or dynamic.

- The Web application can be developed and tested without a Web server. The Try Its in the prior chapters of this book demonstrate this technique.

- No special application needs to be installed on the Web server. This is especially important if a third-party Web hosting service hosts your Web application.

Disadvantages of a Client-Side Architecture

The down sides of a client-side architecture include:

- With all of the processing on the client, differences between browsers and browser versions must be carefully considered.

- Data cannot easily be collected from the user and stored to a database. One workaround for this is to build a feature into a Web page that e-mails the user-entered values to a particular e-mail address, though this workaround is less than optimal.

- Data cannot be obtained from a database and displayed on the page unless the data is regularly converted into an XML file.

Server-Side Architecture

Just as it is possible to build an entire Web application using only client-side technologies, you can build an entire Web application using only server-side technologies. This may be desired if your Web application needs to support any browser on any platform and you don't want to handle the browser differences. A server-side architecture defines how the server-side technologies work together to provide the functionality required by the Web application.

A server-side architecture performs all of the processing on the Web server and downloads generic HTML as the result. The Web browser client on the user's computer simply receives the result of the server-side processing and displays it to the user. The Web browser client does not perform any logic or processing; it just displays information, which is the reason this style of architecture is sometimes called a *thin client* architecture. Figure 15-2 shows a common server-side architecture pattern.

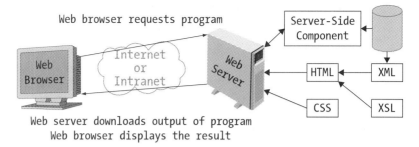

Figure 15-2. A server-side architecture provides all of the processing on the Web server; the Web browser simply displays HTML.

The key difference between client-side architectures and server-side architectures is that server-side architectures support server-side components. A *server-side component* is an application executed in response to a Web browser request. The application can process information obtained from the Web browser, perform any needed logic, or access a database. It can also dynamically generate HTML that is downloaded to the Web browser client for display. Just as a client-side Web application is comprised of any number of HTML pages, a server-side Web application is comprised of any number of server-side components.

Common Server-Side Architecture Applications

A server-side architecture is great for collecting and processing information from HTML forms and optionally storing the results in a database. It can also be used to dynamically generate HTML based on information from a database and download that HTML to the Web browser.

Some of the common uses of a server-side architecture include:

- **Data collection**. An HTML form is presented to the user for entry of information. That information is submitted to a server-side component that processes the information and stores it in a database. Some data collection examples include contact information for a mailing list, survey information, and customer support questions.

- **Order processing**. A retailer (or *e-tailer*) presents a form for the user to place an order. When the user submits the order, a server-side component processes it. The most common metaphor for order form processing on the Web is the shopping cart where users can select many different items, place them in a shopping cart, and then order the items all at once. Another example of order processing is making hotel or airline reservations.

- **Dynamically generated catalogs**. A server-side component can access a database to retrieve information for a catalog and build HTML based on that information. This can be done with server-side component code that reads the database values and concatenates strings to build well-formed HTML. Alternatively, the server-side component can obtain the database values as XML and use XSL to translate the data into well-formed HTML. In either case, the dynamically generated HTML is downloaded to the client for display in the browser.

- **Dynamically generated status information**. A server-side component can access a database to retrieve status information and build HTML based on that information. For example, a user could check the status of an order, the status and balance of a bank account, or the status of a flight.

- **Online bill paying**. A server-side component can build pages containing a list of bills that are due. The user can select to pay bills and specify the amounts to pay.

- **Data maintenance pages**. A server-side component can build an HTML form with data from a database and display the form to the user. The user can update the form values and submit the changes to the server-side component to save back to the database. For example, a salesperson updates customer contact information, a consultant updates time tracking information, or an underwriter updates an insurance policy.

With all of the processing on the server, a server-side architecture does not provide for any client-side processing. A server-side architecture cannot validate data before sending the data to the server. It also cannot provide for interactivity with the user such as changing the data-entry fields displayed based on the user's response. To get the best of both worlds, combine server-side processing with client-side processing as described later in this chapter.

Server-Side Technologies

A server-side architecture requires that you partition your Web application into a set of files, primarily server-side components, which can be processed by the Web server. The Web server invokes these files when requested by the Web browser. The result of the processing is often HTML that is downloaded to the Web browser for display.

Many different server-side technologies are available for developing these files. Let's look at some common server-side technologies and how they are used within a server-side architecture.

HTML

A server-side architecture may have some HTML files that are downloaded directly to the Web browser for display. The remainder of the HTML for the user interface is generated by server-side components either programmatically, by concatenating well-formed HTML strings, or by using XSL to transform XML into HTML.

CSS

Regardless of the Web application architecture, CSS is always a good idea. You can use styles from the CSS file in any HTML, including HTML files, HTML created by a server-side component, or HTML generated as a result of an XSL transformation. The Try Its in Chapter 12, "Using XSL," demonstrate how to include CSS in HTML generated as a result of an XSL transformation.

CGI

The Common Gateway Interface (CGI) is the specification for interfacing a Web server with server-side components. CGI makes it possible for a Web server to execute a server-side component. CGI also provides the communication between the server-side component and the client browser, passing values from the browser to the server-side component and passing HTML back to the browser. CGI is so important for server-side processing that a server-side component is often called a *CGI application.*

A Web browser requests a server-side component if the user enters the Uniform Resource Identifier (URI) of an application into the address area of the browser, if the user clicks on a hyperlink that identifies the URI of an application, or if the user submits a form that specifies the URI of an application.

For example, a Web application displays a data-entry form to collect information for a mailing list as described in Chapter 6, "Building Forms." The HTML contains the following form element:

```
<form name="MailingList" method="post" action= "/cgi-bin/ProcessMailing.cgi">
```

The action attribute defines the name and location of the requested server-side component. In this case, the server-side component is ProcessMailing.cgi.

CGI executes the defined server-side component and passes data from the Web browser client to the application. This data can be system information, such as the user's browser type, information appended to the URI, and any information entered on an HTML form. When processing forms, the method attribute defines how the data is passed to this server-side component for processing.

In the mailing list example, the data is posted as part of the Hypertext Transport Protocol (HTTP) request.

The Web browser then waits for the server-side component to complete its processing. This processing can involve parsing strings received from the client and storing them into a database or building HTML strings from a database. The result of the processing is frequently HTML. CGI passes the HTML back to the client for display in the browser.

CGI applications can be *programs* written in any number of languages such as C, C++, Java, or Microsoft Visual Basic. However, capturing and processing data from forms and building HTML can be a tedious and repetitive process with these languages. Application Programming Interface (API) functions are available for these languages to make CGI programming easier. These APIs include Netscape Server Application Programming Interface (NSAPI) and Microsoft's Internet Server Application Programming Interface (ISAPI).

CGI applications can instead be *scripts* written in scripting languages such as Perl. CGI scripts are often easier to create and maintain than CGI programs because the scripting languages are often easier to learn than the programming languages and the scripts are not compiled.

Writing either CGI programs or scripts requires knowledge of yet another language. In addition, the amount of work required to process form data and build HTML strings can be cumbersome, and the result can be hard to debug.

As a result, a number of technologies have evolved that incorporate server-side scripting directly into the HTML. These technologies support a variety of scripting languages that can be intermixed with HTML to form a hybrid page processed by the Web server to produce HTML. This HTML is then sent to the browser for display. Three widely used server-side scripting technologies are Active Server Pages (ASP), PHP, and JavaServer Pages (JSP).

NOTE   *In the beginning, PHP was an acronym for Personal Home Page because it was written to track users of a Web page. Its functionality has grown significantly since then. Now PHP is normally defined to be PHP Hypertext Processor, basically a recursive acronym.*

These server-side component technologies and languages are discussed further in the following sections.

C/C++

C and C++ are full-featured programming languages. You can develop a server-side component with C or C++, compile it, and install it on your Web server.

Because C and C++ programs are compiled, they execute faster than server-side components written with scripting languages. However, both C and C++ are complex languages and require a significant amount of training. For these reasons, C and C++ are frequently not the most productive choice for Web application development.

Java

Java is also a full-featured programming language. You can develop a server-side component with Java and install it on your Web server. Applications written in Java specifically for the Web server are called *Java servlets*.

Java is not compiled into machine code; rather, it is executed by a JVM. This can make it more easily portable to different Web server platforms. However, Java is also a complex language and requires a significant amount of training.

According to Sun's Java architecture guidelines, servlets should be used as Web server extensions, providing specialized functionality such as authentication. They should not normally be used as the primary server-side component. Rather, use JSP as discussed later in this section. The JSP can then call servlets as needed for the specialized functionality.

Visual Basic

Visual Basic is also a full-featured programming language. You can develop a server-side component with Visual Basic, compile it, and install it on your Web server.

It is possible to write Visual Basic code to read information from the Web browser, process it, and build HTML (see the "Additional Resources" for sample code). In most cases, the developers use the ISAPI libraries to handle much of that processing. More commonly, however, Visual Basic developers forgo Visual Basic and use ASP and VBScript for server-side components, as described later in this section.

Perl

Perl is one of the most widely used languages for server-side components. It is a scripting language that is supported by most Web servers.

Perl is well known for its ability to parse and process text. Because the purpose of most server-side components is to build HTML strings from a database or parse strings from a form and store them into a database, good text processing is critical.

CGI scripts written in Perl frequently have an extension of .pl or .cgi. These scripts are invoked to perform a particular function, such as tracking the number of visitors to a Web site or processing data from forms. For example, a form on an HTML page that posts data to a Perl script defines the script as follows:

```
<form name="MailingList" method="post" action= "/cgi-bin/ProcessMailing.cgi">
```

When the user submits the form, the form data is posted to the ProcessMailing.cgi script. Listing 15-1 presents the Perl code that processes the MailingList form. This code generates a time-appropriate greeting and then displays the information obtained from the data-entry page. See Chapter 6, "Building Forms," for the complete HTML used to create the form processed by this server-side component.

Listing 15-1. This Perl code is for the Apache Web server running under Linux.

```perl
#!/usr/bin/perl
#
#ProcessMailing - perl version of the mailing list request processor
#
# Determine greeting to display
sub Greeting
{
    local($hour) = pop(@_);
    if ($hour < 12 ) {
      $greeting = "Good morning";
    }
    if ( ($hour >= 12) && ($hour < 17 ) ) {
      $greeting = "Good afternoon";
    }
    if ( $hour >= 17 ) {
      $greeting = "Good evening";
    }
    $greeting;
```

```
}
# Parse the fields from the form
sub parse_data
{
    local (*FIELD_VALUES) = @_;
    local ($how_sent, $query, @value_pairs, $field, $value,  $field_value);
    # store the information the form fields and values in $query
    $how_sent = $ENV{'REQUEST_METHOD'};
    if ( $how_sent eq "GET") {
        $query = $ENV{'QUERY_STRING'};
     } elsif ( $how_sent eq "POST" ) {
        read (STDIN, $query_string, $ENV{'CONTENT_LENGTH'} );
    }
    # split the string into an array of fields and values
    @value_pairs = split( /&/, $query );

    foreach $field_value ( @value_pairs)
    {
        # get the field and value
        ($field, $value ) = split(/=/, $field_value);
        # replace + with space and %xx with the actual character
        $value =~ tr/+/ /;
        $value =~ s/%([\dA-Fa-f][\dA-Fa-f])/pack ("C", hex($1))/eg;
        # save the values into the array the caller pased in
        if ($defined{ $FIELD_VALUES{$field}})
        {
            $FIELD_VALUES{$field} = join("\0", $FIELD_VALUES{$field}, $value);
        } else
        {
            $FIELD_VALUES{$field} = $value;
        }
    }
}
# Output the page
# Get the pieces of the current time
($sec, $min, $hr) = localtime(time);
#  Load the array of values passed
&parse_data( *values );
# let the browser know what is coming
print "Content-type: text/html", "\n\n";
# start the document and the body
print "<html>\n";
print "<body>\n";
```

```
print "<h1>",&Greeting($hr)," ",$values{ 'FirstName' }," ",$values{ 'LastName' };
print "</h1>\n";
print "\n", "Thank you for signing up for our mailing list.";
print "We save the following information for you:", "\n";
print "<table>\n";
print "    <tr>\n";
print "        <td>Name:</td>", "\n";
print "        <td>", $values{ 'FirstName' }, " ", $values{ 'LastName' }, "</td>\n";
print "    </tr>\n";
print "    <tr>\n";
print "        <td>Email Address:</td>", "\n";
print "        <td>", $values{ 'Email' }, "</td>\n";
print "    </tr>\n";
print "    <tr>\n";
print "        <td>Referred by:</td>", "\n";
print "        <td>", $values{ 'Referral' }, "</td>\n";
print "    </tr>\n";
print "</table>\n";
print "</body>\n";
print "</html>\n";
```

NOTE   *If you want to try this Perl code, you need to have Perl installed and you need to copy this file to a Web server directory. See the "Additional Resources" section for a link the site where you can download Perl.*

ASP

ASP is a technology that allows you to add server-side scripting directly into an HTML file. ASP is a Microsoft product provided with Microsoft's Internet Information Server (IIS) and bundled with server versions of the Microsoft Windows operating system.

An ASP file contains HTML and server-side scripting. The scripting language used within ASP is usually VBScript, but you could use JavaScript. To identify which statements within the ASP file are HTML and which are server-side script statements, a special tag is used around all server-side script statements:

```
<% %>
```

When the Web browser requests an ASP file, IIS parses the server-side script. When the parsing is complete, the resulting HTML is downloaded to the browser for display.

For example, the form created in Chapter 6, "Building Forms," could submit the form data to an ASP page by modifying the form element as follows:

```
<form id="MailingList" method="post" action="http://localhost/ProcessMailing.asp">
```

The form data is then posted to the ProcessMailing.asp file. Listing 15-2 presents the ASP code that processes the MailingList form.

Listing 15-2. ASP code is comprised of both HTML and server-side scripting.

```
<%@ Language="VBscript" %>
<%option explicit %>
<!DOCTYPE html PUBLIC "-//W3C//DTD XHTML 1.0 Strict//EN" "DTD/xhtml1-strict.dtd">
<html>
<head>
<title>Process Mailing list request</title>
<link rel="stylesheet" type="text/css" href="TrainingStyle.css" />
</head>
<body>
<%
    dim cHour
    dim cNow
    dim Greeting
    cNow = Now()
    cHour = Hour(cNow)
    if ( cHour < 12 ) then
       Greeting = "Good morning"
    end if
    if ( (cHour >= 12) and (cHour < 17) ) then
       Greeting = "Good afternoon"
    end if
    if ( cHour >= 17 ) then
       Greeting = "Good evening"
    end if
%>
    <h1><%=Greeting & " - " & Request("FirstName") & " "%>
    <%=Request("LastName") %></h1>
    <p class="normal">
    Thank you for signing up for our mailing list.
    The following information has been saved for you.
```

```
    </p>
    <table>
        <tr>
            <td>Name: </td>
            <td><%=Request("FirstName") & " " & Request("LastName") %></td>
        </tr>
        <tr>
            <td>Email Address: </td>
            <td><%=Request("EMail") %></td>
        </tr>
        <tr>
            <td>Referred by: </td>
            <td><%=Request("Referral") %></td>
        </tr>
    </table>
</body>
</html>
```

NOTE   *If you want to try this ASP code, you need to have IIS installed and you need to copy this file to a Web server directory.*

ASP .NET

ASP .NET is Microsoft's newest version of ASP. It is part of the new Microsoft .NET platform and comes with the Microsoft Visual Studio .NET integrated development environment.

There are several key differences between ASP and ASP .NET. You can use VBScript or JavaScript to build your ASP. With ASP .NET, you can use any of the .NET languages, including Visual Basic, C# (pronounced *C-sharp*), and JScript. In addition, you can use any of the .NET Framework class libraries, such as those for data access and XML processing. ASP .NET is compiled, improving performance.

PHP

PHP is similar in concept to ASP in that it provides for server-side scripting inserted directly into HTML. Unlike ASP, however, PHP is open source and supported on Linux machines running Apache servers and any other Unix or Windows platform running Netscape or Microsoft Web server software.

A PHP file contains HTML and server-side scripting. The scripting language used within a PHP file is PHP. To identify which statements within the PHP file are HTML and which are server-side script statements, a special tag is used around all server-side script statements:

```
<?php ?>
```

When the Web browser requests a PHP file, the Web server parses the server-side script. When the parsing is complete, the resulting HTML is downloaded to the browser for display.

For example, the form created in Chapter 6, "Building Forms," could submit the form data to a PHP page by modifying the form element as follows:

```
<form id="MailingList" method="post" action="http://localhost/ProcessMailing.php">
```

The form data is then posted to the ProcessMailing.php file. Listing 15-3 presents the PHP code that processes the MailingList form.

Listing 15-3. PHP code is comprised of both HTML and server-side scripting. Notice how similar this is to the ASP code.

```
<!DOCTYPE html PUBLIC "-//W3C//DTD XHTML 1.0 Strict//EN" "DTD/xhtml1-strict.dtd">
<html>
<head>
<title>Process Mailing list request</title>
<link rel="stylesheet" type="text/css" href="TrainingStyle.css" />
</head>

<?php
    // get the components of the time
    $date_time = getdate();
    $hr = $date_time['hours'];

    // Determine the greeting to display
    if ($hr < 12 ) {
        $greeting = "Good morning";
    }
    if ( ($hr >= 12) && ($hr < 17 ) ) {
        $greeting = "Good afternoon";
    }
    if ( $hr >= 17 ) {
        $greeting = "Good evening";
    }
?>
```

```
<body>
    <h1><?php print "$greeting - $FirstName $LastName"; ?></h1>
    <p class="normal">
        Thank you for signing up for our mailing list.
        The following information has been saved for you.
    </p>
    <table>
        <tr>
            <td>Name: </td>
            <td><?php echo $FirstName ?> <?php echo $LastName ?></td>
        </tr>
        <tr>
            <td>Email Address: </td>
            <td><?php echo $Email ?></td>
        </tr>
        <tr>
            <td>Referred by: </td>
            <td><?php echo $Referral ?></td>
        </tr>
    </table>
</body>
</html>
```

NOTE *If you want to try this PHP code, you need to have PHP installed and you need to copy this file to a Web server directory. See the "Additional Resources" section for a link the site where you can download PHP.*

JSP

JSP is Sun Microsystems's variation of ASP and PHP. JSP combines HTML with Java scriptlets to build platform-independent server-side components. Scriptlets are written in Java and normally encapsulate the logic that generates the content for the Web page.

JSP looks similar to ASP and PHP. For specific JSP examples, see the "Additional Resources" section at the end of this chapter.

XML/XSL

Much of the power of XML and XSL cannot be fully realized within a client-side architecture because of the lack of consistent browser support for either technology. You can better utilize these technologies in a server-side architecture.

Before there was XSL, a server-side component could access a database on the Web server or any other database server, retrieve the data in a native format, and process it. This processing normally involved a large number of concatenation operations to build the HTML strings and generate the Web page.

This type of processing is not required if you use XML and XSL. Instead, a server-side component could access data in XML format. If your database does not support an XML format, you can retrieve the data in native format and convert it to XML. Frequently, XML on the server-side is handled as an in-memory string, not an on-disk XML file.

The server-side component uses XSL to translate the in-memory XML data into HTML. The resulting HTML is downloaded to the browser. With the transformation-by-example style of XSL, using XSL is usually significantly easier than programmatically building the HTML strings within the server-side component. Using XSL also makes it easier to update the look of a Web page without changing anything but the XSL.

For example, you could write ASP code that retrieved information for a selection box from a database, converted it to XML, and transformed the XML to an HTML select box using XSL. If the users later want all text within all select boxes to be blue, you could simply change the XSL, and all of the Web pages that were generated using the XSL code to reflect the new user-requested style.

This approach essentially separates the presentation (within the XSL) from the logic (in the server-side component) and from the data (within the XML).

There are many articles on accessing XML and XSL from server-side component technologies such as PHP and ASP. See "Additional Resources" at the end of this chapter for more information.

Putting It All Together

As you can see, there are many different server-side technologies. This list summarizes the common uses of key technology in a server-side architecture:

- **HTML**. Build one HTML file for any static Web page shown to the users.

- **CSS**. Build one CSS file to contain the common formatting styles used in the Web pages of the application. Notice that both the ASP and PHP code (Listings 15-2 and 15-3) use a CSS file.

- **ASP/VBScript, PHP, JSP, Perl**. Build one server-side component for any Web page that requires server-side scripting. For consistency and expandability, some Web applications use the same technology for the static pages as well. The selection of the technology is largely based on the expected Web server system (ASP only runs with Microsoft IIS, for example), on the anticipated features of the Web application, and on developer preference. To simplify development and maintenance, select one of these technologies for use within one Web application.

- **XML/XSL**. Create one XSL file for any Web page or portion of a Web page that is more easily generated with XML and XSL than with a server-side component. For example, tables containing dynamic data are often easier to generate using XSL than ASP, PHP, JSP, or Perl.

Advantages of a Server-Side Architecture

The primary benefits of a server-side architecture are:

- Data can be collected from the user and stored in a database.

- Data can be obtained from a database and dynamically displayed on the page.

- Because the processing is performed on the Web server, there is less concern about differences between browser and browser versions.

- XSL can be used to convert XML data to HTML for download to the browser without downloading or processing the XSL or XML on the client, thereby allowing use of XSL without concern over browser features.

Disadvantages of a Server-Side Architecture

The down sides of a server-side architecture include:

- Any processing requires a trip to the server. For example, to sum a column of numbers a Web page must be submitted to the Web server. This adversely affects response time and can overburden the server.

- There is no client-side reactivity.

- Web server software such as Internet Information Server (IIS) or Apache is required to execute the server-side component.

Server-Side with Client-Side Architecture

Combining client-side and server-side architectures gives you the best of both worlds. This type of architecture provides client-side processing for validation and interactivity and server-side processing to store user-entered information and to dynamically build Web pages based on database values.

A combined architecture, shown in Figure 15-3, is a common pattern for Web applications. The Web server executes server-side components and downloads the resulting HTML and any other needed files, including JavaScript, to the Web browser client. The Web browser displays the HTML and processes the JavaScript on the client for better interaction with the user.

This architecture uses all of the technologies available for server-side processing along with those available for client-side processing. The primary difference between this architecture and the server-side only architecture is the ability of the Web browser to perform some of the processing.

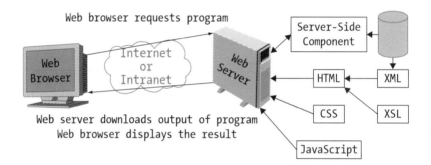

Figure 15-3. A combined architecture provides the best of client-side and server-side technologies.

The Web browser processing can be done using JavaScript or an applet such as an ActiveX control or a Java applet. These technologies were covered in detail in "Client-Side Architecture" earlier in this chapter.

Advantages of a Combined Architecture

The primary benefits of a combined architecture are:

- Data can be collected from the user and validated before it is posted to the Web server.

- The validated data can be stored in a database.

- Data can be obtained from a database and displayed on the page.

- JavaScript or applet code can be generated and/or added to the page before it is downloaded to the client browser.

- XSL can be used to convert XML data to HTML for download to the browser without downloading or processing the XSL or XML on the client, thereby allowing use of XSL without concern over browser features.

Disadvantages of a Combined Architecture

The down sides of a combined architecture include:

- Because some of the processing is performed on the Web client, there is again concern about differences between browser and browser versions.

- You need to know many different technologies, languages, and techniques.

As a small example of the last point, imagine that you have selected a combined architecture with ASP as the primary server-side technology. The ASP code could contain HTML for basic display of information, CSS code to define styles particular to the page, JavaScript for client-side scripting, VBScript for server-side scripting, use of an object model to work with XML, and use of XSL to convert the XML to a table to add to the page. Now you want to simply add a comment in the ASP. Sounds easy enough.

If you put the comment in the HTML part of the ASP, the comment looks like this:

```
<!-- Here is a simple comment -->
```

If you put the comment in the CSS part of the ASP, the comment looks like this:

```
/* Here is a simple comment */
```

If you put the comment within the JavaScript part of the ASP, the comment looks like this:

```
// Here is a simple comment
```

If you put the comment within the VBScript, the comment looks like this:

```
' This is a simple comment
```

You need to know four different techniques just to add a comment! Learning all of the different technologies, keeping track of which syntax is valid for which technology, and ensuring you use the right technology for each part of the architecture add up to make Web application development with a combined client-side and server-side architecture challenging (but fun!).

Three-Tiered Architecture

Another way to look at any software architecture is as a set of tiers. A *tier* in this context is a logically separate and encapsulated set of processes. The server-side architectures covered so far in this chapter have two tiers:

1. **User interface tier**. The first tier is the user-interface tier or presentation layer. This is the code that generates and presents the application's user interface. Many server-side components are often considered to be part of the first tier because their primary responsibility is to generate and process the user interface.

2. **Data tier**. The second tier is the database that stores the data required by the application. This database may run on the Web server or on a physically separate server called a database server. Frequently, the code needed to access the database is also considered to be part of the data tier.

It may seem that two tiers would be enough for any Web application, but frequently this is not the case. Consider a Web application that displays a catalog and takes orders. At first glance, it would seem that the first tier of this application would generate and display the catalog pages and retrieve user-entered order information; the second tier would store the entered data. But if you look at this process with respect to a business operation, this is not enough.

Following along the same example, the placement of the order may not simply be data in tables. Rather, it may trigger a set of business processes. For example, inventory needs to be checked to ensure the item is available and then decremented based on the quantity ordered. Fulfillment needs to be notified so the order can be prepared and packaged. Shipping labels need to be generated and so on.

All of this processing could be achieved within server-side components. However, it may make more sense to build true business application components to handle more complex business processes. These business applications form a middle tier of processing. The middle-tier components can be written using a full-featured development language more suited to business application development than a scripting language. The middle-tier components can run on the same computer as the Web server or the database server, but frequently they are installed on a separate server called an *application server*.

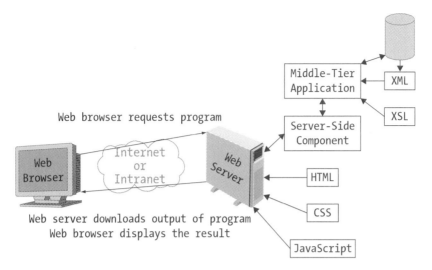

Figure 15-4. A set of middle-tier applications provide business processing in a three-tiered architecture.

Figure 15-4 presents a three-tiered Web application architecture. Table 15-1 describes the pattern commonly used to divide the processing.

Common Three-Tiered Architecture Applications

Three-tiered architectures are great to use any time your Web application does something more than just store and retrieve data. If the Web application involves business processing, that processing can be developed within a business application component instead of within the server-side component.

A business component could be an existing application, such as an accounting application used to adjust financial accounts based on user-entered values. Or it could package processing that is reusable for both browser-based and Window-based applications.

Middle-Tier Technologies

The applications in the middle-tier are built as components that can be accessed from server-side components.

You can build these components using Microsoft's Component Object Model (COM) and the C++ or Visual Basic programming languages. You can use ASP to access these COM components and execute the business logic of your application.

Alternatively, you can build the middle-tier components using Java technologies. You can use Java servlets to access JavaBeans for the business logic of your application.

Table 15-1. A three-tiered Web application architecture divides the processing between the user interface tier (Web browser and server-side components), the middle-tier (middle-tier components), and the data tier (database).

WEB BROWSER	SERVER-SIDE COMPONENT	MIDDLE-TIER COMPONENT
The Web browser provides a mechanism for the user to navigate between the pages. A user requests a page by clicking on a link or entering a URI. The request is submitted to a Web server.	The server-side component is responsible for generating the HTML to be displayed on the Web page. The server-side component calls the middle-tier component to retrieve the data that it needs to display the page.	The middle-tier component is responsible for retrieving the data. It converts it to XML if it cannot natively retrieve the data in XML format. This component can also perform any other processing, such as setting default values or analyzing the data.
The Web browser is responsible for parsing the HTML and displaying the Web page to the user.	When the server-side component receives the XML, it builds the HTML for the page using data from the XML and leveraging XSL wherever possible to generate tables or other display of the data. The resulting HTML, along with any required JavaScript or CSS files, are downloaded to the client and displayed in the Web browser.	The middle-tier component passes the resulting XML to the server-side component.
The Web browser is responsible for collecting user input and waiting for the user to submit the page. Upon submit, the Web browser can execute any client-side script code to validate the input.	The server-side component builds the HTML for the page and is responsible for passing the updated data to the middle-tier component.	The middle-tier component is responsible for doing any final validation, performing business processing, and updating the database with the user-entered values.

Putting It All Together

This list summarizes the common uses of key technology in a three-tiered architecture:

- **HTML**. Insert HTML within the ASP, PHP, JSP, or XSL to format each page.

- **CSS**. Build one CSS file to store all of the styles used on the Web pages of the application.

- **JavaScript**. Build one JavaScript file for each kind of common processing used by the Web pages of the application. This client-side scripting file is downloaded to the client. JavaScript is also common within an ASP, a PHP, or a JSP page to perform logic unique to that page.

- **XML**. Define XML for transferring data between the tiers.

- **XSL**. Create XSL files for formatting and transforming the XML into HTML.

- **ASP/VBScript, PHP, JSP, Perl**. Build one server-side component for any Web page that requires server-side scripting. The selected technology needs to be able to call a middle-tier component.

- **C++/Java/Visual Basic**. Build or leverage business applications and other middle-tier components to provide all of the business processing and database access for the application.

Advantages of a Three-Tiered Architecture

The primary benefits of a three-tiered architecture are:

- The processing is more modular, making it easier to modify or replace a component of the Web application without affecting the others.

- The middle-tier applications are usually compiled; the server-side components are not. Moving complex processing to a middle-tier application can make a significant difference in performance.

- The middle-tier components can be reused for other applications. For example, a middle-tier inventory component can handle all of the business rules regarding inventory tracking, reordering, stocking, and so on.

This component is used by one page of the Web application to check availability of an item. Another page of the Web application uses the same component to decrement inventory when an item is purchased. A Windows application that tracks reorders uses the same component.

- Separating functionality into tiers provides for load balancing, allowing support of many more users.

Disadvantages of a Three-Tiered Architecture

The down sides of a three-tiered architecture include:

- A three-tiered application requires more design to ensure that the division of responsibility between the tiers of the application is clear. Otherwise, it can be difficult to locate and maintain specific functionality in a three-tiered application.

- There is yet another set of technologies to learn.

What Did This Cover?

This chapter covered several Web application architecture patterns. The majority of this book focused on client-side technologies. This chapter showed where those technologies fit into an overall Web application architecture.

There were no Try Its in this chapter because this book was written with the assumption that the reader did not have access to a Web server. However, several server-side technology examples were presented that could be used as exercises.

At this point, you should be ready to design your Web application, architect it following one of the patterns presented in this chapter, and code the HTML, CSS, JavaScript, XML, and XSL as detailed in this book.

Good luck!

Additional Resources

One chapter could not begin to cover everything there is to know about Web application architectures, especially with the large number of server-side technologies available. This section provides some additional resource suggestions by way of books, articles, and links to Web resources.

The books, articles, and links all existed at the time of this writing. There is a good chance that the books and articles still exist as you read this. However, the same cannot be said of Web links. Ignore the suggested links if they no longer exist.

Books and Articles

Blexrud, Christopher et al. *Professional Windows DNA: Building Distributed Web Applications with VB, COM+, MSMQ, SOAP, and ASP.* Birmingham, UK: Wrox Press, 2000.

The book looks at the Microsoft suite of Web application development tools.

Gilmore, W.J. *A Programmer's Introduction to PHP 4.0.* Berkeley, CA: Apress, 2001.

The book begins with a introduction to PHP's syntax and basic functionality and then moves onto advanced issues like PHP's role in database manipulation, sessions, and user interactivity. The book also examines how PHP can work with XML, JavaScript, and COM.

Kurniawan, Budi. *Internet Programming with VB.* Berkeley, CA: Apress, 2000.

This book provides information on using Visual Basic with Microsoft Internet Information Server.

Links

`http://download.cnet.com`: The downloads section of this site provides access to a large library of ActiveX controls, Java applets, and other Web development products.

`http://java.sun.com/products/jsp/`: This is the primary JavaServer Pages site.

`http://java.sun.com/products/servlet/`: This is the primary Java Servlet site.

`http://msdn.microsoft.com`: This site provides access to Microsoft's view of Web development.

`http://msdn.microsoft.com/net/`: Microsoft's .NET site covers all facets of .NET, including ASP .NET.

`http://www.cgi-resources.com`: There are many server-side scripts available from this site, most of which are free. These scripts are written in languages such as Perl, C++, Visual Basic, or VBScript (ASP).

`http://www.devx.com/dotnet/`: This developers exchange site provides many articles and links to other .NET resources.

`http://www.gotdotnet.com/default.aspx`: This site contains many articles and links about .NET.

`http://www.topxml.com/parsers/`: This site contains links to XML parsers that provide for handling XML and XSL from C, C++, Java, and Visual Basic.

`http://www.perl.com`: This site contains links to many Perl resources. You can also download Perl from this site.

`http://www.php.net`: You can download the PHP scripting language from this site.

Index

SYMBOLS AND NUMBERS

& (ampersand)
  in character entities, 55
  character entity for, 56
  in URIs, 149, 305
&& (ampersands) operator in JavaScript, 233
< > (angle brackets)
  for HTML tags, 28–29
  for XML tags, 312
' (apostrophe) character entity for, 56
* (asterisk)
  in regular expressions, 282
  in XSLT stylesheets, 357
@ (at sign) in XSLT stylesheets, 358
! (bang) operator in JavaScript, 233
!= (bang and equal sign) operator in
      JavaScript, 233
{ } (braces)
  in regular expressions, 283
  for statement blocks in JavaScript, 202
  for style rule declarations, 71, 77
^ (caret) in regular expressions, 251, 282,
      283
: (colon)
  in namespaces, 327, 386
  in style rule declarations, 71, 102
  in URLs, 4
  in XML, 311
$ (dollar sign)
  in regular expressions, 251, 283
  for string in XSLT stylesheets, 376
. (dot)
  in object model, 173–174
  for style classes, 80
  in XSLT stylesheets, 357
= (equal sign)
  for HTML attributes, 31, 36, 71
  operator in JavaScript, 202, 232

  for XML attributes, 314
== (equal signs) operator in JavaScript
      202, 233
> (greater than sign)
  character entity for, 56
  for HTML tags, 29
  operator in JavaScript, 233
  for XML tags, 312
>= (greater than or equal to) operator in
      JavaScript, 233
< (less than sign)
  character entity for, 56
  for HTML tags, 29
  operator in JavaScript, 233
  for XML tags, 312
<= (less than or equal to) operator in
      JavaScript, 233
- (minus sign) operator in JavaScript, 202,
      231
-- (minus signs) operator in JavaScript,
      231
-= (minus and equal signs) operator in
      JavaScript, 232
* (multiplication sign) operator in
      JavaScript, 231
*= (multiplication and equal signs) oper-
      ator in JavaScript, 232
  (non-breaking space character),
      35, 56
  in empty table cells, 109, 141
| (pipe character)
  in regular expressions, 283
  in XSLT stylesheets, 366–367
|| (pipe characters) operator in JavaScript,
      233
+ (plus sign)
  operator in JavaScript, 202, 231
  in regular expressions, 251, 282
++ (plus signs) operator in JavaScript, 231

Apress Titles

ISBN	PRICE	AUTHOR	TITLE
1-893115-01-1	$39.95	Appleman	Appleman's Win32 API Puzzle Book and Tutorial for Visual Basic Programmers
1-893115-23-2	$29.95	Appleman	How Computer Programming Works
1-893115-97-6	$39.95	Appleman	Moving to VB. NET: Strategies, Concepts, and Code
1-893115-09-7	$29.95	Baum	Dave Baum's Definitive Guide to LEGO MINDSTORMS
1-893115-84-4	$29.95	Baum, Gasperi, Hempel, and Villa	Extreme MINDSTORMS
1-893115-82-8	$59.95	Ben-Gan/Moreau	Advanced Transact-SQL for SQL Server 2000
1-893115-99-2	$39.95	Cornell/Morrison	Programming VB .NET: A Guide for Experienced Programmers
1-893115-71-2	$39.95	Ferguson	Mobile .NET
1-893115-90-9	$44.95	Finsel	The Handbook for Reluctant Database Administrators
1-893115-85-2	$34.95	Gilmore	A Programmer's Introduction to PHP 4.0
1-893115-17-8	$59.95	Gross	A Programmer's Introduction to Windows DNA
1-893115-62-3	$39.95	Gunnerson	A Programmer's Introduction to C#, Second Edition
1-893115-10-0	$34.95	Holub	Taming Java Threads
1-893115-04-6	$34.95	Hyman/Vaddadi	Mike and Phani's Essential C++ Techniques
1-893115-50-X	$34.95	Knudsen	Wireless Java: Developing with Java 2, Micro Edition
1-893115-79-8	$49.95	Kofler	Definitive Guide to Excel VBA
1-893115-56-9	$39.95	Kofler	MySQL
1-893115-87-9	$39.95	Kurata	Doing Web Development: Client-Side Techniques
1-893115-75-5	$44.95	Kurniawan	Internet Programming with VB
1-893115-19-4	$49.95	Macdonald	Serious ADO: Universal Data Access with Visual Basic

ISBN	PRICE	AUTHOR	TITLE
1-893115-06-2	$39.95	Marquis/Smith	A Visual Basic 6.0 Programmer's Toolkit
1-893115-22-4	$27.95	McCarter	David McCarter's VB Tips and Techniques
1-893115-76-3	$49.95	Morrison	C++ For VB Programmers
1-893115-80-1	$39.95	Newmarch	A Programmer's Guide to Jini Technology
1-893115-58-5	$49.95	Oellermann	Architecting Web Services
1-893115-81-X	$39.95	Pike	SQL Server: Common Problems, Tested Solutions
1-893115-20-8	$34.95	Rischpater	Wireless Web Development
1-893115-93-3	$34.95	Rischpater	Wireless Web Development with PHP and WAP
1-893115-24-0	$49.95	Sinclair	From Access to SQL Server
1-893115-94-1	$29.95	Spolsky	User Interface Design for Programmers
1-893115-53-4	$39.95	Sweeney	Visual Basic for Testers
1-893115-29-1	$44.95	Thomsen	Database Programming with Visual Basic .NET
1-893115-65-8	$39.95	Tiffany	Pocket PC Database Development with eMbedded Visual Basic
1-893115-59-3	$59.95	Troelsen	C# and the .NET Platform
1-893115-26-7	Troelsen		Visual Basic .NET and the .NET Platform
1-893115-54-2	$49.95	Trueblood/Lovett	Data Mining and Statistical Analysis Using SQL
1-893115-16-X	$49.95	Vaughn	ADO Examples and Best Practices
1-893115-83-6	$44.95	Wells	Code Centric: T-SQL Programming with Stored Procedures and Triggers
1-893115-95-X	$49.95	Welschenbach	Cryptography in C and C++
1-893115-05-4	$39.95	Williamson	Writing Cross-Browser Dynamic HTML
1-893115-78-X	$49.95	Zukowski	Definitive Guide to Swing for Java 2, Second Edition
1-893115-92-5	$49.95	Zukowski	Java Collections

Available at bookstores nationwide or from Springer Verlag New York, Inc. at 1-800-777-4643; fax 1-212-533-3503. Contact us for more information at sales@apress.com.

Apress Titles Publishing SOON!

ISBN	AUTHOR	TITLE
1-893115-73-9	Abbott	Voice Enabling Web Applications: VoiceXML and Beyond
1-893115-48-8	Bischof	The .NET Languages: A Quick Translation Reference
1-893115-67-4	Borge	Managing Enterprise Systems with the Windows Scripting Host
1-893115-39-9	Chand/Gold	A Programmer's Guide to ADO .NET in C#
1-893115-47-X	Christensen	Writing Cross-Browser XHTML and CSS 2.0
1-893115-72-0	Curtin	Building Trust: Online Security for Developers
1-893115-42-9	Foo/Lee	XML Programming Using the Microsoft XML Parser
1-893115-55-0	Frenz	Visual Basic for Scientists
1-893115-36-4	Goodwill	Apache Jakarta-Tomcat
1-893115-96-8	Jorelid	J2EE FrontEnd Technologies: A Programmer's Guide to Servlets, JavaServer Pages, and Enterprise JavaBeans
1-893115-49-6	Kilburn	Palm Programming in Basic
1-893115-38-0	Lafler	Power AOL: A Survival Guide
1-893115-89-5	Shemitz	Kylix: The Professional Developer's Guide and Reference
1-893115-40-2	Sill	An Introduction to qmail
1-893115-43-7	Stephenson	Standard VB: An Enterprise Developer's Reference for VB 6 and VB .NET
1-893115-68-2	Vaughn	ADO Examples and Best Practices, Second Edition

Available at bookstores nationwide or from Springer Verlag New York, Inc. at 1-800-777-4643; fax 1-212-533-3503. Contact us for more information at sales@apress.com.

apress™

books for professionals by professionals™

About Apress

Apress, located in Berkeley, CA, is an innovative publishing company devoted to meeting the needs of existing and potential programming professionals. Simply put, the "A" in Apress stands for the "Author's Press™." Apress' unique author-centric approach to publishing grew from conversations between Dan Appleman and Gary Cornell, authors of best-selling, highly regarded computer books. In 1998, they set out to create a publishing company that emphasized quality above all else, a company with books that would be considered the best in their market. Dan and Gary's vision has resulted in over 30 widely acclaimed titles by some of the industry's leading software professionals.

Do You Have What It Takes
to Write for Apress?

Apress is rapidly expanding its publishing program. If you can write and refuse to compromise on the quality of your work, if you believe in doing more then rehashing existing documentation, and if you're looking for opportunities and rewards that go far beyond those offered by traditional publishing houses, we want to hear from you!

Consider these innovations that we offer all of our authors:

- **Top royalties with *no* hidden switch statements**
  Authors typically only receive half of their normal royalty rate on foreign sales. In contrast, Apress' royalty rate remains the same for both foreign and domestic sales.

- **A mechanism for authors to obtain equity in Apress**
  Unlike the software industry, where stock options are essential to motivate and retain software professionals, the publishing industry has adhered to an outdated compensation model based on royalties alone. In the spirit of most software companies, Apress reserves a significant portion of its equity for authors.

- **Serious treatment of the technical review process**
  Each Apress book has a technical reviewing team whose remuneration depends in part on the success of the book since they too receive royalties.

Moreover, through a partnership with Springer-Verlag, one of the world's major publishing houses, Apress has significant venture capital behind it. Thus, we have the resources to produce the highest quality books *and* market them aggressively.

If you fit the model of the Apress author who can write a book that gives the "professional what he or she needs to know™," then please contact one of our Editorial Directors, Gary Cornell (gary_cornell@apress.com), Dan Appleman (dan_appleman@apress.com), Karen Watterson (karen_watterson@apress.com) or Jason Gilmore (jason_gilmore@apress.com) for more information.